Cartography by: Jon Van Coops, New World Designs
P.O. Box 191646, San Francisco, Ca 94119, Nov. 1999

Jewish Communities
in Exotic Places

To Elizabeth + Jerry,

Wishing you the best!

Ken Blady

Jewish Communities in Exotic Places

KEN BLADY

foreword by
Michael Pollak

introduction by
Steven Kaplan

JASON ARONSON INC.
Northvale, New Jersey
Jerusalem

The author would like to thank the following for granting permission to use material reprinted in this book:

Commentary for permission to reprint from S. D. Goitein's "The Transplantation of the Yemenites," 1951.

Smithsonian Folkways Recordings for permission to reprint from "Bukhara: Musical Crossroads of Asia" (SF40050), 1991.

UBS Publishers' Distributors, Ltd. for permission to reprint from S. Muthiah's *The Splendour of South India*, 1992.

John Murray (Publishers) Ltd. for permission to reprint from John Keay's *Into India*, 1973.

Keren T. Freidman for permission to reprint from "The Rabbi with the Long White Beard," 1973.

The Red Sea Press, Inc. for permission to reprint from Teshalo Tibebu's *The Making of Modern Ethiopia*, 1995.

This book was set in 11 pt. Perpetua by Alpha Graphics of Pittsfield, New Hampshire and printed and bound by Book-mart Press, Inc. of North Bergen, NJ.

Copyright © 2000 by Ken Blady
10 9 8 7 6 5 4 3 2 1

Library of Congress Cataloging-in-Publication Data
Blady, Ken.
    Jewish communities in exotic places / by Ken Blady.
        p.   cm.
    Includes bibliographical references and index.
ISBN 0–7657–6112–2
1. Jews—Asia. 2. Jews—Africa. 3. Jewish diaspora. 4. Jews,
  Oriental—History. I. Title.
DS135.A85B53 2000
950'.04924—dc21   99-34824
                                     CIP

Printed in the United States of America on acid-free paper. For information and catalog write to Jason Aronson Inc., 230 Livingston Street, Northvale, NJ 07647-1726, or visit our website: www.aronson. com

This book is dedicated to my nieces,
Techiya and Jenni,
and to my good friend, Roger Silver.

Contents

Part IV

Part V

Part VI

Part VII

Part VIII

Part IX

Part X

Part XI

Part XII

Part XIII

Part XIV

Illustrations

Foreword
by Michael Pollak

One might argue, I suppose, that the Jewish Diaspora began with the flight of Jacob and his family from the famine-stricken regions of Canaan to Egypt, but we generally attribute the origins of the Jewish exile, the *galut*, to the Assyrian conquest of the Northern Kingdom of Israel in 722 B.C.E and the forced dispersion of the people now known as the Ten Lost Tribes of Israel to the Mesopotamian area and beyond. The next substantial Jewish population shifts, some self-imposed for economic, political, or military reasons brought about as the consequence of the Babylonian, Greek, and Roman conquests of the Southern Kingdom of Judea, drove many more Jews eastward, as well as to the lands abutting the Mediterranean. In succeeding centuries, the need to seek refuge from persecution became still another factor in extending the range of the Diaspora, and in the five centuries since the expulsion from Spain and the discovery of the Americas that Diaspora has spread to virtually every inhabited part of the globe.

Understandably, Jews have always been interested in searching for the presence of Jewish communities wherever they might be. These searches were perhaps most intense insofar as the Ten Lost Tribes were concerned, notwithstanding the statement made by Rabbi Akiba nearly 1,900 years ago that these tribes were irretrievably lost. To give one example, a large part of the Jewish world was stirred up not only by the claim of the ninth-century traveler Eldad ha-Dani to be a member of the Lost Tribe of Dan, but also by his assertion that he had personally encountered other Lost Tribesmen elsewhere in the world, one of them being, interestingly, an Isaacharite merchant who ransomed him from a band of cannibals who had brought him to China. Eldad was by no means the only traveler who sought out, and even pretended to have visited, regions peopled by various components of the Lost Tribes—there were uncounted numbers of others. So one finds the English, the Americans, the American Indians, the Germans, Scandinavians, Koreans, Okinawans, Japanese, Maoris, and, for that matter, nearly every ethnic and national group in the world identified at one time or another as being of Lost Tribes origin. It may be pointed out that although the Anglo-Saxon-Celtic peoples of Britain are identified by the British Israelitic movement as descendants of the tribe of Ephraim, the members of the same three ethnic groups who sailed from England to Colonial America and settled there are presently linked genetically by the American Israelitic movement to the tribe of Manasseh.

This is not to say, of course, that there are today absolutely no people on the earth whose roots do not go back at least in part to the inhabitants of ancient Israel, but no documentory evidence supporting that possibility and providing credible genealogical evidence has yet been discovered that justifies the assignment of such a heritage to any particular group.

Whatever the case, the Diaspora, as we ordinarily think of it, is constituted of thousands of Jewish communities whose members unequivocally speak of themselves as the physical and spiritual heirs of the tribes of the Southern Kingdom of Judea—of the tribes, that is, of Judah, Benjamin, and, to a lesser extent, Levi. Among these Jews, we may surmise, there must be a large percentage of individuals who carry a greatly diluted bloodline inherited from those of the inhabitants of the Northern Kingdom who escaped being exiled by the Assyrians to distant lands, and who, finding refuge with their kinfolk in Judea, eventually intermarried with them.

In this work, Ken Blady has focused his attention on seventeen scattered communities whose very existence, let alone their histories and cultures, remain unknown to the overwhelming majority of the mainstream Jews with whom they claim kinship. We tend to think of these alleged outposts of Israel (if and when, that is, our attention happens to be called to them) as "exotic," an adjective that we all too often equate with "peculiar," and serves to conceal the fact that we know so little about these communities. Their stories, it follows, deserve to be told, if only to satisfy our curiosity and fill in some of the voids in our understanding of diasporic history.

But there is more to the matter, for the need to clarify the identities and religious dispositions of these peoples brings us face-to-face with the nagging and contentious question of "Who is a Jew?" We are then compelled to decide for ourselves which, if any, of them should be considered truly Jewish, whether by descent, way of living, or both. And if we judge them to be Jewish, are they entitled to take advantage of the right of return that is guaranteed to all Jews by the State of Israel, regardless of where they happen to live? Moreover, what impact would the incorporation of perhaps millions of these "lost" Jews—most of them, seemingly from Third World countries—have on the state?

While this book of Ken Blady's is by no means the only work that has been written in recent decades about "exotic" Jewish communities, its intriguing approach to the subject and its comprehensive descriptions of such Jewish enclaves make it indispensable to all those Jews and non-Jews who are interested in Judaic history, whether they be specialists in the field or laypersons. We have every reason to be grateful to the author for the information and insight he has provided to us in this remarkable volume and for the skillful manner in which this work has been arranged and presented. Perhaps he will now consider writing a sequel dealing with other putative, "exotic" claimants to a place in the tent of Jacob, such as the Knanaya people of Kerala and the Crypto-Jewish groups that still exist in various Latin American countries, and in the Iberian peninsula and elsewhere.

Preface

Jewish Communities in Exotic Places deals with seventeen Jewish communities that are referred to generically in Hebrew as *edot ha-mizrach* (Eastern or Oriental Jewish communities). These are small pockets of Jewish habitation situated in remote places on the Asian and African Jewish geographical periphery, which over the centuries became isolated from the major centers of Jewish civilization. These communities are neither Ashkenazim nor technically Sephardim, since this latter Hebrew word specifically refers to Jews who are descended from medieval Jews of the Iberian Peninsula. The polyglot, cultured, and dynamic Sephardim who migrated to these areas after the cataclysmic events of 1391 and 1492 tended to look down upon the indigenous Jews. In some cases, as in North Africa and India, the local Jews were treated as a race apart. Therefore, referring to the *edot ha-mizrach* as Sephardim is, to say the least, a misnomer, and deprives them of their unique histories and their own rich diversity of customs and practices.

Some of these *edot ha-mizrach*, specifically the Jews of Yemen and the Jews of Tripoli, might be more appropriately designated as Mista'arvim. The Mista'arvim are the ancient Middle-Eastern, Judeo-Arabic-speaking Jews (with all their regional nuances), invariably living in Sunni Muslim Arab countries, who make up the great majority of the *edot ha-mizrach*. These Mista'arvin at first coexisted in uneasy juxtiposition with the Iberian Jews who settled among them in places like Syria, Egypt, and Algeria, but because of their lower cultural and economic level were gradually submerged into the Sephardi milieu, which numerically and qualitatively overwhelmed them. Of course, mainstream Sephardi culture of the Eastern Mediterranean, in turn, assumed an Oriental coloration.

It should be mentioned, however, that the Yemenite Jews (who were the only Arabian Jewish community to live under protracted Shiite rule) and the Libyan Jews of the lowlands (living among the Arabs as opposed to the cave-dwelling Jews of Tripolitania living in a Berber environment), for at least the last thousand years, maintained only tenuous links with the major vortexes of Sephardi-dominated rabbinic learning in the Islamic world such as Cairo, Fez, and Safed. For these and other reasons discussed in the text, Mizrachi Jews in "exotic" places (exotic being variously defined to mean "different" in a way that is striking or fascinating, and "strangely beautiful") evolved traditions that were at great variance even with "mainstream" Oriental Jewry.

Only with the arrival of travelers, *shelichim* (emissaries, often from Palestine), and the periodic Jewish refugees who found safe haven in their midst were the *edot ha-mizrach* in these far-flung places brought up to date on the latest halakhic rulings (responsa) and other prevailing tendencies in normative Judaism.

There is no fundamental difference among the religious beliefs of the various Jewish ethno-geographic groupings: Ashkenazim, Sephardim, Romaniotes (Byzantine), Mizrachim (See Appendix A). Life for traditional Jews the world over centered around the Torah and the fulfillment of the law. However, among the isolated *edot ha-mizrach* communities under autonomous decentralized spiritual leadership, the religious observances, *minhagim* (customs), *takhonots* (rabbinic enactments), and social conventions often diverged in radical and fascinating ways. Some retained traditions long discarded and forgotten by Sephardim and Ashkenazim. For example, the Yemenite *mesorah* (oral tradition) of being able to identify and render as kosher various species of locusts and grasshoppers mentioned in the Bible. Some practiced customs that outright contradicted rabbinic teaching. For instance, one of the more glaring examples was the Libyan cave-dwellers' tradition of never inviting guests to share the Passover seder. Under the influence of the peoples among whom they settled, some communities embraced aspects of the dominant culture. For example, the Daghestani (Northeastern Caucasian) practice of *qan alma* (vendetta), or the Indian caste system, both of which are perceived as peculiar and bizarre; and outright anathema to "normative" rabbinic-Jewish values. For that matter, so were certain mores and folkways of the Persian Jews—an apt example being the custom of an unmarried girl at a *brit millah* eating the foreskin of a newborn male-child's circumcised penis in order to bring about a *segulah* (boon) for fertility.

Ancient Jews, exiled from Israel intermittently from 722 B.C.E. to the Bar Kochba revolt in 135 C.E., were scattered over thousands of cities and towns spanning three continents, and were splintered into numerous groups. In the course of their migrations many Jewish tribes disappeared. Those able to resist conversion, disease, starvation, or massacre as they passed through the experience of being subjugated by Persia, Greece, Rome, and Islam, were scattered as the Mongols and the Turks rampaged through Central Asia and the Near East. Many centuries later, as a result of the revival of Jewish life in Israel, contacts were re-established. Peoples who had persisted in the most unexpected places—tattooed, black, proto-Mosaic hut-dwellers from the remote highlands of northwestern Ethiopia; locust-eating, dagger-wielding polygamists from the Southern Arabian Peninsula; conjuring cave-dwellers from the mountain escarpments above the Sahara sporting feathered tufts that looked like mohawks, golden earrings, and *peot* (earlocks)—these and others all claimed descent from the patriarchs and the Ten Lost Tribes. Today, the overwhelming majority of the *edot ha-mizrach* have relocated to Israel and are under the purview of the Sephardic Chief Rabbinate. Scattered remnants still survive in Central and South Asia, the Caucasus, North Africa, the Horn of Africa, and the Southern Arabian Peninsula.

This book chronicles the history of these *edot*. It traces their survival and explores aspects of their Jewish, religion, and folklore, stressing both the continuity and diversity of Jewish life in different times and places. The *edot* are examined with an appreciation that these people found beliefs, rituals, and richness of community as Jews, each in their own way, according to their circumstances and isolation.

A special feature of this book is a Background Information section on each country, which serves as an introduction at the beginning of every chapter. Because any discussion of these *edot* needs to be placed in the context of the larger culture, some of the more pertinent and interesting aspects of the geography, history, and ethnology of the country are outlined. Wherever Jews lived, they clung tenaciously to their religious and national traditions and did not lose their uniqueness. At the same time, they were strongly influenced by the customs and social behavior of the dominant culture and shared its traditional outlook. Having lived in these regions since ancient times (in fact, in some places legend has it that the Jews formed the first nucleus of the native population), their fate was inextricably intertwined with that of their neighbors.

Acknowledgments

I would like to acknowledge the valuable contributions of friends, colleagues, and scholars, which brought this book to completion. A number of scholars read and commented on parts of the manuscript in their areas of expertise: Dr. Reuben Ahroni, Keren T. Friedman, Dr. Steven Kaplan, Michael Pollak, and Dr. Yona Sabar. To these scholars who took the trouble to read the manuscript and offer their comments, I am most grateful.

I would like to thank the following people for consenting to be interviewed (formally and informally): Rabbi Yitzchak Amadi; Dr. Shoshana Ben Dor; Peretz Eliyahu; Itamar and Shemesh Ephrati; Dr. Emmanuel Friedman; Tenghiz, Larisa, Teah, and Irakli (may he rest in peace) Iosebashvili; Maatuf Saadia Ben Yitzchak; the Honorary Mesfin Fanta, esq., former Health Minister of Ethiopia; Dr. Ted and Peggy Meyers; Bracha Serri; Haviv Shimoni (also deceased); and Shimshon Shimshon.

Readers will observe in reading the book that I owe an immense intellectual debt to many specialists whose names and works appear in the text and the bibliography. Since neither I, nor anyone else I know, is able to read or speak Neo-Aramaic, Tashilhait Pashto, Malayalam, Ge'ez, Tadjiki, Juhuru, or Judeo-Crimean Tatar, etc., the scholarly writings of Dr. Harvey Goldberg, Dr. Nathan Katz, Dr. Laurence Loeb, Dr. Jeff Halper, Dr. Norman Stillman, Dr. Wolf Leslau, Reuven Kashani, Dr. Tudor Parfitt, Dr. Michael M. Laskier, Dr. Amnon Netzer, Dr. Michael Zand, Dr. Shlomo Deshen, and many others too numerous to name here were indispensable to the research.

Research and preparation for writing this book required work in various libraries in Israel and the United States. This work could not have been done without the cooperation of a large number of individuals and institutions. Their willingness to provide me with recondite sources and to guide me to others was invaluable. Assistance with research, literature, photo-archival material, map-making, and translation came from the following people and institutions: Michel Abitbol and Shimon Rubenstein at the Ben Tzvi Institute of Jerusalem; the staff of the Judaica Division at The Hebrew University of Jerusalem; Ora Schwartz Beeri and Orpa Slapak at the Israel Museum in Jerusalem; Zalman Alpert and Tzvi Erenyi, librarians at the Yeshiva University Judaica Library in New York City; Lily Arbel at the Beth Hatfootsuth in Tel Aviv; Bill Chayes at the Judah L. Magnes Museum in Berkeley, California; Keren T. Friedman; and Nadine Rossignol. Also thanks to head librarians Phillip Miller of Hebrew Union College, New York; Louis Shub of the University of Judaism, Los Angeles; Harvey Horowitz of Hebrew Union College, Los Angeles; Phyliss Brickner of the Sausalito, California, Library;   and the staff at the Jewish Community Library of San Francisco, especially Fred Isaac, former head librarian, for graciously procuring various materials. Others who assisted in various capacities are Nachshon Lustig, Xavier Thienpont, Ophira Druch, and Doris Tseng, Chinese Collection Librarian, International Center, San Francisco Main Library, San Francisco, California.

Two good friends read and corrected portions of the manuscript from a literary standpoint at different stages in its preparation—Vida Marks and Dr. Elliot Isenberg revealed an unflagging attention to detail.

I consider myself graced to have two extremely competent computer support persons as dear devoted friends. Gary Dugger's one-mindedness and meticulous work habits helped make the manuscript presentable. Brandon Shugrue also lent a hand.

Special thanks to my literary agent, Devorah Harris, for making the *shidduch* (match) with Arthur Kurzweil of Jason Aronson Inc.

Finally, I would like to thank a number of relatives and friends who were not directly involved in my work but who made the process of conducting the research and interviews far more agreeable through their love, hospitality, and assistance: Dr. David Blady and his wife Ann, Ling "Kitty" Miao, David Golden, Keiko Masuda, Anat and Amrom Magori, Marc Kallis, Benyamin Tsedaka, Xavier De Costa, Susan Zeibig, and Klaus-Ullrich Rotzscher.

While the creative intelligence and constructive suggestions of all these wonderful people have greatly improved the text, I alone take ultimate responsibility for the interpretations and for any errors that remain.

Introduction
by Steven Kaplan

The tattered *American College Dictionary* that I received as a bar mitzvah present defines *exotic* as: "of foreign origin or character; not native; introduced from abroad, but not fully naturalized or acclimatized." This definition forms an excellent starting point for the consideration of exotic Jewish communities. The designation of a people or place as exotic assumes, of course, that there are others (or, "us") who are not foreign, but native, indigenous, naturalized, and acclimatized. *Exotic* is, in the final analysis, a relative term, and it is this relativism that permits me, a descendant of German and Eastern European Jews born in the United States and living in Israel, to view *others* as "of foreign origin, not native . . . and not fully naturalized."

I can at least comfort myself in having a venerable pedigree. Throughout history people have studied those in distant lands, not only to comprehend the other, but also to use them to achieve a better understanding of themselves. The Jewish people are no different in this respect. Each new discovery of Jewish groups who live far away from major Jewish centers or who have been separated from other Jewish groups produces a body of literature that both illuminates the group in question and deepens our appreciation of the richness and variety of Judaism as a whole.

In this vein, I wish to use this introduction to highlight some of the broader concerns that I believe are implicit in Ken Blady's fascinating survey of exotic Jewish communities. In particular, I shall attempt to consider three themes that I believe lie at the heart of modern Jewish and, particularly, Israeli affairs—race, history, and culture—and demonstrate their relevance to the study of the groups discussed in this book. The challenge, I would suggest, is to understand these exotic communities while at the same time preserving the rich individuality that makes them so fascinating.

RACE: FUNNY THEY DON'T LOOK JEWISH!

On the most immediate level, even before we know anything about their history or culture, members of exotic Jewish communities challenge our concept of who is a Jew and raise basic questions about Jewish identity. Although it is generally conceded today that Jews are not a race, we frequently expect them to have many of the characteristics that we attribute to racial groups: to *look* Jewish or to somehow reveal distinctive Jewish characteristics.

It is certainly not my intention to argue that Jews are indeed a race. I would, however, like to question the meaningfulness of the assertion that they are not a race, and contend that those who deny the racial characteristics of Jews often contradict themselves on the level of practice.

The first challenge to the claim that Jews are not a race comes from much of the recent research on the subject of race itself. Over the past few decades, scholars from a variety of disciplines have increasingly questioned the existence of race as a meaningful scientific concept.[1] For example, race is not as is often popularly assumed, something that can be seen. The external characteristics that are so frequently cited as markers of specific racial groups (skin color, hair texture, and other facial features) are arbitrarily chosen and are no more accurate an indicator of a person's identity than such nineteenth century favorites as cranial measurements, the shape of the skull, or the angle of the forehead. Nor do genetics offer any support for the claim that the human species is today or was ever in the past divided into distinct races. According to recent research, genetic factors vary as much within so-called racial groups as they do between them.

Racial categories are, according to a growing consensus, socially constructed. They vary from period to period and from culture to culture. Groups such as the Irish, Italians, and Jews find themselves defined as "white" in late twentieth century America, but not in historical literature from earlier periods. Ethiopian Jews who, like other peoples of northern Ethiopia, describe themselves as "reddish-brown" find themselves depicted as "black" in Israel.

If there is no race in any biological sense of the term, it is obviously rather meaningless to state that Jews are not a race. However, the discussion does not end here. The fact that race does not exist does not keep people from believing in them and acting upon their existence. Government policies are frequently formulated on the assumption that distinct racial groups exist, and a belief in the existence of race forms the cornerstone of any racist theory. Moreover, race is a real cultural entity. For many people, membership in a racial group constitutes an important part of their social identity and self-image.[2]

In this context of a cultural definition of race, it becomes obvious that there are the numerous ways in which Jews deny the existence of a Jewish race, yet they often use racial categories when identifying as Jews and with other Jews. If popular concepts of Jews were as non-racial as they claim to be, the physical appearance of exotic Jewish groups would not cause the surprise and consternation that they so frequently produce. European Catholics, for example, whatever their feelings regarding Indian, Chinese, or African members of their faith, do not seem puzzled by the existence of such strikingly different-looking believers. (When was the last time you heard: Funny you don't look Catholic?) Similarly, while early Islam had numerous problems with the status of non-Arab Muslims, pilgrims to Mecca from Indonesia (the largest Muslim country in the world), Nigeria, or India merit hardly a second glance. In contrast, the first European Jews who visited Ethiopia desperately sought to find visual proof that the Beta Israel (Falasha) were Jewish, and even cited with confidence their resemblance to Jews in London, Berlin, and elsewhere in the world. Even today, the visual distinctiveness of Jews from Yemen, India, Ethiopia, and China appears as an implicit challenge to the idea of a single Jewish people. It is not surprising, therefore, to find in both rabbinical and Jewish Agency writings claims that Ethiopian Jews are physically distinguishable from their non-Jewish neighbors both by skin color and facial appearance.

Yet, another striking example of the racialization of Jewish identity is the widespread belief that all Jews are of common descent. Several years ago I was asked to offer my scholarly opinion regarding the petition of an Ibo man from Nigeria to be recognized as a Jew. What was remarkable in his case was not the request for citizenship, but the argument on which he based his claim. Having converted to Judaism in an Orthodox ceremony, he was entitled to Israel citizenship. In his petition, however, he requested citizenship not on the basis of his conversion, but by claiming to be of Jewish (Israelite) descent since the Ibo are descendants of the lost tribe of Ephriam.

While this could perhaps be dismissed as the idiosyncrasy of a single individual, the case of the Ethiopians demonstrates its wider application. Given the fairly well-documented evidence for Jewish influences on Ethiopian culture, nothing would appear to be simpler than for Ethiopian Jews to present themselves as ancient converts to Judaism. Indeed, this view has been supported by numerous scholars for many years. Yet, whether they have cited the Pan-Ethiopian myth and presented themselves as descendants of Solomon and the Queen of Sheba or more recent rabbinical views connecting them with the Tribe of Dan, they have been vociferous in their insistence on claiming a physical-biological—racial—link to other Jewish communities.

Whether stated by outside observers or community members, descriptions of common physical characteristics and mythic traditions of shared descent should both be understood as attempts to naturalize and assimilate exotic Jews to the popular image of the Jewish people as a unified group. These descriptions endeavor to make exotic peoples seem somewhat less exotic by accommodating the popular cultural perception that Jews are a racial group, and thus share both physical characteristics and common descent.

HISTORY: WHAT MAKES JEWISH HISTORY JEWISH?

In fact, the domestication of exotic groups is by no means confined to descriptions of their appearance and descent. Those who do not believe that Jews are a racially defined group often contend that their shared identity lies not in biology but in history. Here, too, exotic Jewish groups pose an interesting challenge. Having existed until recently both geographically and symbolically at the periphery of Jewish history and (even more importantly) historiography, such communities had only a limited impact on the construction of the standard accounts of Jewish historical narrative. Living for the most part in countries colonized and dominated by the West, they, like their non-Jewish countrymen, found themselves reduced to an afterthought in the production of a universal (meaning Western) historical narrative. The re-entry of these people into historical consciousness has necessitated both a reshaping of the larger narrative and a rewriting of each group's version of its history.

Of course, it must be remembered that the idea of a common Jewish history as a basis for group identity is itself a problematic concept. As Anthony Appiah notes in his telling critique of W.E.B. DuBois's essay, "On the Conservation of Races," "sharing a common group history cannot be a *criterion* for being members of the same group, for we would have to be able to identify the group in order to identify *its* history."[3]

In the case of exotic Jewish communities, unless carefully drawn (as in the present book) their histories take on a circularity similar to that criticized by Appiah—since they are Jews, they must have participated in a shared Jewish history; since they participated in this shared history, they must be Jews!

All too often the search for a shared Jewish history results in two forms of reductionism. The first kind reduces Jewish history to its lowest common denominator, emphasizing the particular features that the author views as most central at the expense of other, but no less deserving, characteristics. Thus, for example, in many narratives suffering becomes the quintessential Jewish experience. This form of reductionism is often supplemented by another type, which, similar to the legendary beds in Sodom and Gemmorah, stretches and compresses the material to fit a pre-determined narrative. The price one pays for this approach is a homogenization that sacrifices the richness of each group's particular history in order to achieve a single common narrative. The unruly, foreign, and distinctive histories of exotic communities are domesticated, naturalized, and assimilated in the service of the production of a unified group narrative.

HOW DO YOU SAY 'MULTICULTURALISM' IN HEBREW?

So long as these exotic communities remained in distant lands, the issues of history, appearance, and practice were more theoretical than practical. With the "ingathering of the exiles" (yet another expression deriving from the assumption of a shared history), the State of Israel found itself confronted by the challenge of integrating groups with varied cultures and religious traditions.

In the 1950s, Israeli immigrant policy tended to view cultural diversity as an obstacle and treated most immigrants as a *tabula rasa*. The ingathering of the exiles was viewed as a melting pot process in which immigrants groups were turned into Israelis. This approach resembled in many ways French colonial assimilationist policy. Although recent critical depictions of this process have tended to underestimate the genuine limitations faced by absorption officials and overestimate their actual ability to penetrate communal life, the overall picture of an aggressive policy remains accurate. The survival (and politicization) not only of ethnic identities but of distinctive cultural elements is a testimony to the ultimate failure of such assimilationism.

In the 1980s and 1990s Israeli policy toward the Ethiopians and Russians has more closely resembled colonial British indirect rule. Communities have been encouraged to preserve their traditional cultures and tribal representatives have been used to obviate the need to deal directly with diverse populations. Interestingly, if Israeli secular authorities bore the brunt of the criticism for the absorption failures of the '50s, it is the rabbinate and their political allies who have been under fire in recent years. Whether it is the non-rabbinic Judaism of the Ethiopians, the non-Orthodox formulations of many Americans, or the complex family backgrounds of the Russians, Israeli Orthodoxy has found it difficult to accommodate the diversity that is World Jewry today.

The challenge of multiculturalism is, however, not limited to the religious sphere alone. As the book before us richly documents, while almost all Jewish communities used Hebrew for religious purposes, in their daily lives they spoke and wrote a multitude of languages. Some, like Yiddish and Ladino, were Jewish languages; others were simply the vernacular tongues of the people with whom they lived. In contrast to the multi-linguistic United States, Israel has and continues to view modern Hebrew as not only as a national language but as a national treasure. Participation in intensive Hebrew courses known as *ulpanim* is an essential part of the experience of all immigrants to the country, and Israelis often comment with pride at the speed with which young immigrants pick up the language. (Less attention is usually given to the rate at which they lose the facility to speak, read, or write their mother-tongues.) Here too, as in the creation of a unified historical narrative discussed above, it is easy to see the inculcation of a single language as yet another step in the domestication and naturalization of the 'exotic.'

In the final analysis, a significant degree of naturalization and acclimatization may be the inevitable fate of all exotic groups when they migrate to new lands. If so, it is all the more important to document and describe the lives of these communities in their own right. Although Hebrew readers have, for several decades, had growing success to material on these communities through the publications of the Ben Zvi Institute for the Study of Jewish Communities of the Orient and in particular its journal *Pe'amim*, English-speaking readers have only rarely been offered a glimpse into the full diversity of these communities. The book before us is an important contribution in this direction.

NOTES

1. For a particularly good survey of recent scholarly opinions on this topic from a variety of perspectives, including physical anthropology and genetics, see "Contemporary Issues Forum: Race and Racism," Guest Editor, Faye V. Harrison, *American Anthropologist* 100,3 (September 1998).

2. Matt Cartmill, "The Status of the Race Concept in Physical Anthropology," *American Anthropologists 200*, 3 (September 1998): 659.

3. Kwame Anthony Appiah, *My Father's House: Africa in the Philosophy of Culture* (New York and Oxford: Oxford University Press, 1992), p. 32.

Part I

Jewish Girl from Habban, South Yemen
Credit: Yad Ben Zvi Archives

From the Land of Frankincense and Myrrh

BACKGROUND INFORMATION

The Republic of Yemen is situated in the southwest corner of the Arabian Peninsula. Surrounded by high craggy mountains, it is bounded to the north by Saudi Arabia, to the east by Oman, to the south by the Gulf of Aden, and to the west by the Red Sea. Yemen is the most fertile part of Arabia (which is why the Romans referred to Yemen as Arabia Felix or "Happy Arabia"). It is also the most populous country, with a total population estimated at ten million. Yemen is about sixteen hundred miles from Israel.

In the late 1950s Yemen joined the United Arab Republic, forming a federation of states with Egypt and Syria. In 1961 the UAR collapsed and a protracted civil war ensued between rival Yemeni forces. This eventually led to the formation of two separate countries, the Marxist People's Democratic Republic of Yemen (South Yemen) and the pro-Western Yemen Arab Republic (North Yemen). The Republic of Yemen was formed in May 1990 with the reunification of the two Yemens.

Yemen is believed to be the birthplace of the Arab people. According to legend, Yoktan, the father of the Arabs, was born in southern Yemen about 2250 B.C.E. San'a, the capital, is one of the oldest inhabited cities in the world. According to Islamic belief, San'a was founded by the sons of Kathan, a descendant of Shem, the eldest son of Noah. The Yemen of antiquity was known as Sabaea, or Sheba. The visit of the legendary Queen of Sheba to King Solomon is described in the Torah. However, "[t]he idea that the Queen of Sheba ruled in southern Arabia," writes Thomas W. Goodhue, "has been pretty well demolished by H. St. John Philby. . . . The gold and precious stones she is reported to have brought with her to Jerusalem, for example . . . are not found in southern Arabia, but they are in East Africa."[1]

The harbors of Sabaea were a central point for an extensive trade carried on with Egypt and India. The Sabaeans were famous for their cultivation and export of frankincense and myrrh. The aromatic gum resins derived from these spices were used for healing, embalming, personal grooming, and in palaces and temples as a sweet-smelling incense and burnt offering.[2] Another South Arabian people, the Himyarites, overthrew the Sabaeans in the early second century C.E. The Himyarite dynasty lasted until 525 C.E., when the Ethiopians occupied the country. The Ethiopians, in turn, were driven out by the Persians in 575 C.E. In 628 C.E. the Persian satrap of Yemen converted to Islam and the whole of Yemen soon followed suit.

In 897 C.E. a descendant of Mohammed, Yahya ibn al-Hussayn al-Qasim ar Ras, established the Shiite-Zaydi dynasty in northern Yemen. The Zaydis are a sect within Shiite Islam who base their absolute rule on their claim of direct descent from the Prophet. Unlike the main body of Shiites, the Yemeni sect does not accept Mohammed al-Baqir (d. 731 C.E.) as the fifth imam (successor to the founder of Islam), but recognizes his brother Zayd instead. This Shiite Zaydi theocracy lasted almost continuously in northern Yemen until the revolution that established a republic in 1962.

Insurrections against corrupt and oppressive Turkish rule (1538–1636, 1849–1918) caused great upheaval in Yemenite society. In 1905 Imam Yahya ibn Mohammed organized a successful revolt against the Turks and established himself as the undisputed leader of Yemen. The Turks finally retreated from Yemen in 1918 after World War I had stripped the Ottoman state of its power. Yahya was assassinated in 1948 and was succeeded to the throne by his eldest son Saif al-Islam Ahmad. In 1839 the British had taken the Port of Aden by force from the Ottoman Turks and all the sultanates of Western and Eastern Aden became British protectorates. From 1937 until 1962 the Port of Aden was a British crown colony.

Until the middle of the twentieth century, Yemen was still very much a relic from medieval times. Its geographical remoteness made it one of the most unexplored lands in the world. It was one of the few remaining parts of the Arab world where Western influence and technology were hardly known. There were few Yemenite doctors, no industries, no paved roads, and no railway system. Illiteracy among Muslims hovered around ninety-five percent. During the periodic droughts large percentages of the population died from starvation, and the infant mortality rate was appallingly high. The most common malady was trachoma, an eye disease spread largely by flies. Leprosy, malaria, smallpox, and plague were also widespread. In some ways, like India across the Arabian Sea, Yemeni society was based on castes and rigid social classes. Each class and caste fulfilled a specific economic role, and each was separated from the others through a prohibition of intermarriage and eating together. However, the great majority of the Yemeni Muslim tribespeople have usually been free farmers and warriors.

Lacking natural resources, Yemen is still one of the most backward countries in the Middle East and "the physical health of the people . . . is one of the worst in the world. The major causes of the high mortality rate are undernutrition and infections and parasitic diseases."[3] Only with the overthrow of the imamate in 1962 did the isolation of Yemen end. With the discovery of oil in 1986, Yemen is beginning to enter the modern world and become part of the global economic community.

Although considered moderate relative to their counterparts in Persia, the Shiite Muslims of Yemen were notorious for their fanaticism and utter intolerance toward all other religions, including non-Shiite Muslims. The *shariya*, or corpus of Islamic religious codes regarding unbelievers, were rigidly enforced. A source of interminable conflicts in Yemen was—and to this very day is—the mutual antagonisms between the Shiites of the central and northern highland regions and the Shafa'i Sunni Muslims of the lowlands in the south and west. Until the early part of this century, "Yemen was marked by administrative and governmental chaos, with centralized rule only for brief periods in its history."[4]

THE JEWS OF NORTH YEMEN

> Even though the Arabs curse the Jew, swear at him and then beat
> him up for want of anything else to do, deep inside themselves
> they regard the Jew with a certain respect. It is the glowing
> religious fervor of the Yemenite Jew—his personal sacrifices to
> the complicated ritual of his faith, his frequent holidays with their
> varying significance—which makes the Arab look upon the Jew as
> a sort of superman. I have never and nowhere, neither at the
> Wailing Wall in Jerusalem, nor in the crammed ghetto streets of
> Warsaw, seen men practice their religion with more sincere
> devotion and ascetic self-denial than do the Jews in the Yemen.
> —Ladislas Farago, *Arabian Antic* (1938)

> I was astonished to learn that sites for synagogues and Jewish
> cemeteries . . . were sometimes donated by pious Moslems,
> particularly in the smaller villages. . . . [O]n Saturdays the Jews
> spent almost the entire day in the synagogue in prayer and study,
> so that the Jewish community was surrounded by an aura of
> holiness which did not fail to impress its neighbors. I recently
> heard of a Moslem clairvoyant who reported that she had seen the
> Jews in Paradise, sitting and studying the sacred books; she was
> terribly beaten, since the proper place for unbelievers is of
> course Hell, not Paradise; but she insisted that she had seen
> rightly, and no doubt her vision expressed the feelings of many.
> —S. D. Goitein, *The Transplantation of the Yemenites* (1951)

The Yemenites are considered one of the most ancient of Jewish tribes.
Spread out across the length and breadth of northern Yemen in more than one
thousand towns and villages, many of them purely Jewish, they were at various
times institutionally and geographically segregated from their Arab compatriots. Despite only sporadic contact with the outside Jewish world for at least a
thousand years and periodic cruel and heavy-handed treatment at the hands of
the fanatical Shiite clergy, these long-suffering but proud, dignified, and God-
fearing Jews remained unswerving in their religious beliefs. The Jews of Yemen
managed to preserve ancient and unique traditions in a relatively unadulterated
form up to the present day. By virtue of their punctilious adherence to the bib-

lical commandments, their preservation of the Babylonian pronunciation of Hebrew, and their great emphasis on the spiritual dimensions of Judaism, they have been dubbed by one leading scholar as the "most Jewish of all Jews."[5]

In the early centuries of the Common Era, the Yemenites were under the purview of the Babylonian Gaonate. Though cut off from the rest of world Jewry, especially after the rise to power of the xenophobic Shiites in the tenth century, the Yemenites never entirely lost contact with the major centers of Jewish learning such as Baghdad, Jerusalem, and Cairo. They were periodically visited by wandering rabbis and *shelichim* from the Holy Land and elsewhere, more frequently after the seventeenth century. They possessed not only the Talmud, but also the *Shulchan Aruch*, the major Biblical commentaries, and the kabbalistic texts emanating from Safed. In more recent times they somehow even managed to procure sacred books from places as remote as Frankfurt and Vilna. For reasons to be explained later, the Yemenite especially loved and revered the great Sephardi sage Moses Maimonides, and diligently studied his texts. In every generation there arose among the Jews of Yemen great rabbis, philosophers, poets, and mystics. This leadership sustained the Jewish community morally and spiritually, and consoled them with the promise of Redemption during periods of great adversity.

Although solid evidence of Jewish settlement in Yemen exists only from the second century of the Common Era, some communities ascribe their arrival to the period when the Israelites were still wandering in the desert. According to this account, some malcontents, derelict in carrying out Moses' order to wipe out the entire tribe of Amalekites, were forbidden to enter the Promised Land and were exiled to Yemen.

Several local legends harken back to events during Solomonic times. One story has it that King Solomon sent Jewish merchant marines to Yemen to prospect for gold and silver with which to adorn his Temple. According to this view, Jewish colonies in Yemen may have been established during King Solomon's joint naval and commercial ventures with the renowned shipbuilding king Hiram the Phoenician. Another account relates that during her visit to King Solomon, Bilqis, Queen of Sheba, requested from the wise ruler that he send to her land a contingent of skilled Jewish craftsmen. It is not unlikely that in addition to imbibing King Solomon's wisdom, the Queen of Sheba may have come to establish diplomatic and commercial ties with Jerusalem as well as "to secure safe passage through his realm or protection from his expansionist policies, perhaps by offering some form of voluntary tribute."[6] If an historical Queen of Sheba did exist, these various accounts are plausible. However, as pointed out above, recent studies indicate that the gold and precious stones that the Bible tells us the Queen of Sheba brought with her to Jerusalem are found in the Horn of Africa, not in the South Arabian Peninsula.

Other stories hold that the Yemenites are descended from those Jews who fled Judah before the destruction of the First Temple by Nebuchadnezzar in 586 B.C.E. However, there is a legend among the Yemenites that some of their tribe migrated to Yemen many years before this cataclysmic event. Heeding Jeremiah's prophecy of doom for Jerusalem, they fled the holy city. Later, when the Temple was being rebuilt, they were visited by Ezra the Scribe, who summoned them to come back "home," but the Yemenites declined the invitation because they had a strong premonition that the Second Temple, too, would be destroyed. Thereupon, a furious Ezra cursed the Yemenite Jews, prophesying that they would always remain wretched and poverty-stricken.[7] The conclusion of the story is that the Yemenites cursed him back, condemning him to being buried outside the Holy Land. Ezra is believed to be buried in Basra, Iraq.

Many Yemenites attributed all of their later misfortunes to Ezra's curse. Because of their bitter resentment toward him, the Yemenites never name their boys "Ezra." However, some Yemenite sages in Israel today emphatically reject this story as myth—if not outright blasphemy. They insist that Ezra be addressed in the same reverential terms as the other biblical prophets. "The Yemenites' social degradation," Reuben Ahroni soberly informs us, "stems from the extreme primitive and underdeveloped life in Yemen in general, and from the constant rooting out of the Jews from significant economic posts in particular. [The] occasional outbreaks of violence, the pervasive atmosphere of hostility and contempt cultivated by religious fanaticism, are the real causes of the Jews dwindling into insignificance and destitution."[8]

What is certain is that during the Second Temple period Jewish merchant caravans penetrated into southern Arabia. We know this because archeological finds indicate that the Jews in this area were transporting their dead to be interred in Israel. These communities were augmented by exiles who fled the razing of the Second Temple in 70 C.E., the Bar Kochba Revolt in 135 C.E., and the persecutions in the Persian dominions circa 220 C.E. In the centuries before the advent of Islam, Jewish Bedouin tribes of the Southern Arabian Peninsula were numerous and powerful.[9]

In pre-Islamic times, the pagan Arabs of Himyar were polytheistic, worshipping a moon god and other deities. But so successful was Jewish spiritual and political power, and so active were the Jews in proselytizing in the region, that many Arab tribal chieftains adopted Judaism and brought their entire tribes into the Jewish fold. According to De Lacy O'Leary, the proselytes possibly outnumbered the Jews of Judean descent.[10] Ethiopia made numerous attempts to occupy Himyar, with varying degrees of success. In 350 C.E., for example, a Himyarite king named Wakia converted to Judaism, but after the encroachments of the Ethiopians, he opted for Christianity. More successful was Abu-Kariba Asad-Toban (c. 390–420), who, after converting to Judaism, actively campaigned to spread the religion throughout the country.[11] Centuries before Christian missionaries began to spread the gospel in Yemen, Judaism had already made a profound impact on southern Arabian civilization.

Even more dramatic was the conversion of Abu-Kariba's grandson, Zar'a, who reigned from C.E. 518 to 525. Legend ascribes his conversion to his having witnessed a rabbi extinguish a fire worshipped by some Arab magi, merely by reading a passage from the Torah over it.[12] After changing his religion, he assumed the name Yusef Ash'ar, but gained notoriety in history by his cognomen Dhu Nuwas ("Lord of the Curls," possibly because he wore his *peot* long). For some years Dhu Nuwas was successful in staving off Ethiopian incursions and preserving Jewish Himyar's independence. Informed by some Jewish advisors in Tiberias of atrocities perpetrated against Jews in Roman lands, the overzealous proselyte decided on a course of revenge: He executed some Byzantine Christian merchants who were traveling through Himyar on their way to Ethiopia. This outrage led to a rebellion among his Christian subjects in the city of Nejiran, which Dhu Nuwas suppressed with great cruelty. He is said to have cast twenty thousand Christians into pits filled with flaming oil.[13] The massacre and forced conversions of thousands of Christians at Nejiran infuriated Constantine, the Byzantine emperor. As he was occupied in a war with Persia, Constantine sent ambassadors to his Ethiopian Christian ally, King Caleb, entreating him to intervene on behalf of their Arabian coreligionists. With a formidable force of sixty thousand men (some say one hundred twenty thousand), Caleb crossed the Red Sea and attacked the Jewish king. In a fierce battle in 525 C.E. the invaders won a decisive victory. His queen captured and his capital laid waste, Dhu Nuwas chose to escape what was sure to be a cruel death by riding horseback off a cliff into the sea.

Though they had lost their royal state and some Jewish tribes in the region entirely disappeared from the scene, the survivors continued to maintain fierce independence and wielded much influence over their Bedouin Arab compatriots. With the advent of Islam in the seventh century, the political status of Jews underwent a radical change for the worse: They were relegated to the status of second-class citizens. As *Ahl al-Kitab*, neither believers nor infidels but one of the Peoples of the Scriptures, the Jews were assured freedom of religion only in exchange for the *jizya*, payment of a poll tax imposed on all non-Muslims in lieu of military service. Because of the vital services the Jews had provided Mohammed during his conquest of the South Arabian peninsula, the father of Islam issued strict orders not to forcibly convert the Jews of Yemen.[14] Christians, on the other hand, were forcibly converted en masse, and those who wanted to avoid conversion fled to neighboring Ethiopia.

Active Muslim persecution of Jews did not gain full force until the Shiite-Zaydi clan seized power early in the tenth century. In the more traditional orthodox Sunni Muslim countries, such as in Moorish Spain and the Ottoman Empire, Jews and other *dhimmis* generally enjoyed broad religious and social freedoms. Many of the restrictions stipulated by the Pact of Umar, the code of conduct imposed by the Islamic State on its subject "Peoples of the Scriptures" (Christians, Farsis, and Jews), were oftentimes ignored by the rulers. In radical sections of Shiite Islam, such as Persia and Yemen, however, the *shariya* laws regarding the *dhimmis* were interpreted more literally and enforced far more rigidly. Racial and religious intolerance was given legitimacy by the high caste Shiites.[15]

As the only visible outsiders, the Jews of Yemen were treated as pariahs, third-class citizens who needed to be perennially reminded of their submission to the ruling faith. Only some of the more egregious restrictions will be enumerated here. The Jews were considered to be impure, and therefore forbidden to touch a Muslim or a Muslim's food. They were obligated to humble themselves before a Muslim, to walk on his left side, and to greet him first. They were forbidden to raise their voices in front of a Muslim. They could not build houses higher than the Muslims' or ride a camel or horse, and when riding on a mule or donkey, they had to sit sideways. Upon entering the Muslim quarter, a Jew had to take off his footgear and walk barefoot. No Jewish man was permitted to wear a turban or carry the *jambiyyah* (dagger), which was worn universally by the free tribesmen of Yemen. If attacked with stones or fists by Islamic youth, a Jew was not allowed to defend himself. In such circumstances he had the option of fleeing or seeking intervention by a merciful Muslim passerby. According to *shariya*, if a Muslim killed a Jew, his only punishment was an obligation to pay blood money to the victim's family—but even this was done only if two Muslim witnesses could produce evidence against him. Needless to say, the offender would often get away with murder, because no self-respecting Shiite would testify against a brother Muslim for the sake of an unbelieving Jew.

It has been generally assumed that the Yemenite Jews let their *peot* grow long because, as tradition-bound pietists, they were fulfilling the biblical injunction "Ye shall not round the corners of your heads, neither shalt thou mar the corners of thy beard" (Leviticus 19:27) *lefnim meshurat ha-din* ("beyond the prescription of the law"). In fact, according to some authorities, the wearing of the long dangling *peot* (and bald head) was originally a source of great shame for the Yemenites. It was decreed by the imams to distinguish the Jews from the Muslims, so that Jews were not killed by mistake in times of war. The Jews perceived their *peot* as "two long coiling snakes protruding from the cheekbones" and referred to them as *simonim* (distinguishing marks).[16] Later generations, of course, imputed great religious significance to the *peot* by growing them long and devoting time to grooming them. According to Ahroni, this revisionist attitude "only underscores the marvelous ability of the Jews to adapt to their environment and to transform curses into blessings."[17]

Even more degrading and insulting to the religious sensibilities of the Jews were the *Atarot* (Headgear) and Latrine Decrees. The former was a seventeenth-century injunction designed to humiliate the Jews by forbidding them to wear a headcovering. Since the Talmud says "Cover thy head, so that the reverence of Heaven be upon Thee" (*Shabbat* 156b), walking under the open skies and especially praying in the synagogue without some form of headcovering constituted a grave transgression. Only after much pleading, and greasing the palms of the local sheikhs, did the latter yield somewhat; they allowed the Jews to wear rags over their heads. The *Atarot* Decree remained in effect until 1872, after the Turks reconquered Yemen.

The Latrine Decree was a nineteenth-century edict forcing the Jewish community to take responsibility for cleaning out the public toilets and baths and to remove animal carcasses from the streets. "Most members of the community soon evaded the decree," writes Yehuda Nini,

> since there were few who were willing to carry out the task. . . . As a result there emerged a socially inferior group, almost a caste of untouchables. . . . They [and their children] were not called up to read the Torah . . . there was no intermarriage with them. [They] often caused problems to the community. They sometimes went on strike, or fled to one of the nearby villages. The community leaders would conciliate them with gifts . . . but during their absence the task was imposed on the entire community, from scholars to tradesmen, rich and poor, with no exceptions. The Muslim authorities . . . considered the entire community responsible for clearing the dung.[18]

Most devastating and terrifying of all to the pious Jews were the so-called orphan decrees that were periodically instituted: Any child under the age of thirteen whose father died was to be forcibly removed from the Jewish community and brought up in a mosque as a ward of Allah. Although the Jews were generally extremely submissive and obedient, and scrupulously adhered to other degrading edicts, the state-sanctioned kidnapping and conversion of their children to Islam was resisted bitterly. In resisting the "orphan decrees" the Jews were more than willing to die *al kiddush haShem* (to consecrate God's name). One method of circumventing the enforcement of this law was to marry off the child even if he or she was at an extremely tender age (a common practice in Shiite countries) and send him or her to live in the home of the father-in-law. Another way was to hustle the boy off to those Jewish villages in the countryside where the Muslim tribes tended to be both sympathetic to the Jews and hostile toward the imam, and where he could be adopted by relatives, friends, or well-to-do Jews.[19] In more recent times another option was to smuggle the youngster to the British-controlled Port of Aden, which contained a large and prosperous Jewish community.[20] The Shiite practice of abducting and forcibly converting children wreaked havoc on the Jewish community. It also created a subculture of "marranos" with divided loyalties, who lived out their lives in fear and ambivalence.[21]

While there were periodic outbursts of physical violence perpetrated by Muslims against Jews, conscientious Shiites considered such behavior contrary to Islamic law. In fact, it was considered a noble deed to protect, defend, and show mercy toward subject "Peoples of the Scriptures." A person cursing a Jew could theoretically be hauled off to jail and made to pay a fine. Killing or harming a Jew was considered a shameful, mean-spirited act. Relations between Jews and Muslims were generally more amicable in the rural areas. In these territories the Muslims "had preserved the pre-Islamic tribal laws [*taghut*] under which the Jews were considered *jar* [protégé], a status superior to that granted to Jews as a protected minority under orthodox Islamic Law. Persecution, expulsion, and occasionally death threatened only the Jews of San'a, where the ancient tribal laws had lost much of their force."[22] In the rural and mountain areas of Yemen it was not unheard of for Muslim tribesmen to go on the warpath if harm or death befell a Jew attached to their tribe. As long as they paid their *jizya* and adhered strictly to Islamic *dhimmi* laws, the Jews were given complete freedom of worship and full autonomy in communal affairs.

The largest concentration of Jews was situated in the urban centers of San'a and Aden. The rest of the Jews were dispersed over more than a thousand rural towns and mountain villages in Yemen. The Jews of San'a, who claimed to be the progeny of the sentinels who had guarded the Holy Temple in biblical times, tended to look condescendingly on the Jews of the villages. They believed the latter were descended from proselytes and slaves.[23] The Jews living in cities and towns were confined to their own quarters (the *Qa'al Yahud*), separate from the rest of the population. According to Hayyim Cohen, Yemen had the second largest percentage of Jewish farmers in the world[24] (Kurdistan had the largest percentage). In more tolerant times Jewish landowners even hired Muslim *fellahin* to plow their fields.

Although treated as inferiors by the Muslims, the valuable services the Jews provided made them indispensable to Yemeni society. Jews lived all over the country because they were needed everywhere. Islam forbids the faithful from working in the crafts, and manual labor is considered undignified to caste-conscious Shiites. Therefore, the Jews had a virtual monopoly on skilled handicrafts and the trades. Over the centuries the Jews refined their skills and developed a reputation as silversmiths and precious metal workers, and, to a lesser degree, they excelled as potters, tailors, shoemakers, weavers, embroiderers, carpenters, and stonemasons. Some Jews were employed exclusively by the royal palace or by local tribal sheikhs. Others bartered farm implements, weapons, ornaments, and clothing with the surrounding Muslim peasantry for a portion of their harvest yield; if the Muslims' harvest failed, many Jews died of starvation. Still others were itinerant peddlers who sold their wares in Bedouin villages, returning home only for the Sabbath or the holidays. Occupations usually were handed down from father to son.

Because it was so difficult, in a poor country like Yemen, to eke out a living from one trade alone, many Jews mastered a number of different trades. The great Jewish historian of Yemenite Jewry, S. D. Goitein, once wrote about encountering a Jew who was proficient in some thirty crafts, one of which was writing *segulot* (magical Hebrew formulas) for sick cows.[25] Following the example of Hillel (a woodchopper), Shammai (a carpenter), Yochanan the Sandal Maker, and many other talmudic sages, even rabbis in Yemen invariably earned their daily bread by working with their hands. Women's domestic chores included grinding corn, drawing water from wells, painting walls, and repairing furniture. In addition, women contributed to the family coffers, or made money for personal expenses, by weaving, embroidering, making kitchen utensils and brooms, and selling directly to Muslim women.

Yemenite Jewry was never centrally organized. Each community had a headman called an *aqil* (*nasi* in Hebrew) and a *mori*, or rabbi. The *aqil* usually was a worldly and wise elder who had connections with the local tribal chieftain. It was the *aqil*'s responsibility to collect taxes from, and mediate disputes within, the community. He also protected Jewish interests vis-a-vis the government. The headman was elected by the elders of the patronymic groups, and he was paid for his services. The *mori* was responsible for the community's internal affairs. He served as *ma'lameh melamid* (*cheder* teacher), *shochet* (ritual slaughterer), *mohel* (circumciser), and *gabai* (treasurer) of the synagogue. He performed all these functions in addition to working for a living. The highest authority in the land for the Jews was the *beit din* (literally "house of judgment"; actually religious court), a tribunal of three *hakhamim* (sages) presided over by the *av beit din*. During the period of Turkish occupation the Turkish authorities recognized the *hakham bashi* of San'a as the official representative regarding Jewish communal affairs in Yemen. There was at least one occasion when the *hakham bashi* concomitantly served in the capacity of *av beit din* as well.[26]

While illiteracy was almost universal among the Yemenite Muslims, it was a rarity to find a Jewish man who could not read. In addition to the pure Arabic that they spoke in the street, amongst themselves the Jews spoke a hybrid Arabic heavily interspersed with Hebrew. With the exception of some bumpkins in the remote mountain villages, almost every Jewish male exhibited mastery in speaking Hebrew and reading the Torah. "A Yemenite does not desert his studies until his dying breath," writes Noach Mishkowsky.[27] Another observer has remarked that "Even their *am haratzim* (ignoramuses) are scholars."[28] Every Jewish man was expected to be able to perform all the Jewish rituals flawlessly, without need for a professional rabbi. Tremendous emphasis was placed on education and *derech eretz* (moral rectitude and upright behavior). There was a pervasive fear among the Yemenites that a father who died without having provided his sons instruction in the Torah would be deprived of his share in *olam habah* (the World to Come). Fathers who were derelict in their responsibilities to their sons were treated as outcasts by other Yemenite Jews. For example, the *shochet* might refuse to slaughter for them, so that the family was deprived of meat, and the father would not be counted as part of the *minyan*.[29]

In the larger Jewish communities, such as San'a and Sad'a, boys were sent to *ma'lameh* when they turned three. After being given his first haircut, leaving only the *peot* intact, a Yemenite boy was wrapped in his father's tallit (prayer shawl), and carried off to the *ma'lameh*. After the father and the *mori* exchanged blessings, the *mori* handed his new charge a piece of candy. The child then was seated in a circle of his peers on the dirt floor of a room in the back of the synagogue. One early-twentieth-century observer described these classrooms as dirty and poorly ventilated.[30] The boys were taught by mechanical repetition to memorize the prayers and the Torah by heart. Memorization was extremely important in impoverished Yemen because there was such a great scarcity of Holy Books. The few books that were available for students in *ma'lameh* were placed in the center of the circle so that six or eight children were obligated to read from one book. Thus Yemenite Jewish children developed the marvelous ability to read the text not only right side up, but sideways and upside down as well.

Boys attended *ma'lameh* from early dawn to sunset Sunday through Thursday and until noon on Friday. Testing usually took place on Wednesday, and woe unto the youngster who could not recite the text flawlessly. He was considered to be possessed by demons who were distracting his attention from Torah studies, and he would be beaten with a stick or a strap for every mistake. Fathers literally pleaded with the *mori* to take whatever punitive measures were necessary to drive the evil demons out as long as he did not injure the child. It is no wonder that by the time they were ready to leave the *ma'lameh*, many Yemenite boys could recite by heart the entire Torah; whole sections of *hilchat shechita*, the talmudic tractate pertaining to the laws of ritual slaughtering; and Maimonides' *Mishneh Torah* (Code of Law). It was common to find in Yemen certified ritual slaughterers who had not yet reached their teens. It was also common to find children aged nine or ten who functioned as teaching assistants, or even as master teachers. Many of these children were orphans or runaways who were available to travel even to the remote villages to teach. More often the *mori* was someone who, for whatever reason, never learned a trade or was an elderly man who had taken up teaching upon reaching retirement.[31]

Because Yemenite Jewish families tended to be large and poor, boys were usually taken out of school at twelve or thirteen, or even earlier, and apprenticed to their fathers or some other relative.[32] Oftentimes this transition was met with a great deal of resistance from the boy's mother. Although completely illiterate herself, the Yemenite Jewish mother ardently believed that studying Torah was the highest merit a man could attain and therefore her greatest fulfillment in life was to raise a *talmud hakham* (talmudic scholar). She would fight her husband hammer and tongs to prolong her child's Jewish education.

The concept of childhood was almost nonexistent among the Jews in Yemen. There were no rites of passage such as the bar mitzvah ceremony for a boy, and there was no fixed age for donning *tefillin* (phylacteries). A boy began to put on *tefillin* when his father decided the boy was mature enough, which in Yemen could be as young as eight or nine. Since, according to halakha (rabbinic law), a father is not obligated to provide for his sons after they have reached the age of six, many youngsters who came of age were placed on their father's or other relative's "work-study" program: As he sat side by side with his boy, teaching him the intricacies of his craft, the father would at the same time engage him in discussions of the Holy Texts. By engaging in Torah and work simultaneously, writes S. D. Goitein, Yemenite Jewish men "realized the ancient Jewish ideal of embodying in everyday life the combination of productive manual labor with a preoccupation with the intellectual sacred tradition."[33]

Goitein's statement also explains why *yeshivot* and *kolellim* (post-rabbinical academies like those in Eastern Europe) did not exist in Yemen. Another reason is that there simply was not an economic class that could undertake to support large numbers of young men, many of them with wives and children. The term "yeshiva" in Yemen meant something entirely different from the institution that evolved in the Eastern European milieu. "The San'a yeshiva did not offer instructions, but engaged solely in clarifying religious problems and passing judgment . . . and [served as] a high court of appeal."[34] Adult education, where it existed, was of the "night school" variety: After work the men would go to the local *bet hamedrish*, or House of Study, to attend a *mori*'s lecture on the Talmud or some mystical tract, and then they would pair off and review the text. Yemenite Jews, as a general rule, did not excel as talmudists. Emphasis was placed on mastering the *Mishnah* only. *Gemurah* (discussions and elaborations of the *Mishnah*) with *mefurshim* (additional comments on the Talmud) were an extracurricular course of study engaged in almost exclusively by those who were studying for the rabbinate.

"Yemenite Hebrew literature," writes Ahroni, "reflects the enormous spiritual fortitude and courage which Yemenite Jewry manifested in the face of the incredible horror of reality."[35] Much of the creative literature produced by Yemenite Jews was of an ecclesiastical nature and was greatly influenced by Maimonides and the Sephardi masters of Hebrew verse. Lurianic mysticism emanating from Safed reached Yemen through *shelichim* (emissaries) from Palestine who periodically came to Yemen to raise funds for various charitable projects. The spiritual prestige of the Holy Land was enhanced by the visitors and, as a consequence, some outstanding Yemenite sages felt impelled to make *aliyah*. Rabbi Shalom Shabazi is universally recognized as Yemenite Jewry's greatest poet and saint. Born in Ta'izz, South Yemen, in 1619, he earned his living as an itinerant weaver. He is said to have written thousands of hymns and poems, only some five hundred and fifty of which survived the infamous Mawza Decree (see below). The great preponderance of his poems, written in Hebrew, Aramaic, and Arabic, are spiritual in nature and deal primarily with the themes of exile and redemption, eschatology, the Jewish life cycle, and ethics and morality. Yehuda Ratzaby estimates that about half the poems of the Yemenite *diwan* were composed by Shabazi.[36] The *diwan* is a collection of poems that are intended to be sung or chanted. In most *mizrachi* lands these *diwans* are preserved in writing, but the music and dances that accompany them are transmitted orally.

According to musicologist Avner Bahat, the Yemenite *diwan* is the "richest and most valuable of all."[37] Rabbi Shabazi is believed to have died in Ta'izz in 1681. He was revered as a *tzaddik* (saint) and miracle worker by Jew and Arab alike, who made pilgrimages to his grave to receive his grace.

Education for men and boys was considered essential, but Jewish women in Yemen were kept illiterate. There was a pervasive belief that should girls ever be taught to read, crime would proliferate and the world would be deluged with torrential rainstorms.[38] A popular Yemenite proverb states that one who reads aloud to his mother will never make a mistake, because his mother would never know the difference.[39] Only in rare cases, where a father had no sons, would he give his daughter or daughters a formal Jewish education. Women were required to have thorough knowledge of the laws pertaining to *kashrut* and *taharat mishpachah* (family purity), and life cycles. Some women even mastered the laws of *shechita*, thereby acting as ritual slaughterers. These laws and a whole repository of oral traditions, proverbs, and songs were passed down through the generations from mother to daughter.[40]

In Yemen it was common to find a thirteen-year-old girl already a mother. Customarily, girls married between the ages of ten and twelve. Boys married between the ages of thirteen and fifteen. Early marriage was believed to be literally a prophylactic for *mowtzy zerah levatalah* (masturbation) and lascivious thoughts. Since the commandment to "be fruitful and multiply" was taken seriously in Yemen, bachelors and old maids were virtually nonexistent. The desire to have sons was especially great because Yemenite Jewish parents wanted to have someone to say *kaddish* for them when they died.[41] In the more urbanized and relatively more prosperous communities the parents generally decided who was an appropriate match, but they sometimes conferred with their child before proceeding with the negotiations.

The marriage festivities were a lavish fourteen-day affair, beginning a week before the wedding and lasting through the following seven days of banqueting known as *sheva bruchot*, or seven blessings. During the wedding and the ensuing banquets, men and women sat and danced in separate areas. Sometime prior to the wedding ceremony, the bridesmaids would smear henna dye on the palms and soles of the bride, to assure her good fortune. The bride's female entourage was dressed exactly like the bride herself so that the *shaidim* (demons), who are always presumed to be intent on harming the bride, would be confused.[42] A unique and touching aspect of the Yemenite wedding "was the solemn moment when the door leading from the room of the women to the hall of the men was opened and the bridegroom walked up to his mother and kissed her knee, asking her forgiveness for all his sins in word and deed against her."[43] By custom, newlywed women were not allowed to leave their husband's abode for two months. The rationale was that a young bride would become homesick for her parents and run away from her husband.[44]

Like most other *edot hamizrach* in Islamic lands, the Yemenites never accepted the *herem Rabbainu Gershom*, an eleventh-century decree named after the authoritative Ashkenazi rabbi who outlawed polygamy. Those who could afford to had multiple wives. Joseph Halevy encountered Jewish men in Yemen in the nineteenth century who had eight to ten wives.[45] If a man's first wife was barren, or had borne only daughters, the man would take a second wife. Sometimes the motive was solely sexual gratification.[46] In the villages it was common for an older man, with children and even grandchildren, to buy a very young girl from her father. He would serve as her guardian and raise her until she reached the customary age for marriage, at which time he would marry her. A Muslim researcher who visited the Jewish community of Yemen before the mass migrations of the late 1940s encountered one Jew of nearly fifty years old who had nine wives, the youngest only eight.[47]

Urban Yemen is the original home of the high-rise buildings, many of them dating back to the early centuries of the Common Era. These freestanding structures are as much as twenty stories high. Made of brick and stone, they were decorated with whitewashed details. Jewish urban dwellings were lower than those of their Muslim neighbors, and generally not more than four stories tall.[48] Carl Rathjens believes that it was Jewish arrivals of the early C.E. period who brought with them the idea of the "Mediterranean style" house with an open court in the center.[49] One of the distinguishing features of the Jewish house in San'a was that a room, or several rooms, on the top of the house could be easily converted into a *sukkah*.[50] In the villages, Jews lived in clay huts or even in caves like their Muslim neighbors. Beds, chairs, and tables were unknown in Yemen. People ate and slept on palm mats and carpets. Foreign travelers who visited the Jewish quarter in San'a observed that the Jews were less prone to diseases than the Muslims, because their streets and houses were generally cleaner and less insect infected.[51] So as not to arouse the envy of the Muslims, Jewish dwellings appeared very modest from the outside.

For similar reasons, the Jews were extremely inconspicuous in their dress, especially when venturing outside the Jewish quarter. On weekdays they were outfitted entirely in black, like peasants. Even wealthier Jews dressed modestly so as not to draw resentment and hostility from the Muslims. Men wore a long strip of cloth that was fitted like a skirt. In Yemen, only women wore trousers. Only relatively affluent urban Jews, both male and female, could afford to wear a type of leather shoe. A dark-colored *gargush* (cowl) embroidered with silver ornaments was a woman's traditional headdress. Though not veiled like Muslim women, Jewish women pulled the shawl across their faces when approached by strangers. On the Sabbath and holidays, when the gate to the *Qa'al Yahud*, the Jewish quarter, was closed off to the outside world, Jews were less inhibited and donned their best finery. The men would wear white robes with fancy multicolored belts, and the women were attired in beautifully embroidered shawls and exquisite jewelry.[52]

Locusts are the most widely prized and heavily consumed insect in the Third World.[53] In Yemen, they were an integral part of the staple diet, eaten "seasonally" by all the inhabitants. Leviticus (11:21–22) mentions four species of locusts that are kosher to eat.[54] Because later rabbinical authorities did not have a *mesorah* (oral tradition) and had forgotten how to recognize these kosher locusts, they rendered all forms of the species taboo. The Yemenite Jews had a way of identifying the pure varieties of locust, and this was passed down through the generations. They could identify four types by sight: the reddish locust, which was considered the creme de la creme, followed in descending order of quality by the spotted grays, the yellows, and the whites. The last variety was much too meager and fibrous to make a hearty meal.

When swarms of locusts were sighted in the hills, Jews would send scouts late at night to locate their nesting areas. The scouts would light bonfires in the general vicinity of the nests to serve as a beacon. Before dawn the next morning, when the locusts were covered with frosty dew, entire families, carrying sheepskin sacks and backpacks, large sticks to use as crutches, threads and needles (in case the sacks tore), and some breakfast, would ascend the hills in the direction of the bonfires. The docile insects were collected until the sacks were full. Sometimes a team effort was required. When multitudes of locusts were in the trees, one person would climb up and shake the branches while those below hastily scooped them up. The supply of locusts was then divided equally among them all.

The locusts were spread out on the rooftop or in the yard to dry, and stored in large containers. They were usually baked in a stove until crisp. Sometimes the locusts were boiled and then dried in the same manner as described above. They would be sautéed in a clay pot after being boiled, and then spiced with salt, black pepper, and ground cumin. Sometimes dessicated locust was ground to a powder then mixed with milk or kneaded with flour, and this paste was seasoned with salt and butter.[55] The legs and wings, which are tasteless, were plucked, and the head, which was decapitated (thereby removing the guts), was never eaten. In *Black Tents of Arabia*, written in 1947, Carl R. Raswan gives us a "taste" of locusts from the perspective of a Westerner's palate:

Boiled, I did not like locust; they had the taste of particularly insipid cabbage or some such vegetable. Roasted, I found them more palatable; crisp outside, and inside something like tender spinach. In neither case did they taste at all like meat. They are clean animals and as food not at all unpleasant, but one gets very tired of them, when one has to eat nothing else day after day. . . . Men and women, dogs and camels, fed on them—but only for a few days; after that they turned one's stomach. But what was left was carefully preserved for other and leaner times, for when the locusts swarm in vast numbers, one can safely predict drought and famine.[56]

Among the privileged Yemenite Jews, locust was usually eaten as a dessert; for the destitute, especially in times of drought, they often served as a main course as long as they were plentiful.

In Yemen, as in the Horn of East Africa, the ancient custom of chewing *catha edulis*—or qat leaves—continues to this day. The Islamic masses, forbidden from drinking alcohol, chew the tender oval leaves and fiber from young shoots of the qat plant. This sour-tasting mountain shrub, referred to by the cognoscenti as the "Flower of Paradise," is a minor narcotic, which the locals believe suppresses the appetite, gives added strength, increases alertness, eases bowel movement, is a cure for melancholia and depression, alleviates vomiting in early pregnancy, and acts as a slight aphrodisiac. However, according to a 1988 study in the *Journal of Substance Abuse Treatment*, long-term consumption causes chronic insomnia, emotional instability, anorexia and gastric disorders, and loss of sex drive, among other things.[57] Far from being illegal, the use of qat in Yemen is "socially sanctioned and even prestigious, and . . . many houses have a special room devoted to regular sessions of khat chewing."[58] The qat habit has reached almost epidemic proportions. In the heyday of Nancy Reagan's "Say No to Drugs" campaign, the Yemeni consul in San Francisco, with a somber, almost apologetic tone informed me that currently about half of his countrymen were habitual chewers. Other sources put the estimate as high as ninety percent.[59] The typical consumer prefers to take his or her qat in social situations, usually after the noon meal. The leaves are not swallowed, but are rolled into a little ball like chewing tobacco and tucked between the cheek and gums. After chewing them for up to an hour, the user spits the residue into a basin. While blissfully chewing the leaves, one usually also partakes of the *nargila* or water pipe, strong mocha with sugar, and plenty of bottles of spiced cold water to relieve the parched mouth that qat causes. A typical Yemeni spends about a third of his income on qat.[60]

The Yemenite Jews habitually chewed qat in the synagogue for inspiration during study and prayer sessions, and also when the men and women were socializing. Many inspired *diwans* and kabbalistic tracts were presumably written under its influence. At wedding ceremonies, circumcisions, and other festivities, qat was usually "highballed" with shots of homemade *aragi* (barley brandy). According to a number of scholars and medical researchers, some elderly Yemenite Jews who were interviewed for this book, and from me personal observations among recent arrivals in Israel, there were many habitual users and abusers of the qat and alcohol combination among the Jews of Yemen.[61]

"As in any other Jewish community," writes Bat-Zion Eraqi Klorman, "Yemeni Jews were not isolated from their surrounding environment and were not free of its social and cultural influences. . . ."[62] It is no coincidence that when Yemen was governed by a dynasty of rulers who had *mahdist* (messianic) pretensions and who actively sought the coming of the messianic age, messianic hopes were intensified among the Jews."[63] The Jews of Yemen had absolute faith in the coming of their Messiah. The relentless persecutions and social upheavals that so often wreaked havoc on their lives made the Jews of Yemen especially susceptible to pretenders, some well meaning, who passed themselves off as the Messiah or heralded his coming. In one such case, the Jews' joy in the Redemption underwent a radical turnaround when one particularly influential charlatan was caught by the Yemenite Muslim authorities and beheaded. In the aftermath, many Jews were forcibly converted to Islam, while many others lost their faith in Judaism and voluntarily converted. Upon hearing of their great distress, Maimonides sent the Jews of Yemen an epistle, exhorting them to stay faithful to the Jewish God. His passionate and brilliant letter, dated 1172 c.e., did much to uplift the spirits of the Jews and stemmed the tide of conversion.[64] Out of gratitude to the great Sephardi sage, the Jews of Yemen include his name when reciting the *kaddish* and diligently study his texts.

Like Jewish communities the world over, the Yemenites responded with great enthusiasm to the call of that most infamous of Jewish false messiahs, Shabbatei Zvi (1626–76). Under his influence, many Yemenites made preparations to leave for Palestine. When word of their intentions reached the ear of the imam, he promptly rounded up the ringleaders and the Chief Rabbi of San'a and mockingly paraded them through the streets before torturing them to death.

During the turbulent period of the second Turkish occupation of Yemen, no fewer than three self-styled harbingers of the Messiah appeared on the scene. Shukr Kuhayl, an extremely pious ascetic from a village west of San'a, claimed that Elijah the Prophet had appeared to him and exhorted him to announce the Messiah's arrival. Multitudes believed him and followed him. Even many of the leading rabbis of San'a were sympathetic to his cause, and did not denounce him outright because he was earnestly enjoining the Jews to repent. In the end, the imam had him shot and his head hung at the gate of the Jewish quarter. Four years after Shukr Kuhayl was executed another aspirant appeared, this time from San'a. He claimed to be Shukr Kuhayl reincarnate, an emissary of the Messiah resurrected by none other than Elijah the Prophet himself. Shukr Kuhayl II had even greater ambitions than his predecessor and sent letters to Jews in neighboring countries—Aden, India, Egypt, even Palestine—informing them of his mission. Like Shukr Kuhayl I, he called upon the Jewish masses the world over to repent and punctiliously observe the *mitzvot*, but he also demanded that the Jews send him their tithing, which he made compulsory. European Jews who visited Yemen around this time accused Shukr Kuhayl II of distributing some of this money to Muslims in order to bribe them to convert. One Palestinian rabbi wrote a very incisive letter in the style of Moses Maimonides' "Epistle to Yemen" that lambasted the pretender. Shukr Kuhayl II eventually was apprehended by the Turkish authorities and sent to prison in Constantinople. Still another false messiah, Yosef Abdallah, appeared in 1893 and, like Shukr Kuhayl, was very popular with Jewish inhabitants of the villages. But the rabbis of San'a nipped this apocalyptic's career in the bud.[65]

Whereas the condition of the Jews in other parts of the world were markedly improved under Ottoman occupation, for the most part Turkish rule of Yemen marked the advent of their darkest period. The Ottomans were unable to maintain more than nominal control of Yemen after conquering the country in 1538. During the incessant power struggles between the Zaydi imams and the Turks, the Jews invariably sided with the latter, and for this act of perfidy they paid a heavy toll in deaths and incarcerations. Communications with world Jewry were severely hampered, and the Yemenite Jews were more isolated than ever. The Zaydis temporarily succeeded in driving out the Turks in 1676, and their next move was to exact revenge upon the Jews. In what is infamously known as the "Decree of Mawza" (1679), all San'aian Jews who did not convert to Islam had their houses and property confiscated and were sent into exile to live in a desolate, malaria-infested area on the Tihama coast called Mawza. Compassionate, pious Muslims along the way, including the district governor, provided them with sustenance and protection. A year later some tribal chieftains from San'a interceded with the imam on the Jews' behalf. They argued that the Jewish craftsmen were indispensable to the capital, and warned him of divine retribution if the Jews were harmed. The imam acceded to their demands, but the Jews were not permitted to return to their original homes. Instead, they were compelled to settle in a special quarter outside the city limits. During this period of exile three-quarters of San'a's Jews perished, and most of their sacred texts were destroyed.[66]

In 1762, the imam al-Mahdi Abbas ordered the destruction of all synagogues. Thirty years later his son, al-Mansur Ali, whose decadent lifestyle had depleted the state treasury, permitted the Jewish community to rebuild the synagogues upon payment of large fees. In 1818 the tribes of the Bakil and Hashed confederation rebelled against the weak central government in San'a. They sacked the city and left it in ruins. The population of Yemen was greatly depleted during the incessant hostilities and the ensuing famines, which were inevitably followed by an outbreak of plague. Because the Jews of San'a did not own land, they invariably were the first to starve to death. Only a small fraction of the already decimated Jewish population of San'a had managed to survive when the Turks reoccupied Yemen in 1849. Their arrival was welcomed by the Jews, and during this short but relatively liberal period of Turkish rule (actually, the Ottomans did not consolidate their rule over Yemen until 1872), the Jews were able to reestablish contact with their coreligionists around the world. Many of the severe restrictions that had been imposed on the Jews by the Zaydis, such as the Latrine Decree, were temporarily relaxed. Jews were given permission to build a new quarter and to erect synagogues in their new neighborhoods. However, after intense Shiite pressure was brought to bear on the Turks, these privileges were rescinded.

The years preceding their mass migration to Palestine were difficult ones for the Jews of Yemen. Turkish rule was never stable, and continuous battles raged between the occupying army and the imam and the local tribal chieftains. The Jews suffered greatly during the chaos and anarchy caused by this protracted struggle. The Turks exacerbated Jewish woes by forcing the already greatly impoverished Jewish community to lodge soldiers in their homes, and by requiring the Jews to grind flour for storage in their army depots. In 1905, a year of heavy drought, the strife between Imam Yahya and the Turkish overlords resulted in the deaths of 20,000 Yemenite Jews from starvation—6,000 alone in beleaguered San'a. In the end, the imam gained the upper hand, the Turks were forced to relinquish the capital, and the imam was given control over the country's internal affairs. At his inauguration the Imam Yahya reinstituted a strict Shiite theocracy and restored many of the old *dhimmi* laws that had been enforced only loosely by the Turks.

Throughout the centuries, Jews of Yemen maintained close links with the Holy Land. Zionist propaganda began to infiltrate Yemen in the 1870s, and a small vanguard colony of Yemenite Jews existed in Jaffa in 1875, seven years earlier than the arrival of the noted BILU group from Russia. But the real beginning of a substantial Yemenite presence in the Holy Land commenced in 1882. Yemenite Jews considered that year an auspicious time to make *aliyah* because they had calculated by gematria that the Jewish year 5542 (1882) would be the year of Redemption. Also, at that time, false rumors had spread among the Jews of San'a that Rothschild, king and spiritual leader of the Jews [*sic*], was buying up land from the Turks in Palestine to give to Jews, and that the Ottomans were maintaining an open door policy for any Jews who wanted to settle there.

In a perilous journey during 1882 that took months, Jews trudged across the desert by foot and caravan to the ports of the Red Sea. Many died en route. Some ran short of money and had to return to Yemen. Those who did arrive safely were in for a bitter disappointment. Penniless, they could not afford to pay rent for lodgings. Entire families were compelled to sleep outdoors under the trees in the summertime, and during the rainy season they found shelter in crevices beneath the city walls of Old Jerusalem. Shunned by the surrounding Jewish population as dark-skinned primitives, the Yemenites survived by undertaking the most demeaning, back-breaking tasks, those that no one else would accept. Eventually, after a journalistic outcry, a rich Baghdadi Jew came through with funds to erect a housing project on the Mount of Olives in Jerusalem. A second wave of immigrants from the rural parts of North Yemen arrived in 1907. This hardier group chose to live in the new agricultural settlements in Rehovot, Petach Tikva, and Gedaira, all near Tel Aviv. The influx of large groups of Yemenite proletarians were of great ideological and personal concern to the leaders of the Poalei Zion movement, especially the future first prime minister of Israel, David Ben Gurion. They feared that the "apparently tractable and uncomplaining [Yemenite] workers were being exploited and given second-class status . . . [and] that their lack of secular socialist ideology would water down and weaken the Zionist workers' movement."[67] Some Zionists found it troubling that the Yemenites were being used merely as a tool in "conquering" Jewish labor from the Arabs.[68] After 1912, Palestinian emissaries curtailed their Zionist activities among the Yemenites, and *aliyah* stopped completely with the onset of World War I.

Despite the fact that the Imam Yahya had reenacted the notorious "orphan decree," Yemenite Jews spoke of him with a certain fondness and respect.[69] Yahya reinstituted a strict Islamic theocracy and the rampant lawlessness and wild disorder that had existed under the Turks, which had brought great ruin upon the Jewish community, was ruthlessly suppressed. Imam Yahya was a benevolent tyrant who protected his Jews and gave them a sense of security. He gave them unprecedented freedoms, such as the right to live outside the walls of the ghetto and to sell their wares in the Arab *suqs*. Swift and harsh Islamic justice was applied to those Muslims who reviled, cheated, harmed, or murdered a Jew. But the imam also was vehemently opposed to the Jewish emigration to Israel. He therefore forbade them from selling their property and houses when leaving the country. According to Ladislas Farago, the *London Chronicle* correspondent who visited Yemen in the late 1930s, "The imam needed his Jews, who are the country's only artisans and darn good rent collectors; he needed them as an example of clean life and sober ideals. His refusal to let them go was misunderstood by the Zionists. They believed the imam wanted to keep them in tyranny, and so illegal means were sought to help them slip out of the country to Aden, where the Jewish Agency had established a branch office to help these refugees reach Palestine."[70] Imam Yahya's prohibition against emigration proved very difficult to enforce. By the end of World War II, some 40,000 Yemenite Jews were living in Palestine.

Following the establishment of the State of Israel and its ensuing victories against the combined Arab forces in 1948, the successor to the throne, Saif al-Islam Ahmad, permitted the Jews to leave Yemen. Perhaps it was because he was more tolerant and magnanimous than his father Yahya, or maybe he feared reprisals from the Israelis if he refused to let them go. In any event, the Jews were permitted to leave only on the condition that they first teach their crafts to the Muslims. In some places the local tribal chieftains were in great fear that the Jews would leave without imparting their skills to the Muslims, so they put Jewish artisans in chains to prevent this from happening.[71]

Entire Jewish communities from hundreds of towns and hamlets in Yemen made the tortuous trek of hundreds of miles through the wilderness, on foot or by donkey, to the Hashed transit camp outside the British-controlled Port of Aden. The more affluent Yemenite Jews supported those who were traveling penniless. Sultans upon whose territory the Jews needed to trespass had to be bribed, and Arab bandits lurked in the mountains waiting to attack the Jewish caravans. Those who survived the ordeal arrived at the Hashed transit camp ill from various tropical diseases, and psychologically debilitated.[72] Arriving in the swampy Hashed camp, Jews found thousands of coreligionists who had fled years earlier because of a famine in Yemen but had not yet transferred to Palestine due to the restrictive immigration policies of the British government. Also swelling the numbers in the camp were some 1500 Adeni Jews who had been evacuated from the Jewish quarter there after Arab marauders had perpetrated a pogrom against them following the United Nations partition of Palestine in 1947.

Geula, as the Hashed camp was called, was set up by the Israeli government with assistance from the American Jewish Joint Distribution Committee.

This camp originally was meant to accommodate one thousand, but it soon brimmed to a crisis point with twenty times that number. There was a constant fear of typhus and other epidemic diseases. To expedite the evacuation of the refugees from the camp, the Joint Distribution Committee leased six big Skymaster planes from Alaska Airlines to fly between Aden and Lod. While in the camps, the Yemenite Jews were given a crash course in Western ways. Men who had never seen a pair of pants learned the knack of putting them on by standing on one leg at a time without falling down. A bed, the Joint social workers kept insisting, was something one slept upon, not under. When the Yemenites first heard a radio, they ran around shrieking hysterically about boxes talking at them.[73] They enjoyed the showers so much they would stand under them for hours and literally would have to be dragged away kicking.[74]

In his book *Operation Magic Carpet*, Israeli journalist Shlomo Barer gave a lively and entertaining account of what he observed in this tent city in the desert:

> They were issued new clothes with the result that shrinking Patriarchs of the Bible were sporting rainbow-striped sweatshirts and tennis shorts with perhaps a towel for headgear. The women, to cover the shame of bare legs, would lengthen their new dresses by fastening a towel around their knees. . . . They were afraid and suspicious of white men and long serf-dom had bent their backs and made them servile and herd-like.
>
> The nicest of all stories were about their childlike belief in God and the Bible. God had written "signs in the sky" to let them know that the exile in the Yemen was over, whereupon they had packed up and left. And though they came from a world still unconquered by the machine age and its ways of transport, none had been in the least surprised to find giant flying machines waiting for them; for is it not written in the Book of Exodus, "Ye have seen how I bore you on the wings of eagles," and had not the prophet Isaiah foretold, "They that wait upon the Lord . . . shall mount up with wings as eagles?"[75]

Operation On Eagles' Wings (condescendingly dubbed Operation Magic Carpet by Israeli bureaucrats and social workers on the scene), commenced in December 1948 and was concluded in September 1950. Almost 49,000 Yemenite Jews were airlifted to Israel. Because their average weight was under ninety pounds, up to 150 passengers could be put on a plane meant to carry about sixty. Many carried on board little more than their Torah scrolls, other sacred objects, and the clothing on their backs. Three babies were born during Operation On Eagles' Wings flights. It has been said that the planes that brought the Yemenites to Israel spanned not only a thousand miles but also a thousand years. By 1953 there were an estimated 100,000 Yemenites in Israel.

Some Yemenites swear that Israeli government officials swindled and robbed them of hundreds of Torah scrolls, Holy Books, and other artifacts they had brought with them from the Old Country. These were priceless historical antiquities. Upon entering Israel, the Yemenites were informed that these items would be stored for them until they settled in their new homes. Some Yemenites found that when they attempted to retrieve their sacred items, they could not be located—and they never did get them back. Considering the chaotic circumstances and conditions of the Yemenite arrival and resettlement, perhaps it is inevitable that at least some of these items would be stolen or lost. The Yemenites and a segment of the *chareidim*, or ultra-Orthodox, believe that the missing objects found their way into the international underground antiquities market.[76]

Far more tragic is the disappearance of Yemenite children who arrived in Israel in 1949–50. At the time of their arrival the Yemenites were living in makeshift transit camps called *ma'abarot*. Infants were plucked from their (often very young) nursing mothers' arms and ostensibly taken to hospitals, where they "died." Parents never saw the body, the grave, or the birth certificate. It is firmly believed by the Yemenites themselves that these kidnapped babies were adopted by Ashkenazi families who had lost their children in the Holocaust, or possibly to childless American Jews.[77] Estimates of the numbers of disappeared babies range from twenty-two (the government figure) to 4,000 (allegations made by Yemenite militants). This is a festering problem that surfaces now and again in response to public outrage by the families of the disappeared children and their sympathizers. In May 1994 a shootout took place between the police and Waco-style Yemenite cult leader Uzi Meshulam and forty of his heavily armed followers. They barricaded themselves inside a synagogue complex, demanding a commission of inquiry into the disappearance of the children. After an exchange of gunfire, in which one of the militants was killed, Meshulam and his followers agreed to surrender after some sympathetic MP's promised them a more aggressive investigation.[78] As of late 1999 the mystery of the disappeared children remains unsolved.

When they first arrived in Israel, the Yemenite newcomers were quarantined, sprayed with DDT, vaccinated, and provided with new sets of clothing. Their first employment in Israel was as farm workers, picking oranges. The Yemenites established a reputation for being industrious and diligent, but were treated like inferiors and exploited by their fellow Jews. Almost from the very outset, Jewish life in Israel proved to be a bad dream for the Yemenites who had wanted only to live in holiness. In the early 1950s Raphael Patai made the following observation about the way in which the lives of the Yemenite Jews were radically changed by their move to the Holy Land:

> In Palestine . . . [the Yemenites] were forced to do the bidding of others. They were regarded as unskilled laborers who must be prepared to work hard and to earn little. . . . [T]hey were treated by the other Jews as if they were an inferior tribe, lacking in education as well as descent. Their life was hard. They had to hurry to work early in the morning, remain far away from home all day long, eat an unsatisfying meal squatting in the field under a tree or in the narrow shade of an unfinished wall, and run after new employment in the evening. . . . Gone were the days when they could spend unhurried hours in the synagogue, teach their children Torah and artisanry, and take their leisurely meals in the company of wife and child. The inadequacies of a man's earnings soon forced also his wife to seek employment, and as the only work to be found was domestic help, she too was lifted out of her home for the duration of the entire day, leaving her smaller child in the care of the six-and seven-year-olds. Another year or two and the oldest girl too had to go to work to serve in the house of some Ashkenazi *giveret* (madam) while the boy was taken out of the Torah school and forced to fend for himself in the streets. The family was dispersed, paternal and maternal authority was broken down, and the home, once the proud, safe and sequestered castle of the family turned into the occasional meeting-place for people who were becoming more and more estranged.[79]

The mass influx of Ashkenazim fleeing Fascism in Eastern Europe before and after the Holocaust had squeezed many Yemenites from the earlier *aliyot* out of even the lowliest jobs. Some Yemenites joined underground terrorist groups, while others turned to black marketeering and hooliganism.[80] It was said that the Yemenites were the brains behind the Israeli mafia, while the Moroccans provided the muscle.

Over time, the Yemenites have blended successfully into the Israeli melting pot. They are estimated to number around 200,000, of whom approximately forty percent live in the greater Tel Aviv area. They are well represented in the professions and have the lowest rate of criminality of all the *edot*—or ethnic Jewish communities—in Israel. No other non-Ashkenazi group has influenced Israeli culture the way the Yemenites have. Constituting only five percent of the population (before the recent arrival of masses of Russian and Ethiopian Jews), the Yemenites have always been disproportionately well represented in the arts. Their music and dance are considered to be the most ancient and authentic form of Middle Eastern artistic expression.[81] Many Israeli folk songs are based on Yemenite religious poetry and musical themes. Traditional Yemenite folk dance has become synonymous with popular Israeli dance. Much of the craftwork thought of as "Israeli" is of Yemenite origin. So highly regarded is this craftwork that the Bezalel Institute in Jerusalem is in large part dedicated to the study of Yemenite arts and crafts.

Today there are an estimated 500 to 1,000 Jews left in Yemen. They are spread out all over the country, with the largest concentrations in the mountain town of Beideh, near the Saudi border, and in Raida. Many of these Jews are believed to have stayed behind during Operation On Eagles' Wings because they were held in chains and forced to teach their trade to low-caste Muslims, or did not want to leave elderly or sick relatives behind. There are no Jews left in the capital. In 1962, just before the republican revolution broke out, a couple of hundred Jews from Hajjeh, northwest of San'a, were brought to Israel. From that point until 1992, the Jews were forbidden to emigrate. The Jews in Yemen are under the protection of the local tribal chieftains. Although occasionally harassed by the local population and, before the Oslo Accords, by Palestinian fighters who found refuge in Yemen, the Jews live in relative harmony with their Muslim neighbors. They remain traditionally Jewish, and are still distinguished from their compatriots by their long, dangling *peot*.

The Yemeni government no longer restricts emigration to Israel. Since the early 1990s, the Yemeni government has shown concern for the religious needs of the Jewish community. Some assistance has been forthcoming for the building of religious edifices, such as a sorely needed *mikvah* (ritual bath). American Jews of Yemeni origin periodically visit Yemen and bring new supplies of religious texts and ritual articles. The vehemently anti-Zionist Satmar Chassidic sect and their Neturai Karta allies in Israel, intent on intensifying their campaign of polarization and paranoia, tried to frighten off the Yemenites from making *aliyah* by alerting them to the spiritual dangers of living in Godless Israel. The Satmar, who see Zionist conspiracies everywhere, feared that the "*shmadniks*" (apostates) who make up the Israeli establishment would cut off the *peot* of immigrant youngsters and turn them into *Shabbis goyim* (desecrators of the Sabbath). Satmars' hysteria does have some basis in reality. Yemenite boys living on kibbutzim in the early 1950s occasionally did have their *peot* snipped off by overzealous Hashomer Hatzair (socialist) types.[82] To allay the fears of the ultra-Orthodox community in Israel, the Jewish Agency has placed the education of Yemenite children under the purview of the Sephardi Shas party. The Satmars, who have been permitted by the Yemeni regime to enter the country because of their connections with the PLO (according to Yossi Klein Halevi of the *Jerusa-lem Report*), have supplied the community with holy books and artifacts, and established *chedarim* there.[83] Classes in the Satmar-run *chadarim* were taught in Yiddish, a language totally foreign to Arabic-speaking Jews. Some recent arriv-als I interviewed in Rehovot allege that the Satmars absconded with some of their ancient Holy Books.[84]

In the aftermath of the evacuation of the Jews from Ethiopia, the Israeli government assisted in the evacuation of a larger number of Jews from Yemen. According to the July 24, 1993 edition of the *Jerusalem Post*, some 280 Jews were brought to Israel in the preceding year. Among these recent arrivals was one man who had two wives and eight children, and insisted on having the govern-ment help him purchase two homes.[85]

THE JEWS OF HABBAN, SOUTH YEMEN

> Change your dwelling-place often, for the sweetness of life
> consists in variety.
>
>   —popular South Arabian Bedouin saying

One of the smallest and most geographically isolated of Jewish tribes were those of the city of Habban, on the Wadi Habban, in what was formerly known as the (British) East Aden Protectorate in South Yemen. Unlike their brethren to the north, the Habbani Jews rarely experienced persecution in this Sunni Muslim milieu. For many centuries they were considered among the higher castes in the South Arabian hierarchy.

The Jews of the East Aden Protectorate were different from their northern brethren in dress, appearance, *minhagim* (customs), and the fact that there were no *kohanim* and *leviyim* (priests and Levites) among them. The Jews of this region numbered around 700 in the late 1940s, some 450 of whom lived in the city of Habban proper.[86] There were also small colonies of Jews in Lahij, al-Hauta, al-Hidna, and Haura. The Jews of Habban were divided into four clans and were believed to have been descended from a single family. All the Jews of southern Yemen were flown to Israel in the late 1940s and early 1950s, together with their northern coreligionists, in what was known as Operation On Eagles' Wings (more popularly but condescendingly known as "Operation Magic Carpet.")

Habban is a small city lying about 225 miles northeast of Aden and about 150 miles west of the port of Mukalla, the Hadramaut's major link with the rest of the world. In ancient times this area was an important desert crossroads in the spice trade and was known as the "Land of Frankincense and Myrrh." The British colonial officer Harold Ingrams, who traveled extensively in the East Aden Protectorate during the 1930s, referred to the area as "the Land of Genesis," because it is "a world that lives still in the fashion of the Old Testament."[87] The surrounding countryside is wild and underdeveloped. A large percentage of the people were (and still are) traditionally nomadic.

Laurence Loeb has pointed out that the Jews of Habban have been erroneously referred to as the "Jews of the Hadramaut."[88] Wadi Hadramaut actually lies about 100 miles to the northeast. In fact, the Hadramaut was off limits to the Jews because the tomb of the Arab prophet Hud is located there. The Hadramaut is the only portion of the South Arabian Peninsula that was never known to have had a documented Jewish population.[89]

The Jews of Habban were virtually unknown to the outside Jewish world, but maintained tenuous links with the Jews of northern Yemen and Aden. The nearest Jewish settlement was located more than seventy miles to the east. The Habbani Jews did not come to the attention of world Jewry until 1912, when the Zionist emissary Shmuel Yavnieli penetrated the area. Yavnieli's caravan was attacked by eight Bedouin highwaymen in southern Yemen. They captured him, stole his money and blankets, and accused him of being a Christian and a spy. When the Jews of Habban became aware of his plight, they sent an Arab mediator to negotiate his release and graciously provided him with funds to travel back to Aden.[90] Yavnieli writes: "The Jews in these parts are held in high esteem by everyone in Yemen and Aden. They are said to be courageous, always with their weapons and wild long hair, and the names of their towns are mentioned by the Jews of Yemen with great admiration."[91]

The Jews of South Yemen maintained traditions that reflected the antiquity of their origin. One legend has it that they arrived in this area nearly 3,000 years ago, in the retinue of the Queen of Sheba. Indeed, some historians are of the opinion that the Queen of Sheba was neither Ethiopian nor from the northern portion of Yemen, but came from the ancient town of Shabwa, in the Hadramaut, about 130 kilometers from Habban.[92] Another conjecture is that South Yemen's Jews originally came from Babylonia and converted the local tribes to Judaism.[93] The prevalent local version has it that they are descended from a tribe of Judeans who settled in the area before the destruction of the Second Temple. These Judeans belonged to a brigade dispatched by King Herod to assist the Roman legions fighting in the region. According to this view, some of these Jewish soldiers may have settled in South Yemen. However, the total absence of *kohanim* and *leviyim* makes other scholars suggest that they are descended from the ten tribes of Israel or may have descended from Himyarite proselytes converted by Babylonian Jews dating from the Jewish king Abu Dhu Nuwas's time, around 525 C.E.[94]

According to local Jewish folklore a Jew advised the Sultan of Habban on the successful prosecution of a war some four hundred years ago. Because of this, the Jews henceforth enjoyed a privileged position in the region. The details of the struggle and the Jews' contribution were described as follows:

A rebel named Badr Abu Tuwarik was at war with Bin Abid al-Wachidi, Sultan of Habban. It took Abu Tuwarik a year to capture the town. During the state of siege, the inhabitants suffered gravely because there was an acute shortage of water.

The Sultan called all his advisors together. One of them was a Jew named Shlomo al-Hakim. Al-Wachidi asked each of his advisors to chart stratagem. When asked, Shlomo al-Hakim advised him not to show his weakness but to display a facade of strength. "You must collect the left-over water from the reservoir and plaster the side of the palace facing the enemy. Bring green vegetation from Hadda and give it as a gift to Abu Tuwarik's horse, which has just given birth. Commence negotiations with Abu Tuwarik regarding *soolcha* (a festive meal to mend fences). In the meantime dig ditches along Wadi Habban and fill them up with gunpowder. The ditches should be covered with straw mats. Then surprise the enemy with an attack that will force them to flee across the wadi. They will fall into the ditches filled with gunpowder and you will throw lit torches into the ditches. Those who try to escape will be shot."

This stratagem proved successful. The army of Badr Abu Tuwarik was routed. Badr Abu Tuwarik tried to escape. He was caught at the gates of his hometown Etzbeon and was slaughtered. Abu Tuwarik's wife was pregnant, and when her son was born she named him Bin Sidi, or Son of the Entrance Gate. Because of his sage advice, the sultan decided to reward Shlomo al-Hakim. "Anything you wish will be granted," he proclaimed. Shlomo requested a special Jewish quarter in the part of town called Chafet Bar Be'eira. Later the name was changed to Chafet al Yahoud, or the Jewish quarter.[95]

The Jewish quarter was situated on a foothill opposite the sultan's palace. Their clusters of tower-shaped houses, which ranged from two to five stories in height, were built from mud. The houses of the settlement formed a half-circle and were built on top of rocks, with their backs to the precipice, so that they enjoyed a sheltered position.

The Habbani Jews were fairly well-to-do and possessed land and property. When R. B. Serjeant visited the area in the 1940s, they still possessed the title deeds to the land. Their land had been recently expropriated by the sultan and they were left only with a cemetery and the meaningless title deeds.[96]

In this extremely caste-conscious part of the South Arabian Peninsula a man is recognized as a fully accepted member of the higher castes if, among other things, he is allowed to wear a belt and carry the richly decorated curved dagger known as the *janbiyya*. As honored citizens, the Jews were permitted by the grateful sultan to wear the belt and carry the vaunted weapon. The sultan required only that the Jews pay a poll tax amounting to fifteen percent of their crops and earnings in return for their position as *dhimmi*. Over the centuries the Jews of Habban established a reputation as a fierce fighting force in the sultan's legions and lived in relative security.

Perhaps characterizing the Jews as living in relative security is an overly idyllic description of their situation. Hostility between the various Muslim clans in the region "was chronic, often aggravated by protracted blood feuds and offenses against the norms of tribal honor."[97] The Jews were always a small minority in the region, and it is probable that their numbers were further diminished due to the interminable tribal wars and the malarial diseases that were a continual problem in the region.[98]

In southern Yemen there was a strong Islamic tradition of giving protection to the Peoples of the Scriptures. This was an economic as well as cultural imperative, because the tribes of the area relied heavily on the Jews to produce their implements and weapons. "In South Arabia it was a shameful act to kill a Jew, as it would be to kill a woman."[99] If a Jew of one tribe were to be harmed by a Muslim of another tribe, the Muslims of his tribe would retaliate. Sometimes a Jew from a warring tribe was killed in revenge for the death of *yehudina* ("our Jew"). A Muslim who insulted a Jew was obligated to pay a fine and slaughter an animal. The slaughtered animal was distributed among the poor.[100] In Habban proper, the Jews were under the protection of the Mashiach and Kabail tribes. With the rise of Arab nationalism in the region in the 1940s, the Jews' status in southern Yemeni society began to deteriorate. Rabble-rousing tribal chieftains helped foment contempt for the Jews, but they met with success only in the cities.

In the countryside, the Muslims tended to be more in awe of the Jews. They believed that the Jews could foretell the future and knew when the rains would fall. The Jews were believed to have a special pipeline to Allah and therefore were able to miraculously heal the sick. They were brought in to serve as advisors, negotiators, and umpires among the bickering tribes. Feuding Muslim parties preferred to have the Jews arbitrate among them and work out truces.

There were some cobblers and herdsmen among the Habbani Jews, but the predominant occupation was itinerant silversmithing. Craftmaking was a family affair. The Jews specialized in decorating weapons for Muslim men and fashioning household utensils and jewelry for the women. Jewish men would sell their wares around the villages and encampments of the Bedouin in the desert. They covered their routes by forming camel and donkey caravans travelling from the borders of Wadi Hadramaut to the Port of Aden. When sojourning in a town, they would usually lodge at the *murabbas* (rest homes) of the local sheikhs. They would eat only food they had prepared or slaughtered themselves. While the peddlers were away their women and children stayed home, with only the old men in residence. The peddlers usually came home in time for the holidays. It was common for the Jews to be attacked by highwaymen and return home empty-handed, with nothing to show for their efforts.

The Jews spoke the colloquial Arab dialect of the region, but were also fluent in Hebrew. Every Habbani man was literate in biblical Hebrew. There were no ordained rabbis in Habban, but many were *talmudai hakhamim* (talmudic scholars), well versed in the laws. The commandments were scrupulously observed. Many of the men had mastered *hilchat shechita* (laws pertaining to ritual slaughtering) by the age of twelve or thirteen. They were so punctilious in this regard that they refused to eat meat slaughtered by their brethren to the north. As Loeb writes, describing the Hashed refugee camp during Operation On Eagles' Wings in 1950: "The Habbani were so appalled at the ritual slaughter and inspection of other Yemenite slaughterers, they forcibly evicted them and resorted to their own slaughter."[101] The Habbanim possessed, in addition to the Torah and Talmud, the works of Maimonides, the *Orah Hayyim*, the *Shulchan Aruch, Bereshit Rabbah Tanchumah, Ein Ya'akov*, and *Pirchay D'Rabbi Eliezer*. They also had copies of the *Zohar* and the writings of the great Sephardi poets and mystics.

Like the indigenous south Yemeni Arabs, the Habbani Jews tended to be wiry, of small stature and swarthy complexion. But in contrast with their brethren to the north, the Habbanim seemed to journalist Shlomo Barer " . . . taller and more muscular . . . and walk[ed] with a manlier gait."[102] The proud and extremely pious Habbani men wore kilts; only the women were attired in trousers. Like their Muslim compatriots, the men were accustomed to grow beards, but never cut their hair. The Habbanim say they wore their hair long to commemorate the *churban bayit shaini* (the destruction of the Second Temple). Their long, flowing hair was tied with an oiled bonnet of indigo into which were placed green incense leaves. They did not grow *peot* or mustaches but, like the Muslims, plucked them out. They walked around barechested with a blue tallit wrap thrown over the shoulders. Perhaps in many ways Habbani men resembled Jews from biblical times.

Habbani women wore their hair in little braids and covered their heads with nets decorated with silver jewelry. Women often sported a red beauty spot on their foreheads, a local custom probably imported from India, on the other side of the Arabian Sea. Jewish women, like their Muslim counterparts, covered their faces with a veil when out in public. They rarely left their homes unaccompanied by male relatives.

Habbani Jews had a unique way of embracing each other upon meeting. One person would clasp the hand of the other and then raise the back of the hand and kiss it. They would address each other, and then the process would be reversed. This procedure was repeated several times, accompanied with the sniffing of the hand, neck, and forehead.[103]

Some of the unique aspects of the Habbani wedding ceremony are noteworthy, as well as practices concerning childbirth and children's education.[104]

Girls married at twelve and boys at sixteen. The groom was obliged to purchase his future wife from her parents. All arrangements and dates were set by the parents. The groom did not meet his wife until the marriage day. Wedding ceremonies began eight days before the *chuppah* with a formal announcement known as *al-shiduch*. A *sheliach* (messenger) assigned by the groom's family would go to the bride's house and announce the groom's wish to marry. He would give a coin to the bride's father, pour oil on the bride's head before two witnesses, and announce that a formal marriage had taken place. Eight days later (i.e., seven "clean days" after the bride's menses was completed), the wedding took place.

The day after *al-shiduch* was known as *ilmud*. On this day the groom's gifts were brought to the bride's house. Two people were assigned the task of acting out the role of merchants. They would stand at the door of the bride's house pretending to measure and argue over the groom's gifts.

The *vichli* ceremony was a women-only affair and invariably took place on Friday. A *koovri* (bridal attendant) was assigned the task of dressing the bride and her entourage, and setting up the wedding ceremony. The *koovri* made thin braids of the bride's hair, except for one large braid on the top of her head. During the braiding process her hair was rubbed with a perfume and spice mixture to make the braids stiff. This kept the bride's hair in place until the early part of the following week, when the bride attended the *mikvah* (ritual bath).

The Sabbath before the wedding was known as *shabbat chatan*. The groom, covered with his tallit, accompanied by his *shoshbinim*, two best men, was escorted into the synagogue by the beadle. His forehead was rubbed with an oily perfume and spice mixture that was prepared by his mother. Then the same application was rubbed on his best men's heads. Later, a second application was rubbed on the groom and his best men, and on all the men in attendance.

The henna ceremonies took place on the fifth day, invariably on a Sunday morning. Stripes and circles were formed by binding pieces of cloth on the bride's hands and feet. There was singing and dancing until midafternoon, when the henna was washed off. The henna ceremony, the ritual bath, and the hair braiding were repeated on the sixth day. Also on the sixth day the groom's henna ceremony took place. The groom and his best men carried, on their backs, bags of raisins and candy prepared by the groom's parents. Incense was burnt, and those who washed and painted the groom's hands and feet would recite their family trees and offer blessings. That evening the guests sat down to a festive meal. The bride's and groom's henna was not removed until the next morning. At this point the female relatives arrived. They would shake their braids while singing special melodies and kissing the groom's head.

On the afternoon of the seventh day the groom would go off to the *mikvah* (ritualarium). A tallit shaped like a large pocket was draped over his shoulders, and the guests placed gifts of money or jewelry into it. They would dress him in lavish finery, wind a strip of glossy red ribbon around his head, and splash him with perfume. To commemorate the destruction of the Temple, they would rub ashes on his head and he would intone the prayer "If I Forget Thee O Jerusalem May My Right Hand Be Forgotten."

On the eighth day the bride, dressed in a traditional white headdress, with cuffs and large bracelets tingling with silver coins, was brought to the home of the bridegroom. She was escorted by all the womenfolk of her family, bearing torches of smoking incense. The bride rode on a camel or donkey adorned with colorful rugs, accompanied by the village populace. Muslim as well as Jewish friends danced, played flutes and drums, and fired welcoming shots in the air.[105]

During the *chuppah* ceremony the bride was separated from the groom by a partition. After making *kiddush* (the sacramental blessing) over wine, the groom sat down next to the bride and placed his knee on top of her knee, indicating that the bride was now subordinate to her husband. A goat was then slaughtered at their feet. Instead of a ring, the groom gave the bride a coin and then kissed her. The *ketubah* (marriage contract) was written on red and green parchment.[106]

When a woman gave birth, a ewe lamb was killed in her honor and passed three times over her head. Two days before the *brit* people were invited to the *ilmispar* preparation. An animal skin decorated with colorful illustrations was stretched over a round dish. When the colors on the skin were dry, the preparers would cut around the dish and remove the round-shaped skin, which would serve as a diaper. During the *brit* the men would don their *tefillin* (phylacteries) and read from the *Zohar*.[107]

In the period before their departure to Israel there were two synagogues in Habban, with elementary schools attached to each. Habbani boys commenced *cheder* at age three or four. The *mori* (teacher) was oftentimes an old man who had retired from itinerant peddling. An occasional visitor from the north might sometimes serve as teacher when sojourning in the area. A verbal agreement was worked out with the parents to pay the *mori* either a salary or in kind. The *mori* would often take his meals at the student's parents' home. A child who had mastered the *aleph-bet* was given a painted egg to eat as a reward for his accomplishment. During the lessons the *mori* gave each child time to go to the bathroom or take a break, and he would spit on the wall. If the spit dried before the boy returned to the classroom, the youngster was sure to get a paddling.[108]

Only the more gifted children continued formal religious studies beyond nine or ten years of age. This elite group was especially trained to master the laws of ritual slaughtering. The rest were apprenticed to their fathers or uncles to learn the smithing trade. As was common among Jews everywhere in Yemen, the Habbani father would engage his son in Torah discussion while they were working together. Even the most erudite of young Habbanim mastered the smithing trade sooner or later. In the period before *aliyah*, young girls attended *cheder* with the boys. In contrast to northern Yemeni Jewish women, who were universally illiterate, some Habbani women of the pre-*aliyah* generation were taught to read and write.[109]

The bar mitzvah was not a special occasion. A boy under thirteen could be called up to the Torah, except for the *shacharit* (morning) service. However, a young man could not be called up to the Torah on Shabbat, Yom Tov, or for the morning service unless he was married.

Other aspects of daily life that were unique to the Jews of Habban can best be illustrated by the following vignettes.

On Shevuot, the time of the Giving of the Law, the Habbani Jews had a custom of pouring water over each other. The reason for doing this is that water symbolizes Torah. A special cake called *myatsuba* was eaten on this holiday. *Myatsuba* was made from wheat dough fried in a pan with sesame oil, butter, and honey. It was eaten with milk because the Torah is compared to milk and honey.[110]

On all the roofs of Habban (and also in North Yemen), there was a special space designated for a *sukkah* (tabernacle). The space was built in when the edifice itself was erected. Because *etrogim* (citrons) are not available in this region, the Habbani Jews weren't able to fulfill the mitzvah of the "Four Species" during Sukkot. (The other symbols include the branch of the date palm, or *lulav*; myrtles; and willows. Worshippers march around the interior of the synagogue in a processional circle bearing these four plants during the recitation of Psalms of Thanksgiving.)[111]

On Purim, Jewish youngsters would shoot off firecrackers that were provided to the community by the local sultan. A scarecrow representing Haman was placed on the rooftop of one of the tallest buildings and burned in effigy.[112]

On Chanukah, after the candle lighting, the women and girls would braid their hair with silver bells, then shake their heads from side to side, causing the bells to ring.[113]

When a member of the tribe passed away, the entire tribe would visit the bereaved. At the end of the *shiva* period (eight days of grieving), goats and sheep were slaughtered, and a meal was prepared for the family and guests. Graveyards possessed no tombstones. Graves everywhere in Yemen were marked with piles of simple stones with no indication of the names of the deceased.[114]

A small contingent of Habbani Jews made *aliyah* in 1945, and a second group arrived in Israel in 1948. "Even after news trickled back to Habban of the massive *aliyah* from all over Yemen," writes Loeb, "no one expressed real desire to leave. . . . [T]he convincing arguments were not those of religious or political Zionism, but the fear of real isolation that they would remain the last Jews on the Arabian peninsula."[115] Those who reached Israel in 1945 and 1948 traveled the 230-mile journey across the desert and along the shore of the Indian Ocean to get to the Hashed camp in Aden. They had to cross three sultanates, pay a variety of tolls and taxes, and grease many palms. Those who remained in Habban were subjected to persecution and confined to a ghetto by the ruling sultan.

The ostensible reason for this unprecedented behavior toward the Jews was their failure to pay tribute. The real reason was that the new sultan, Nasr ibn Abdullah, was swayed by Arab League anti-Jewish propaganda. He imposed exorbitant taxes on the Jews and even demanded their conversion. "It was later discovered that a secret plan had been underway to wipe out the Jewish community, but the local Arab population did not want to implement it."[116] The Muslims complained that the Jews owed them money and feared that they would leave the country without having repaid their debts. The Jews acknowledged the debt, but claimed that the amount owed was considerably less than that demanded. A Jewish Agency emissary named Yosef Tsadok was sent to Habban in the summer of 1950 to assist the Habbani Jews in their dealings with the Muslims. Tsadok ironed out a compromise with the debtors and managed to ransom the Jews from the sultan upon payment of a lump sum. Almost 350 people were crammed into a convoy of large trucks and driven to the Hashed camp in Aden.[117]

"They were the only group among the many thousands who had passed through the camps whose behavior was that of free men," Shlomo Barer observed.

They were a distinctly organized society, albeit after an archaic pattern. They had their spokesmen and appointed representatives in the elders of three family groups. . . . They did not look or feel helpless like the rest of the camp inmates. They took a keen interest in Hashed's unfamiliar installations, and their elders came to inspect the hospital, gazed at the microscope in the laboratory shed, and asked questions. They, too, had brought ancient Torah scrolls with them, and when, two months later, they were flown to Israel in time to celebrate Rosh Hashanah . . . they were the delight of photographers as they stood in the open in the former R. A. F. camp and prayed—the tall, long-haired warriors, white cotton robes hanging from their shoulders, with a certain harsh nobility in their dark faces, going through the old rites with the dignity of ancient priests.

. . . The thing that beats me is how this tiny remnant, marooned for ages among the Bedouin, war-loving like the Bedouin, and in many other respects obviously part and parcel of the life of the desert in one of the darkest recesses of dark Arabia, have preserved a knowledge of Hebrew and old religious customs, so that today they still say the same prayers as their emancipated brethren in Poland or in Palestine.[118]

It was in the transit camps that the Habbani Jews began wearing the long dangling *peot* of their northern coreligionists. Jews from the surrounding Protectorate villages were brought out shortly thereafter. By 1952 there were no Jews left in southern Yemen.

In Israel the Habbanim settled in two *moshavim* (farm cooperatives): K'far Shalem near Tel Aviv and Bareket, two miles from Ben Gurion Airport. One elderly informant that I interviewed in 1989, who had arrived at Moshav Bareket at the age of forty, learned early that at least some of the old ways would have to end. Luxuriating in his new environment, he decided that it was time to marry a second wife. Although this was before 1952, the year in which Israel outlawed polygamy, his wife would hear none of this. She grabbed a knife, ran up to him, and held it against her throat. Tearfully, she made him swear he wouldn't take a second wife or she would slit her throat on the spot. With still a touch of sadness in his voice, this man said he had to resign himself to settling for one wife.

Soon after their arrival in Israel, the Lubavitcher Chassidic movement began to aggressively proselytize among the Habbanim. The "conversion" to Ashkenazi pietism appears to have been an entirely volitional act on the part of the Arabians. "We wanted to provide a religious education for our children," one Habbani told me. "We were living in *ma'abarot* (temporary shacks) at the time. A *sheliach* (emissary) from Lubavitch told us that Mapai (the Labor Government) are *goyim,* and if we want *da'at* (religion) we should follow Chabad."

Another Habbani explained it this way:

The Torah and Halakha are the same for everyone. When we came to Israel, we saw other types of Jews. In general we felt different and inferior to other Jews. We were impressed with the Torah knowledge of the Chabadniks. We liked what they had to say. We were very religious, but our *rav* [Ma'atuf Shalom Yitzchak] had passed away, and we needed spiritual direction. We wanted to raise our children as *yirat shumayim* (God-fearers), so we sent the children to study at the Chabad Yeshiva. The children influenced us. This caused a generational problem. Even today we have differences of opinion between the generations.

Loeb has described the influence of the Lubavitchers on the Habbani Jews as a case of "cultural imperialism." "While HaBad motivations may initially have been largely altruistic, intending to defend the Habbani . . . community from the encroachment of Israeli secularism, they ultimately resulted in cultural self-aggrandizement and consequent denial of the validity of indigenous Habbani values and norms."[119]

One of the *edot ha-mizrach* most resistant to assimilation, the Habbanim continue to practice ancient mores and folkways in Israel. Gideon Russack once observed the following peculiar custom of the Habbanim at Moshav Bareket:

> While visiting a friend or relative, they sit in a crouching position in such a way that the legs are pulled back to the breast and the belt is girdled to the knees. The effect of this is that it holds the legs up without having to support them with the hands, and puts the pressure upon the back, helping to straighten it as well as the whole body. This practice of two thousand years duration could be called today, in modern medical rehabilitation, "isometrics."[120]

The Habbanim in Israel now number around 1,600. They continue to maintain strong family ties, and until recently married primarily among themselves.

NOTES

1. "The Queen of Sheba's Children," *Congress Monthly* 58:5 (July–August 1991), p. 7.

2. Nigel Groom, *Frankincense and Myrrh: A Study of the Arabian Incense Trade* (London: Longman, 1981), esp. pp. 22–37.

3. P. Underwood, *Health and Culture in a Traditional Community in Yemen, Arabia.* (unpublished doctoral dissertation, University of Western Australia, 1983), cited in Michael A. Weingarten, *Changing Health and Changing Culture: The Yemenites in Israel* (Westport, Conn.: Greenwood, 1992), p. 59.

4. Yehuda Nini, *The Jews of Yemen: 1800–1914* (Chur, Switzerland: Harwood Academic Publishers, 1991), p. 4.

5. S. D. Goitein, "The Jews of Yemen," in *Religion in the Middle East: Three Religions in Concord and Conflict*, vol. 1, *Judaism and Christianity*, edited by A. J. Arberry. (Cambridge: At the University Press, 1969), p. 228. Goitein's statement has to be construed strictly from a religious point of view because genetic studies conducted over the last two decades indicate that today's Yemenite Jews are probably descended from Bedouin converts to Judaism in the fourth and fifth centuries C.E. See Batsheva Bonne-Tamir, "Oriental Jewish Communities and Their Genetic Relationship with South-West Asian Populations," *Indian Anthropologist* (1985), p. 168.

6. Nigel Groom, *Frankincense*, p. 53.

7. Lawrence Resner, *Eternal Stranger: The Plight of the Modern Jew from Baghdad to Casablanca*, 1st ed. (Garden City, New York: Doubleday, 1951), pp. 155–56.

8. *Yemenite Jewry: Origins, Culture, and Literature* (Bloomington: Indiana University Press, 1986), p. 6.

9. Allen H. Godbey, *The Lost Tribes a Myth: Suggestions Towards Rewriting Hebrew History* (Durham, N.C.: Duke University Press, 1930), p. 178.

10. *Arabia Before Muhammad* (London: Kegan, Paul, Trench, Trubner, 1927), p. 172.

11. For scholarly attempts to construct a chronology of the various Jewish monarchs of the Himyarite period see H. Philby, *Arabian Highlands* (Ithaca, N.Y.: Cornell University Press, 1952), esp. pp. 258–61; and Robert L. Playfair, *A History of Arabia Felix or Yemen* (Amsterdam: Philo Press, 1970), pp. 45–66.

12. Playfair, ibid., p. 62.

13. W. G. Greenslade, "The Martyrs of Nejran," *Moslem World* (July 1932), p.8.

14. Before he had formulated a position vis-à-vis the *dhimmi* Mohammed had expelled or annihilated the three powerful Jewish tribes in the vicinity of Medina and the fertile oasis towns of Khaibar and Nejran. They had rejected his claims to being the last and greatest prophet.

15. For an in-depth study of the concept of *dhimmi* see Bat Ye'or, *The Dhimmi: Jews and Christians Under Islam* (London: Fairleigh Dickinson University Press, 1985).

16. Menachem Kapoliak, "Di Yidn in Teiman," *Di Goldene Keyt* 23 (1955), pp. 184–85; Ahroni, *Yemenite Jewry*, p. 112; R. A. B. Hamilton, "The Social Organization of the Tribes of the Aden Protectorate," *Journal of the Royal Central Asian Society* 30:2 (May 1943), p. 151.

17. Ahroni, ibid., p. 112.

18. Nini, *The Jews of Yemen*, p. 25.

19. Tudor Parfitt, *The Road to Redemption: The Jews of the Yemen 1900–1950* (Leiden: E. J. Brill, 1996), pp. 67–68.

20. Aviva Klein-Franke, "The Orphans, Their Plight and Their Immigration to Israel," in *Yemenite Paths*, edited by Shalom Ben Sa'adya Gamliel, et al. Jerusalem: Shalom Research Centre, 1984, pp. xxxi-xxxii; Parfitt, *The Road*, pp. 70–71.

21. Ladislas Farago, *Arabian Antic* (New York: Sheridan House, 1938), p. 303.

22. Yehuda Nini, "Yemen," in *Zionism in Transition*, edited by Moshe Davis (New York: Arno Press, 1980), p. 211.

23. Dana A. Schmidt, *Yemen: The Unknown War* (New York: Holt, Rinehart, and Winston, 1968), pp. 107–08; Parfitt, *The Road*, p. 112.

24. *The Jews of the Middle East, 1860–1972* (Jerusalem: Israel Universities Press, 1973), p. 103.

25. S. D. Goitein, "The Transplantation of the Yemenites," *Commentary* 12:1 (July 1951), p. 26

26. Nini, *The Jews of Yemen*, p. 106.

27. *Etiopia: Yidn in Afriki un Azieh* (New York: Borochov Yugent Bibliotek, 1936), p. 108.

28. Kopoliak, "Di Yidn," p. 184. According to Joseph Schectman, "[even] the least-educated [Jewish men] knew large portions of the Bible by heart, and the more oppressed they were, the more ardently did they cling to and cultivate the exalted spiritual vision of their people." See *On Wings of Eagles: The Plight, Exodus, and Homecoming of Oriental Jewry* (New York: T. Yoseloff, 1961), p. 46.

29. S. D. Goitein, "The Social Structure of Jewish Education in Yemen." In *Jewish Societies in the Middle East: Community, Culture, and Authority*, edited by Shlomo Deshen and Walter P. Zenner. (Lanham, N.Y.: University Press of America, 1982), p. 229.

30. See the Alliance Israelite Universalle emissary Yomtov Semach's description, translated into English, in Cohen, *The Jews of the Middle East*, p. 148.

31. Cohen, ibid, p. 151.

32. Many children, especially those living in the small, isolated villages, received little if any formal Jewish education.

33. This statement by Goitein is cited and paraphrased by Yael Katzir in "Preservation of Jewish Ethnic Identity in Yemen: Segregation and Integration as Boundary Maintenance Mechanisms," *Comparative Studies in Society and History* 24:2 (April 1982), p. 276.

34. Nini, *The Jews of Yemen*, p. 111.

35. "Tribulations and Aspirations in Yemenite Hebrew Literature," *Hebrew Union College Annual* 49 (1978), p. 293.

36. "Shalem Shabazi," vol. 14. (Jerusalem: Keter, 1973), p. 1215.

37. *The Yemenite Jews* [*Sound Recording*] *Jewish-Yemenite Diwan*, publisher # D8024 (France: Auvidis-Unesco, 1990), p. 2.

38. Lisa Gilad, *Yemeni Jewish Women* (unpublished dissertation, Cambridge University, 1982), p. 62. See also Michael M. Caspi, *Daughters of Yemen* (Berkeley: University of California Press, 1985), p. 6.

39. Goitein, *Jewish Education*, p. 125.

40. In spite of the limitations Jewish male society imposed on her, "the Yemenite woman is one of the most cultured human types I have ever encountered," wrote Goitein in 1951. "[I]f culture is defined as perfection of the soul, i.e. an instinctive, unerring moral discernment and aesthetic judgment, then the Yemenite woman comes very close to that ideal." *Jewish Education*, p. 126.

41. The *kaddish* is an acclamation of God's greatness. When recited in memory of a loved one, it is believed to merit that loved one in the World to Come.

42. Johanna Spector, "Bridal Songs and Ceremonies from San'a, Yemen," in *Studies in Biblical and Jewish Folklore*, edited by Raphael Patai, et al. (Bloomington: Indiana University Press, 1960), p. 161.

43. Goitein, *The Social Structure*, p. 223.

44. Caspi, *Daughters of Yemen*, p. 8.

45. *Travels in Yemen: An Account of Joseph Halevy's Journey to Najran in the Year 1870*, written in Sa'ani Arabic by his guide Hayyim Habshush, edited by S. D. Goitein (Jerusalem: Hebrew University Press, 1941), p. 51.

46. Erich Brauer, "The Yemenite Jewish Woman," *Jewish Review* 4 (1933), p. 41.

47. Cited in A. Shivtiel, et al., "The Jews of San'a," in *San'a: An Arabian Islamic City*, edited by R. B. Serjeant and Ronald Lewcock (London: World of Islam Festival Trust, 1983), p. 424.

48. Yemenite-Israeli poet Bracha Serri reminisces that the Jewish houses in San'a were connected at the roofs, and it was possible to wander around the whole Jewish quarter via the roofs.

49. *Jewish Domestic Architecture in San'a, Yemen* (Jerusalem: The Israel Oriental Society, 1957), p. 65.

50. Ibid., p. 6.

51. Carsten Niebuhr, "Travels in Arabia," in *Voyages and Travels in All Parts of the World by John Pinkerton*, vol. 10 (London: Longman, 1811), p. 69; Ameen Rihani, *Arabian Peak and Desert: Travels in Al-Yaman*, (London: Constable and Co., 1930), pp. 184–185. See also Rathjens, *Jewish Domestic*, p. 17. Hugh Scott observed that "Jewish houses in San'a showed a high degree of cleanliness [but] the same cannot be said of Jewish houses in outlying places." See *In the High Yemen* (London: John Murray, 1942), p. 136.

52. For a detailed study of Yemenite Jewish finery see Esther Muchawsky-Schnapper, *The Jews of Yemen: Highlights of the Israel Museum Collection* (Jerusalem: The Israel Museum, 1994).

53. Ronald L. Taylor, *Butterflies in My Stomach: Insects in Human Nutrition* (Santa Barbara, Calif.: Woodbridge Press, 1975), p. 36.

54. Much of the information on the role of locust in Yemenite Jewish culinary culture is derived from Rabbi Amram Yihya Korah, *Sa'arat Teman: Qorot ha-Yehudim be-Teman*, edited by Shimon Garidi (Jerusalem: Harav Kook Institute, 1954), p. 94.

55. L. Du Couret, *Life in the Desert* (New York: Mason Brothers, 1860), p. 116.

56. *Black Tents of Arabia* (New York: Creative Age Press, 1947), pp. 74–75.

57. Peter Kalix, "Khat: A Plant with Amphetamine Effects," *Journal of Substance Abuse* 5 (1988), pp. 163–169.

58. Ibid., p. 164.

59. John G. Kennedy, *The Flower of Paradise* (Dordect, Holland: D. Reidel Publishing Company, 1987), p. 78; Tomas Gerholm, *Market, Mosque, and Marfaq* (Stockholm: University of Stockholm, 1977), p. 183.

60. Deonna Laurence, *Yemen* (Washington, D.C.: Three Continents, 1991), pp. 107–108.

61. Norman Stillman, *The Jews in Arab Lands: A History and Sourcebook* (Philadelphia: Jewish Publication Society, 1979), p. 85; Norman Stillman, "The Moroccan Jewish Experience: A Revisionist View," *The Jerusalem Quarterly* 9 (Fall 1978), p. 120; Parfitt, *The Road*, p. 115. According to Weingarten, alcohol is usually imbibed as an antidote to the insomnia qat induces. The combination of alcohol and qat can trigger a marked form of hallucination. See *Changing Health*, pp. 38, 102–103.

62. Bat-Zion Eraqi Klorman, *The Jews of Yemen in the Nineteenth Century: A Portrait of a Messianic Community* (Leiden: E. J. Brill, 1993), p. 54.

63. Ibid., p. 21.

64. An English translation of Maimonides' Epistle to Yemen can be found in *Masterpieces of Hebrew Literature: A Treasury of 2000 Years of Jewish Creativity*, edited by Curt Leviant (New York: Ktav Publishing House, 1969), pp. 308–331.

65. On the Yemenite Jewish messianic pretenders of the 19th century see Eraqi Klorman, *Jews of Yemen*, pp. 104–164; Nini, *Jews of Yemen*, p. 136–153; Ahroni, *Yemenite Jewry*, pp. 145–154.

66. Ahroni, *Yemenite Jewry*, p. 132.

67. Herbert S. Lewis, *After the Eagles Landed: The Yemenites of Israel* (Boulder: Westview Press, 1989), p. 47.

68. Yehuda Nini, "Immigration and Assimilation: The Yemenite Jews," *The Jerusalem Quarterly* 21 (Fall 1987), p. 90.

69. F. Goitein's observation is found in Parfitt, *The Road*, p. 134.

70. Farago, *Arabian Antic*, p. 305.

71. Barer, *The Magic Carpet*, p. 148; S. D. Goitein, "The Transplantation of the Yemenites," *Commentary* 12:1 (July 1951), p. 26.

72. According to Weingarten 15,000 to 20,000 of 49,000 Yemenite immigrants who made *aliyah* during this period had malaria. *Changing Health*, p. 66.

73. Zecharia Nissim, "A Yemenite Boy in Israel," in *Sound the Great Trumpet: The Story of Israel Through the Eyes of Those Who Built It*, edited by Moses Z. Frank (New York: Whittier Books, 1955), p. 376.

74. Constantine Poulos, "In the New Land," *Commentary* 12 (1951), p. 31.

75. (London: Secker and Warburg, 1952), p. 28.

76. *Der Yid* (31 May 1991), p. 3. For an in-depth discussion of the stolen Yemenite possessions see Parfitt, *The Road*, chapter 14.

77. Yossi Klein Halevi, "Where Are Our Children?" *The Jerusalem Report* 6:23 (21 March 1996), pp. 14–19; Weingarten, *Changing Health*, p. 93.

78. Felice Maranz, "The Jews Who Slipped Off the Magic Carpet," *The Jerusalem Report* 5:2 (2 June 1994), pp. 16–17; Yossi Klein Halevi, "Rage in the Land of the Lost Children," *The Jerusalem Report* 8:11 (2 October 1997), pp. 26–30; *Israel Yearbook and Almanac* 49 (1995), pp. 201–202.

79. Raphael Patai, *Israel Between East and West: A Study of Human Relations* (Philadelphia: Jewish Publication Society, 1953), p. 197.

80. Poulos, "In the New Land," p. 32

81. On Yemenite dance see Gurit Kadman, "Yemenite Dance," in *The Jews of Yemen: An Exhibition Organized by the Maurice Spertus Museum of Judaica*, edited by Grace Cohen Grossman (Chicago: Spertus College of Judaica Press, 1976), pp. 6–8. On Yemenite music in Israel see Uri Sharvit, "The Yemenite Music in Israel," ibid., pp. 9–12.

82. Sarah Honig, "Tug-of-War over the Yemenites, 40 Years Ago," *The Jerusalem Post* (28 June 1991), pp. 9–10. See also Al Ellenberg and Tom Sawicki, "Magic Carpet II," *The Jerusalem Report* 3:25 (22 April 1993), p. 34; Tom Segev, *1949: The First Israelis*. New York: The Free Press, 1986, pp. 213–214.

83. (27 July 1994), p. 20. See also *Jerusalem Post* (23 July 1993), p. 7.

84. See also Yossi Klein Halevi, "A Battle for Souls," *The Jerusalem Report* 4:19 (27 January 1994), p. 20; and Robin Gilbert, "Satmar's Trap," *The Jerusalem Report* 5:5 (14 July 1994), p. 54.

85. "Agency Discloses Secret Immigration from Yemen," pp. 1, 4.

86. Maatuf Saadia Ben Yitzchak, "Habban (Hadramaut) Jewry in the Last Generations" (M. A.thesis, Department of History, Bar Ilan University, Ramat Gan, Israel, 1984), p. 1.

87. *Arabia and the Isles*, 3rd ed. (London: John Murray, 1966), p. 133.

88. "Jewish Life in Habban: A Tentative Reconstruction," in *Proceedings of a Regional Conference of Association for Jewish Studies*, edited by Frank Talmadge (Cambridge, Mass.: Association for Jewish Studies, 1980), p. 202.

89. Manfred W. Wenner, *Modern Yemen: 1918–1966* (Baltimore: Johns Hopkins University, 1967), p. 29; *Western Arabia and the Red Sea* (Great Britain: Naval Intelligence Division, 1946), p. 391.

90. Shmuel Yavnieli, *Massa le'Teman* (Tel Aviv: Am Oved, 1951), pp. 126, 227.

91. Quotation cited in Dvorah Hacohen and Menachem Hacohen, *One People: The Story of the Eastern Jews* (New York: Adama, 1986), p. 152.

92. Richard H. Sanger, *The Arabian Peninsula* (Freeport, N.Y.: Cornell University Press, 1970), p. 238.

93. Aviva Klein-Franke, "The Jews of Yemen," in *Yemen: 3000 Years of Art and Civilization in Arabia Felix*, edited by Werner Daum (Innsbruch: Pinguin-Verlag, 1987), p. 272.

94. Loeb, "Jewish Life," p. 202–204; Klein-Franke, "The Jews," p. 270.

95. This story was narrated to me by Maatuf Saadia Ben Yitzchak at Moshav Bareket in September of 1989. This account can also be found in "Habban Jewry," pp. 18–19.

96. "A Judeo-Arab House Deed from Habban," *Journal of the Royal Asiatic Society* (1953), p. 123.

97. Robert W. Stookey, *South Yemen: A Marxist Republic in Arabia* (Boulder: Westview Press, 1982), p. 5. See also R. A. B. Hamilton, "Social Organization of the Aden Protectorate," *Journal of the Royal Central Asian Society* 30, Part 3–4 (September 1943), esp. pp. 271–272.

98. Sanger, *The Arabian Peninsula*, p. 215.

99. Serjeant, "A Judeo-Arab House Deed, p. 119.

100. Ibid.

101. "Folk Models of Habbani Ethnic Identity," in *Studies in Jewish Ethnicity: After the Ingathering*, edited by Alex Weingrod (New York: Gordon and Breach Science Publishers, 1985), p. 203.

102. *The Magic Carpet* (London: Secher and Warberg, 1952), pp. 94–95.

103. Yavnieli, *Massa le'Teman*, p. 228; Loeb, "Jewish Life," p. 210.

104. The information on wedding customs is drawn primarily from Maatuf Saadia, "Habban Jewry," pp. 103–106.

105. Tuvia Ashkenazi, "Yehudai Hatzramut," *Edoth* 2:1–2 (October 1946–January 1947), p. 66.

106. Ibid., p. 64.

107. Maatuf Saadia, "Habban Jewry," p. 99.

108. Ibid., p. 37.

109. Laurence Loeb, "Gender, Marriage, and Social Conflict in Habban," in *Sephardi and Middle Eastern Jewries*, edited by Harvey E. Goldberg (Bloomington: Indiana University Press, 1996), p. 263.

110. Maatuf Saadia, "Habban Jewry," p. 92–93.

111. Ibid., p. 93–4.

112. Ibid., p. 97.

113. Ibid.

114. Tudor Parfitt, *The Road to Redemption: The Jews of the Yemen 1900–1950* (Leiden: E. J. Brill, 1996), p. 100.

115. Loeb, "Folk Models," p. 205.

116. Maatuf Saadia, "Habban Jewry," p. iv.

117. Joseph B. Schechtman, *On Wings of Eagles: The Plight, Exodus, and Homecoming of Oriental Jewry* (New York: Thomas Yoseloff, 1961), p. 86.

118. Barer, *The Magic Carpet*, p. 249.

119. Loeb, "Folk Models," p. 208.

120. "The 'Habanim'—One of the 'Tribes of Israel,'" *Jewish Affairs* 22:9 (September 1967), p. 137.

Part II

Djedid al-Islam (Crypto-Jews) of Meshed, Iran, 1912
Credit: Judah Magnes Museum

Pariahs among Ayatollahs

BACKGROUND INFORMATION

Persia, or, as it is called today, the Islamic Republic of Iran, is bounded by the Caspian Sea, the Transcaucasus, and the Central Asian Republic of Turkmenistan on the north; by Afghanistan and Pakistan on the east; by the Persian Gulf and the Gulf of Oman on the south; and by Iraq and Turkey on the west. Most of the Iranian plateau is arid desert and oppressively hot in the summertime, with temperatures easily reaching 120°. Resting between the Asiatic steppes and the Fertile Crescent, Persia has always been a stepping-stone between East and West. Iran traditionally played a pivotal role as the central point in the silk trade between China and the West. Desert oases such as Isfahan and Shiraz in the south were originally manufacturing centers along the way of the caravan routes. The population of Iran is estimated at sixty-six million, with more than six million living in the capital, Teheran.

Ethnically, Iran, "Land of the Lion and the Sun," is a conglomeration of many different groups who migrated to the Iranian heartland during the course of history. "Iranian society" writes John W. Limbert, "resembles a mosaic or a Persian carpet in which varied languages, religions, and tribes, like distinct colors and textures, form an intricate yet coherent design. Within this ethnically heterogeneous society, the Islamic religion and the Persian language have been the dominant cultural strains."[1]

The Iranian people, including the Kurdish element who comprise about ten percent of the population, are of Indo-European, or Aryan, stock. An estimated fifteen percent of the population are ethnic Turks. Ninety percent of Iranians are Shiites of the Twelver sect, and Shiism is the state religion of Iran. The remaining ten percent are almost exclusively Sunni Muslims, primarily Turks and Kurds. Non-Muslims make up tiny percentages of the population; these consist of Christians—mostly Orthodox Armenians—Jews, Zoroastrians, and followers of the Bahai sect. The national language is Farsi.

In 558 B.C.E. Cyrus the Great founded the Persian Empire. The Achaemenid dynasty, as it was known, lasted for more than two centuries, and succeeding monarchs such as Darius and Artaxerexes expanded the empire as far as India, Ethiopia, and the Aegean Sea. Alexander the Great overthrew the Achaemenids in 330 B.C.E., and he and his Seleucid successors ruled Persia for more than a century. Around 129 B.C.E. the Parthians, an Aryan nomadic tribe from the north, overwhelmed the Greeks. During its existence, Parthia was almost continuously at war with Rome and prevented Roman expansion beyond the Euphrates. The Parthian dynasty was finally eclipsed in 224 C.E. by the rise of the Sasanians, who modeled their government after the Achaemenids. Under Sasanian rule, Zoroastrianism was established as the official and exclusive Persian religion, and religious minorities were sometimes persecuted.

The religious system known as Zoroastrianism is based on the teachings of the eighth-century B.C.E. Persian prophet Zarathustra. According to the *Avesta*, the Zoroastrian Bible, all the world is a struggle between two spirits: a god of light and good called Ahura Mazda and a God of evil and darkness called Ahriman. These two forces are engaged in eternal conflict in which the former always prevails. The struggle for man's soul takes place not only on earth but also in the afterlife, the nature of which is determined by man's behavior on earth. Man has an existential choice to make between good and evil, and will find salvation in the hereafter only if he practices Good Thoughts, Good Words, and Good Deeds. Fire represents the principle of goodness and light and is therefore central to the religion. Zoroastrianism is today one of the world's smallest religions, yet from its pantheon evolved such concepts as good and evil, angels and demons, the resurrection of the dead, the afterlife, and heaven and hell—all of which had a profound influence on the monotheistic religions. It is very likely that the Jews of the postexilic period embraced these Magian notions as well as Zoroastrian practices of ritual purity and pollution.[2]

By the seventh century C.E. the Sasanids were worn down from their seemingly endless battles: first with the Romans, and later with the Byzantine Empire. Therefore, the Arabs had little difficulty conquering Persia when they invaded the country in 641 C.E., and the Persian people were forced to forsake Zarathustra for Mohammed. For the next six hundred years, under the Ummayid caliphate (661–749; capital: Damascus), and Abbasid caliphate (749–1258; capital: Baghdad), Persia became a province of the Islamic world-empire and was a hotbed of Shiite sedition.

The causes of the disintegration of the Arab commonwealth can be attributed in part to the decadent lifestyles of the later Abbasid caliphs; their inability to effectively rule the distant regions of the empire; and their need to rely upon the services of mercenaries, usually Turkish, whose generals accumulated great power and ultimately established dynasties of their own. Under the suzerainty of the Abbasid caliphs the Saffarids (867), Samanids (874), and Buyids (932)— all local Persian dynasties; and the Turkish Ghaznavids (977) and Seljuqs (1038), ruled over vast portions of the Muslim empire, including all or parts of Persia.[3] With the exception of the Buyids, who were Shiites, these conquerors were all at least nominally Sunni. These sultanic dynasties were followed in turn by the rapacious Mongol and the Timurid hordes (1255 and 1384 respectively), both of which devastated Persia. After Tamerlane's death in 1405 his successors could not hold the empire together, and the Persian province was split up by many feuding warlords.

The history of Iran as a reunified nation and the triumph of Shiite Islam begins with the Safavid dynasty founded by Shah Isma'il Safavi (1501–24). Under the Safavids, whose origins are obscure, Persia experienced a renaissance of culture and learning. Non-Muslims were forbidden to enter the country, alien influences were purged, Shi'a Islam was imposed on the country's subjects, and it became the state religion.

Shiism is a heterodox sect within Islam that began as a political dispute over the succession of the leadership of the Muslim community after the death of Mohammed in 632 C.E. The founder of Islam had made no provisions for a successor. The majority recognized Abu-Bakr, Mohammed's father-in-law and uncle, as caliph, but a minority supported the claims of Ali ibn abi Talib, Mohammed's cousin and son-in-law. In 661, Ali was assassinated by a Muslim dissident, and his oldest son Hassan succeeded him as imam (successor to Mohammed). Hassan abdicated in favor of his Sunni rival Mu'awiyah, but Hassan's younger brother Husayn rose in rebellion. Husayn, the "Lord of All Martyrs," was routed and tortured to death by the Sunni followers of Mu'awiyah on the tenth day of Moharram, and this calamity bred Shiism, the first schism in Islam. The Shiites replaced the Sunni term caliph with that of imam and focused their belief on a hereditary line from Mohammed through twelve imams, starting with Ali and his sons from Mohammed's daughter Fatima. Persian Shiites believe that the last imam disappeared in 873 but will resurface in the holy city of Meshed as the harbinger of the Kingdom of Allah. Until that time the imam is represented on earth by eminent doctors of the law called ayatollahs ("signs of Allah"). The imams were recognized as infallible rulers in whom all temporal power resided. From its inception, some scholars hold, Imami Shiism became a nationalist movement for unifying the Persian toiling masses against their Arab overlords and for reviving some of Persia's ancient glory.[4]

Under Shiite domination the position of Christians, Jews, Farsis, and other groups was that of an inferior and often persecuted religious minority. The all-powerful Shiite clergy introduced the concept of *najasa*, which relegated all *kafers* (unbelievers) to the status of untouchables and made anything touched by an unbeliever ritually unclean for a Muslim. A whole assortment of humiliating restrictions and social prohibitions were imposed on the unbelievers to keep them separated from the Shiites, and to remind them of their third-class status.

In 1722, the Safavids capitulated to the Ghilzai Afghan invaders, who were themselves dislodged in 1736 by the Persian brigand who became known as Nadir Shah. A Sunni and religious reformer, Nadir Shah abolished Shiism as the state religion and showed amazing tolerance toward non-Muslims. Desiring to stimulate commerce, he settled Jews in his capital, the Shiite holy city of Meshed. Nadir Shah was assassinated by his adjutants in 1747. The intolerant policies toward religious minorities inaugurated by the Safavids were even more stringently pursued by the Qajars dynasts (1796–1925). The Qajar period is characterized by imperialistic intrusions from many directions, great financial depletion, social unrest, and a resurgence of Shi'a fanaticism and severe persecution of non-Shiites, especially Jews. It was under the Qajars that the capital was transferred to Teheran.

Only after the Persian Revolution of 1905 and the drafting of a constitution one year later were minorities accorded equality of rights. In 1921 a military commander named Reza Khan pulled off a coup d'état, and four years later established the Pahlevi dynasty. Reza Khan modeled himself after Kamal Ataturk, the authoritarian founder and first President of the Republic of Turkey, who in 1923 had abolished the Ottoman Caliphate and instituted a far-reaching reform and modernization program. He drafted a constitution and adopted a Western orientation. The power of the Shiite clergy was broken, and the separation of mosque and state ended discriminatory policies directed at women and religious minorities. In 1935, by official decree, the modern name Iran replaced the ancient name of Persia. Reza Shah's flirtation with the Nazis provoked the occupation of Iran by British and Russian armies in 1941, which led to his ouster and subsequent abdication in favor of his son Mohammed Reza Pahlevi.

Initially a weak monarch, Mohammed Shah was almost toppled from the throne in 1953 by the immensely popular premier Muhammed Mossadegh, but he managed to stave off the opposition with help from the British and the American CIA. He did much to secularize and modernize the country, using the dreaded SAVAK (secret police) to brutally crush dissent. In the end, many factors contributed to the Shah's downfall. These factors included galloping inflation, mismanagement, an antiprofiteering campaign that clamped down hard on the *bazaari*, and the suppression of basic liberties. In addition, there was strong belief by the *ulama* (Muslim clergy) and the typical Muslim man-in-the-street that the shah was supporting international Zionism and Western imperialism.

On February 1, 1979, amid widespread popular acclaim, the Ayatollah Khomeini returned from a seventeen-year exile. Within a week Khomeini announced the formation of a provisional government under a revolutionary council. Under the new constitution of December 1979, Shiite Islam was reestablished as the official state religion, supreme powers were vested in the hands of the *ulama*, and the Ayatollah Khomeini was named the nation's religious leader for life. All opposition to the regime was bloodily swept aside. The Ayatollah Khomeini died in June 1989. In August of that year the leader of the *majlis* (parliament) was elected president of Iran, but real power has been concentrated in the hands of Khomeini's successor, Ali Khamenai. In May 1997 a relatively liberal cleric, Mohammed Khatami, rolled to a stunning, decisive victory over a conservative opponent in the presidential election. As of summer 1999 it is too early to prognosticate if the cautious Khatami, who does not control the police or the military, will be able to carry out his moderate reforms in the face of resistance from the archconservative clerical establishment.

THE JEWS OF PERSIA

> Adam and Eve spoke of their love in Persian, and the angel who
> drove them out of Paradise spoke Turkish.
>
> —Persian saying

Persian Jewry is the oldest documented community of the Diaspora, having been in Persia continuously for twenty-seven centuries. Walter J. Fischel writes, "Jews have been living on Iran's soil from the dawn of the first Persian Empire on, as an inseparable part of Iran's national destiny and development. Jews were the eyewitnesses of all the historical events in Persia under every dynasty . . . and under every ruler. Jews were the contemporaries of all the manifold religious movements and sects that were born on Persian soil . . . ; they were companions of the great classical poets . . . and of all the other great Persian masters of art, literature, and philosophy who made their everlasting contributions to world culture."[5] Yet in no other country of the Diaspora have the Jews suffered from so many centuries of unrelenting oppression and mortifying legal restrictions as did the Jews of Persia. At the instigation of cruel despots and the extremely hostile and fanatical *mujahaddin* (Shiite clergy), thousands of Jews were slaughtered, while those who were allowed to exist lived in conditions of the most brutal penury and dehumanization. On numerous occasions Jewish communities escaped annihilation only by embracing Islam. At one time numbering possibly in the millions, the entire Jewish population of Persia was several times brought almost to the brink of extinction.

In talmudic times Persian Jewry was intricately intertwined with the spiritual life of Mesopotamian Jewry and its great rabbinical academies, and submitted to the jurisdiction of the *resh galuta* (Babylonian Exilarch). By medieval times Persian Jewry had developed a distinct mode of worship (Persian *nusach* or rite) and a rich Judeo-Persian literature, but because of the decline of scholarship due to the Mongolian and Timurid upheavals, turned to the Chief Rabbis of Baghdad and Jerusalem on matters of law. With the rise of the Shiites in the sixteenth century, formal links between Persian Jews and the Baghdadi and Sephardi centers of learning abroad were abruptly cut off. As a result, Persian Jewish culture collapsed and in its stead there evolved a pious but extremely superstitious religiosity that had little resemblance to normative Judaism. Contributing to Persian Jewry's demise was the lack of a centralized authority, a great dearth of educated clergy, and the almost complete absence of an affluent class to support Jewish educational institutions.[6] Another important contributing factor was the wholesale destruction of books by the fanatical Shiites during the periodic pogroms.[7] Because of their great isolation, Persian Jewry had few outside sources from which to obtain replacements. It is for these reasons that Persian Jewry of the last five hundred years made only a nominal contribution to the development of halakha or religious life. "In an atmosphere of hatred and violence, of suffering and persecution," writes Fischel, " . . . all the energies and efforts of Persian Jews had to be concentrated on mere physical survival."[8]

Yet despite their meager intellectual output and lack of unity, the Jews of Persia demonstrated a fierce determination to keep the Jewish spark alive. To a great extent this can be attributed to the paternalistic, authoritarian, and clannish nature of the Jewish extended family whose ties were binding and strong, and actually had little need for formal organization. Despite their relatively small numbers, the Jews added a special color and richness to Iran's life and culture. "With the inherent conservatism of a dispersed minority," writes John Limbert, "they have preserved Iranian folkways and cultural traditions—in food and music, for example—that have been forgotten by the Muslim majority."[9]

It is possible that Israelite exiles first reached Persia during the population exchanges that began with the Assyrian conquest of the Northern Ten Tribes in 721 B.C.E. Local Jewish legend has it that when the Jews were driven into exile by Nebuchadnezzar in 586 B.C.E., they carried with them samples of earth and water from Jerusalem. When they arrived at the Persian city of Isfahan, they found that the earth and water weighed the same as that which they had brought with them from the Holy City. The Jews decided to settle there and renamed the town Al-Yahudiya (City of the Jews). They cultivated the soil and prospered.[10]

Cyrus the Great (558–528 B.C.E.), the first of the Achaemenid kings of Persia and conqueror of Babylonia, made Shushan Habiru (modern-day Susa) his capital. Recognized as one of history's most righteous of Righteous Gentiles by the Jews, Cyrus was tolerant of all religions in his realm, but especially benevolent toward the Jews. This may have been due in part to the services the Jews rendered him. It might also have been a realization that sooner or later his armies would clash with Egypt, and that it would be advantageous to have a faithful Jewish community both in Jerusalem and within his wide empire. In 538 B.C.E. he issued a proclamation permitting the exiles in his domain to return to Palestine and rebuild their Temple, but by this time the Jews in the Persian Empire were affluent and secure and perhaps a touch too complacent. Only an estimated 50,000 Jews returned to the Holy Land with their leader Zerubbabel. It was not until the reign of Darius I (522–486 B.C.E.), after much sabotage and intrigue by the Samaritans, Idumiens, and others, that the *beit hamikdash* (Holy Temple) was rebuilt.

The first persecution of Jews in the Persian Empire is recorded in the *Megillat Esther*. From the Purim story we learn that during the reign of Achash-vairosh (believed to be Artaxerexes I, who reigned from 404–361 B.C.E.), an attempt was made by Haman, his grand vizier, to annihilate Persia's Jewish minority. Fortunately Esther, the Jewish queen, managed to persuade the king to side with the Jews. Led by Esther's uncle Mordechai, the Jews defended them-selves and vanquished the enemy. According to popular local belief, Queen Esther and Mordechai founded a Jewish settlement in Hamadan, and both are buried there.

During the period of Parthian rule, Jewish life in Persia and Mesopotamia was vigorous and flourishing. The Parthians sided with the Maccabees against the Seleucids, and later against the Romans. Jews fleeing Greek and Roman oppression in Palestine found a safe haven in Parthia. Estimates are that the Jews' numbers may have swelled to as many as two million in the early centuries of the Common Era.[11] The Parthian dynasts recognized the office of *resh galuta* (Prince of the Exile) and its holder, the scion of the House of David, who offi-cially represented the Babylonian Jews to the authorities.

The rise and fall of the Sasanids roughly encompasses the period of the com-pilation and redaction of the Babylonian Talmud by the *amorites* in 500 C.E. Al-though for the most part the Jews lived in harmony and security and were rep-resented at court, there were also periodic episodes of religious intolerance. According to Armenian sources, during the Sasanian King Shapur's rule (310–339), thousands of Jews were forcibly transplanted from Armenia to Isfahan. During the reigns of Yazdegerd II and his son Firuz in the fifth century, persecu-tion was particularly severe: The Jews were forbidden to observe the Sabbath under the father Yazdegerd II; and the son, Firuz, outdid his father by ordering the ab-duction of Jewish children for the purpose of raising them as Farsis. These out-rages led to a mass flight of Jews to central Asia. The major cause for this harsh attitude toward the Jews is attributed to the great power and influence that was exerted by the Zoroastrian magi on the Sasanian royal court. These militant priests carried on a vigorous campaign against all the other religions in the empire.

According to the Zoroastrian worldview, when Ahura Mazda created the material world, he first produced from Infinite Light a form of fire, out of which all things were to be born. In Zoroastrian temples the magi exalt the sacred fires in which Ahura Mazda is thought to reveal himself. In the Jewish pantheon, fire is also consecrated; for example, by the lighting of candles for the Sabbath and Chanukah. Perceiving this Jewish observance as irreverent and an outright vio-lation of Zoroastrian precepts, the fanatical magi forbade the Jews to light candles for religious purposes. Zoroastrian priests were given license to invade Jewish homes on the Sabbath and extinguish the fires. The issue of burying their dead also brought the Jews into conflict with the Farsi religion. Zoroastrians believe that the earth becomes polluted by burying the dead, and therefore the dead should be exposed on hilltops to be devoured by wild animals and birds. The notion that a menstruating woman would use a body of water—which, like earth, is a sacred material creation—for ritual cleansing also was repulsive to pious Farsis.[12]

Sometimes the Jews tried to resist force with force, which on one occasion resulted in great tragedy. In 472 C.E. two Zoroastrian magi were rumored to have been slain by Jews in Isfahan. A riot broke out, and in an effort to mollify the mob, King Firuz ordered the execution of half of Isfahan's Jews, including the *resh galuta* (Prince of the Exile), and the forcible conversion of all Jewish children. A series of repressive measures were enacted in other parts of the empire, including the temporary cancellation of Jewish self-rule and the closing down of Jewish educational institutions. Many Jews had no choice but to flee the country.

During the reign of Kavadh I (488–531), a movement known as Mazdakism took hold in Persia, advocating a form of communism—including communal wives.[13] The values espoused by Mazdak were embraced by the sovereign himself and were used to undermine his enemies among the landed classes. Mazdakite teachings threatened the Jewish way of life and provoked the exilarch Mar Zutra ben Tuvia into leading an insurrection. His successful revolt brought about the establishment of the Independent Jewish Principality of Mahoza (484–91). This autonomous Jewish state, whose very existence is shrouded in controversy and myth, held out for seven years before being destroyed by the Persians. Mar Zutra and his grandfather were put to death by crucifixion.[14]

The Jews jubilantly greeted the Arabs as liberators when they conquered Persia in 641. Life had become unbearable during the last years of Sasanid rule; *yeshivot* were closed down and the position of exilarch was abolished. An attempt was even made to execute Bustenai, the last man to hold the office of exilarch. In gratitude for their allegiance, the Arab caliph Mu'awiya restored the office of exilarch and gave its holder, Bustenai, a captured Sasanian princess as a gift. The great rabbinical academies were reopened, and the brilliant *geonim* drew young prodigies from all over the Muslim world.

The chaos and sectarian divisions that wracked Islamic society during the latter stages of the Ummayid period in Persia also affected Persian Jewry. Around 755 C.E. a messianic pretender named Abu Isa raised an army of ten thousand

Jews to recapture the Holy Land, but the movement fizzled after the leader was killed on the battlefield. Persia was also a major center of the Karaite movement, which rejected the authority of the Talmud; many of the leaders of this schismatic sect were of Persian birth and background. "It may well be that the absence of some Jewish practices common to normative Judaism, even among traditional Iranian Jews, stems from the influence of Karaism."[15]

The caliphs of the Abbasid dynasty (750–1037) generally tended to disregard the *shariya* laws vis-à-vis the Jews. With the exception of Harun al-Rashid and al-Mutawakkil, the Jews were treated tolerantly. During the fifteen-year tyrannical reign of al-Mutawakkil (847–861), the *zemmi* (*dhimmi* in Arabic) laws were rigidly enforced. Synagogues were demolished and Jews (and other non-Islamic religious minorities) were compelled to wear yellow clothes and paint Satan's picture on their houses, and were disbarred from all government posts.[16]

The Golden Age of Imami Shiism, which existed under the Buyids, came to a violent end with the Seljuq conquest of Persia in 1037. The Seljuq sultans, who like their predecessors ruled in the name of the Abbasid caliphs, reestablished Sunni orthodoxy; but valuing order and stability, the state entered into a partnership between the Turkish "warriors of valor" and Persian Civil administrators, many of whom were men of great distinction. Literature, science, and religion flourished under the enlightened Seljuqs. It was in Seljuq times that the Jews of Persia, to a considerable extent a nomadic people, settled among the sedentary population of the burgeoning cities and towns of the empire, where they underwent a degree of acculturation and assimilation. New Persian (the Persian language revived in Islamic form) gradually supplanted Arabic as the literary language of Persian Jewry, but to preserve their religious and national heritage Jews used Hebrew letters in writing the Persian language. Nevertheless, from time to time there were periods of persecution and upheaval. The debacles of the messianic pretenders David Alroy and Abu Sa'id ben Daud in the twelfth century wreaked havoc on the Jewish communities of Kurdistan and Persia. This intense yearning for salvation indicates that life must have been very difficult for Jews at certain times and in some places even under Seljuq rule. It is around the same period that the well-known Jewish traveler Benjamin of Tudela described in his journals four Jewish communities that existed alongside the Hashishim (Assassins) in their impregnable enclaves in northwestern Persia. Like these Isma'ili Shiites who put up a fierce resistance to Sunni rule, the Jews were beholden to no leaders but their own "and descend from these mountains to pillage and to capture booty, and then retire to the mountains, and none can overcome them."[17]

During the rapacious Mongol onslaughts (circa 1256 C.E.), entire Jewish communities in Persia, particularly in the north, were totally decimated. Survivors from these regions fled to other areas of the empire where conditions were more favorable. After the initial devastation, the Mongols settled into a more peaceful lifestyle. Initially indifferent in religious matters, the shamanistic Mongol lords conducted themselves magnanimously toward the various subject peoples in their empire. *Zemmi* laws were abolished, and Jewish scholarship and poetry thrived once again in Persia. The Mongol il-Khans relied increasingly on Christians and Jews to govern their predominantly Muslim lands and a disproportionate number of Jews became members of the ruling circles as court officials, court physicians, and even as ministers of state. "It was the greatest indignity the Muslims of the Middle East had ever experienced," writes Vladimir Minorsky.[18] Arghun Khan appointed his Jewish friend and confidante, the physician Sa'd al-Daula, to be his grand *wazir*. Al-Daula, who flourished from 1284 to 1291, was assassinated by hostile elements within the ruling class who could stomach his harsh anti-Islamic line no longer. Sa'd was accused of poisoning the il-Khan and executed in 1291.[19] Another Jewish physician who came to power as (joint) *wazir*, the apostate Rashid al-Din Fadl Allah (1248–1318), has been described by one modern historian as "a man of intense learning . . . [who] was connected through marriage with many prominent . . . families . . . accumulated an immense fortune . . . patronized the religious classes . . . and used [his] wealth to make charitable foundations. . . ."[20] Like Sa'd al-Daula, he also accumulated many enemies. He, too, suffered from the Muslim reaction to the il-Khan's policy of favoring minorities. Rashid was accused of poisoning the il-Khan and executed together with his sixteen-year-old son. According to one account his head was whisked off to Tabriz, where it was carried around town with cries of "This is the head of the Jew who abused the name of God; may God's curse be upon him."[21] After the conversion of Ghazan Khan to Islam in 1295, Islam once again reigned supreme as the state religion. The Covenant of Umar was interpreted along strict constructionist lines, a multitude of restrictions were imposed on the *zemmi*, and they were dismissed from positions of power.

With the rise of the Safavids in 1501, the state religion shifted from Sunni to Twelver Shiism, with terrible consequences for the Jews. Under the Safavid nation-state the nonconforming Jew was perceived as an outsider and an obstacle to homogeneity. In the rural areas Jewish landholdings were expropriated, and the Jews were reduced to tenant farming. Jews were considered *najasa* (polluted) and Shiite Muslims took numerous steps to avoid contact with them. For example, food touched by a Jew could not be eaten by a Muslim. Because water is an agent of pollution, Jews were forbidden to use Muslim storage tanks or public baths. The possibility that rainwater might splash off a Jew onto one of the faithful led to the prohibition of Jews from walking in public during rain or snow; a Jew caught in the streets on a such a day was certain to receive blows from a young Muslim. If a Muslim insulted a Jew, he had to drop his head and remain silent. A Jew entering the home or shop of a Muslim had to sit on a special rug. Jews not only were forbidden to own a shop in the marketplace, but they usually avoided the marketplace altogether, because if a piece of merchandise was touched by a Jew it became contaminated—and then the Jew would be obliged to purchase the item even if the Muslim demanded ten times the price. If a Muslim took money from a Jew, he had to wash it before he could put it in his pocket. To avoid defiling the Muslims, the Jews were required to wear identifying clothing such as the "hat of serfdom," a tall dunce cap constructed of many colors; mismatched shoes; and a special red badge on their chests.[22]

A host of other discriminatory measures were directed against the *zemmi* during the Safavid period and later reinstituted under the Qajars. A Jew could not build a house taller than a Muslim's. He was forbidden to ride a horse, because his head always had to be positioned lower than the believers'. He could not raise his voice when he spoke to a Muslim. If a Muslim decided to sell a house to a Jew, he could demand a price five times its worth. Even after the transaction was completed, the Muslim could find various loopholes to reclaim his property. As decreed by the Law of Apostasy, any Jew who converted to Islam inherited all the goods and property of his Jewish relatives who had remained Jews.[23] The murderer of a Jew was subject in most cases only to a fine, even if Muslim witnesses stepped forward on behalf of the victim. If the murderer claimed that he killed a Jew who was in the act of drinking a distilled liquor, he could get away scot-free.[24] The entire Jewish community was held responsible for the misdeeds of individuals. Jewish legal evidence being impermissible in Islamic courts, the Jews would go to great lengths to avoid action there.[25]

In some localities the Shiite population held a superstitious belief that rain could be induced by burning the bodies of exhumed Jews and reciting certain prayers. They believed that scattering the dust of a disinterred Jew would break a drought.[26] There was also a conviction that the Jews had killed Ali, the son-in-law of Mohammed, and therefore it was dangerous for Jews to go out on certain holidays.[27] At public festivals the Jews often experienced great humiliation. A highlight of such events, and a source of great entertainment for the shah and his entourage, was the spectacle of watching Jews being thrown into a tank filled with water and mud, and then making the half-drowned unfortunates crawl out on hands and knees.[28]

Throughout Persia the Jews were segregated within the confined walls of the *mehallah* (ghetto). Nineteenth-century observers such as viceroy of India Lord Curzon, and Eleanor Roosevelt writing in the late 1950s, and many others have graphically described the stench and sordidness they encountered while "touring" these ghettos. The inhabitants were variously depicted by these writers as "unspeakably wretched," "sickly and short-lived," and "social pariahs," who were living in hovels that were infested by scorpions, snakes, rats, cockroaches, and other disease-carrying vermin. The *mehallah* in Teheran was depicted as the most despicable of despicable Middle Eastern slums.[29]

The first Safavid shah Isma'il, Amnon Netzer tells us, had his own mother executed and watched her die. This cruel tyrant also ordered that any Jew who came within his sight should have his eyes gouged out.[30] During the early phase of the reign of Shah Abbas I, however, the Persian Jews seem to have enjoyed relative economic and religious freedom. Under the enlightened monarch Shah Abbas I (1558–1629), reforms were introduced to curb the power of the Shiite clergy. Abbas I opened his doors to Jews in adjoining countries to come settle in his capital, Isfahan. According to one source, because the Georgian Jews had assisted Shah Abbas in his wars with the Ottomans, he granted them the right to settle on Persian soil. The city of Farahabad on the Caspian Sea is believed to have been established by Georgian Jews.[31]

Shah Abbas's attitude toward the Jews changed radically toward the end of his reign. A *shochet* (ritual slaughterer) in Isfahan was accused by his patrons of tampering with the weight of meat. Vindictively, he converted to Islam and intimated to the shah that the Jews were using magic to conjure up his death. Community elders were brought before a Muslim religious court, and, refusing to convert to Islam, were thrown to the dogs. The Holy Books were burned in the village square, and the whole community, to avert a massacre, converted to Islam. This activity spread to other parts of Persia, and in order to alleviate their great oppression, a large number of Jews converted to Islam. A sizable proportion of the Muslim population of Shiraz is believed to be of Jewish origin. Some Jews were permitted to come out in the open during the reign of Shah Saf'i (1629–1642), although many communities remained Muslim.

During the reign of Shah Abbas II (1642–1667) a wave of anti-Jewish persecution reached its most brutal heights. His grand *wazir*, Muhammed Beg, ordered that the Jews, without exception, be given the option of embracing Islam or leaving the country empty-handed. A reward was offered to the new converts in the form of a fixed sum of money for each Jewish family. Most Jews obstinately clung to their religion but played the Muslim game in public for economic survival. When the Shiite clergy learned of this Jewish duplicity, they realized it was futile to make the Jews stay faithful to Islam and pleaded with the Shah to permit the the Jews to return to their religion. An edict was issued by Abbas II in 1661 allowing the Jews to openly return to their ancestral faith, on condition that they wear a red patch on their chests.[32]

Another attempt was made by the clergy under the last of the Safavids to forcibly convert all nonbelievers to Islam. Fortunately, the Jews and other minorities were saved from physical and spiritual annihilation by the rise of Nadir Shah, an enlightened ruler who overthrew the Safavids in 1736. Upon ascending to the throne, the great conqueror abolished Shiism as the state religion and treated all religious minorities with great tolerance. Several of the largest Jewish communities in Persia—specifically Teheran and Meshed—date from Nadir Shah's time.

Under the Qajars (1796–1925) the situation for Persian Jewry was as gloomy as ever. *Zemmi* laws were energetically enforced, and once again the Jews were under the heavy yoke of the Shiite clergy. Numerous repressive measures were imposed on them, such as arbitrary tax exactions and the meting out of collective punishment for the crimes of an individual. As the most despised element in Persian society, their position deteriorated even further. They were subject to periodic blood libels and ritual murder charges. Sometimes a dead child would be placed in front of a Jewish home to support the accusation. In one such case in 1910 the mob unjustly avenged itself against the Jews of the Shirazi *mehallah,* leaving virtually the whole community of six thousand homeless and badly bloodied.[33]

During the late Qajar period (from the 1870s onward) some contact was established with European and American Jewry. *Shtadlanim* (intercessors) such as Moses Montefiore, Baron De Hirsch, Adolph Cremieux, and other powerful and influential Jews began to pressure the English and French governments to intervene on behalf of Persian Jewry, with slightly positive results. Shah Nasr al-Din (1848–96) made an earnest attempt at protecting the Jews and ameliorating their condition. For example, in Hamadan in 1892 a massacre of the entire community was averted when the shah, hearkening to the alarmist voices of the (Paris-based) Alliance Israelite Universelle, sent in his troops to shield the barricaded Jews from an enraged mob. To some degree he was motivated by a belief that these powerful "Court Jews" would help him broker advantageous business deals with Western governments and venture capitalists. A remarkable exchange between Baron Rothschild and the shah, in 1873, was recorded in the shah's diary. In exchange for a large sum of money the shah suggested that Rothschild finance a Jewish state, possibly located in Iran, for the world's Jews. "You yourself would become their chief and rule over them peacefully, so that they would no longer be scattered and driven about."[34] Rothschild is not known to have responded to this idea.

Beginning in the latter part of the nineteenth century the Alliance established schools for Persian Jews. Classes were taught in French and English as well as in Persian. The Alliance helped counter the conversionist activities aggressively carried on by Christian missionaries.

English and French Jewish philanthropical institutions did much to ameliorate the condition of the Persian Jews and educate their children. Unfortunately this relationship could be described as a Jewish variation of the "White Man's Burden," since the European educational institutions placed great emphasis on teaching Western values. Alliance communal workers tended to be condescending toward things culturally Iranian. The non-Orthodox practices of many of them, and their decidedly non-Zionist orientation, offended the religious sensibilities and aspirations of the Iranian Jewish masses. As a consequence, those Persian Jewish youth under Alliance influence "were detached not only from their Jewish roots, but from Persian culture as well."[35]

Before the rise of the Safavids in the sixteenth century, the Jews were, to a large extent, merchants and traders who served as middlemen between their country and India, Arabia, and the Ottoman Empire. Under the Shiite dynasts the Jews were removed from positions of power and wealth and forbidden to open businesses in the marketplace. Many impecunious urban Jews were glad to obtain work even as sewer cleaners and wool carders. Most barely eked out a living as itinerant peddlers. They would travel around the countryside selling an assortment of dry goods such as clothing, carpets, amulets, and utensils. They generally left their homes after the Sabbath and returned home the following Friday before sundown. Sometimes they would be gone for weeks or even months. The lonely peddler who trudged through the scorching desert to remote villages to sell his merchandise lived a precarious existence, and there was never a guarantee that he would return home with the minimum money needed to feed his family. S. Landshut explained the Jews' predicament thusly: "Usually peddlers obtain their wares on loan from Muslim or Jewish retailers at exorbitant rates of interest. The peddler's return scarcely suffices to pay off his debts, and he is consequently always at the mercy of the merchants. In turn, the peddler must extend credit to the peasants, and the collection of debts in the villages is a difficult and often dangerous task."[36]

In certain regions, such as in Isfahan, entire Jewish clans engaged in specialized crafts such as tanning, weaving, tailoring, and jewelry making. Because Muslims are forbidden to sell gold and silver at a greater value than the metal is worth, the smithing crafts were wholly in Jewish hands. In stiff competition with the Armenian Christians, some Jews engaged in money lending and in the illegal and often dangerous manufacture of intoxicants. Some Jews operated subterranean drinking establishments; others were opium dealers. (It should be remembered that while the Koran condemns the use of alcohol, no such restrictions are placed on the use of opiates.) Womenfolk contributed to the meager family coffers by assisting their husbands with craftwork. They also served as midwives, fortune tellers, amulet writers, advisors to the ladies of the harem on beauty and health issues, and as dispensers of love potions. Some were ladies of the harem themselves.

As the most despised class in Persian society, the Jews supplied the ranks of the public dancers, singers, and entertainers—professions considered beneath the dignity of any self-respecting Shiite Muslim. The Jews played mostly before Muslim audiences, in the courts and the caravansaries, and were considered the finest musicians in all the realm. The Jews of Shiraz are said to have best preserved the classical Persian music traditions. Because the Jews had a virtual monopoly in the entertainment field, Persian music and dance became synonymous with Jewish music and dance.[37]

Although the Muslim masses were generally hostile and condescending toward the Jews, there were times and places when they coexisted harmoniously. For example, there is documentation that in the town of Yazd in the seventeenth century the Jews were threatened with forcible conversion. Coming to the defense of their Jewish neighbors, an outraged Muslim citizenry, for economic reasons, sent a petition to the shah on the Jews' behalf when the Jews threatened to evacuate the city en masse if His Majesty persisted in converting them.[38] In certain cities such as Kashan, a city halfway between Teheran and Isfahan, the Jews tended to feel physically and economically secure. Kashan is a silk manufacturing center, and the Jews there had a virtual monopoly on the dyeing process. Because of their long-standing reputation for honorable dealings and superior products, the Jews were treated respectfully by the Muslims. Here the Jews walked erect with their heads high, were not obligated to wear the red badge, and didn't shrivel up upon the approach of a Muslim, as did Jews in Shiraz and other parts of Persia.[39]

"Medicine is little known, but is reverenced in Persia . . . ," writes the nineteenth-century traveler Frederika Freygang.[40] Whatever measure of respect the Jews obtained from their Muslim neighbors, it was had in the capacity of physician and herbal therapist. Although there were many Jewish *hakims* in Persia, few had formal academic training, acquiring knowledge of the profession from experience. A Jewish *hakim* was perceived as "almost supernatural in his wisdom. Muslims who refused to eat Jewish food would take his medicines."[41]

A *hakim* with great curative powers therefore also wielded power and influence in Muslim society, and was often in a position to intercede on behalf of his fellow Jews in times of tribulation.[42]

In some parts of Persia in the nineteenth century, Jewish women were obliged to wear black veils instead of white ones in public; in other areas they were not permitted to cover their faces in public at all. Jewish women, like their Muslim compatriots, were heavily bejeweled with bracelets on the arms and ankles, necklaces, earrings, nose rings, and finger rings. Turquoise and carnelians were the most common jewelry worn, because they were considered lucky stones. Jewish women in the urban centers were not permitted to wear the *chador*, a large square cloth designed to disguise a woman's curves. The prohibition thus imposed, writes Sorour Soroudi, was "intended to place Jewish women on the same level as prostitutes."[43]

Jewish men were rarely seen in the street with their wives for two reasons. For one thing, Persian men were rarely seen in public with their spouses because this is contrary to Shiite etiquette. For Jews there was an additional problem: the possibility of having to come to the defense of their womenfolk in the not-unlikely scenario that they were assaulted by a Muslim. Should a Jew intervene on behalf of his wife, he would surely be seriously beaten, if not killed. Because Jewish women could be easily identified, they were often vulnerable to molestation or kidnapping. Even though in patriarchal Persian culture men are the guardians and defenders of family honor (an act of machismo called *gheirat* in Farsi), Jewish women had no one to rely on for assistance and had to defend their honor by themselves when attacked. Islamic men often ganged up on Jews in the streets. In Shiraz it was said that when a Jew was beaten up, he would immediately begin to scream and feign excruciating pain, claiming he had been wounded to death. The Muslims called these histrionics *jud baazi* (the Jew game).[44] Laurence Loeb asserts that as an intimidated and oppressed minority, the Jews tried to make themselves as invisible as possible, because an individual who was visible to the authorities was usually singled out for punishment. This caused even the slightly more prosperous to dress and act like impecunious beggars, shirk social responsibility, and not take care of their own poor. As a result, the notion of giving *tzedakah* (charity) was unknown in many parts of Persia. "The pattern of affecting poverty, necessitated by the fear of theft as well as a desire to hide wealth from potential Jadid al-Islam (apostate) heirs, fostered a reluctance among the wealthy to donate to charity. . . . Personal insecurity . . . encouraged an ethos in which labor is not considered a virtue, because its fruits are likely to be stolen."[45] Heavy drinking and opium and hashish addiction were once common among the poorer strata of Persian Jewish society. In some regions, especially in Shiraz, there was prostitution, and there were even cases of husbands pandering for their wives and sisters.[46]

Until the late nineteenth century there were virtually no Jewish schools of higher learning in Persia. It was rare to find a Jew, including *hakhamim*, who had knowledge of *Gemurah* and *mefurshim* (exegesis).[47] Most Persian Jews were functional illiterates who never attended *maktab* (*cheder*). For those who did attend *cheder* the curriculum was primarily geared to making the youngster an active participant in synagogue life. Schooling usually lasted for about five years, around ages five to ten. A youngster who was sent to *cheder* might first be taught the Hebrew alphabet and to read from the *siddur* (prayer book). He then was taught by rote to translate the *Tanach* into Judeo-Persian, and to chant from the Torah in the synagogue. If he had progressed this far in his studies and wished to continue, he might be taught some *Mishnah* and *Midrash*, but rarely *Gemurah*.

In addition to the "pure" local tongue and Judeo-Persian (which employed Rashi script), Jews all over Iran spoke a special dialect called *Letra'i* (not-Torah-like). *Letra'i* is the language of the marketplace, a mixture of Hebrew and Persian, written with Hebrew letters like Yiddish and Ladino. Because it is heavily laden with Hebrew, it is incomprehensible to the Muslims.[48] Few, if any, Jews could speak pure Hebrew.

Jewish communal affairs were administered by an elected representative body of seven family heads called *anjumman kalimian*. These community chieftains appointed a *kadkhuda* (*nasi* in Hebrew) to represent the community vis-à-vis the authorities. The *kadkhuda* was usually the wealthiest and most respected member of the community—oftentimes a *hakim*—and his primary responsibility was the prompt payment of the *jizya* to the authorities. The *kadkhuda* was assisted in this task by a *mullah* or rabbi. In addition to his political role, the *mullah* served as all-round religious functionary—*rav, dayan, mori, chazan, mohel*, and *shochet*. There was no organized countrywide rabbinical body in Persia, the *mullah* of each locality being the ultimate authority on issues pertaining to Jewish law. To support the upkeep of the synagogue and the educational institutions, the *mullah* could impose a special internal tax known as *geballa*. Invariably the *mullahs* knew little more than the rudiments of Judaism; in practice they were more like shamans and wizards. The position of *mullah* was handed down from father to son.

The custom of making pilgrimages to the tombs of holy men is popular among all Persians, including Jews. Jewish pilgrimages were made to the tombs of great biblical figures who died on Persian soil, such as the mausoleums of Queen Esther and Mordechai in Hamadan and the tombs of the Prophets Daniel in Susa and Zecharia in Hamadan. These pilgrimages were usually undertaken by the faithful to fulfill a vow made upon recovery from illness or after the birth of a son.

Persian Jews married off their children very early: boys at ten or twelve, and girls at the very tender age of six or seven. Some girls were mothers by age twelve or thirteen. Polygamy was practiced only by men who could afford more than one wife. It was common for a prepubescent girl to marry a man who was old enough to be her grandfather. As John Wishard points out, there must have been an inordinate number of young widows.[49] Upon entering her husband's house, a bride would bang her head against the doorpost, to indicate her submission to her husband.[50]

On the whole, the Persian Jews tended to be extremely superstitious. There was a pervasive fear of *shaydim*, believed to be angels who are demoted to the rank of demons. These *shaydim* (called *gazand* in Persian) were believed to be capable of stealing children and causing humans—especially pregnant mothers—much bodily harm. Amulets, magic protective circles, and prayer services over new mothers were a common practice. For instance, during the first eight days after birth a mother with a newborn son would sleep with a sword and an assortment of charms under her pillow for protection against evil spirits. The American Jewish journalist Ida Cowen observed that at the conclusion of the Yom Kippur service, the Persian Jewish men would crowd around a synagogue official who passed out bits of the candle that had been lit in the synagogue for Yom Tov. The men gave these pieces of candle to their childless women, who would eat the wax as a *segulah* (curative) for barrenness.[51]

To ward off the evil eye during the *brit*, the infant's head was covered with a white hood, to which was attached a gold-encased cube of salt. The infant was placed on the lap of the *sandaq* (godfather) and the *mohel* would rub some ash on the baby's penis. The foreskin of the penis was then cut with a very sharp razor. At this point an older man would pour some wine or *arak* (a distillation made from raisins) on his middle finger and place it on the infant's mouth to suck on.[52] A woman who could not conceive a male child would sometimes grab the foreskin of a newly circumcised boy and swallow it in the hope that her next child would be a boy.[53] Among Persian Jews, as among the rest of the population, if a mother was told that her child was beautiful, she would immediately begin preparing its *tachrichim* (burial clothes), because such a remark was certain to bring disaster from the evil eye.[54]

The Persian Jews had many unique holiday traditions. *Chumetz* was not burned but thrown into water. At the Passover *seder* all participants would wash their hands. The act of ritual pouring was considered a special *mitzvah*, and the girl or woman who performed this act was thought to enhance her chances of finding a good husband or bearing a child. The water used for washing hands was saved, and if a childless woman dabbed drops of it on her head forty times, it was believed to improve the possibility of conception. The wine spilled out during the recital of the ten plagues, combined with the water used for washing hands, if saved, could be used to punish enemies. Splashing this mixture at the foe's doorstep would cause his family to split up. It was customary during the Passover *seder* for a few of the participants to slip away and return carrying bundles on their shoulders. Answering their knock, the head of the household would ask: "From where are you coming?" and they would reply: "From Egypt." They would then be brought to the center of the room to recite the story of the Exodus. During the recitation of *Dayeynu* when they came to the words *illuh hoitzionu memitzraim* ("if He only had taken us out of Egypt") all the *seder* participants would take a green onion, and when they came to the word *Dayeynu*, all the other seder participants would hit each other on the back with the onion to recall the Egyptian taskmasters' beating of the Jewish slaves.

On the day after Passover, Iranian Jews celebrated a festival called Ruz-e bagh. On *mowtzie yom tov* (after sundown of the eighth day and conclusion of Passover) families would prepare a festive meal. They would put their silver and gold in a pot of water and mount a big mirror nearby. The reflection was thought to symbolize the hope for a year of prosperity. There followed a day of picnicking at which young men and women would hope to find a future spouse. [55]

Moed Qatan ("Little Festival") was a special holiday celebrated by the Jews of Shiraz. This holiday commemorates how the Jews were saved after the exposing of an apostate. This recreant, who felt insulted by his fellow Jews, decided to avenge himself and reported to the Shiite clergy that on the Islamic holy day of Ashura the Jews placed a dog's head inside a Torah scroll with a sign saying "Hussein." The night before the holiday the caretaker of the synagogue had a nightmare that the Torah scroll was burning. He raced into the synagogue and found the planted evidence inside the Torah scroll. He immediately disposed of the dog's head and the sign. The next day an angry mob stormed the synagogue and threatened to kill all the Jews. The Muslims, who expected to find the dog's head and sign inside the Torah scrolls, discovered that there was nothing there. Frustrated and angry, they left the synagogue without doing the Jews any harm. [56]

The Jews of Persia were primarily an urban people residing in every large city in the country. Until the nineteenth century the major Jewish communities were concentrated in Tabriz, Shiraz, Isfahan, and Hamadan. Massacres, combined with a number of plagues that ravaged Shiraz and other Persian cities throughout the nineteenth century, forced the Jews to stream into the new capital, Teheran. By the late 1970s an estimated half of the 80,000 Iranian Jews were living in the capital. Thousands of Persian Jews began to make *aliyah* to the Holy Land in the last two decades of the nineteenth century. A sizable number were from Shiraz, which contained the most pious and learned of Persian Jews. These religious-idealistic elements managed to enter Palestine in spite of the restrictions imposed by the Ottomans. They contributed heavily to the construction of Jerusalem as it was expanding outside its city walls. Between 1948 and the rise of the Ayatollah Khomeini in 1979 an estimated 70,000 Iranian Jews emigrated to Israel in five waves. Those who migrated to Israel, especially during the early phases, were generally from the poorer strata of the Jewish community.

"The Jewish flirtation with Bahai," writes Daniel Elazar, "reflects the universal problem of modern Jewish assimilation."[57] Whereas the Protestant missionaries were able to make relatively few converts among the Jews of Persia, the Bahai had greater success. Founded in 1863 by a Persian nobleman named Baha'u'llah, the Bahai religion attracted thousands of Persian Jewish adherents to its fold. The Bahai movement, with its emphasis on the oneness of mankind, the unity of all religions and races, and eradication of prejudices and superstitions, had a great appeal to those educated Persian Jews who (like their Islamic counterparts) were alienated from what they perceived to be the spiritual vacuousness and fossilization of the ancestral faith.

As no formal conversion is required, the Jewish community never wrote them off outright as *meshumadim* (apostates); yet as sectarian Muslims (the Bahai were officially registered as Muslim), they were no longer regarded as *najasa* and could mingle freely in Islamic society.[58] The converted Jews of Hamadan "[formed] the kernel of the Bahai organization, and . . . in later years [were] the most fanatic and ardent propagandists of the Bahai religion."[59] Before the rise of the Ayatollah Khomeini, upwardly mobile Iranian Jews oftentimes found it socially and economically expedient to convert to the Bahai religion in much the same way that some American Jews have tried to "pass" by embracing Unitarianism or Episcopalianism. In the aftermath of the Shiite revolution in 1979, the 350,000 Bahai, whom the ayatollahs consider to be *mahuar al-damm* (apostates whose blood can be shed with impunity), have been experiencing much more severe repression than the Jews, and the Jews who have converted suffer even more than prior to their conversion.[60]

When Reza Shah Pahlevi came to power in 1925, the various indignities that had been inflicted on the Jews were abolished. No longer *najasa*, the Jews were now free to leave the confines of the *mehallah*. They were no longer subject to the discriminatory poll tax and other impositions. Islamic education was abandoned in state public schools, and Jewish children were for the first time allowed to attend these schools along with Muslims. Jews could also attend schools of higher learning and branch out into the professions, but were not allowed to rise to the top. Periodically, when the hostile Muslim religious leaders stirred up their followers against the Jews, Reza Shah Pahlevi protected the Jews—using the army, if necessary, to forcibly suppress violence. However, in the period leading up to World War II the shah sided with the Nazis, and all Jewish officials were removed from government posts.

Under Mohammed Shah Pahlevi, the last shah, the Jews were afforded even greater opportunities for social, economic, and intellectual achievement. According to Daniel Elazar, this was due in part to the support many wealthy Jews had given the shah in helping depose the leftist premier Muhammad Mossadegh.[61] Many Jews prospered in trade and industry, especially in the export of petroleum and plastics, where they were engaged in personal dealings with the shah and his family. Some attained positions in the civil service, while a small number attended universities and became successful attorneys, doctors, engineers, and technocrats. Zionist organizations and Jewish educational institutions proliferated. The shah publicly recognized Israel, and relations with Israel were generally good.

While in exile the Ayatollah had written that the Jews "are wretched people who wish to establish Jewish domination throughout the world,"[62] and during the period leading up to the overthrow of the shah, Khomeini's supporters fulminated against the Jews, accusing them of collaborating with the Zionists and of depleting the country of its resources. There was much animosity directed at the shah because of his intimacy with the Jews. Attacking the Israeli consulate in Teheran became an acceptable form of anti-shah defiance. At the time of the "Black Friday" massacres in Jaleh Square in September 1978, rumors were spread by the Khomeiniites that the shah had flown in Iranian-Israeli troops to help maintain order and that fanatics in the crowd were instigating a massacre of the Jews.[63] "During the Ayatollah Khomeini's exile in Paris in 1978," writes David Sitton, "a delegation of Jews visited him asking for his protection from Shiite fanatics. Khomeini promised them full protection and said that when he returned to Iran, the Jews would not be harmed. Upon his return from exile in Paris on February 1, 1979, an estimated one million [some sources say three million] Iranians gathered at the airport to welcome him. Among them were 5,000 Jews led by Chief Rabbi Shofet. The Jews held aloft a picture of the Ayatollah with the slogan 'Jews and Muslims, brothers.'"[64]

In 1979, seven prominent Jews, including Habib Elghanian, the multimillionaire president of Iranian Jewry, were accused of being Zionist spies and/or drug dealers and executed. Jews in government posts and at the universities were dismissed from their positions, and Jewish religious schools were closed down. The former Israeli mission in Teheran was turned over to the PLO.[65] Some Jews were so fearful for their lives that they placed ads in the Islamic newspapers announcing that they were converting to Islam. It appeared that the unrestricted life the Jews had become accustomed to was rapidly coming to an end. "However, once the revolution had succeeded, there was a radical change in Khomeini's pronouncements regarding the Jews. Venemous attacks gave way to more balanced and tolerant statements. This was in keeping with the new regime's general policy towards religious minorities."[66] The government of Israel (or private Israeli companies representing the government) seem to have secured the safety of the remaining Jews by tacitly agreeing to sell arms to the Iranians, with a value of approximately $150 to $500 million annually, and as long as Israel sent a steady flow of arms to Iran, Jews would be free to emigrate to the west.[67] Some 55,000 have left since 1980, the overwhelming majority settling in the United States. An estimated 30,000 Iranian Jews live in the Beverly Hills area of Los Angeles (jokingly referred to as "Irangeles").

During the height of the Iran-Iraq War the world witnessed the hideous spectre of fanatical Shiites sending children into the trenches and (for the first time since World War I) the use of poison gas. Several dozen Jewish soldiers were known to have been killed in the war with Iraq. Many Jews were forced to emigrate in 1986–87 after Iraq's aerial bombing of Shiraz, Isfahan, and Kermanshah, where the majority of the Jewish community was concentrated. Hundreds of Jews arrived every month at refugee centers in Europe, primarily Vienna. Many carried tales of growing persecution and official discrimination: eviction from government posts, confiscation of property, wholesale roundups, and incarceration for the purpose of extorting ransom.

Since mosque and state are one in Iran, Jewish youngsters attending public schools were constantly bombarded with Islamic, anti-Zionist propaganda, and attending classes on the Sabbath and holidays was compulsory. After morning prayers, which Jewish pupils were not obligated to take part in, various slogans that reviled the U.S. and Israel were spewed in the classrooms. Jewish students were ordered to shout in unison with the other students "Death to Israel and death to America."[68] To prove their loyalty to the regime, Jewish communal leaders were also regularly forced to condemn Israel and Zionism.

The Jews are recognized by the Constitution of 1979 as an "official" protected religious minority entitled to representation in the Iranian *majlis* (National Consultative Assembly). Many secular Jews are therefore kept in the religious fold, because their children must obtain some form of Jewish education, and the Islamic republic requires all citizens to register as belonging to a religious community for purposes of marriage and inheritance. The Jews in Iran today are less prosperous than they were under the shah. About two-thirds are self-employed, principally in retail and manufacture, and another fifteen percent are professional. Fearing the Revolutionary Guards and the periodic accusations of "associating with Zionism" and being scapegoated for all the evils that beset the country, many Jews anxious about their future in the Islamic republic have surreptitiously left Iran.[69]

At present, Jewish life in Iran is looking bleak, and the Jews are living in a perennial state of fear. In the past five years there have been five Jews killed by the Iranian government, two of whom were explicitly charged with Zionism. In April 1999 Iranian security forces arrested thirteen Jews, and charged them with spying for Israel and the United States. These detainees, including rabbis, religious teachers, community leaders, and a sixteen-year-old boy who was seized from his classroom, come from the southwestern towns of Shiraz and Isfahan, where a substantial number of Iran's estimated 27,000 Jews live.

The consensus among observers is that these are trumped-up charges made by hardliners who are using the Jews as unfortunate pawns in an ongoing power struggle between reform-minded moderates, including President Mohammad Khatami, and the deeply unpopular arch-conservative camp led by Ayatollah Ali Khamenei, which is tenaciously clinging to its threatened supremacy and resisting any significant improvement in relations with the West. Fearful that elections in the parliament that are scheduled for spring 2000 will cost them control of the legislature, the clerical oligarchy is determined to do all they can to stymie the forces of change. Bringing up allegations of espionage against foreign nationals or members of vulnerable religious minorities, such as the Bahai and Jews, gives the hardliners a pretext to justify repressive measures at home and to undermine efforts to establish détente with the United States.

Facing possible execution if convicted, the thirteen Jews are unlikely to get a fair trial. Hope for their release now rests on international diplomatic pressure.

THE DJEDID AL-ISLAM (NEW MUSLIMS) OF MESHED

> I one morning saw a fakeer take an old [Meshedi] Jew by the beard as
> if he would have pulled it from his face, and accuse him of having been
> party to selling him to the Toorkmuns, nor did he release the terrified
> old man till he promised to pay a few reals, the crowd looking on as
> Englishmen do at badger-baiting, and thinking it capital sport.
> —Arthur Connolly, *Journey to the North of India* (1838)

At various times and places in the Diaspora, Jewish communities in hostile Christian and Muslim environments were faced with a bitter choice: conversion or annihilation. Tens of thousands of Jews boldly defied peril and force
and died *al kiddush haShem* (for the sanctification of God's name). Myriads more,
finding that they were no longer bound by the impediments that restricted them
as Jews, embraced the religion of their oppressors. Still thousands upon thousands more converted unwillingly, but maintained allegiance to Judaism. At a
more propitious time, such as a change in the political climate, or by fleeing to
a freer, more tolerant environment, they would surface again as Jews. These
clandestine Jews are variously referred to as "conversos" or *anusim* (Hebrew for
"the forced ones").

In a famous epistle to North African Jewry, Moses Maimonides (1135–
1204) justified apostasy to Islam in times of persecution. Maimonides' family,
along with thousands of other Sephardim, were compelled to go underground
during the fanatical Almohades rule in Spain. According to Maimonides, Judaism was theologically closer to Islam than to Christianity, since Islam is free from
the personification of the deity, and it is a lesser perjury to testify that Mohammed
was the Prophet of God than to proclaim Jesus as the Son of God. Therefore,
according to Maimonides, "if one were to inquire, 'Shall I be slain or utter the
[Islamic] formula?' the answer should be, 'Utter the formula and live.'" Since
worshipping images of Jesus and Mary is outright *avodeh zara* (idol worship), it
was imperative for a Jew to make the ultimate sacrifice rather than convert to
Christianity. But feigning conversion to Islam in order to survive was permissible provided one took the earliest opportunity to flee the land of forced conversion and return to Judaism.[70]

Unlike the conversos of Spain and Portugal, most of whom eventually were
forcibly assimilated into the Christian milieu, the so-called Djedid al-Islam, or
New Muslims of Meshed (pronounced Mash-had), remained staunch Jews at
heart. For generations the Djedid al-Islam lived a precarious double life, out-

wardly appearing to be good and faithful Muslims, but in their souls remaining fervently Jewish. Though cut off spiritually from their fellow Jews in other parts of Persia, they assiduously resisted absorption into the surrounding Muslim population, mingling as little as possible. Intent on practicing their ancestral faith, despite a relentless Shiite campaign to make them conform, they devised an assortment of artifices to outwit their tormentors. Because of their decades-long communal ordeal, the conversos developed extremely close bonds of friendships. This extreme form of communal bonding enabled them to remain more traditional and loyal to Judaism than other Persian Jewish communities. When conditions permitted, they fled Meshed and openly returned to their ancestral faith.

The holy city of Meshed is the capital of the province of Khorasan, in northeast Iran, near the Afghani border. Meshed, which means "place of martyrdom" in Persian, owes its very existence to Reza, the eighth of the twelve Shiite imams, who is interred there. Reza is believed to have died there in 813 C.E., either from eating poisonous grapes or from having been stabbed with a poisoned dagger. The Imam Reza's tomb is considered a most holy place for Shiites, and Shiite canon goes so far as to allow Muslim pilgrims to substitute the obligatory pilgrimage to Mecca with a pilgrimage to the sacred tomb of this Persian saint. The prophet Ali ibn abi-Talib, son-in-law of Mohammed, is also reputed to be buried there. Every year tens of thousands of believers converge on Meshed from all over Asia and the Near·East. In former times, the shrines of Meshed were *bast* (sanctuary) for Muslims who were accused of crimes and fleeing their pursuers.[71] Even unscrupulous characters, fleeing their debtors, once safely ensconced within the confines of the holy sites, were protected by the Shiite clergy and shielded from litigation. "From the security of his retreat, he can then make terms, and settle the ransom with which to purchase his immunity if he comes out."[72] With the accession of the Safavid Shiites in the sixteenth century, all infidels, including Jews, were forbidden to enter Meshed, let alone live there.

After his conquest of India in 1736, Nadir Shah returned to his hometown province of Khorasan and supplanted Isfahan with Meshed as the seat of government. Meshed was chosen as the capital because of its vital strategic importance and because it was a crossroads of trade between Persia and Central Asia, Afghanistan, India, and China. To fortify the capital and make it economically viable, the man who is described by modern historians as the "Napoleon of Iran" settled various ethnic minorities there, including some forty Jewish families from other parts of Persia. By increasing the permanent population, the shah, who is believed to have been a Sunni Muslim of Turkish descent, would not have had to rely on the local Shiite population, whose loyalty he could not count on.

The great conqueror was also a religious reformer. Although a Sunni, he is said to have been something of a religious universalist. He abolished Shiism as the state religion and treated all religious minorities as equals. All previous decrees discriminating against Jews were revoked, and the Jewish community was allowed to carry on business activities unimpeded. Magnificent carpets and rugs manufactured by Jewish industries were exchanged for glass and porcelain from Teheran, shawls from Kashmir, lambskins from Bukhara, cloaks from Kabul, pearls from the isles of the Indian Ocean, silk from China, and tea leaves from Ceylon. Almost the entire import-export trade of Khorasan was concentrated in Jewish hands.[73]

Jewish wealth was greatly envied and bitterly resented by the local population, and the settlement of *najasa*s (ritual polluters) on holy soil infuriated the clergy. In constant fear of the Muslims, the Jews constructed large gates in entrances to their neighborhoods and dug tunnels under their homes for safe escape in case they were attacked. While Nadir Shah was still alive, there was little the Shiite faithful could do about "the Jewish problem." However, after his assassination in 1747, and the reimposition of restrictive laws under the Qajars a half-century later, the Jews of Meshed were exposed to persecution, and their position began to deteriorate. Disaster finally struck in 1839 in the form of a massacre known as the Allahdad. The circumstances were as follows:

According to local Jewish tradition the massacre took place during the month of Muharram.[74] The Muharram, which corresponds with mid July, is a period of grieving and mourning for pious Shiite Muslims. It is a time to commemorate the martyrdom of their greatest leader, Ali, the son-in-law of Mohammed. The tenth day of the Muharram, known as the *ashura*, is considered the holiest and most solemn day of the Islamic calendar. On this day, the Shiites memorialize the torture and slaying of the Imam Husayn, Ali's second son, along with seventy of his followers, at the hands of the Sunni enemy. During this month the Shiites assemble in their mosques and grieve for the loss of their leaders with lamentation and fasting. Everyone from the shahs and ayatollahs down to the poorest of poor is attired in black rags. The Shiites parade through the streets, displaying religious frenzy by bloodily flagellating themselves and each other with knives, whips, and sticks.

In 1839 on the day of *ashura*, so one story goes, a Jewish woman in Meshed was suffering from a severe case of rheumatism of the hand. As was wont in those days, the woman visited a local healer whose "prescription" called for soaking the ailing hand in the blood of a freshly killed dog. The woman hired a Muslim street urchin to catch a stray dog and kill it in her backyard. A heated dispute over payment flared up, and the young rogue began to run around the streets spreading a rumor that the Jews deliberately killed a dog, whom they called Ali, in mockery of the Islamic holiday. An infuriated mob from a nearby mosque rushed into the Jewish quarter and, incited by the *cadis* and *mullahs*, set fire to a synagogue; burned the Torah scrolls; pillaged Jewish homes; murdered thirty-five men, women, and children; and injured many more. Those Jews who managed to escape found their way safely to Afghanistan, Central Asia, and Turkey. A massacre of the survivors left in Meshed was averted only after a local *cadi* made the Jews convert to Islam on the spot. These unfortunates, some four hundred families in number, were henceforth referred to as Djedid al-Islam (New Muslims).

As Djedid al-Islam, the Jews were no longer stigmatized as *zemmi* and *najasa*, and the restrictions that they had operated under as Jews were now removed. They were no longer required to wear the special Jewish badge or pay the *jezziya*. During the initial period of terror, the *anusim* dwelt under constant scrutiny; the enforcers of *shariya* were observing their every move. Fully aware that their behavior was being monitored, they were nevertheless intent on maintaining their Jewish identity.

Over time the *anusim* concocted an assortment of ruses in order to be able to carry out, as much as possible, the practice of their ancestral faith. In constant terror, they were obliged to forego certain rites and ceremonies that could easily draw attention to themselves. Obliged to attend services in the mosque, they peered at the Koran and recited the Islamic confession of faith out loud. But the words they were silently uttering in their hearts were *tehillim* (psalms) in Hebrew. For *minyan* in earnest, they established makeshift synagogues in underground tunnels and cellars of private homes. Because Shiite etiquette considers it improper for one of the faithful to enter a home where women are present, a Jewish woman was stationed at the entrance during prayer services to function as a lookout. The holidays were scrupulously observed, but understandably with a modification of performances and duties. It goes without saying that the *shofar* could not be blown nor could a *sukkah* be built. Chanukah candles were lit, but the *menorah* was never placed near a window. The reading of the *megillah* on Purim took place "in hushed silence."[75] On Passover only *matzah* was eaten, but bread was bought in the market to avoid suspicion.

The Jews of Meshed are fond of recounting the various and sundry ways they cleverly outwitted their Muslim oppressors. For instance, they would buy meat from the Muslim butchers, but would throw it to the dogs. Every Friday, the *shochet* would go from home to home to provide the Djedidim with kosher meat. In one case a man was caught by surprise in the performance of his office;

he was hacked to death and thrown to the dogs.[76] The Djedid al-Islam kept their stores open on the Sabbath but no sales were made. A child would stand behind the counter and when a customer attempted to purchase something he was told that the proprietor, his father or uncle, was away on business, and he had no idea as to prices. The customer was told to come back "tomorrow." In this way no business was transacted on the Sabbath.

Every male child was duly circumcised, but not necessarily on the eighth day, since the Muslims forbade the operation on that day. Jewish children were given two names, one Muslim and one Hebrew. When they were mature enough, Jewish boys would accompany their fathers to a secret study chamber where they were taught Hebrew and the Torah. "Each member of the community from childhood on was instilled with the feeling of responsibility and respect, not only for his family, but for the community at large. As soon as a child was able to think, he was taught that whatever he did—good or bad—reflected on the whole community."[77]

It was fortunate that in this part of the world children are betrothed to each other, sometimes even when they are still in their mothers' wombs. It was also quite common to contract marriages between children who had barely passed the infant stage. In order to avoid having to give their daughters in marriage to the Muslims, the girls became engaged at an extremely tender age. If a Muslim proposed the marriage of his son to a Djedidi girl, her parents would politely inform him that their little girl was already engaged. On the wedding day, two ceremonies were held. One took place in a mosque before a Muslim *cadi*, with the marriage contract written up in Persian. Later that evening, a second ceremony was surreptitiously performed at home, this time in accordance with Jewish law and rituals.[78]

When a death occurred, Ida Cowen informs us, it was customary for Shiites "to carry the coffin to the courtyard of the Imam Reza Mosque, circle the mosque several times, all the while reciting verses from the Koran. The Djedidim perfunctorily carried out this public ritual, but interment of the dead was invariably in a cemetery of their own in accordance with Jewish custom."[79]

Outwardly "orthodox" Muslims, some of the conversos even attained the honorific status of *hajji*. In order to protect themselves and the community, it was incumbent upon the Djedid al-Islam to make a pilgrimage to Mecca and Medina, like other Muslims. Some stories tell of Jews who had the *chutzpah* to bring their *tallitim* and *tefillin* along and secretly pray there with them. When they returned, they were conferred as *hajji*. These *hajji* enjoyed great prestige and were able to use their enhanced position in the interests of the Jewish community. Others managed to steal away from the pilgrim caravans to visit Jerusalem, ostensibly to visit the Islamic holy shrines there, but really to pray at the Western Wall and at the graves of the *tzaddikim*. A colony of Djedid al-Islam settled in Jerusalem, where they openly reclaimed their religious identity. Keeping themselves apart from other Jews, they built their own synagogues in the Bukharan Quarter and established a cemetery on the Mount of Olives.

The Muslims always suspected the Djedidim of deceitfulness, but were afraid to expose them. As the economic backbone of the city, the Jews provided much of the goods and services to the thousands of pilgrims who came to visit the Imam Reza's shrine every year. Because adherents of other creeds are expressly forbidden to tread near the holy spot, it was imperative for local Muslims to conceal the fact that the Imam Reza's shrine was being defiled, or be accused of a dereliction of religious duty. Making a scandal would have been tantamount to shooting themselves in their collective foot because this would have put the Islamic tourist industry out of business.[80] Amicable relations with their Muslim neighbors also proved a check to religious fanaticism. Sometimes a little *baksheesh* to local officials was necessary. As long as the Djedidim maintained the veneer of Islamic conformity in public, the Muslims made themselves oblivious to Jewish duplicity.

As Djedid al-Islam, they had some freedom of movement and many eventually fled from Meshed. Many migrated to Iraq, Russian Central Asia, and Afghanistan, where they immediately resumed their lives as free and open Jews. Some found haven in British India, where they formed tiny colonies in Peshawar, Bombay, and Calcutta. In the heyday of the Great Game (as spying was called), the great imperial struggle was taking place between the Czar and the British for hegemony in Central Asia. A number of Meshedi Jews served the British in a variety of capacities: as moneylenders, translators, envoys, and "as the eyes and ears of the service . . . to gather information in an inconspicuous way concerning the attitude of the rulers and the people towards Russia and Britain, and to win support for the British policy."[81] Especially notable were the exploits of the brothers Ibrahim and Mussa Nathan, who at great peril to themselves funneled money to British officers and facilitated in ransoming British hostages.

It is reported that, during the imprisonment of the British officers and troops at Cabul, Ibrahim, in an attempt to get in touch with them, disguised himself and succeeded in meeting with some of them. But being without ink or pencil, British officers scratched their skins in order to write, with their blood, messages on tiny scraps of paper which Ibrahim concealed in the hollow part of a hen's feather and stuck in his turban. By thus getting the messages safely into the hands of the commanding officer, Ibrahim paved the way, actually, for the rescue of the prisoners. On his journey back to the British camp, a spear was hurled at him and wounded his arm, leaving him scarred until the day of his death. He and his brother's daring spirit led to their own imprisonment by the Emir of Afghanistan . . . from which they were released only after a heavy fine.[82]

According to Fischel, this intertwining with, and strong affinity for, the British by Central Asian Jewry is attributed to the perception by the latter that the British were their protectors and saviors who would help them return to their ancestral homeland.[83]

Wherever they went, the Meshedi Jews clung together, but also remained bound by closest kinship to the Meshedi Jews whom they had left behind. A network of trading posts was established among the Meshedi refugee communities along the commercial highways, and many became quite wealthy. "Their ordeal," writes Dan Ross, "produced a sense of solidarity, and they trusted each other to a degree few other merchants achieved."[84] Some of the money they accumulated was used to aid poorer Jews in other Persian cities. Until World War I the majority of the Meshedi diaspora was concentrated in Russian Turkestan (Bukhara). During the Bolshevik Revolution (1917), the Meshedis were deprived of their traditional occupations and castigated as reactionary bourgeoisie. Many migrated to Europe, the United States, and Palestine.

The situation in Meshed began to improve in 1925 when Reza Shah Pahlevi ascended the throne. In an attempt to jolt his country into the twentieth century, the Western-oriented shah broke the absolute power of the Shiite religious authorities and abolished the various indignities imposed on non-Muslim minorities, including Jews. Many Meshedis settled in other parts of Persia, especially in the capital, Teheran. Some even returned to Meshed openly Jewish. During the period between World War I and World War II, some two hundred Meshedi families emigrated to Palestine, settling mainly in Jerusalem on the fringe of the Bukharan quarter. Most of them were well-to-do and continued to carry on trade in carpets and karakul furs with their brethren in Meshed. They built their own synagogues and, as elsewhere, tended to keep themselves separate from the other Jewish communities.

In 1941, after Reza Shah was deposed by the allies because of his pro-Nazi sentiments, Russian forces occupied Iran. The departure of the Russian troops in 1946 was followed in Meshed by a blood libel. This occurred not so coincidentally on a Shiite day of mourning, which resulted in a mob attack on the Jewish quarter. Fortunately, the British consulate appealed to the Islamic clergy, and the violence was stemmed. After Israel became a state in 1948, a large majority of the estimated ten thousand Meshedi Jews, most of whom were residing in Teheran, made *aliyah*. When the issue of the Jewishness of the former *anusim* was raised, the Israeli Chief Rabbinate concluded that they should be regarded as Jews under the terms of the Law of Return. Since the Meshedis had never abandoned Judaism throughout the period of their ordeal, they did not even require symbolic re-conversion. Mordechai Zar, who had lived as a Djedid al-Islam in Meshed, served as Deputy Speaker of the Knesset in the early 1970s.

Before the rise of the Ayatollah Khomeini in 1979, there were still an estimated 3,000 Meshedi Jews in Iran, all concentrated in Teheran. The Iranian revolution that year drove out the rest. This last group settled among already existing Meshedi communities in Tel Aviv, where an estimated half of the Meshedi community in Israel lives. There are also communities in Istanbul, Bombay, Hamburg, Milan, and New York. In New York, most Meshedi Jews are concentrated in the Upper West Side of Manhattan and in Kew Gardens, Queens. Their principal occupation is dealing in rugs and carpets. Wherever they live, the former Djedid al-Islam tend to be extremely clannish. Until recent times, ties between Meshedis were so strong that the men would travel halfway around the world to obtain a Meshedi bride. Today, more and more are marrying non-Meshedis. All told, today's entire worldwide Meshedi community totals about 20,000. There are no Jews left in Meshed today (1999).

NOTES

1. John W. Limbert, *Iran: At War with History* (Boulder: Westview Press, 1987), p. 19.

2. Firoz Davar, *Iran and Its Culture* (Bombay: New Book, 1953), pp. 232–33; Jamsheed K. Choksy, *Purity and Pollution in Zoroastrianism: Triumph Over Evil* (Austin: University of Texas, 1989), p. 50.

3. By Seljuq times the caliph had become little more than a glorified religious figurehead, and, some might say, a virtual puppet of the Seljuq sultans.

4. For succinct and useful studies on the Shiite creed see Etan Kohlberg, "The Evolution of the Shi'a," *The Jerusalem Quarterly* 27 (Spring 1983), pp. 109–126; Roger M. Savory, "Iran: A 2,500-Year Historical and Cultural Tradition," in *Iranian Civilization and Culture*, edited by Charles J. Adams (Toronto: McGill University Institute of Islamic Studies, 1973), pp. 77–89; Albert Hourani, *A History of the Arab Peoples* (New York: Warner Books, 1991), esp. pp. 181–88.

5. Walter J. Fischel, "Israel in Iran," in *The Jews: Their History, Culture, and Religion*, ed. Louis Finkelstein (Philadelphia: The Jewish Publication Society, 1960), p. 1149.

6. Vera B. Moreen, *Iranian Jewry's Hour of Peril and Heroism: A Study of Babai Ibn Luft's Chronicle (1617–1662)* (New York: The American Academy for Jewish research, 1987), p. 155.

7. Salo W. Baron, *A Social and Religious History of the Jews*, vol. 18. 2nd ed. (New York: Columbia University Press, 1983), p. 334.

8. "The Jews of Mediaeval Iran from the 16th to the 18th centuries: Political, Economic, and Communal Aspects," *Irano-Judaica* (1982), p. 290. See also Vera B. Moreen, *Iranian Jewry's*, p. 155; and Eli Smith and H. G. O. Dwight, *Missionary Researches in Armenia* (London: George Wightman, Paternoster Row, 1834), p. 358.

9. *Iran: At War With History*, p. 33.

10. Walter J. Fischel, "Isfahan: The Story of a Jewish Community in Persia," *The Joshua Starr Memorial Volume: Studies in History and Philology* (New York: Jewish Social Studies Publications, 1953), p. 113.

11. Daniel E. Spector, *A History of the Persian Jews*, unpublished dissertation, University of Texas (Ann Arbor, MI: University Microfilm, 1975), p. 28.

12. Robert Brody, "Judaism in the Sasanian Empire: A Case Study in Religious Coexistence," *Irano-Judaica* 2 (1990), p. 58; E. Denison Ross, *The Persians* (Oxford: Clarendon Press, 1933), p. 32

13. Cecil Roth, *A History of the Jews: From the Earliest Times Through the Six Day War* (New York: Schocken Books, 1973), p. 122. On the Mazdakite heresy; see Josef Wiesenhofer, *Ancient Persia: From 550 BC to 650 AD*, translated by Azizeh Azodi (London: I. B. Tauris and Co., 1996), pp. 199–216.

14. On the various schools analyzing the *Seder 'Olam Zuta*, which deals with the subject of Mar Zutra and the Jewish enclave of Mahoza, see Jacob Neusner, *Israel and Iran in Talmudic Times* (Lanham, Md.: University Press of America, 1986), pp. 217–227.

15. Daniel Elazar, *The Jewish Community of Iran* (Jerusalem: Center for Jewish Community Studies, 1975), p. 5.

16. Percy M. Sykes, *A History of Persia*, vol. 2 (London: Macmillan and Co., 1915), p. 14; Richard N. Frye, *The Golden Age of Persia* (London: Weidenfeld and Nicolson, 1975), pp. 135–36.

17. Elkan N. Adler, *Jewish Travellers in the Middle Ages: 19 Accounts* (New York: Dover Publications, 1987), pp. 53–54.

18. "Iran: Opposition, Martyrdom, and Revolt," in *Unity and Variety in Muslim Civilization*, edited by Gustave E. von Grunebaum (Chicago: University of Chicago Press, 1955), p. 191.

19. On the rise and fall of Sa'd al-Daula see Walter J. Fischel, *Jews in the Eco-*

nomic and Political Life of Medieval Islam, vol. 22 (London: Royal Asiatic Society, 1937), pp. 90–117.

20. Ann K. S. Lambton, *Continuity and Change in Medieval Persia* (London: I. B. Tauris and Co., 1988), pp. 65 and 307–08.

21. Ibid., p. 309.

22. Laurence Loeb, *Outcaste: Jewish Life in Southern Iran* (New York: Gordon and Breech, 1977), pp. 292–293; David Littman, "Jews Under Muslim Rule: The Case of Persia," *The Weiner Library Bulletin* 32 (1979), pp. 2–15.; Sorour Soroudi, "The Jews in Islamic Iran," *The Jewish Quarterly* 21 (Fall 1981), pp. 99–114.

23. Elkan N. Adler, *Jews in Many Lands* (Philadelphia: The Jewish Publication Society, 1905), p. 194; Fischel, "The Jews of Mediaeval Iran," pp. 277–78.

24. Hayyim J. Cohen, *The Jews of the Middle East: 1860–1972* (New York: John Wiley and Sons, 1973), p. 57.

25. Nehemiah Robinson, *Persia and Afghanistan and Their Jewish Communities* (New York: Institute of Jewish Affairs, 1953), p. 18.

26. Henry A. Stern, *Dawnings of Light in the Middle East; with Biblical, Historical, and Statistical Notices of Persons and Places Visited During a Mission to the Jews in Persia, Coordistan, and Mesopotamia* (London: C. H. Purday, 1854), p. 263.

27. I. J. Benjamin, *Eight Years in Asia and Africa, from 1846 to 1855*. 2nd ed. (Hanover: n.p., 1863), p. 256.

28. C. J. Wills, *Persia As It Is; Being Sketches of Modern Persian Life and Character* (London: Sampson, Low, Marston, Searle, and Rivington, 1886), p. 230.

29. George N. Curzon, *Persia and the Persian Question* (New York: Barnes and Noble, 1892), vol. 1, p. 333, 510, 567, and 570; vol. 2, p. 493; Yehuda Kopellowitz, "Letter from Abroad: The Jews of Persia," *Menorah Journal* 18 (January 1930), pp.42–43; Joseph B. Schechtman, *On Wings of Eagles: The Plight, Exodus, and Homecoming of Oriental Jewry* (New York: Thomas Yoseloff, 1961), p. 242.

30. "The Fate of the Jewish Community of Tabriz," in *Studies in Islamic History and Civilization*, edited by M. Sharon (Leiden: E. J. Brill, 1986), p. 413.

31. Fischel, "The Jews of Mediaeval Iran," p. 268.

32. Walter J. Fischel, "Israel in Iran," in *The Jews: Their History, Culture, and Religion*, 3rd ed., ed. Louis Finkelstein (Philadelphia: The Jewish Publication Society, 1960), p. 1170. For contemporary accounts of the persecutions see Ezra Spicehandler, "The Persecution of the Jews of Isfahan Under Shah Abbas II (1642–1666)," *Hebrew Union College Annual* 46 (1975), pp. 331–345.

33. Laurence Loeb, *Outcaste*, p. 1.

34. Cited in Fischel, "The Jews of Persia, 1795–1940," *Jewish Social Studies* 12:2 (April 1950), p. 134.

35. Amnon Netzer, "Iran," in *Zionism in Transition*, edited by Moshe Davis (New

York: Arno Press, 1980), p. 226. See also Avraham Cohen, "Iranian Jewry and the Educational Endeavors of the Alliance Israelite Universelle," *Jewish Social Studies* 48:2 (Spring 1986), pp.15–44; Amnon Netzer, *The Jews of Persia and the Alliance in the Late Nineteenth Century: Some Aspects* (Jerusalem: The Hebrew University of Jerusalem/Ben-Zvi Institute, 1974), p. 22.

36. S. Landshut, *Jewish Communities in the Muslim Countries of the Middle East: A Survey* (London: The Jewish Chronicle, 1950), p. 64. See also Robinson, *Persia and Afghanistan*, p. 20.

37. Sorour Soroudi, "The Concept of Jewish Impurity and Its Reflection in Persian and Judeo-Persian Traditions," *Irano-Judaica* 3 (1994), p. 162.

38. Wilhelm Bacher, "Les Juifs en Perse au XVIII et au XVIII siecle d'apres les chroniques poetiques de Babai Louft et de Babai b. Farhad," *Revue de etudes Juives* 51 (1906), p. 247, cited in Loeb, *Outcaste*, p. 286; Amnon Netzer, "Persecution of Iranian Jewry in the 17th Century," *Pe'Amim* 6 (1980), pp.53–54.

39. Stern, *Dawnings*, pp. 179–181.

40. *Letters from the Caucasus and Georgia* (London: John Murray, 1823), p. 346.

41. Sadok Masliyah, "Persian Jewry—Prelude to Catastrophe," *Judaism* 116, 29:4 (Fall 1980), p. 394.

42. Even though the Jewish physicians were oftentimes able to establish close connections with the ruling circles and the Islamic clergy, "their success was not remarkable." Amnon Netzer, *The Jews of Persia and the Alliance*, p. 7.

43. "Jews in Islamic Iran," *The Jerusalem Quarterly* 21 (Fall 1981), p. 104.

44. Loeb, *Outcaste*, p. 18.

45. Laurence Loeb, "Dhimmi Status and Jewish Roles in Iranian Society," *Ethnic Groups* 1 (1976), p. 101. Daniel J. Elazar also points out that the Iranian Jews, with the exception of those in a few localities, did not care for their poor. See *People and Polity: The Organizational Dynamics of World Jewry* (Detroit: Wayne State University, 1989), p. 456.

46. Loeb, "Dhimmi Status," p. 94.

47. Kopellowitz, "Letter," p. 49; Hayyim Cohen, *The Jews of the Middle East*, p. 141.

48. Loeb, *Outcaste*, pp. 14–15.

49. *Twenty Years in Persia* (London: Fleming H. Revell Co., 1908), p. 244.

50. Loeb, *Outcaste*, p. 204.

51. *Jews in Remote Corners of the World* (Englewood Cliffs, NJ: Prentice Hall, 1971), p. 255. Kopellowitz had observed the same custom in a synagogue in Teheran four decades earlier. See "Letter," p. 49.

52. Loeb, *Outcaste*, p. 199.

53. Ibid.

54. Wishard, *Twenty Years In Persia*, p. 242.

55. Ken Schachter, "Out Of Exile," *Jerusalem Post Magazine* (1 April 1988), p. 9.

56. Loeb, *Outcaste*, p. 195.

57. Elazar, *People and Polity*, p. 454.

58. Masliyah, "Persian Jewry," pp. 401–02.

59. Netzer, *The Jews of Persia*, p. 12.

60. On the persecution of the Bahais under the Shiites see John Simpson and Tira Shubart, *Lifting the Veil* (London: Hodder and Stoughton, 1995), esp. pp. 221–228; and Richard W. Cottam, *Nationalism in Iran* (Pittsburgh: University of Pittsburgh Press, 1964): 87–89. One member of Iran's elite in the 1970s summed up anti-Bahai sentiment in this way: "The Jews are an economic people who share the same holy books with us. They live and work side by side with other Iranians. The Bahais, however, are not part of our traditions. They are spies for the English and want us to forsake our nationalism to serve Haifa [the headquarters of the Bahai faith]." See Marvin Zonis, *The Political Elite of Iran* (Princeton: Princeton University Press, 1971), p. 276.

61. Elazar, *People and Polity*, p. 453.

62. Cited in Simpson and Shubart, *Lifting the Veil*, p. 232.

63. Jerrold D. Green, *Revolution in Iran* (New York: Praeger, 1982), p. 98; Amir Taheri, *The Unknown Life of the Shah* (London: Hutchinson, 1991), p. 266.

64. David Sitton, *Sephardi Communities Today* (Jerusalem: Council of Sephardi and Oriental Communities, 1985), p. 182.

65. On Khomeini's perceptions of the Jews see Ervand Abrahamian, *Khomeinism: Essays on the Islamic Republic* (Berkeley: University of California Press, 1993), esp. pp. 120–124.

66. David Menashri, "The Jews of Iran: Between the Shah and Khomeini," in *Anti-Semitism in Times of Crisis*, edited by Sander L. Gilman and Steven T. Katz (New York: New York University Press, 1991), p. 362.

67. For details on Israeli arms deals with the Khomeini regime see Sohrab Sobhani, *The Pragmatic Entente: Israeli-Iranian Relations 1948–1988* (New York: Praeger, 1989), pp. 141–151.

68. *Encyclopaedia Judaica Yearbook 1988/89* (Jerusalem: Keter, 1989), p. 292.

69. In 1992 an elderly Jew was hanged after it became known that he tried to contact his two sons in Israel. See *Anti-Semitism World Report 1995* "Iran" (London: The Institute of Jewish Affairs and the American Jewish Committee, 1995), p. 258.

70. Solomon Zeitlin, *Maimonides: A Biography* (New York: Bloch Publishing Co., 1935), pp. 5–17.

71. C. E. Yates, *Khorasan and Sistan* (London: William Blackwood and Co., 1900), pp. 334.

72. George N. Curzon, *Curzon's Persia* (London: Sidgwick and Jackson, 1986), p. 48.

73. J. P. Ferrier, *Caravan Journeys and Wanderings in Persia, Afghanistan, Turkistan, and Beloochistan; with Historical Notices of the Countries Lying Between Russia and India*, 2nd ed. William Jesse, trans., H. D. Seymour, ed. (London: John Murray, 1857), pp.124–5.

74. Other sources say the Allahdad took place on the Muslim feast day of Kurban Bayram, on the tenth of the month Dhu 'l-Hijja. See Raphael Patai, *Jadid Al-Islam: The Jewish "New Muslims" of Meshhed* (Detroit: Wayne State University, 1997), pp.56–57.

75. Joseph Reuveni, "The Secret Jews of Iran—Memories of Meshed," *Jewish Life* (December 1959), p. 22.

76. I. J. Benjamin, *Eight Years in Asia and Africa; from 1846 to 1855*, 2nd ed. (Hanover: n.p., 1863), pp.241–42.

77. Reuveni, "The Secret Jews," p. 23.

78. Reuven Kashani, *The Crypto-Jews of Mashad*. (Jerusalem: n.p., 1979): 20–21.

79. "The Secret Jews of Meshed: Marranos Who Came Back," *Hadassah Magazine* 62:6 (February 1981), p. 27.

80. Ida Cowen, "The Secret Jews," p. 28.

81. Walter Fischel, "Mulla Ibrahim Nathan (1816–1868): Jewish Agent of the British During the First Anglo-Afghan War," *Hebrew Union College Annual* 29 (1958) pp.333.

82. Ibid., p. 346.

83. Ibid., p. 336.

84. Dan Ross, *Acts of Faith: A Journey to the Fringes of Jewish Identity* (New York: St. Martin's Press, 1982), p. 75.

Part III

Kurdistani Jewish Men in Traditional Garb, Sandur, Kurdistan
Credit: Judah Magnes Museum

Lost in the Land of Assyria

BACKGROUND INFORMATION

Kurdistan is a rugged mountain territory in central southwest Asia, about 600 miles north to south, and 150 miles east to west. It is a landlocked region, containing large and fertile plains and valleys. Kurdistan possesses many rivers, the most important of which are the Euphrates and the Tigris. It is a harsh place to live, the winters being very cold and the summers oppressively hot. Boiling cataracts, whirlpools, and ravines form many dangerous and impassable areas in the mountains. In the valleys, which are more pleasant, there once were forests and meadows covered with much lush vegetation and colorful flowers. The sweet dew common to many parts of Kurdistan is identified with the manna of the Bible. Until about a hundred years ago, lions, bears, hyenas, and other wildlife, including a species of leopard, inhabited this area. Iraq's Saddam Husein's use of napalm, germ warfare, and chemical agents are only the latest measures used against the insurgent Kurds in the twentieth century. These attacks combined with intensive deforestation and erosion have resulted in the ecological degradation of much of Kurdistan's countryside.[1]

The Kurds are primarily an Indo-European (Aryan), not an Arabic, people. After the Arabs, Turks, and Persians, they are the most numerous of Near Eastern people, with a population estimated between seven million and twenty-five million (depending on who's doing the counting). Before the Arab invasions in the seventh century, the Kurds adhered to the Zoroastrian religion. Today they are predominantly Sunni Muslims of the Shafi'a school of law, except in Iran and parts of Iraq, where many are Shiites. Arabs and Turkomans form the largest ethnic groups among the non-Kurdish Muslims. The Kurdish elite have generally been tolerant of their Yezidi,[2] Jewish, and Christian (Nestorian, Assyrian, Armenian, and Chaldean) minorities. Many dialects of Kurdish—an Indo-European tongue related to neo-Persian and Afghani—are spoken, the two primary dialects being Sorani and Kurmanji.

The precipitous mountain fastnesses of Kurdistan provided asylum for people from the Near Eastern plains and deserts who were fleeing religious and political persecution, and also served as a hideout for bandits. Until fairly recent times, Kurdistan was isolated and quite inaccessible to the outside world. As a result, the Kurds preserved a lifestyle that was hardly different from the way people lived thousands of years ago.

William R. Hay has characterized the Kurdish tribe as "a community or a collection of communities which exists for the protection of its members against an external aggression and for the maintenance of the old racial customs and way of life."[3] Tribes were traditionally organized and confederated politically along feudal lines, lesser *aghas* (chieftains, or feudal barons) being subservient to more powerful ones. Most Kurds in the mountain villages belonged to a tribe whose *aghas* were perpetually at war with each other. "Tribal wars and bloodshed [were] occasioned . . . by old blood feuds, the kidnapping of women, the seizure of flocks and arms, [and] disputes regarding the ownership of pasture-grounds. . . ."[4] Even though their land has been conquered by many invading powers, the Kurds have never had feelings of allegiance to anyone except their own tribal chieftains.

Mehrdad Izady writes:

> To a Kurd the mountain is no less than the embodiment of the deity: mountain is his mother, his refuge, his protector, his home, his farm, his market, his mate, and his only friend. . . . Such a thorough attachment to and indivisibility from their natural environment is the source of many folk beliefs that all mountains are inhabited by the Kurds. . . . Kurds living in the plains cities are seldom considered to be Kurds by those living in the highlands, and are not trusted to be leaders. To know the secrets of the mountains, the passes, rivers, and caves; to know the tribal customs; and to be brave, are the essential characteristics of Kurdish chiefs and leaders.[5]

Throughout their history, the Kurds have had a reputation for being powerful and fearless mountain guerrilla fighters, and born horsemen. They are described by the early twentieth century traveler Pierre Ponafidine as "an independent, hospitable people, loving their liberty and true to their given word, or to 'bread and salt.'"[6] The region's nomadic and semi-nomadic tribes "depended on attacking and pillaging neighboring villages. . . . As a result, Kurdistan was long a center of tribal warfare and lawlessness."[7] Today most Kurds are sedentary village dwellers.

A Kurdish origin myth has it that one day King Solomon, ruler over the supernatural world, called together five hundred genies and ordered them to fly north and bring back five hundred of the most beautiful maidens they could find. By the time they returned the wise king had died, so they kept the maidens for themselves. These maids became the mothers of the Kurdish people.[8]

There is evidence in Sumerian records that, as far back as 2000 B.C.E., Kurdish tribes occupied what is known today as Kurdistan. Some authorities and the Kurds themselves, believe they are the progeny of the ancient Medes. The Kurdish tribes staved off the onslaughts of the Sumerians, Hittites, Assyrians, and Babylonians, and helped the Persian king Cyrus (538–529 B.C.E.) conquer Nineveh and Babylon. Later the Kurds resisted the Greek Seleucids, Persian Parthians and Sasanians, Armenians, Arab caliphates, and Mongol and Turkish tribes, although the latter two rendered desolate much of Kurdistani civilization. In recent centuries Russia, Britain, France, and Iraq occupied large portions of Kurdish territory.

The period from the tenth to the twelfth century in the political history and life of the Islamic heartland should rightfully be called Islam's Kurdish centuries, as the Kurds ruled and defended the Islamic heartlands against the Byzantines, the Rus, and finally the Crusaders.[9] Ironically, Salah-ed-Din (1137–1193), founder of the Ayyubid dynasty and Kurdistan's most celebrated son, was born not in Kurdistan but in Takrit, Iraq, on the alluvial plains near the Tigris. This legendary Muslim warrior unified the kingdoms of Egypt, Syria, Palestine, the South Arabian Peninsula, and Mesopotamia. Then he defeated Richard the Lion Hearted in 1192, and thereby drove the Crusaders out of Palestine. Although his empire was vast, Kurdish land remained outside his dominion.

There are two primary reasons for the decline of Kurdistan. One is the discovery by Vasco da Gama in 1497 of a continuous sea route from Europe to India via the Cape of Good Hope. "This date marks the beginning of the rapid shift of international commerce . . . away from the long-established land routes like the Silk Road between East and West. The heavy traffic in goods and technology between Europe and the Orient . . . suddenly ceased to cross Kurdish lands, bypassing its markets altogether. Kurdistan quickly became a mountainous irrelevancy."[10]

Another reason for Kurdistan's decline is the fact that over the centuries Kurdistan has been subjected to great power shifts. The critical period occurred

early in the sixteenth century. In 1514 a raging battle between the regional su-
perpowers, the Ottomans and the Persians, was fought inside the Kurdish heartland. Kurdish tribes fought on both sides, frequently against each other. At the
war's conclusion the frontiers between the regional powers were drawn so as
to leave three-quarters of Kurdistan under Ottoman control and the rest under
the jurisdiction of the Safavids. The Ottoman rulers, making a pitch for Sunni
solidarity, granted the Kurdish princes in their protectorate a degree of independence and protection in return for joining forces against their common enemy, the Safavid Shiites.[11]

The corrupt Ottomans played the Kurdish tribal chiefs against one another.
But they were themselves manipulated by the powerful chieftains who took advantage of the centuries-long Persian-Ottoman conflict to throw off the yoke of
their oppressors and consolidate their own positions. The social disorder fomented
by plundering nomadic tribes, combined with the incessant uprisings of the tribal
chieftains who refused to be subjected to taxes and military service, compelled
the Ottomans to forcibly uproot entire populations and destroy the means of agricultural production by employing a scorched earth policy.[12] With the rise of the
Safavid Shah Tahmasp (c. 1525) similar attacks against the Kurds were carried out
on the Persian side. By the late nineteenth century the last of the old Kurdish principalities in both Turkish and Persian areas were virtually wiped out.

Following the dismantling of the Ottoman Empire after World War I,
and the Treaty of Lausanne in 1923, political control of Kurdistan was divided
among Turkey, Iraq (which was under British mandate), and Iran, with small
overlaps into Syria and the Transcaucasus region of the former Soviet Union, in
what are today the Independent Republics of Azerbaijan and Armenia.

An attempt to create an independent Kurdistan, the Republic of Mahabad
in the Iranian sector of Kurdistan, which was sponsored by the Soviets in 1946,
was quickly quashed by the armies of the shah. It is not difficult to understand
the geopolitical reasons for denying the Kurds a homeland, considering Kurdistan's close proximity to the former Soviet Union and the fact that many of the
richest Near Eastern oilfields are situated inside Iraqi-Kurdish territory. Saddam
Hussein has deported entire populations of Kurds living near the petroleum
refineries and supplanted them with an Arabic component. Within the Turkish
boundaries, where the largest percentage of Kurdish Muslims live, the authorities until 1990 suppressed the Kurdish language and culture and euphemisti-
cally referred to the Kurds as "Mountain Turks." Saddam Hussein's use of napalm, germ warfare, and chemical agents are only the latest measures used against
the insurgent Kurds in the twentieth century. The Kurds can be characterized
as a Fourth World people oppressed by Third World dictatorships.

THE MOUNTAIN JEWS OF KURDISTAN

Behold! From Arabia to Georgia is the Kurdish home. But when
the Persian ocean and the Turkish seas get rough, only the
Kurdish country is splattered with blood.
—lyricist Ahmad Khani, *Mem o Zin* (1694)

Kurdistan is one of the few Islamic lands where Jews rarely experienced
anti-Semitism. It is also one of the few places in the Diaspora in which Jews
were permitted to own land and engage in agriculture. The Kurdish Jews were
the only Jewish community in the world to have retained agricultural roots
from Babylonian times. And Kurdistan is the only area in the world where
the Jews preserved Lashon haTargum (Hebrew for neo-Aramaic, and called
Suriyani in Kurdish) as a living spoken language.[13] Lashon haTargum is related to the Aramaic of the Babylonian sages who wrote the Talmud almost
two thousand years ago.

In sharp contrast with most other Jewish communities in the Diaspora,
the Jews of Kurdistan had little use for learning. The great isolation, difficult
work, onerous taxation, famine, disease (especially malaria), and interminable
Muslim tribal wars had a retarding effect on the spiritual and cultural life of the
Jewish communities in Kurdistan. Additionally, there was always a great shortage of qualified rabbis and teachers. The few outstanding rabbis who lived among
the Kurdistani Jews came from Baghdad, the Ottoman Empire, and the Holy
Land. Many of the locally educated *hakhamim*, or learned men, were—in truth—
usually terribly uninformed and superstitious.

The preponderance of Kurdistani Jews were concentrated in some two
hundred small towns and villages, scattered and vastly removed from each other.
The percentage of Jewish communities in Kurdistan by country was the following: fifty percent Iraq, thirty-five percent Iran, ten percent Syria, and five percent in the Turkish sector. Cities with the largest populations were Amadiyah,
Arbil, and Zakho in Iraqi Kurdistan; Sanandaj, Kermanshah, and Urmia on the
Iranian side of the border; and Urfa and Diyarbakr in the Turkish area. In some
towns the Jews were a minority, in others a majority. In some they made up the
entire local population. They generally lived voluntarily in segregated Jewish
quarters. Before they emigrated to Israel en masse in the early 1950s, during
an airlift known as Operation Ezra and Nehemiah, there were an estimated
25,000 Jews in Kurdistan, the majority from the mountainous region of northern Iraq.

There is an ancient belief among the Kurdistani Jews (as well as Kurdish Muslims and Christians) that Mount Ararat, in northeastern Kurdistan, is the resting place of Noah's Ark. There is also a widespread folk belief that the city of Urfa, in the Turkish part of Kurdistan, is the Biblical Ur of the Chaldeans, the birthplace of Abraham, father of the Jewish people.

It is not known exactly when the Jews first settled in Kurdistan. As the Kurdish Jews have no written history, they are one of the least known of all Diaspora communities. The earliest written record of Jewish life in Kurdistan we have today comes from the famous Jewish traveler Benjamin of Tudela, who visited the area in the twelfth century.

The Kurdistani Jews have an ancient belief that they are the descendants of the ten tribes who were banished from the Kingdom of Israel by the Assyrians in 722 B.C.E. These tribes were followed by the exiles from Judah after the destruction of the First Temple by the Babylonians in 586 B.C.E. In 1989, in Jerusalem, I met Kurdistani Jews who claimed to have direct lineage from the tribe of Benjamin (part of the Kingdom of Judah). Other oral traditions maintain that some Jews also arrived during Ezra the Scribe's time, in the third century B.C.E. The tomb of Ezra is said to have been located near the Kurdish town of Kurna.

To these small communities were added a number of converts belonging to the Royal House of Adiabene. This small pagan kingdom, situated in the upper Tigris region of Iraqi Kurdistan, was a major power within the Parthian Empire. Sometime around 30 C.E., Queen Helena and her favorite son, Crown Prince Izates, converted to Judaism. Soon after Izates was circumcised he was accused of betraying the pagan religion of his people, and a revolt broke out in the court. The Prince crushed the revolt and ruled peacefully over his kingdom for thirty years thereafter. Many of the inhabitants of Adiabene are believed to have followed their ruler in converting to Judaism. The Talmud tells us that Helena and her son provided the Jews of Palestine with food during the periodic droughts. And Izates sent five of his sons to study in the *yeshivot* in Jerusalem. During the great Jewish revolt against the Romans in the period leading up to the destruction of the Second Temple in 70 C.E., battalions of soldiers from Adiabene fought valiantly alongside the Jewish rebels. The Jewish kingdom of Adiabene lasted until 115 C.E., when it too was destroyed by the Roman legions.[14]

Jews from Syria and Palestine fleeing the approaching Crusaders in the twelfth century found refuge among the mountain Jews of Kurdistan. So, too, did Jews from Iraq who were escaping from the Mongol invasions a century later. As a result, Jewish spiritual life experienced a revival of sorts in Kurdistan. In the course of his travels, Benjamin of Tudela said he encountered in the town of

Amadiya, in northern Kurdistan, a community of 25,000 Jews (scholars say a gross exaggeration) who spoke the Aramaic language of the Talmud. He mentions that they were pious and learned men.[15]

Amadiya is also the city that gave birth to a great messianic movement in the twelfth century. This movement, led by David Alroy, was a heroic attempt to bring redemption to the persecuted Jews in the Diaspora. Alroy was possessed of great courage and charisma. He mobilized an army of Jewish warriors and prepared to wrest Jerusalem from the Crusaders. Before he was able to undertake this venture, the Persian king crushed the movement. Alroy was murdered in his sleep, allegedly by his father-in-law. But so great was his popularity that his followers continued to believe he was the Messiah. Immortalized by Benjamin Disraeli's fictional account of his life, David Alroy is the most famous person in Kurdistani-Jewish history.

For centuries the Kurdistani Jews longed to return to Palestine, the land of their forefathers. Rabbis from Palestine would periodically visit the Jews of Kurdistan and strengthen their connection with the Holy Land. Kurdistani Jews were among the earliest to immigrate to the Holy Land. As early as 1812 small settlements were established by Kurdistani Jews in Jerusalem. During the Ottomans' campaign of reconquest (1834–39, 1842–47)—a period in Kurdish history that Stephen Pelletiere calls "The Phase of Fire and Sword"[16]—the position of the Jews in Kurdistan began a marked deterioration. Repression of the Kurds took the form of massacres and the torture of tens of thousands of innocent victims—Muslims, Christians, and Jews. Entire districts, including the Jewish quarters, were razed and plundered. Pogroms carried out by Kurdish Islamic zealots against the Christian minorities (with the approval of the Ottomans) were soon expanded to include all infidels, Jews, and non-Sunni Muslims.

Armed conflicts between Kurdish units struggling for independence against the Turkish, Iranian, and Iraqi regimes persisted sporadically between World War I and World War II. Each insurrection was suppressed, with great loss of Kurdish life. Famines and epidemics ravaged the Kurdish countryside. There were also interminable and protracted power struggles and blood feuds between warring Kurdish Muslim tribes; and the Jews, often caught in the cross-fire, suffered many losses. As a consequence, more and more Jews began to emigrate to Palestine.

Among the early pioneers was a group of Kurdistani Jews who founded the village of Alroy near Haifa. Almost 4,000 more arrived in the 1920s and 1930s. Following the revolt in 1941 of Iraq's pro-Axis head of state, Rashid Ali, against the British, many Kurdistani Jews were murdered and Jewish communities were looted. With the help of their Muslim friends, many Jews successfully made their way to Palestine. After the establishment of the State of Israel, Kurdistani Jews were accused of "Zionism" and persecuted by the Iraqi government. Many sold their farms and houses for a small fraction of their worth, concluded their affairs, and set out for Baghdad to await their turn to migrate to Israel. The entire community of Kurdistani Jews, estimated at 25,000, was evacuated together with the Jews of Iraq in the airlift designated Operation Ezra and Nehemiah in 1950–51. Kurdistani Jews fleeing pogroms in Kermanshah, in Iranian Kurdistan, made *aliyah* via Teheran with the Persian Jews.

Historically, for the most part, relations between Jews and Muslims were amicable, and both groups worked and socialized together. Kurdistani Jewish oldtimers in Israel still speak nostalgically of Muslim compatriots who treated them well and looked out for their interests. They strongly identify with the Kurdish people's plight during and following the Gulf War in 1991 and have carried out demonstrations supporting independence.

Dress restrictions imposed on Jews in other parts of the Islamic world were not decreed in Kurdistan. Like their Muslim neighbors, Jewish men wore brightly colored baggy trousers with a cummerbund, a short embroidered tunic, collarless cotton shirts with wide Turkish sleeves, and flowery scarves. What distinguished Jewish men from other Kurds sartorially was the *tzitzit* (fringes) the Jews wore underneath their clothes. Women wore splendid silk and satin garments consisting of a gown with wide sleeves, a corset-like vest "with armholes shaped like a horseshoe," loose-fitting trousers, and a long quilted coat described by Brauer as a combination of long-sleeved bodice and wide pleated skirt.[17] Men wore large tasseled turbans with a gray checked pattern while women employed a white silken cloth that was folded around their heads and under which they wore a black felt skullcap with only the side curls exposed. Women's turbans were decorated with jewels and precious stones.

Women, young and old, adorned themselves with silver or gold earrings, nose rings, hand bracelets with three cornered charms worn around the wrist and forearm, and facial and body tattoos. Many of these ornaments and talismans were supposed to possess protective qualities and ward off the evil eye. Only rich people in Kurdistan could afford to buy shoes. Since almost all the Jews were poor, they wore sandals or went barefoot. In Kurdistan most people would often sleep in their work clothes for many days.

All Kurdish mountain people, Muslims as well as Jews, were subject to the whims and temperament of the powerful tribal chieftains, the *aghas*. Like typical oriental despots, these *aghas* had absolute power of life and death over the people they ruled.[18] The Jews, as *dhimmi*, a protected non-Muslim minority, and belonging to no tribe, were at a great disadvantage. They were forced to pay heavy taxes and bribes to the *agha*s in order to be protected from other chieftains and from bandits. In a crunch, the *agha*s would sell some of their Jewish chattel into slavery. They could sell an individual Jew, or his or her entire family. Sometimes an *agha* would give a Jew away to another tribal chieftain as a present. Jews living under oppressive *agha*s might flee to other, more powerful, *agha*s who offered better protection, or to the larger, more stable cities. There were many *agha*s who treated their Jews well and would not allow harm to befall their chattels. With tongue in cheek, the early twentieth-century traveler and historian W. A. Wigram gives us an apt example of *agha* "protectionism."

[The Agha] of Chal is noted for being on the whole the most crafty murderer in the country-side. . . . [B]ut perhaps this is not the most remarkable thing about this Agha. He is the only man of the writer's acquaintance who really keeps a large herd of domestic Jews. . . . The writer has known a case, where the unfortunate Israelite, who was owned in this fashion by one Agha, was robbed of every penny and rag he possessed by that Agha's rival. Poor Ibrahim complained, of course, to his natural lord, on the ground that it was *iyba* to that master himself, if his property was robbed in this style. The chief had to admit that there was something in the argument; but redress by force of arms (the obvious method) was impossible, because the robber was far too nearly his equal in strength. "Your face is blackened, my Lord," pleaded the poor Hebrew. "It is indeed," said the Agha; "but I can't go to war with him notwithstanding." Presently he had a brilliant inspiration. "Look here Ibrahim; I have it! I'll go and rob his Jew myself."[19]

According to Walter J. Fischel, being a Jew in some ways was actually an advantage in Kurdistan. Since they did not belong to any Muslim tribe, the Jews were the only ones who could move among the feuding tribes without being harmed. Many Jews therefore took to peddling as an occupation. They would travel from village to village in companies of two or more, on muleback, selling clothing, foodstuffs, tools, and other merchandise. This occupation was very dangerous because the routes were often infested with murderous thieves. Many Jews lost their lives at the hands of Kurdish brigands.[20]

In the cities, towns, and villages of the transverse valleys and plains many Jews engaged in commerce, occupying stalls in the local bazaars. Many occupied themselves with the crafts, such as tanning, weaving, carpentry, shoemaking, and precious metals. Payment was sometimes by barter and sometimes partly in kind and partly in cash. Like the Jews of Yemen, the Kurdistani Jews had a reputation among their Muslim neighbors as honest, and superior, gold and silversmiths.[21] Many Jews living alongside the riverbanks worked as lumberjacks in pine, oak, and poplar forests and hauled the cut timber on rafts up and down the rivers. These jobs required great strength and endurance, which made them uncharacteristic occupations for Jews, who did not traditionally engage in hard physical labor.

In the isolated villages of the mountain slopes and plateaus many Jews were engaged in agricultural occupations. "Kurdistan," wrote the second President of Israel, Yitzhak Ben-Zvi "is practically the only exile in which there remained a solidly agricultural Jewish population with villages completely inhabited by Jews engaged in agriculture. . . ."[22] In some places, such as Acra and Sandur, the Jews were freeholding farmers who possessed their own land and cattle, but more generally they tilled the soil either as tenant farmers or as seasonal agricultural laborers on land belonging to absentee landowners. Jewish farmers raised crops such as corn, wheat, rice, barley, beans, grapes, and tobacco. They also raised herds of goats, fat-tailed sheep, and cattle. Using mule-driven wooden frame plows, and short-handled sickles, the men would harvest the crop. The women would gather the grains and haul them to the threshing floor. Beekeeping was a specialty in certain villages. A portion of the yield—sometimes as much as fifty percent—in addition to the profits and *koda* (an animal tax for flock owners) would automatically go to the *agha*. Jewish farm laborers who did not produce a winter crop would engage in the petty trades or weaving and other crafts.

In the course of his journeys across the Jewish enclaves of Kurdistan, the nineteenth-century traveler Rabbi David D'Beth Hillel observed that in some places some Jews were quite well-to-do and living in "a land flowing with milk and honey."[23] Most Jews, however, were poor and oppressed. Nevertheless, even the most impecunious of Jews rarely suffered a shortage of food at home. Almost everyone in the village had orchards and gardens. Grains, meat, and dairy products were cheap and readily available.

On weekdays an assortment of lamb and chicken dishes were eaten cold. On festive occasions cold, cubed chicken was usually served as hors d'oeuvres. A favorite dish of the Kurdistani Jews was *yiprak*, rice balls mixed with raisins and wrapped in vine leaves. Another unique Jewish food was *kuba*, flat ground wheat or rice cakes stuffed with fried meat, or its sweeter and *pareve* version, which was filled with raisins, dates, and preserves. On the Shabbat, a special dish called *maboteh* was eaten. This stewed delicacy can be compared to the *cholent* with *kishkah* of the Eastern European Jews. Its primary ingredients consisted of chicken, lamb, cow's intestine, wheat, chickpeas, and spices. *Maboteh* was baked before sunset on Friday and kept warm on the stove until lunch time on the Sabbath. On Shevuot, when traditionally only milk products are eaten, the Kurdistani Jews substituted *medira*, crushed wheat boiled in sour milk, and *katulai*, dumplings stuffed with flour and rancid butter, for the meat dishes. More than ample quantities of *zachlawi* (brandy) and *alubaluh* (old fermented cherry wine) were consumed at all festivities.

The social unit of father-mother-child was nonexistent in Kurdistan. The primary unit of traditional Kurdistani Jewish social life was the co-residing family or household. The oldest male in every household was the family head. He made all the decisions, and no one dared to question him. Kurdistani Jews, like other Kurds, were patrilocal regarding postmarital residence; sons with their wives and children continued to dwell in their father's residential compound, or in close proximity to it. Usually all the males worked together in one occupation and shared the profits.

Houses in the typical hamlet in Kurdistan were usually clustered together on a steep slope and provided accommodation for several families. A typical lodging was constructed of sun-baked mud bricks, or built of stone and lime. Flat roofs made from mud and supported by horizontal rafters of poplar poles provided special protection against the sun and were used for drying fruits.[24] For purposes of defense, house and garden were completely encircled by a mud brick wall. Kurdish houses contained no glass in the windows, nor a door to close the entrance. Houses were usually one story high and consisted of only one room. The interior was devoid of furniture; felt rugs and embroidered tapestry served for functional purposes as well as for aesthetic design.[25] During the frosty winter months, the family huddled together in the living room next to the hearth. During the hot summer months, when highly venomous scorpions abounded in the dark crevices of the interior, people preferred to sleep on the rooftop or on the terrace. Jewish villages were invariably situated next to a river or spring, so that the people could perform their ritual ablutions.

In the selection of a life partner for their children, Kurdistani parents would exercise utmost care and solemnity. In selecting a bride for their son, parents looked for a girl who would be dutiful and care for them in their old age.[26] Agnatic (patrilineal parallel) cousin and paternal uncle-niece marriages were preferred. One reason for preferring a blood relative for their son was that a girl from the same family would naturally be more loyal and loving than if she came from a family of strangers. Marriages were especially important for another reason. In a land as violent and anarchistic as Kurdistan, clan cohesion was a survival necessity; a man was considered powerful if he had many men to back him up in a fight. By marrying his daughter within the clan, the patriarch could be assured that his brother or nephew who was now also his son-in-law would fight along-side him in case he was attacked.

The marriageable age for girls was twelve; boys married at fifteen. Jewish parents usually arranged marriages for their children, the father of the groom formally requesting the bride's hand from her parents.[27] Although marriages were usually arranged, if the parents of the bride objected to the groom, "the groom simply 'kidnapped' his beloved and the consent usually followed."[28]

The marriage arrangement was like a business deal. After much bargaining, the father of the prospective groom would pay to the father of the intended bride a *mahr* (bride price), in either cash or merchandise. When the fathers of the prospective bride and groom agreed, the engagement became official. Candy would be distributed amongst the guests, and festivities would begin.[29] The men would gather around the groom and the veiled bride and form a chain dance. Standing side by side, holding hands and shoulder to shoulder, they would move in a semicircle. Those at the end of the chain would wave colorful scarves in their free hands. The steps would radiate toward the center of the semicircle and then out again. Dances were accompanied by singing, and fife and drum provided the music.

During the *kiddushin* (formal betrothal) ceremony, the groom would give the bride a coin or ring. The unveiling of the bride usually marked the first time the groom got a glimpse of his future wife. During the unveiling, the female guests would make joyful trilling sounds to ward off the evil spirits. A few days before the wedding a women-only henna ceremony took place. After the ritual bath, the bride and her attendants would remove all superfluous hair from her body. Amidst much singing and dancing, the bride's female relatives would paint auburn dye on the bride's hair, hands, fingers, and toes. A powdered antimony called *kel* was applied as an eye makeup. On the day of the wedding, the bride and groom would be led separately from their parents' homes to the village square. When the two parties met, a loaf of bread was broken over their heads.[30] The *chuppah* (canopy) ceremony was arranged by the family of the groom. Wedding festivities, which included mock sword dances and war motifs, took place both at the house of the groom and the house of the bride and usually lasted for seven days and seven nights.

Among all Kurdish people the bride's virginity was highly esteemed. Immediately upon the deflowering of the bride, the bloodstained sheet was triumphantly exhibited. The demand that the bride be a virgin was so absolute that if it was dishonored, the girl was put to death by her father or brothers.[31] In the extremely unlikely scenario in which a woman was caught in the act of adultery, "she was either killed by her husband, or, if he was more law abiding, he would immediately divorce her, whereupon they would cut off her hair, seat her backwards on a donkey, make her hold on to the donkey's tail as a bridle, and let her ride in the streets while the children would beat her and pour sour milk over her."[32]

Polygamy was permitted by the Jews of Kurdistan. However, only wealthy Jews could afford to have more than one wife, and only in rare cases where the first wife could not have children did the husband take a second wife.

If a child was born on a Jewish holiday, it would be named after a great hero or sage identified with that holiday. For example, a boy born on Chanukah might be named Judah, after Judah Maccabee; a girl born on Shevuot or Purim would be named Ruth or Esther. As the Jews of Kurdistan were very superstitious, the room of the mother and her newborn infant was always covered with amulets to ward off the evil eye.

Few boys ever attended *knishta* (*cheder*). The Jewish communities of Kurdistan were too small and too poor to maintain schools, and the few schools that did exist were woefully lacking in books. According to Dina Feitelson, the *knishta* was "viewed not so much as an institution which imparts learning, as a place where the boy is kept under supervision and thus out of mischief."[33] The general length of attendance for the boys was less than four years. Boys were first taught to read the *Chumash* (Five Books of Moses) without translation. In his book *The Vanished Worlds of Jewry*, Raphael Patai describes the severe abuse to which children in *knishta* were subjected by their teachers: An insubordinate child would be hung up head down from the ceiling. A heap of dung was placed beneath the head of the child and set fire to. With the acrid smoke rising into his face the poor victim would be ordered to recite the weekly portion of the Torah.[34] By the time he was ready to learn the translation of the text, the boy was withdrawn from school. Once he left school, a boy was apprenticed to his father or an older brother to learn the family trade.

Women and girls rarely left the house. The only occasion for going outside might be to draw water from a well (an exclusively female chore), to collect manure for fuel, or to go on a family picnic. Many women helped their farmer husbands during the planting and harvesting seasons. There were no schools for girls. Reciting a few blessings by heart was generally the extent of female religious training. Girls assisted their mothers with domestic chores and with weaving and embroidering.

As everywhere else in the traditional Jewish world, the Kurdistani Jewish woman was subservient to the dominating personality of her husband. Prior to the 1940s, there was almost no information available concerning the way the Kurdistani Jewish men treated their wives. Raphael Patai wrote that Kurdistani

Jewish women were so severely abused in the Old Country that many became permanently bedridden,[35] basically reiterating the view taken by the Jewish anthropologist Erich Brauer, who visited Kurdistan in the early 1940s. Brauer remarked that, as in the dominant Muslim male culture, there was a tendency among Jewish men to be harsh to their wives, to beat them and abuse them.[36] "Since to dominate one's wife was considered proper behavior," Patai notes, "the husband did not hesitate to beat his wife even in public," in order to demonstrate to his family and neighbors that he still "wore the pants" in the house.[37] More recent research has shown that the wife-beating and abuse were not at all endemic to Kurdistani Jewish society. The current understanding is that Dr. Brauer focused on a number of the most extreme instances and applied them to characterize an entire culture.[38]

A number of early-twentieth-century Westerners who traveled extensively in Kurdistan in the early 1900s described the Kurdish wife as the "pillar of the house," who had remarkable freedom, and noted that Kurdish men treated their womenfolk with greater respect than men in other places in the Muslim Middle East.[39] Kurdish women worked and fought alongside their men and did not wear the veil that was obligatory elsewhere in the Near Eastern Islamic world. Donna Shai, a Hebrew University anthropology professor, in the course of her field-work and research among Kurdistani Jews in Israel, was told by informants that in the Old Country when it came to household matters the matriarch was the "dominant figure whose authority went unchallenged even by the men of the household.[40] . . . The image which emerges from the folksongs [of the Kurdistani Jews] is that of a strong and dynamic personality."[41]

What is unique about Kurdistan is that a Jewish community that fostered universal illiteracy among women once gave rise to an outstanding rabbi who happened to be a woman. Asenat Barazani was born around 1590. Her father, Rabbi Shmuel, was dean of the rabbinical academy of Barazan. He was a great scholar and mystic who founded a number of *yeshivot* in Kurdistan. During her early childhood, Asenat sat on her father's lap while he was lecturing. When she was older, she married a talmudic scholar who succeeded her father as *rosh yeshiva* (dean of the rabbinical academy). Apparently she was permitted a seat at the rabbinical academy, for at the time of her husband's death, she was *bekki'a beshas*, which means that she had mastered the whole compendium of talmudic law and lore. This level of brilliance and achievement prompted the rabbinical authorities of the city of Mosul to offer the *"tannai'it,"*[42] the position of dean of the seminary there. It was at Mosul that she established a reputation as a great sage and miracle worker. When the Jewish community of Baghdad requested that she send one of her top students to serve as chief rabbi there, she sent her own son.

Although most Jews could not read the Hebrew prayers, many knew large portions of the *siddur* (prayerbook) by heart. The *hakham*, who might be the only one in the community who could read, would have to pray for all. Synagogues were always built near a river or stream so that the congregants could bathe before entering the holy place. Since in many of the scattered villages the Jewish families were few and isolated, there were no *knishtas*, no *minyanim*, no *hakhamim*, and no *shochetim* (ritual slaughterers). Not infrequently a visiting rabbi or *sheliach* (emissary from the Holy Land) would sojourn among them, and during this period there was an upgrading in the standards of the Jewish community's practices and religiosity. Visiting rabbis oftentimes were the community's only link with the outside Jewish world. In many of these isolated mountain villages, ritual slaughter was available only once a year. Families would dry enough meat until a *shochet*'s next visit.

The *mukhtar/hakham* was the temporal and ecclesiastic head of the Jewish community. In the capacity of *mukhtar* he would represent the interests of the community to the tribal government. He might also serve as the "house Jew" to the local or regional chieftain in the capacity of treasurer, tax farmer, book-keeper, etc. In the capacity of spiritual leader of the community, the *hakham* also served as principal of the *knishta*, cantor, circumciser, ritual slaughterer, herbalist, healer, dream interpreter, and fortuneteller.

Being highly superstitious, the Jews believed in devils and evil spirits. When they or their children were ill or experienced something terrible, they blamed their troubles on the evil eye. To rid themselves of the evil eye, they would go to the *hakham* for a blessing and receive a *kameah*, an amulet or other piece of jewelry containing kabbalistic formulae from the *Sefer Reziel*. *Kameot* were written in Hebrew because the Jews believed that Satan did not understand the Holy Tongue.[43] David Becker, in researching his thesis on the Kurdistani Jews, found that sea shells, wolves' teeth, and birds' wings were also believed to ward off bad luck.[44]

Like Jews in other parts of the Near East and North Africa, the Jews of Kurdistan during the Jewish festivals would make yearly *ziyara* (pilgrimages) to the shrines of great biblical prophets and *hakhamim* located in Kurdistan. The most widely known were the tombs of the Prophets Jonah in Nineveh, Nahum in Ailkush, Daniel in Kirkuk, and several caves reputedly visited by Elijah. On these sacred grounds they would pray for their own and their family's well-being, and beg the holy souls to plead before God on their behalf.

The Jews of Kurdistan preserved ancient Jewish traditions not found in other Jewish communities. For example, the Shabbat was announced with the blowing of a *shofar*. All activities would come to a halt, and the women would light the Sabbath candles. Probably the most unusual holiday custom was observed by the well-known traveler J. J. Benjamin II who visited the town of Alquosh during festival of Shevuot in the 1840s. Very early in the morning all the men would go up to the top of a mountain armed with guns, daggers, and swords. After reciting the holiday prayers, they would come down from the mountain, and—like a dress rehearsal for a theater performance—the men would begin to engage in simulated physical combat. Amidst the sound of blood-curdling war cries, gunshots were fired in the air and weapons rattled and clashed. This dramatic act symbolized the great combat that the Jews will have to carry on against those nations who—when the Messiah comes—will attempt to deter them from entering the Promised Land.[45] Another unusual Shevuot custom "was to spray water from the roof-tops on passersby below."[46]

Benjamin II also made the following observation during his sojourn in Kurdistan:

> When a Chacham from Jerusalem comes into these parts, which occurs but very seldom, they go out solemnly to meet him, kiss his shoulders, his beard, and even his feet. . . . [T]hey then carry him in triumph to the house of the Nasi, bare his feet and wash them, and the water used for that purpose is collected for drinking. . . . The highest people of the place have the first right to partake of this water; the rest is divided up among the women and children; and this unclean beverage is considered to be a preventative of all illnesses.[47]

The Kurdistani Jews may have been unsophisticated and naive in many ways, but they did possess a rich folk literature whose subjects were often drawn from the Bible, rabbinic sources, and local oral traditions. These satirical stories, fables, songs, nursery rhymes, proverbs, and anecdotes—many of them quite humorous—were handed down orally from father to son and mother to daughter. UCLA professor Yona Sabar, who is a Kurdistani Jew, has compiled a wonderful collection in his book *The Folk Literature of the Kurdistani Jews: An Anthology*.[48] This is the first time that a collection of folktales from such a little-known Jewish community has been translated from neo-Aramaic into English and collected in a single volume. Although no doubt much of the flavor is lost in the translation here are a few examples of proverbs and popular sayings: "Your fire did not warm me, but I was blinded by your smoke." (Said of people who cause only suffering.) "A hundred (good) people can live together without quarreling, but two dogs (i.e., bad people) in one place will (always) quarrel." "A mountain does not need another mountain, but a person needs another person." (Since people need each other, they should be kind to each other.)

In addition to observing the Jewish holidays, the Kurdistani Jews celebrated secular holidays called *saharanei*. *Saharanei* were nature trips and family picnics lasting for several days, coinciding with Passover, Shevuot, Sukkot, Chanukah, and Purim. On these days family members dressed up in splendid festive garb adorned with their finest jewelry. Tents were pitched at the festival site. Festivities included much eating, drinking, praying, singing, and dancing around the campfire. Out in the fields, children were given horseback riding lessons.[49] While the Jews were away, their Muslim neighbors would station guards to protect the empty Jewish homes during the festival. They believed that the Jews left for *saharanei* in search of Moses' cane. On their return, the Jews were welcomed by their Muslim friends with wine and cheese.[50] In Israel today a variation of this festival has gained much popularity among the Kurdistani Jews as a celebration of their heritage. The *saharanei* in Israel, "performs the function of ensuring communal solidarity and continuity."[51]

Today there are an estimated 125,000 Jews of Kurdistani origin in Israel. Many of them live in predominantly Kurdistani neighborhoods around Machneh Yehudah and in the hilly parts of Jerusalem. Many others settled in cities such as Tel Aviv, Holon, Haifa, and Tiberias, or development towns and agricultural communities such as Kiryat Shmoneh, Kiryat Malachi, Mevaseret Tzion, and Kiryat Ata.

"When someone in Israel tells you you're behaving like a Kurdi, the implication is derogatory," writes Jerusalem Post reporter Greer Fay Cashman. "Few of the ethnic ingredients in Israel's sizzling melting pot have been as cruelly maligned as the Kurds. The deprecating image of a hot-tempered, illiterate primitive is so deep seated that for years many Israelis of Kurdish extraction denied their origins and identified with other national groups."[52]

Heavy-boned and muscular, the Kurdish Jews have tended to gravitate to occupations requiring physical strength, although they are now fairly well integrated in all areas of the Israeli economy.

NOTES

1. The Kurds were history's first civilian targets of bomber aircraft, when the RAF dropped their cargo on villagers in central Kurdistan in the 1920s. See Robert

Olson, *The Emergence of Kurdish Nationalism and the Sheikh Zaid Rebellion, 1880–1925* (Austin: University of Texas Press, 1989), p. 163; Philip Kreyenbrock and Christine Allison, *Kurdish Culture and Identity* (London: Zed Books Ltd., 1996), p. 13.

2. The Yezidis have erroneously been described as devil worshippers but really are a syncretistic Islamic sect with strong Zoroastrian antecedents and some Jewish, Christian, and pagan elements.

3. *Two Years in Kurdistan: Experiences of a Political Officer, 1918–1920* (London: Sidgwick and Jackson, 1921), p. 65.

4. Arshak Safrastrian, *Kurds and Kurdistan* (London: The Harvill Press, 1948), p. 65.

5. Mehrdad R. Izady, *The Kurds: A Concise Handbook* (Washington, D.C.: Crane Russak, 1992), p. 188.

6. Pierre G. Ponafidine, *Life in the Moslem East* (New York: Dodd, Mead and Co., 1911), p. 48.

7. Edward Ghareeb, *The Kurdish Question in Iraq* (Syracuse, N.Y.: Syracuse University Press, 1951), p. 31.

8. C. J. Edmonds, *Kurds, Turks, and Arabs.* (London: Oxford University Press, 1957), p. 4.

9. Izady, *The Kurds*, p. 43

10. Ibid., p. 49.

11. A. R. Ghassemlou, *People Without a Country* (London: Zed Press, 1980), p. 22.

12. Izady, *The Kurds*, p. 102.

13. The Nestorian and Assyrian Christians of Kurdistan also speak Aramaic.

14. On the conversion of Queen Helena and her son Izates, see Jacob Neusner, *A History of Babylonia: The Parthian Period* (Chico, Calif.: Scholars Press, 1984), pp. 61–73; and Sidney B. Hoenig's "Conversion during the Talmudic Period," in *Conversion to Judaism: A History and Analysis* (New York: Ktav Publishing House, 1965), pp. 44–47.

15. Elkan N. Adler, ed., *Jewish Travellers in the Middle Ages: 19 Firsthand Accounts* (New York: Dover Publications, 1987), p. 50.

16. *The Kurds: An Unstable Element in the Gulf* (Boulder: Westview Press, 1984), p. 37.

17. Erich Brauer, *The Jews of Kurdistan*, completed and edited by Raphael Patai (Detroit: Wayne State University Press, 1993), pp. 88–89; Shifra Epstein, "The Jews of Kurdistan," *Ariel* 51 (1982), p. 71.

18. On relations between the nontribal Kurds with the *aghas* see Martin van Bruinessen, *Agha, Shaikh and State* (London: Zed Books Ltd., 1992), pp. 66–67, 105–09.

19. *The Cradle of Mankind: Life in Eastern Kurdistan* (London: Londres and Bloch, 1914), pp. 317–18.

20. "The Jews of Kurdistan: A First-Hand Report on a Near Eastern Mountain Community," *Commentary* 8:6 (1949), p. 556.

21. See Ora Schwartz-Be'eri, "Kurdish Jewish Silvercraft," *Israel Museum Journal* 7 (Spring 1988), pp. 75–88.

22. "Lost and Regained: They That Were Lost in the Land of Assyria," *Phylon* First Quarter (1955), p. 59.

23. *Unknown Jews in Unknown Lands: The Travels of Rabbi David D'Beth Hillel (1824–1832)* (New York: Ktav Publishing House, 1973), p. 79.

24. Henny H. Hansen, *The Kurdish Woman's Life: Field Research in a Muslim Society* (Copenhagen: National Museets, 1961), p. 27; Glenn M. Fleming, "The Ecology and Economy of Kurdish Villages," *Kurdish Times* 6:1–2 (Summer–Fall, 1991), pp. 28–29.

25. Ora Schwartz-Be'eri, "Jewish Weaving in Kurdistan," *Kurdish Times* 6:1–2 (Summer–Fall, 1991), p. 90.

26. Dina Feitelson, "Aspects of the Social Life of Kurdish Jews," in *Jewish Societies in the Middle East: Community, Culture, and Authority*, edited by Shlomo Deshen and Walter P. Zenner (Lanham, N.Y.: University Press of America, 1982), p. 264.

27. Donna Shai, "Family Conflict and Cooperation in Folksongs of Kurdish Jews," in *Jewish Societies in the Middle East: Community, Culture, and Authority*, edited by Shlomo Deshen and Walter P. Zenner (Lanham, NY: University Press of America, 1982), p. 276.

28. Dvorah and Menachem Hacohen. *One People: The Story of the Eastern Jews* (New York: Adama Books, 1986), p. 15.

29. Donna Shai, "Wedding Customs among Kurdish Jews in (Zakho) Kurdistan and in (Jerusalem) Israel," *Folklore Research Center Studies* 4 (1974), p. 253.

30. Hacohen, *One People*, p. 15.

31. Hansen, *Kurdish Woman's Life*, pp. 131, 133.

32. Raphael Patai, *The Vanished Worlds of Jewry* (New York: MacMillan, 1980), p. 159.

33. "Aspects of the Social Life," p. 268.

34. Patai, *Vanished Worlds*, pp. 157, 159.

35. Ibid., p. 159.

36. *The Jews of Kurdistan*, pp. 179–180.

37. Patai, *Vanished Worlds*, p. 159. "The greater the importance of the family," Brauer wrote, "the more extreme does this behavior become." See *The Jews of Kurdistan*, p. 179.

38. Conversations with Professor Yona Sabar of UCLA, May 1993 and December 1997.

39. E. B. Soane, *To Mesopotamia and Kurdistan in Disguise* (London: John Murray,

1912), pp. 396–97; Mrs. Linfield Soane, "A Recent Journey to Kurdistan," *Journal of the Royal Asian Society* 22:3 (July 1935), p. 410; Hay, *Two Years*, p. 43.

40. Shai, "Family Conflict," p. 5.

41. Ibid., p. 8.

42. The feminine form of an especially reverential title since this appellation was conferred on the rabbis of the early talmudic period.

43. Austin H. Layard, *Nineveh and Babylon: A Narrative of a Second Expedition to Assyria During the Years 1849, 1850, and 1851* (London: John Murray, 1882), p. 519.

44. *The Jews of Kurdistan: An Historical and Ethnographic Study* (Bachelor's Honors Thesis, State University of New York at Binghamton, 1986), p. 32.

45. I. J. Benjamin, *Eight Years in Asia and Africa: From 1846 to 1855* (Hanover: n.p., 1859), pp. 72–73.

46. Hacohen, *One People*, p. 19.

47. Benjamin, *Eight Years*, pp. 98–99.

48. *The Folk Literature of the Kurdistani Jews: An Anthology* (New Haven and London: Yale University Press, 1982).

49. Emil Murad, *My Friends from Kurdistan* (Tel Aviv: Yesod, 1977), p. 33.

50. Jeff Halper and Henry Abramovitch, "The Saharanei As a Mediator of Kurdish-Jewish Ethnicity," *World Congress of Jewish Studies* 8:4 (1982), p. 80.

51. Halper, unpublished notes on the Saharanei provided the author.

52. "The Pride of Being Kurdish," *Jerusalem Post* (21 August 1983), p. 14. See also, Harvey Goldberg, "The Changing Meaning of Ethnic Affiliation," *The Jerusalem Quarterly* 44 (Fall 1987), p. 49.

Part IV

Krimchak Chief Rabbi Chaim Chezkiyahu Medini with Family
Credit: Yad Ben Zvi Archives

On the Russian Riviera

BACKGROUND INFORMATION

The Crimean peninsula of southern Ukraine lies between the Black Sea and the Sea of Azov. Noted for its picturesque beauty and mild, subtropical climate, the Crimea was referred to as the "Riviera" of the former Soviet Union. The population of the Crimea is approximately three million; its capital is Simferopol.

Inhabited since the most ancient times, the Crimea has been a battlefield throughout the centuries: Phoenicians, Scythians, Greeks, Romans, Goths, Huns, Byzantines, Khazars, Turkish Kipchaks, and Mongolians swept over the heavenly peninsula and left charred ruins in their wake. In the thirteenth century the Venetians and the Genoese established colonies along the port cities of the Crimean peninsula that traded with Byzantium and the Mediterranean countries.

In 1239 C.E., the Tatars, an assortment of nomadic Turks from the Volga region, invaded the Crimean peninsula. The Tatars were auxiliary troops under the command of the Mongol chieftain Batu (Genghis Khan's grandson) and comprised the bulk of the Golden Horde. The Tatar princes, who claimed descent from Genghis Khan, established a khandom (principality) in the Crimea, at first independently, then under Ottoman Turkish suzerainty. The Genoese and Venetian colonies on the Black Sea were tributaries to the Tatars before they were driven out in 1475. Under the Ottomans, the Tatars served as a military force in Eastern Europe and as a defensive buffer in the north. The Tatars were originally shamanists who believed in good and evil spirits. Around the early fourteenth century, they converted to Islam. The Tatars belong to the Hanifa sect of Sunni Islam.

Under the Tatar Khandom (1449–1796) the Crimea became a major slave-trading emporium. Ransoming slaves became a profitable offshoot of the slave trade. During the khanate period, the Tatars enjoyed personal freedoms and passed for a friendly and hospitable people. "Women were entitled to personal property, and took part now and then in public life, diplomatic negotiations or even in military expeditions. . . ."[1]

The Crimean peninsula was annexed by the Russian empire in 1783. Anti-Russian and anti-Christian feelings were strong among the Tatars and an estimated 300,000 took refuge in Turkey. In place of the Tatars came ethnic Russians, Ukrainians, and other Eastern European peoples, including Jews.

During World War II some Tatars allegedly collaborated with the Nazi invaders. After the Crimea was liberated by Soviet forces, the entire population of Crimean Tatars (a quarter of a million people, or twenty percent of the total population) was deported to Central Asia under a decree by Joseph Stalin. Tens of thousands died en route. "Those punished included thousands of innocent victims, including many who had fought courageously against the Nazis."[2]

Crimean Tatars began to trickle back to the Crimea after a 1967 decree of the Presidium of the Supreme Soviet restored the constitutional rights of the innocent victims of Stalinist persecution. Only a fraction of the Tatars, about 60,000, had relocated to the Crimea by 1997. The Crimea originally belonged to the Russian Socialist Federative Republic, but in 1954 was annexed by Ukraine.

THE KRIMCHAKS OF THE CRIMEA

> The whole of the south coast of the Crimean peninsula, with its
> romantic valleys and mountains, well deserves to be termed the
> Switzerland of Russia; while the pretty villages of the Tatars,
> with their tiny mosques and minarets, embosomed in the foliage
> of their rich orchards, adds a novel and peculiar feature to the
> scenery.
>
> —Captain Spencer, *Turkey, Russia, the Black Sea,*
> *and Circassia* (1854)

The Krimchaks, or Tatar Jews of the Crimean peninsula, are perhaps the
least known of all the *edot ha-mizrach*. The Crimea is considered to be the cradle
of Russian Jewry; from there Jewish settlers from the Near East spread to other
parts of Eastern Europe. The Krimchaks are believed to be descended in part
from the earliest of these Jewish settlers. They have inhabited the Crimea for at
least two millenia, and due to intermarriage with the Tatar peoples, are in many
ways indistinguishable from their Muslim neighbors.[3] Before the Communists
outlawed their language, the Krimchaks spoke Judeo-Crimean Tatar, which is
essentially a Turkish dialect sprinkled with Hebrew and Aramaic words and
traditionally written with Hebrew letters.

No one knows exactly why the Jews of this region are called Krimchaks.
The name is believed to date from the period after the Russian conquest of the
Crimean peninsula sometime in the nineteenth century. The Russian regime
referred to the original Jewish inhabitants of the Crimea as Krimchaks, to be
distinguished from the Ashkenazi Jewish emigrants from Poland and Lithuania,
and from the antirabbinic Karaite Jewish sect. Like the Krimchaks, the Karaites
have been living in the Crimea for many centuries. The entire Jewish population was called by the Tatars *Yakhudelar*. To differentiate the traditionally Orthodox Krimchaks from the sectarian Karaites, the former were referred to as
the *zuluflu chufutlar* (Jews with *peot*), while the latter were called the *zulufsuz
chufutlar* (Jews without *peot*). The Krimchaks referred to themselves as *Srel
Balalary*, or Children of Israel.[4]

Some historians trace the origins of the Crimean Jewish community back
to the Babylonian period. However, we can say with certainty that Jewish colonies existed on the shores of the Black Sea from the second century B.C.E., during the period of Greek rule. These Hellenistic or Greek-speaking Jews came
to the Crimea from Asia Minor to engage in trade and farming, and to enjoy the

freedoms accorded other Greek citizens. Eventually, Jews from Persia, Babylonia, and other parts of the Near East also established themselves in the Crimea. An inscription recently excavated in the Crimea led by a team of American investigators reveals that Jews on the peninsula were involved in the manumission of slaves as early as the first century of the common era.[5]

The Jewish influence in the region must have been widespread, because in the first centuries of the common era there arose among the pagan population cults known as *sebomenoi theon hypsiston* ("Worshippers of the All-Highest God"), who joined the Jewish communities as half-Jews. They attended synagogue, ate kosher, and circumcised their boys, but also retained certain pagan rituals. Some of these cultists were eventually persuaded by zealous Christian missionaries to convert to Christianity, but others adopted normative Judaism as their religious mode.[6]

From the second to the seventh century the Jewish communities on the Black Sea were constantly in upheaval as a result of successive invasions by barbarous hordes from the steppes of Central Asia and Siberia. One such wild, bellicose tribe, the Khazars, overran the Caucasus and the Crimean peninsula and succeeded in subduing all the surrounding nations and tribes. Around 740 C.E. the Khazar ruling class and a sizable portion of the population converted to Judaism. For the next two hundred years Khazaria was a mighty empire and a haven for Jews fleeing persecution in neighboring countries.

The Khazars were ethnically a Finno-Ugrian people related to the Turks, Finns, Huns, and Bulgars.[7] They were originally nomads and shamanists who practiced human sacrifice. According to legend, the Khazar *khagan* (King) Bulan (circa 730–740) experienced a spiritual crisis. An angel appeared in his dream and urged him to find the "One True God." Bulan invited to his court representatives of the three monotheistic faiths, who debated the superiority of their respective religions. During the debate Khagan Bulan realized that the Christian priest preferred Judaism to Islam, and the Islamic *cadi* preferred Judaism to Christianity. This convinced Khagan Bulan that Judaism was the truest of all three religions, and he decided to embrace Judaism.

In reality, the *khagan* adopted the Jewish religion for more practical reasons. The Jewish population of Khazaria was economically and politically powerful and wielded much influence upon the Khazar ruling classes. Squeezed between the two major powers—the Byzantine Christian Empire to the west, and the Islamic caliphate of Baghdad to the south—the *khagan* chose to adopt Judaism in order to be a regional power in his own right.[8]

Khazaria was the most tolerant country of its time and observers were impressed with the liberty and benevolence of her population. All ethnic and religious groups coexisted harmoniously in the empire. Christians, Muslims, pagans, and Jews could live according to their own religious laws.[9] Jews fleeing persecution from the East Roman Empire and the Caliphate flocked to Khazaria for protection and to practice their faith unhindered.

The Khazars were governed by the dual authority of the *khagan* and the *beg*. The *khagan* is believed to have been merely a figurehead and the *beg* the equivalent of a prime minister. "When they wish to enthrone this [*khagan*], they put a silken cord around his neck and tighten it until he begins to choke. Then they ask him: 'How long doest thou intend to rule?' If he does not die before that year, he is killed when he reaches it."[10] Every day the *beg* would enter the presence of the *khagan* barefooted. He would light incense and when it was extinguished, he would sit on the right side of the *khagan's* throne. The *beg* was the caretaker of governmental affairs; the *khagan* himself had no social intercourse with his subjects.

Every *khagan* had a harem consisting of twenty-five wives and sixty concubines. Each of the wives was the daughter of a king who owed him allegiance. The duration of the *khagan's* rule was forty years. If he exceeded this time by a single day, his attendants would kill him. "When evil times befell, the people held the *khagan* responsible and called upon the *beg* to put him to death. . . . The commander of an army who suffered defeat was cruelly treated: His wife, children, and property were sold before his eyes, and he was executed or degraded to menial rank."[11] When the *khagan* died, a great mausoleum with twenty chambers was built for him. In each chamber a grave was dug. Those who buried him had their heads chopped off, so that no one would know in which chamber he was buried.[12]

At first the Khazars, perhaps under Karaite influence, were lax in their practice of rabbinic Judaism. Contrary to Jewish law—Karaite or rabbinic— they continued to sell their women and children into slavery. Only later, during the reign of Khagan Ovadiah in the ninth century, were religious reforms instituted. Ovadiah invited rabbis from Babylonia, Byzantium, and Jerusalem to establish synagogues and *yeshivot* in Khazaria. Additionally, under Ovadiah a policy was instituted that henceforth all *khagans* should have Hebrew names.[13]

The Khazars became a world power around the year 630 C.E., after they assisted the Byzantines in crushing the Persian Empire. At first, relations with the Byzantines were relatively peaceful. Khazaria provided the Byzantines a service on two fronts: by holding back Slavic and Swedish Viking (Rus) raiders from the north, and by serving as a first line of defense against the Turkish barbarians from the east.[14] The Khazars are believed to have founded the city of Kiev in the eighth century, but their greatest contribution to the world was their success in preventing the Muslim hordes from invading Europe for almost two centuries. In 965 C.E., the Byzantines, now enemies of the Khazars, joined with their Russian allies to attack the Khazars. The Khazars suffered a decisive defeat. Approximately ten years later the Khazar capital, Atil, fell into Russian hands.

Some historians believe that a definite end to Khazar independence came then, or within the next century. Others, however, are of the opinion that a considerably shrunken Khazar kingdom continued to exist in the Crimea, with the city of Kerch as its capital. Only after being overwhelmed by the Golden Horde in the thirteenth century did an independent Khazar state entirely disappear from the map.[15]

During their period of decline many Khazars were killed in battle, sold into slavery, or forced to convert to Islam or Christianity. A sizable number probably intermarried with the Crimean Jews. Others fled to the West (meaning Poland and southern Russia) where they intermarried with Ashkenazi Jews. Those who fled to the Caucasus formed distinct Khazar-Jewish sects. For the next two hundred years this region was overrun by barbaric Turkish tribes from Central Asia. These Tatar masters tended to be kindly disposed toward their subjects, including the Jews.

From 1315 to 1475 the Genoese established trading colonies in the southwestern part of the Crimea. In the tolerant atmosphere of this Christian princedom, the existing Jewish population was increased by an influx of Jews from the Mediterranean countries, Eastern Europe, Persia, and the Caucasus. The cultures of the Jewish communities of the Crimea were so diverse and separate that they were soon praying in three different *nusachot:* Sephardic, Ashkenazic, and Romaniot (Greek-speaking Byzantine Jews). Only after Rabbi Moshe Hagolah, the Chief Rabbi of Kiev, settled in the Crimea around 1515 were the different Jewish traditions combined into one. The compromise *machzor* (holiday prayer book) drawn up by Rabbi Hagolah became known as the "Ritual of [the city] Kaffa."

Under the Sunni Islamic Tatars the Jews lived in separate quarters and were granted religious and judicial self-rule in accordance with *millet* (religious community) regulations established everywhere else in the Ottoman empire. Because the Jews were not allowed to serve in the military, they were obligated to pay a capitation tax. Although legally inferior to the Muslims, the Jews were never persecuted. However, when in 1777 the enlightened khan, Sahin, attempted to grant equality of citizenship to his Jewish (and Christian) subjects, the Tatars rose up against him.[16]

Russia annexed the Crimea in 1783, and from that time forward the Jews on the peninsula were subject to the same humiliations and restrictions that were imposed on Jews in other parts of the Russian Empire. They could not work for the government or send their children to high school. They had to pay outrageously heavy taxes and could not live outside the boundaries of restrictive areas called the Pale of Settlement. During the reign of Nicholas II the Krimchaks petitioned the Czar to allow them to be exempt from military service. The Czar asked the Krimchaks if they believed in the Talmud. When the Krimchak delegates replied that they did, the Czar rejected their petition and told them they would have to provide soldiers for his army.

In the nineteenth century a large number of Ashkenazi Jews from Russia and Lithuania settled in the Crimea and established their own communities there. Considering themselves culturally and intellectually superior to the Krimchaks, the new arrivals disparagingly referred to their bucolic brethren as "ignorant sheep heads."[17] Poor Ashkenazim who couldn't find brides in their own community married Krimchak girls. By the end of the nineteenth century there were an estimated 60,000 Ashkenazi Jews in the Crimea as opposed to only about 6,000 Krimchaks.

The Krimchaks, like their Muslim compatriots, were universally illiterate and unsophisticated. This lack of education and sophistication limited the expression of their piety. However, in some ways the Krimchaks were perhaps even more pious than other Jews, especially when it came to practicing good works and deeds. For example, they took care of the poor so that there were no beggars in their midst. Every Thursday money, food, and essential needs such as wood and coal were distributed among the indigent.[18] They treated their elders with great dignity and respect, and their generosity and hospitality was legendary. The term "Krimchak" was synonymous with honesty; a Krimchak was always true to his or her word.

Great emphasis was placed on fulfilling the biblical commandment of *pidyan shevuyin*, the release of Jews from prison and the ransoming of captured Jews in the battlefield or from pirates. During the Cossack pogroms in 1648, when tens of thousands of Jews were butchered in Poland and Ukraine, the Krimchaks provided shelter for those survivors who managed to reach the Crimea.[19]

The Krimchaks had many interesting and unusual traditions and *minhagim*. For example, when they gathered to attend prayer services in the synagogue, they did not enter the threshold until everyone had arrived. They would enter the synagogue in a body, and as soon as they entered they would start the services. This was done in order to prevent people from chattering and gossiping in the Holy Place. No one dared even whisper to one's neighbor while in the synagogue. And just as they entered as a body, so too did they also leave as a body.[20] "Many travelers and scholars who visited the Crimea in the [nineteenth] century," Yevsai Paisach informs us, "wrote that the Krimchaks possessed prayer-books produced 1200 years ago."[21]

Unlike many other traditional Jewish cultures around the world, marriages among the Krimchaks were not prearranged. Boys and girls were free to marry whomever they wished. Girls married as young as ten. Marriages between close relatives, such as an uncle and a niece, were permitted. Widows could never remarry, because it was believed that a woman was inseparable from her husband even after death.[22]

Another peculiar custom was the way in which the bridegroom's friends groomed him for his wedding day after much partying. They would hoist him above their shoulders and carry him off to the bathhouse. Before heaving him into the pool they would auction off the honor of taking his clothes off. For example, one close friend might bid five cents to charity to remove his shirt; another might try to outbid the others in removing his pants. Once the bridegroom was in the bath, his friends would bid against each other for the privilege of washing various parts of his body. When this was completed, they would auction off the privilege of drying various parts of his body. Finally, they would bid to determine who would dress various parts of his body.[23]

The wedding procession would begin at daybreak with the entourage singing, dancing, and making merry. At the synagogue the closest relatives would circle the bride and groom seven times, twirling roosters over their heads, while the rabbi recited the blessings. Afterwards, the roosters were slaughtered and distributed among the poor.[24] Instead of a wedding canopy, the Krimchaks used a prayer shawl. During the *chuppah* ceremony the guests tossed coins at the bride and groom as a symbol of a rich and abundant life. The coins were later gathered up and given to the poor. After the ceremony, the bride and groom were escorted to the groom's house. During the period of *shevah bruchot*, the bride and groom were confined to their room and no one else was allowed to enter.[25]

Being highly superstitious, the Krimchaks conjured up all kinds of remedies to cure the effects of the evil eye. A person experiencing something terrifying would be taken outside the city limits. His friends would lay him down on the ground and draw a circle around him with a cane. Then seven pieces of thread would be tied to the nearest tree, and a pot and copper coin were buried on the place where the distressed person rested. The person was then considered cured.[26]

When burying their dead, the Krimchaks would decorate the tombstone not only with religious symbols, such as menorahs and *shofars*, but also with the symbol of his occupation. For example, if he was a shoemaker a symbol in the shape of a shoe was carved on his tombstone. Ancient tombstones found in the city of Kerch indicate that this tradition dates from the Greek-Maccabean period (135 B.C. E.).[27]

The Krimchaks were simple people who did not require many material possessions. Their houses, which they built with their own hands, were made of clay, usually two stories high. Every house was enclosed with high walls and surrounded by gardens and flower beds. The interior was quite sparse. There was no furniture except for a low round table in the dining room. The Krimchaks, like the Crimean Tatars, had little use for chairs, couches, or beds. All eating and sleeping was done on the floor, which was covered with Turkish carpets.

During medieval times, Crimean Jewish men engaged in international trade involving silk processing and fabric dyeing. The decline of the Ottoman Empire at the end of the seventeenth century contributed to the demise and stagnation of the Jewish community in the Crimea. Up to the twentieth century there were few businessmen among the Krimchaks. Many Jews left for other parts of Europe, and those Jews who remained in the Crimea mostly eked out a living as craftspeople. The majority engaged in occupations such as haberdashery, dressmaking, and shoemaking. Some were involved in farming, gardening, and wine making.

Unlike Jews in most other Muslim lands, there were no special restrictions or codes of dress imposed on the Jews of the Crimea. Both men and women wore the national garb of the Tatar people. Men wore red or black Turkish caps, a wide blue overcoat called *arkbulak*, and a pair of loose pants bound with a wide belt ornamented with silver. Men capable of writing carried a pen and inkwell attached to their belts; everyone else carried a small dagger in a sheath attached to the belt.[28]

Women and girls wore short, brightly colored skirts of floral design. Beneath the skirt they wore long white linen bloomers and colorful slippers with gold or silver trimming. Their adornment consisted of immense earrings and gold and silver chains worn around the neck and over their plush red caps. Krimchak women were renowned for their luxuriant black hair, which they wore in long braids. They twisted into their braids silver threads from which dangled gold and silver coins. The cleansing formula they used was a clay-like soap called *kill*, derived from an indigenous herb called *alabota*. For dyeing the hair they applied a greasy red paint called *kene* (henna).

Favorite Krimchak dishes were *shashlik*, or mutton squares boiled in fat until crisp and eaten with green vegetables and pita bread; *yantach*, a special *erev Shabbat* dish consisting of heavily greased meat pies filled with potatoes, onions, lamb, or mutton; and *tcheberek*, ground lamb and onions fried in a boiling dish of fat. The favorite soft drink, *buzzah*, was made from bran cooked with sugar. In addition to seemingly endless cups of coffee, another favorite drink was a tea made from a wild herbal plant that grew near the banks of the Don. This tea was seasoned with butter, pepper, and salt. Both men and women incessantly smoked tobacco from a pipe. To keep their mouths and teeth fresh and clean they chewed a type of gum called *sazik*.[29]

Beginning in the early nineteenth century the Krimchak community in the Crimea was constantly beset with disasters. A plague in 1813 and a flood in 1815 devastated the community of Karasu Bazaar (nowadays Belagorsk), the largest Krimchak community in the Crimea.

It was the dedication and influence of one saintly, compassionate man who came to live among them that transformed the Krimchaks from illiterates into a people who knew the essentials of Judaism. In *charedi* (ultra-Orthodox) circles referred to as the *melech hamoshiah* (Messiah King), Chaim Chezkiyahu Medini is considered to be one of the outstanding Sephardic rabbis of the nineteenth century.[30] He was the author of an eighteen-volume halakhic encyclopedia titled *Sdai Chemed*. Because of his erudition, great deeds, and modesty, the title of Gaon (Excellency) was conferred upon him.

Rabbi Medini was born in Jerusalem in 1832. He was ordained at thirteen, and shortly thereafter served as rabbi and judge in Constantinople, Turkey. When he was in his mid thirties, a wealthy Krimchak prevailed upon him to accept the invitation to become Chief Rabbi of the city of Karasu Bazaar, the largest Krimchak community in the Crimea. Upon arriving in the Crimea he was so appalled by the spiritual vacuousness he found among the Krimchaks— their great lack of halakhic rigor and their infatuation with witchcraft and the evil eye—that for the next thirty-three years he assiduously devoted himself to educating young and old. He established *chedarim* and *yeshivot*, instituted various *takkanot* (dictums), eradicated customs that contravened Jewish tenets, and raised their spiritual and cultural level to that of Jews in other parts of Russia. Many who were graced to be in Medini's presence experienced his charisma and saintliness. Even Muslims and Christians considered him to be divinely inspired, and often the leaders of these communities would come to pay homage to him.[31]

During World War I there was a civil war in the Crimea in which many Krimchaks were killed, caught in the crossfire between the pro-Czarists forces and the Communist revolutionaries. The famine that followed the war diminished their numbers even more. Some Krimchaks emigrated to Turkey, Palestine, and the United States. To better understand the situation of the Krimchaks under Communism and Nazism, some background on the Crimean Karaites is crucial at this juncture, because the Krimchaks who remained in the Crimea applied a lesson that they had learned from the Karaites.

Around the year 767 C.E., rabbinical sources (perhaps biased) tell us, a sect of Babylonian Jews, led by Anan Ben-David, out of jealousy for being passed up for the prestigious and powerful position of *resh galuta* (exilarch) in favor of his intellectually inferior younger brother, broke away from mainstream Judaism. Rejecting the Talmud as human-inspired, Anan maintained that only the Written Law, the Torah, is of Divine origin—for did not the Torah explicitly state (Deuteronomy, chapter 4): "Ye shall not add unto the word which I command you, neither shall ye diminish from it, that ye may keep the commandments of Jehovah your God which I command you."

In the early stages of the movement the religious practices of these Jewish fundamentalists were extremely rigorous and uncompromising. For example, their literal translation of the Bible compelled them to sit home in the dark, eat cold food, and refuse to perform any semblance of work—not even slicing bread—on the Sabbath.[32] They "demanded an eye for an eye in lieu of the Pharasaic-rabbinic fine. . . . Any violence whatsoever done to parents was to be punished by stoning."[33] They refused medical attention because they believed that God alone could heal. Realizing that such rigid observances made normal living very difficult and was driving away potential followers, the Karaite leaders constructed a Talmud-like halakhic compendium and loosened the laws slightly.

The reformist, intensely nationalistic movement launched by Anan was only the latest in a long line of dissident messianic and sectarian movements beginning with the Sadducees and Essenes from the Second Temple era that resisted the exclusive authority of the rabbinate and the growing oral tradition embodied in the Talmud. The movement drew mainly from the disgruntled intelligensia and from poor, marginalized, and heterodox Jewish elements— especially the more independent-minded frontierspeople living in the sparse, peripheral areas of the Muslim empire, who bitterly resented the oppressive power wielded by the exilarchic political administration emanating hundreds or thousands of miles away in Baghdad. Women also found the Ananist creed appealing since the reformists had expunged the *shelow osani isha*[34] prayer from the *siddur* and given them unprecedented freedoms, such as the right to file for divorce. These Jewish dissident groups were inspired by various incipient Islamic movements in the Caspian provinces that were revolting against the

Caliphate.[35] Early in the ninth century, when they had solidified under the aegis of Benjamin an-Nahawendi, the Jewish reformist elements came to refer to themselves as Karaites, derived from the Hebrew words *B'nai Mikra*, the "People of the Scriptures."

It was Karaism's great misfortune to have begun to make successful inroads among the Jews concomitant with the rise of the brilliant and influential Egyptian talmudist and grammarian Saadia Gaon (892–942). Saadia, who ultimately became rector of the rabbinical academy of Sura (Babylonia), vigorously opposed the Karaites, denouncing them as apostates who must be read out of the Jewish community. Saadia's scathing attacks had the effect of galvanizing the various groups within Karaism; in the tenth and eleventh century the movement crystalized and reached its greatest intellectual heights. Eventually, the Karaites established small communities in Palestine, Egypt, Byzantium, the Ottoman Empire, Poland, and Lithuania. In late medieval times the south of Crimea became the major population center for the Karaites. They formed tightly-knit communities there, marrying within their own group and preserving their own language, religion, and *minhagim*.

In those places where relations between Karaites and Rabbinites were not strained by economic competition they were generally cordial. And despite rigid rabbinical prohibitions that restrained intimate relations with heretics who practiced laws that rendered the child of a remarried woman who had been divorced a *mamzer*,[36] mixed marriages were not uncommon. Ironically, this was most prevalent in Egypt, Saadia's birthplace, even among the wealthier classes.[37] Up to the late eighteenth century the Karaites of Eastern Europe were considered to be an integral part of the Jewish people. When various restrictive laws were passed against the Jews, the Karaites always shared in the suffering of the Rabbinites.

The Crimea was annexed by the Russian Empire in 1783. The Karaites constituted one of many minorities in the Crimea. Their appearance as far as the Russian invaders were concerned was hardly distinguishable from the rest of the population. Capitalizing on this fact, the Karaite leaders tried to evade subjection to the oppressive Pale of Settlement laws. Toward this end they attempted to separate themselves from the rest of the Jewish people by redefining themselves as "Russian Karaites of the Old Testament Faith." They petitioned the Czarina, Catherine the Great, requesting that they be exempted from any legislation affecting the rest of the Jews. They claimed that they were descended from a segment of the Lost Ten Tribes who had settled in the Crimea more than 2,500 years earlier. Therefore, they claimed, they could not possibly have been involved in the crucifixion of Jesus. The anti-Semitic Russian government, always seeking ways to create conflict within the Jewish community, accepted this assertion. The Karaites were given status as a separate ethnic group no longer subject to the same restrictions as the Russian Jews. They were allowed to purchase land like other Russian subjects and were exempt from paying the outrageous taxes imposed upon the Jews of Russia.[38]

During the latter part of the nineteenth century, Abraham Firkovitch (1784–1874), a Crimean Karaite scholar, traveled throughout Russia and other parts of Europe and the Middle East searching for evidence that would support his own redefinition of his people's identity, namely, that they were descended from the Turkish Khazars. He was searching for evidence that would separate the Karaites from the Jewish people and thereby carve out a privileged position for his people. Unsuccessful in his search, he resorted to forging documents and tampering with archeological artifacts in an attempt to prove that the Karaites were descended from the Khazars and not from Semitic peoples of Palestine. As originally Turkish shamanists who adopted the Jewish religion many centuries after the founding of Christianity, Firkovitch asserted, the Karaites could not possible have conspired in the crucifixion of Jesus. During World War II Firkovitch's distortion of Karaite history helped save the Karaite community from annihilation by the Nazis.

After the Russian revolution of 1917, which some Krimchaks took part in, a few Krimchaks were for the first time free to attend universities and enter the fields of medicine, law, and engineering. However, with the rise of Joseph Stalin in the 1930s, the quality of Jewish life in the Crimea markedly declined. A great Russian chauvinist (although a Georgian himself), Stalin was determined to Russify all of the Soviet Union. He accomplished this by ruthlessly suppressing ethnic groups who persisted in maintaining their cultural identities. He decreed that the Krimchaks were forbidden to read and write in the Tatar-Hebrew alphabet; they were ordered to employ only the Russian Cyrillic alphabet. Synagogues and Jewish schools were forcibly closed, and the Krimchaks were compelled to work in factories and collective farms.

When the Nazi forces invaded the Crimea in 1941, they arrived with orders to identify and round up all the Jews in the Crimea. The 67,000 Ashkenazi Jews were easily identifiable. How to deal with the Mongoloid-looking Karaites and Krimchaks was more confounding, and the *Einsatzgruppe* (Nazi Strike Commandos) requested instructions from Berlin. The officials in Berlin determined, based on their pseudoscientific research, that the Krimchaks were descended from Jews who had emigrated to the Crimea from Italy four hundred years earlier, and therefore should be annihilated. The Berlin officials were less familiar with the Karaites and inquired of three Ashkenazi Jewish scholars whether the

Karaites had Jewish origins. These Ashkenazi scholars, realizing that the fate of the Crimean Karaites was hanging on their response, supported the Karaites' view of themselves as not being racially Jewish.[39] This enabled the five-thousand-strong Karaites to survive World War II. Six thousand Krimchaks, or an estimated seventy-five percent of the entire community, were liquidated by the Nazis. Only those Krimchaks who had been evacuated to non-occupied areas in Central Asia, or had joined the Red Army, survived.

In 1944, the Stalinist regime accused all the Crimean Tatars of collaborating with the Nazis, although only some had actually done so. This accusation precipitated deportation proceedings, and all the Crimean Tatars—some 250,000—were rounded up and sent to Central Asia and Siberia. The Red Army soldiers carrying out the deportations had the same confusion as the *Einsatzgruppe* in distinguishing the Mongoloid Krimchaks from the rest of the native population. Some Krimchak houses and properties were confiscated and several hundred families were forced into exile along with the Tatars.[40] Gradually, over a period of years, only a remnant of the Jewish exiles returned to the Crimea.

After World War II, most Krimchaks were indifferent to their Jewish heritage and at the same time concerned about the stigma of being identified as a Jew, especially on their official identification papers. Taking their cue from the Karaites, these Krimchaks began to redefine their history and origins. They claimed that their ancestors were Crimean people who were converted to Judaism by Jews who had arrived on the peninsula in ancient times. They further insisted that since the Soviet Union was an atheistic country, religion should not be the basis for ethnic identification. Therefore, the Krimchaks argued, they should be recognized as an ethnic group whose identity was simply Krimchak. By the late 1950s the Krimchaks were granted their wish, and the official identification papers were stamped "Krimchak" and not "Krimchak Jews." Still, many Krimchaks chose to remain registered as "Krimchak Jews."[41]

Every year on December 11, the designated anniversary of the extermination of the Simferopol Krimchaks, many Krimchaks would gather together to commemorate the Holocaust events of 1941–42. During these gatherings the Krimchaks, who had no rabbis or cantors of their own, would hire an Ashkenazi cantor to say kaddish for them. They would all go to the site where the martyrs were buried and place wreaths on the site.

There are perhaps 2,500 Krimchaks left in what was formerly the Soviet Union. About half live in Ukraine and about a third still reside in the Crimean cities of Simferopol, Sevastopol, Kerch, and Feodosia. The rest live in the Republic of Georgia, the Central Asian Republic of Uzbekistan, Israel, and in the United States. The Krimchaks are rapidly assimilating into the larger Jewish and Gentile populations.

NOTES

1. B. Spuler, "Kirim," *Encyclopedia of Islam*, New Edition, vol. 5 (Leiden: E. J. Brill, 1986), p. 139.

2. Yuri Zarkovsky, "The Return of the Crimean Tatars," *Soviet Life* 2 (February 1990), p. 29. On the Soviet treatment of the Crimean Tatars see also Ann Sheehy, *The Crimean Tatars, Volga Germans, and Meskhetians: Soviet Treatment of Some National Minorities*, Report no 6., new and revised edition (London: Minority Rights Group, July 1973), esp. pp. 7–21. For a detailed study of the Crimea under Nazi occupation see Aleksandr M. Nekrich, *The Punished Peoples: The Deportation and Fate of Soviet Minorities at the End of the Second World War* (New York: W. W. Norton, 1978), esp. pp. 13–35.

3. According to Hakan Kirimli the commonly referred term "TatarJews" is a misnomer because among the Crimean Muslim Tatars even the ancient non-Muslim minorities, who were indistinguishable from the Crimean Muslim Tatars in almost every way except religion, were never considered to be Tatars. See *National Movements and National Identity Among Crimean Tatars (1905–1916)* (Leiden: E. J. Brill, 1996), pp. 26–37.

4. Michael Zand, et al., "Krimchaks," *Encyclopaedia Judaica Decennial Book 1983–1992* (Jerusalem: Keter Publishing House, 1994), p. 266.

5. Robert S. MacLennan, *The Black Sea Archaeological Project* (St. Paul, Min: Macalester College, 1995), p. 2.

6. Simon Dubnow, *History of the Jews: From the Roman Empire to the Early Medieval Period*, vol. 2 (New York: Thomas Yoseloff, 1968), pp. 533–534; Itzak Ben-Zvi, *The Exiled and the Redeemed* (Philadelphia: Jewish Publication Society, 1957), p. 102.

7. On the various theories of the origins and ethnic affiliations of the Khazars see Peter Golden, *Khazar Studies: An Historico-Philological Inquiry into the Origins of the Khazars*, vol. 1. Budapest: Akademiai Kiado, 1980), esp. pp. 51–57; and Kevin Alan Brook, *The Jews of Khazaria* (Northvale, NJ: Jason Aronson, 1999), pp. 1–26.

8. J. B. Bury, *A History of the Eastern Roman Empire: From the Fall of Irene to the Accession of Basil I* (New York: Russell and Russell, 1965), p. 406.

9. See "Extracts from the Book of Lands of Al-Istachri," in C. A. Macartney, *The Magyars in the Ninth Century* (Cambridge: Cambridge University Press, 1930; reprinted 1968), p. 219.

10. This translation of al-Istachri's description is cited in Arthur Koestler, *The Thirteenth Tribe: The Khazar Empire and Its Heritage* (New York: Random House, 1976), p. 53.

11. J. B. Bury, *A History*, pp. 404–405.

12. Ibn Fadlan's description is cited in D. M. Dunlop, *The History of the Jewish Khazars* (New York: Schocken Books, 1967), pp. 111–112; and Koestler, *Thirteenth Tribe*, pp. 44–45.

13. Norman Golb and Omeljian Pritsak, *Khazarian Hebrew Documents of the Tenth Century* (Ithaca, NY: Cornell University Press, 1982), pp. 26–29.

14. Golden, *Khazar Studies*, vol. 1, p. 19.

15. Dunlop, *History*, p. 250.

16. Alan W. Fisher, *A History of the Crimean Tatars* (Stanford, CA: Hoover Institute Press, 1979), pp. 64–65.

17. Raphael Goldstein, *The Krimchaks: Their Life and Origin in the Crimea* (Hebrew Union College Rabbinical Thesis, Cincinnati, 1916), p. 54.

18. Yevsai Paisach, "Krimchakis," *Sovetish Heimland* (July 1974), p. 174; V. Moskovich and B. Tukan, "The Krimchak Community: History, Culture, and Language," *Pe'Amim: Studies in the Cultural Heritage of Oriental Jewry* 14 (1982), pp. 12–13.

19. Ben-Zvi, *Exiled*, p. 106

20. Goldstein, *The Krimchaks*, p. 64.

21. "Krimchakis: Shprach un Folklore," *Sovetish Heimland* (September 1974), p. 138.

22. Zand et al., "Krimchaks," *Encyclopaedia Judaica Yearbook* 1988–89 (Jerusalem: Keter Publishing House, 1989), p. 374; Moskovich and Tukan, "Krimchak Community," p. 13.

23. Goldstein, *Krimchaks*, p. 68.

24. Max Rosenthal, "Krimchaks," *Jewish Encyclopedia*, vol. 7 (New York: Funk and Wagnalls, 1904), p. 575.

25. Rosenthal, *Krimchaks*, p. 68.

26. Goldstein, ibid., p. 50.

27. Ibid., pp. 25–26.

28. Rosenthal, "Krimchaks," p. 574.

29. Goldstein, *Krimchaks,* p. 47–49.

30. "Rebbe Chaim Chezkiyahu Medini z'tzl, Ba'al 'Sdai Chemed,'" *Dos Yidishe Vort* (March–April 1991), p. 34.

31. Leo Jung, *Men of the Spirit* (New York: Kymson Publishing Co., 1964), p. 114.

32. Samuel Kurinsky, *The Glassmakers: An Odyssey of the Jews* (New York: Hippocrene Books, 1991), p. 281.

33. Baron, *A Social and Religious History of the Jews*, vol. 5: *Religious Controls and Dissensions*, 2nd ed. (New York: Columbia University Press, 1957), pp. 240–41.

34. "Blessed are Thou, O Lord, Our God, King of the Universe, who hast not made me a woman."

35. Richard N. Frye, *The Golden Age of Persia: The Arabs in the East* (New York: Barnes and Noble Books, 1996), pp. 115–119. Zvi Ankori, *Karaites in Byzantium: The Formative Years, 970–1100.* (New York: Columbia University Press, 1959), p. 10; Martin A. Cohen, "Anan Ben David and Karaite Origins (Part II)" *The Jewish Quarterly Review* (February 1978), pp. 224–230. "Karaite attitudes were culturally reinforced by an environment which suggested that orthodoxy lay in loyalty to Scripture rather than to interpretive consensus. In Armenia and Persia, the early centers of Karaism, various Shiite groups . . . rejected the *Sunna* of oral tradition and based their way of life on the Koran as interpreted for them by a trusted *imam* (teacher)." Daniel Jeremy Silver, *A History of Judaism*, vol. 1: *From Abraham to Maimonides* (New York: Basic Books, 1974), p. 338.

36. A bastard, and therefore not permitted to enter into "the Congregation of the Lord" for ten generations. "Intermarriage with a Karaite was forbidden, because they violated the rules of forbidden marriages as interpreted by the Rabbinites, based on the laws of incest in the Bible. Their children were regarded as illegitimate as the Karaite sanctification rite at marriage was not according to law, and the *kiddushin* (marriage) was not binding. It was as if no marriage had taken place." See Reuben Kaufman, *Great Sects and Scisms in Judaism* (New York: Jonathan David, 1967), p. 41.

37. Moses M. Shulvass, *The History of the Jewish People*, vol 2: *The Early Middle Ages* (Chicago: Regnery Gateway, 1982), p. 95; Leon Nemoy, "Kafaites," *Encyclopedia of Islam*, New Edition (Leiden: E. J. Brill, 1978), p. 607.

38. Warren Green, "The Fate of the Crimean Jewish Communities: Ashkenazim, Krimchaks, and Karaites," *Jewish Social Studies* 46:3–4 (Summer–Fall 1984), p. 170.

39. Ibid., pp. 169–72. For detailed studies of the Nazi solution to the Karaite "problem" see Philip Friedman, "The Karaites Under Nazi Rule," in *On the Track of Tyranny*, edited by Max Beloff (London: Vallentine, Mitchell, 1960), pp. 97–123; Itzhak Ben-Zvi, *Exiled*, esp. pp. 158–163; Emanuela T. Semi, "The Image of the Karaites in Nazi and Vichi France Documents," *Jewish Journal of Sociology* 33:2 (December 1990), pp. 81–94. According to the evidence in Nazi documentation at Yad Vashem in Jerusalem the Karaite claim was believed to the extent that Karaites were drafted into Nazi units. See Shmuel Spector, "The Karaites in Nazi Occupied Europe as Reflected in German Documents," *Pe'Amim: Studies in the Cultural Heritage of Oriental Jewry* 29 (1986), pp. 90–108. (Hebrew)

40. Warren Green, "The Fate," p. 175.

41. Anatoly Khazanov, *The Krymchaks: A Vanishing Group in the Soviet Union*, Research Paper No. 71 (Jerusalem: The Marjorie Mayrock Center for Soviet and East European Research, The Hebrew University of Jerusalem, 1989), p. 54; Michael Zand, "Notes on the Culture of the Non-Ashkenazi Jewish Communities Under Soviet Rule," in *Jewish Culture and Identity in the Soviet Union*, edited by Ro'i and A. Beker (New York: New York University Press, 1991), pp. 398–399.

Part V

Entrance of a Carpet Shop on Maydon Square
in Tiblisi, Georgia, circa 1897

From the Land of
the Golden Fleece

BACKGROUND INFORMATION

The Great Caucasian Mountains stretch five hundred miles from the Black Sea to the Caspian Sea. Much of this majestic mountain range is heavily forested, with deep valleys and narrow ravines that are extremely difficult to traverse. There are some 150 peaks, many of them virtually inaccessible, the loftiest being the 19,000-foot snow-capped Elbrouz in Daghestan. Throughout history, "the Caucasus . . . divided Europe from Asia, West from East, [and] Christendom from Islam."[1] Northern Caucasia is made up of the republics of Daghestan, Chechnya, North Ossesia, and Kabardino-Balkaria. Southern Caucasia, also known as Transcaucasia, contains the republics of Georgia, Armenia, and Azerbaijan.

The Caucasus is one of the most polyglot regions on earth. Many cultures have met and clashed here for millennia, and the area has some of the oldest continuously settled societies in the world. Over the centuries of documented history many foreign invaders crossed the Caucasus. They came in succession: Greeks, Romans, Persians, Huns, Khazars, Seljuqs, Mongols, Ottomans, Russians, and Soviets. The Caucasus Mountains traditionally have been refuge from attacks perpetrated on the narrow coastal plains and in the valleys. These impenetrable mountains sheltered many peoples, including remnants of surviving tribal peoples.

The Transcaucasus is mostly a semitropical highland region that is rich in flora. Verdant plantations produce an abundance of cotton, tobacco, tea, corn, and fruits of all sorts, especially grapes. The area is famed for its scenic beauty, its therapeutic sulfur springs, and the pure air of its mountain regions. In premodern times this region was frequently ravaged by swamp diseases such as malaria, as well as dysentery, that decimated the population.

The Republic of Georgia is a mountainous country that lies along the Black Sea in the central-west part of Transcaucasia, and is bounded by Russia on the north, Azerbaijan to the east, Armenia to the southeast, and Turkey to the south.

W. E. D. Allen writes:

> The whole mellow land of Georgia lies before, with its fresh meadows and its lusty uplands, its bright vineyards and its sombre woods, its warm gracious sun and sudden looming storms. Georgia, like some other countries, has a colour. Ireland is green and grey. Morocco is all red. Georgia is a fine yellow gold like the white wines of Burgundy. The impression of the colour is partly of the sunlight and partly of the tincture of the soil, but also there is some property in the atmosphere, intangible and not easily described, a bouquet, almost imperceptible, which envelops and caresses, fragrant and soft, insidious.[2]

Georgia has one of the world's most ancient peoples, with a unique and rich culture. The total population of Georgia is estimated at 5,500,000, an estimated two-thirds of whom are Kartvelis, as the Georgian Christians refer to themselves. Armenians, Russians, Azerbaijanis, Persians, Ossetians, Abkhazians, Greeks, Ukrainians, Jews, and Kurds round out the more significant minorities. The capital is Tbilisi, with a population estimated at one million.

The Kartvelis are described as one of the handsomest peoples in the world, traditionally known for their hospitality, chivalrous nature, ferocity in battle, and penchant for gourmet wine. They belong to the Indo-European (Aryan) family of nations, but their language has peculiarities that distinguish it from all other tongues. Although independent, the Georgian church is in communion with the Russian Orthodox Church.

In Greek mythology Georgia is the fabulous land in which Jason and the Argonauts, with Medea's help, found the Golden Fleece. According to local Georgian tradition, Mtzkheta, one of the oldest cities in the world, was founded by the patriarch Karthlos, a great-great-grandson of Japhet, the youngest son of Noah. Another legend has it that Nimrod, the son of Cush, was killed by the Caucasian tribes at the foot of Mount Ararat after he had conquered the whole world.

The Kartvelis are very proud of the fact that their pagan ancestors were one of the first peoples to embrace Christianity. In fact, both Georgian and Armenian traditions emphasize the role played by Jews in the spread of Christianity in the region. According to legend, a wandering Jew from the city of Mtzkheta brought Jesus' Tunic Without a Seam from Golgotha. This coat, the story goes, was buried on Georgian soil, and a tall cedar tree that grew from the spot oozed a fragrant myrrh, which healed the sick. Around 332 CE, Nino, a slavegirl from Cappadocia who spoke Hebrew, originally came to Georgia to convince the Jews there of Jesus' messiahship. While she only made only slight inroads among the Jews, the "Apostle of Georgia" is supposed to have so impressed the Zoroastrian king Mirian and his consort by virtue of her miraculous healing powers that they and their subjects converted en masse to Christianity. Together with Armenia, Georgia became an outpost of Christian civilization in the Near East.

Over the course of three millenia there were successive invasions by Achaemenids, Greeks, Romans, Huns, Sasanids, Arabs, Byzantines, Seljuqs (twice), Mongols, Tartars, Safavids, Ottomans, and Russians. Georgia time and again served as a battleground and a bargaining point for the political rivalries of the mighty regional powers. As a consequence, the Georgians transformed into a battle-hardened, extremely individualistic, fervently nationalistic, and vehemently anti-authoritarian people with a strong abiding sense of family and community. "Even though caught in the middle, the Georgians managed to preserve their country's unmistakably Georgian character, an intriguing blend of East and West."[3]

The Bagratid dynasty, the fountainhead of Georgian national pride, rose to power in the early tenth century during a period when Arab domination of the region began to wane. For the purpose of prestige this succession of Georgian sovereigns perpetuated the myth of divine right to rule by virtue of being descended from the union of the biblical King David and Bathsheba. "On their arms," writes S. C. Malan, "were emblazoned the sling that served to kill Goliath, David's harp, a pair of scales as emblem of the wisdom of Solomon, a lion on which rested Solomon's throne, and our Lord's coat, with this inscription round: 'Now the coat was without seam, woven from the top throughout,' and the great martyr and champion St. George slaying the dragon. All round this coat of arms is the inscription taken from the Psalms: 'The Lord hath sworn in truth unto David, he will not turn from it; of the fruit of thy body will I set upon thy throne.'"[4]

During the eleventh century, beginning with King David the Builder (1089–1125), the unity of the country was temporarily restored, and Georgia became a center of culture and civilization. In 1184, David's great-granddaughter Tamara succeeded her father George III and ruled for twenty-eight years. During her reign, writes K. Salia, "Georgia was one of the most powerful states in the Near East, playing an important dual role in the world political arena—liberator of the eastern countries and protector of western culture."[5] Queen Tamara is considered to be the most popular of all Georgian rulers and the period of her rule is considered the Golden Age of Georgian history.

The thirteenth century witnessed successive incursions by Mongol and Turkic hordes from the Central Asian steppes. "The onslaughts of Tamerlane between 1386 and 1403 dealt blows to Georgia's economic and cultural life from which the kingdom never fully recovered. The countryside was strewn with the ruins of churches, castles, and towns, the people fled to the hills, and the once busy roads were overgrown with grass and bushes."[6]

Georgian society in medieval times was ruled by feudal lords or *patroni*, who were royalty, the nobility, and church officials. Their lands were worked by *kama*, or serfs, who were bound to the land as vassals. Interminable invasions, especially those of the Mongols and the Turks, and internecine warfare decimated the population and ruined the economy. To boost their revenues the *patroni* exploited the peasantry with exorbitant taxes and forbade them from leaving the land they tilled without first getting the *patroni*'s permission.

The Bagratid dynasts ruled feudalistically for almost a thousand years. The last Bagratid king who ruled over a united Georgia was Alexander I, who reigned from 1412 to 1443. After his death, his three sons divided the country into three small kingdoms: Karthli (Central Georgia), Imeretia (Western Georgia), and Kakhetia (Eastern Georgia). The disintegration of the Georgian monarchy was accelerated by the fall of Constantinople in 1453. Transcaucasia became a Turkish lake, and the Christian kingdoms of Armenia and Georgia were completely isolated from western Christendom. For two centuries (from the end of the sixteenth century to the late eighteenth century) Georgia was a battleground in the recurrent Turko-Persian wars. "Massacre, bloodshed, treachery, and cruelty are the staple elements of Georgia during this period, lit up at rare intervals by flashes of heroism and sublime patriotism."[7] Tens of thousands of people, including Jews, were deported to distant regions of Persia.

In spite of persecution from the Islamic invaders, the Georgian people clung tenaciously to their religion and national character. In 1783 Georgia was partitioned in half: Imeretia under Turkish rule and Kakhetia under Persian overlordship. Faced with an imminent Persian threat, the Kakhetian King Irakli II voluntarily ceded his dominions to the Christian Russians. But Catherine the Great violated her agreement with Georgia by allowing the Persians to ravage the Georgian capital, and in 1801 she annexed the war-torn country. Following the Russo-Turkish War of 1877–78, the whole of Transcaucasia was conquered by Russia and governed from Tbilisi by a Russian viceroy. It is during the period of czarist colonialization that a program of forced Russification was instituted: Industrialization accelerated, agrarian reforms were implemented, and the serfs were emancipated.

Joseph Vissarionovich Djugashvili, better known as Joseph Stalin, was born in a hovel in Gori, Georgia. Before joining the socialist underground he had studied for the priesthood in an Orthodox seminary in Tbilisi. With the triumph of the Communists in the civil war (1917–21), Stalin gathered much power. In the capacity of Commissar of Nationalities, he ruthlessly waged a campaign of violent suppression of local nationalism in the Soviet Asiatic periphery. The Red Army, with Stalin directing operations, entered Tbilisi and established a Georgian Soviet Republic in 1921. Georgia became part of the Transcaucasian Soviet Federal Socialist Republic until 1936, when it came to be called the Georgian Soviet Socialist Republic.

During the Stalinist reign of terror in the late 1930s the Generalissimo was no less harsh and brutal toward his fellow Georgians than he was in other areas of the Soviet empire. Many prominent Georgian leaders and intellectuals were liquidated. For the most part, however, the dictators and bureaucrats in Moscow tended to be more sensitive and tolerant toward the nationalistic feelings of the satellite Asiatic peoples. The political tentacles extending from Moscow did not quite squeeze the lifeblood of the Georgian people as tightly as happened in European Russia. Georgia governed itself without much interference from Moscow. After World War II, an underground laissez-faire economy thrived in Georgia, and small-scale private enterprise, if not outright legitimized, was given silent acquiescence by the local Communist apparatchiks. For this reason, Georgia was the most independent-minded of the fifteen Soviet republics, and the Georgian people had the highest standard of living of all the Soviet peoples.

THE EBRAELI OF GEORGIA

Every guest is given to us by God
No matter from which country he may be
Even if clothed in rags
God be with you, God be with you.
                    —popular Georgian song

According to local Jewish traditional belief, a segment of the Lost Ten Tribes that fled the Assyrian invasion of the Kingdom of Israel found asylum in Georgia almost 2,800 years ago. During the many centuries of living there the Jews cultivated warm, amicable relations with the Kartveli people, who considered them a loyal and constituent element within Georgian society. Until the nineteenth century Georgia was one of the few countries in the Christian world where the kind of virulent anti-Semitism that existed in places like Germany, Poland, and Ukraine was rarely experienced.

Historically, the notion of maltreating or forcibly converting the Jews was considered unbecoming of good Georgian Christians. On the contrary, etched into the collective consciousness of the Georgian masses was a sense of gratitude and an appreciation of the Jews for bringing Christianity to their soil. The Georgian Orthodox Church was relatively free of religious intolerance, and this was reflected in the deep and enduring friendships that existed between Georgian Christians and Jews. Also contributing to the absence of anti-Semitism in Georgia was the fact that the role of the universally despised moneylender was played by the Armenian Christian minority and not by Jews. It was only in the late nineteenth century, under Russian czarist instigation, that violent attacks were first perpetrated by the Georgian people against the Jews.

The Georgian Jews refer to themselves as Ebraeli. They have been such an integral and indistinguishable part of the Georgian people that, unlike Jews in so many other places in the Diaspora, they never developed a dialect of their own.[8] They studied the holy texts and prayed in Hebrew, but among themselves they spoke the same Kartveli language as their non-Jewish compatriots. Their family cognomens were virtually the same as those of non-Jews, with last names ending in "shvili" and "adze." Georgian Jewish men, like their Kartveli counterparts, tended to be tall and olive-skinned, with black hair, brown eyes, and a characteristic drooping mustache. In premodern times they wore the bullet-filled bandoleer over their shoulders and across their chests.

The Ebraeli were Georgian in every way except religion. Yet, astonishingly, researcher Yochanan Altman found that virtually all the Georgian *olim* in his study stated that in the Old Country they "would celebrate Christmas together with the Gentiles in the same way: decorating trees, buying presents, putting on fancy dress." In turn their Christian friends would partake as honorary guests at festive Jewish holidays, such as Purim and Simchat Torah.[9] Georgian Jews in Israel share a powerful nostalgia for their country of origin.[10]

In the face of antireligious indoctrination and a dearth of Jewish educational facilities under Communism, the Ebraelis' strong attachment to their ancestral faith and tradition, their rich community life, and tight extended family bonds enabled them to withstand more successfully than other Jewish communities the former Soviet Union unremitting attempts to assimilate them. Under the relatively tolerant local Communist authorities, the Ebraeli managed to retain a greater number of synagogues and *cheders* than their Ashkenazi brethren did in the western regions of the former Soviet Union.

Before the mass migration to Israel in the early 1970s, half the Ebraeli community in Georgia, or an estimated 40,000, lived in Tbilisi. Other major Ebraeli communities were situated in Kutaisi (Georgia's second largest city), Kulashi, Batumi, Sukhami, Poti, and Gori. A sizable number were scattered throughout the highland villages in Georgia. There were also some thousands of Georgian Jews residing in Armenia, Azerbaijan, and Kazakhstan. Between 1969 and 1980, a period when the Ebraeli were vociferously struggling to leave the Soviet Union, some 30,000 managed to get out, the great majority emigrating to Israel. It is estimated that today there are some 75,000 Jews in Israel whose roots are in Georgia. There are only 5,000 Ebraeli left in Georgia today.

According to Georgian and Armenian chronicles, the Jews arrived in Transcaucasia possibly as early as 722 BCE, after the Assyrian invasion of Northern Israel, or possibly with Nebuchadnezzar's exiles in 586 BCE. Whenever their exact arrival, most historians agree that there was a sizable Jewish settlement in the region at the beginning of the Common Era. When Bar Kochba carried out his rebellion against the Romans in 132 C.E., Rabbi Akiva was one of the few talmudic sages who vigorously supported the uprising. To propagate the idea of armed revolt, and to raise funds for Eretz Israel, he is said to have traveled among the Jews of the Babylonian Diaspora, including the Jewish communities of Armenia and Georgia.

From the sixth century onward, waves of Jews fleeing persecution in the Byzantine Empire found refuge in the Transcaucasus. There were also Jewish migrations from Armenia and Persia to Georgia around this time. Very little is known about Georgian Jews in the Middle Ages, or the relationship between Georgian Jewry and the Jewish kingdom of Khazaria. What is known is that Georgian Jews were the principal middlemen in trade with the Persian, the Arab, and the Byzantine world. Georgian Jewish merchants traversed the Silk Route and maintained contact with Jewish centers of learning in Persia and Babylonia. Although some Jews engaged in commerce, most survived by cultivating the land.

The Jews' fortunes took a turn for the worse with the institution of the feudal system in Georgia in the eighth century. Until that time, writes Reuben Ainsztein, "the Jews of Georgia enjoyed almost equal rights with the Christians. But the growth of a feudal system that in time virtually enslaved the peasantry and prevented the creation of a native middle class, combined with growing religious intolerance imposed by the Byzantines, led to a radical deterioration in the situation of Georgian Jewry. To escape the consequences many embraced Christianity and were given certain privileges, or fled the country."[11] During the Mongol invasions in the early thirteenth century, some Jews of eastern and southern Georgia fled to western Georgia. Their plight was greatly exacerbated after the onslaughts of Tamerlane's hordes and by the upheavals caused by the expansionist designs of the Persians and the Ottoman Turks. They were also traumatized by the feuds that raged among the Georgian elites. Their impoverished situation and increasing dependence on, and exploitation by, the *patroni* led to the Jews becoming virtual slaves of their feudal lords.

As vassals of the *patroni*, the Jewish *kama* were obligated to pay exorbitant taxes and perform the most demeaning and backbreaking tasks. They could be bought and sold at the whim of their masters, given away as gifts, or even killed. Families were broken up when some members were transferred to other estates. Young girls were sold to harems of the Muslim rulers. It should be understood that Jewish serfs were generally treated no better or worse than their Christian and Muslim counterparts, although there might have been cases where anti-Semitic Christian *patroni* abused their Jews, and there is documentary evidence that sometimes out of expediency some Jews converted to Christianity in order to escape their serfdom.[12] A Jew who converted to Christianity was given a plot of land and transformed from slave to master.

Jewish *kama* lived in small tight-knit groups on their *patroni*'s estates, separated from other Jewish communities, and were permitted to practice their religion unhindered. Because they were isolated from the outside world and from each other, and were without a religious and spiritual center, their Jewish knowledge deteriorated. Yet despite their seemingly insurmountable problems, the Ebraeli managed to persevere and retain their uniqueness.

Constant warfare and rebellion devastated entire regions of the country in the late eighteenth and early nineteenth centuries. In the highland regions this deprived many Ebraeli yeoman farmers of their property. Many of these Jews were reduced to a semi-servile condition and, consequently, many migrated to the major towns and cities. Jewish serfs who had the means were able to buy their liberation, while some of those who couldn't stealthily fled from their masters. Many of these village Jews were terribly ignorant of religious laws and customs and were condescendingly referred to by the relatively more sophisticated and urbane town Jews as "Canaanites." As a general rule, those former Jewish serfs who migrated to the towns and cities were later joined by their landsmen from the same former fiefdom. They lived in their own separate quarters and established their own synagogue and other Jewish communal institutions. As recently as the early decades of the nineteenth century, there were still a few Jews living on the estates of their feudal lords.

When the Russians first occupied the Transcaucasus in the early nineteenth century, the Ebraeli were so thoroughly integrated into local society that the Russian authorities could barely distinguish between them and the general population. At first no legal distinctions were drawn between Jews and non-Jews, and the draconian decrees promulgated by the Czar in the Pale of Settlement were rarely enforced in Georgia. Some Ashkenazi Jews began to trickle into Georgia after the Russians annexed the country. At first this element of Ashkenazim consisted mostly of artisans and peddlers who settled in the Jewish quarter of the major cities. In the late nineteenth century some Ashkenazi conscripts in the Russian army who were stationed in Georgia also settled there after they were discharged from the military. As seems to be the case wherever Ashkenazim and Sephardim established new roots in the Jewish Third World, relations with the indigenous Jews were acrimonious from day one. The Ebraeli considered the newcomers "as godless or insufficiently observant, while the Ashkenazim often looked down on the Georgian Jews."[13] The large-scale influx of these disparate Jewish groups into the overcrowded, poverty-stricken urban ghettos produced a frightening infant mortality rate and frequent epidemics.

After the autocratic Czar Nicholas I (1825–55) issued an *ukase* (decree) in 1834 that narrowed the Pale of Settlement, all the Jews of Georgia were threatened with expulsion. But the local authorities, realizing that the Jews were a vital element in commerce and agriculture, whose departure would seriously harm the economic stability of the country, prevailed upon the sympathetic local Russian commander-in-chief not to enforce the decree.

Until the nineteenth century, the contagious anti-Semitic virus, which from medieval times had afflicted Western Christendom, never incubated on Georgian soil. The stereotype of the Jew as a diabolical blasphemer and ritual murderer was an alien concept that never resonated within the Georgian people. Only after the Russian invaders arrived and began to foment hatred toward the

Jews within the Georgian population did the phenomena of blood libels take hold in Georgia. According to the *Encyclopaedia Judaica*, the anti-Semitic outbursts of the second half of the nineteenth century can be attributed to the following factors: "[T]he process of urbanization of the Jewish community and the consequent change of occupation by the majority of Jews who now chose trade as their livelihood; from the influence of Russian anti-Semitism and from turning the Jew, a weak outsider, into the object of xenophobia which could not be released against another stranger—the powerful Russian invader."[14]

This animus led to six blood libels in Georgia. The most notorious of these took place in 1878, and was known as the "Kutaisi Trial." Nine Jews from the little town of Sachkere, near Kutaisi, were accused of the ritual killing of a six-year-old Christian girl in anticipation of Passover. The trial of the Sachkere nine actually took place in Kutaisi, hence it was called the "Kutaisi Trial." This trial received much international notoriety, and the accused were defended by a number of noted Russian attorneys. Although the defendants were declared innocent of the charges, the local population remained convinced that the defendants were guilty.

In the decades leading up to the Bolshevik Revolution, a period of intensive industrialization and rapid growth, most of the Jews of the Georgian towns and cities eked out a living as peddlers and shopkeepers. Large-scale commerce was monopolized by the Armenians. In the rural and highland regions some Jews owned land and tilled the soil. Many Jews were excellent artisans and craftspeople. The wealthiest strata of Jews were heavily involved in the import-export business with Russia and the Ottomans and in the production and sale of the famous Georgian wines.

Initially, the establishment of Soviet rule did not seriously affect the Georgian-Jewish bourgeoisie. In the aftermath of New Economic Policies (NEP) promulgated by the Communists in 1921, the Soviet Union was allowed a mixed economy. The large industries were nationalized, but in commerce and small-scale industry, private enterprise prevailed. In Georgia, the production and sale of wine, a virtual Jewish monopoly, was taken over by the state. The expropriation of their industries, combined with exorbitant taxes and severe limitations imposed on small and medium-sized businesses, led to an extreme deterioration in the status of the Georgian Jews. Some suffered to the point of starvation. Thousands migrated to Palestine, Europe, and Istanbul, Turkey, where a Georgian-Jewish community existed from the late nineteenth century.

Attempts by the Communist authorities to forcibly involve the stiff-necked Jews in *kolkhozes* (collective farms) and factory assembly line work did not succeed. An effort was made in 1928 to settle some Georgian-Jewish communities in the so-called Jewish Autonomous Region of Birobidjan, and in the areas of the Crimea designated for Jewish agricultural settlement. These efforts also resulted in fiasco. Communist attempts to eradicate Judaism by the forced merging of Jewish collective farms with non-Jewish farms resulted in a mass desertion by the Jewish farmers. These resettled Jews who deserted the collective farms migrated back to the Georgian cities and towns, where under the auspices of "artisans cooperatives" many established legitimate employment. Many others resorted to smuggling, black-marketeering, and the petty trades. Of the eight Georgian-Jewish *kolkhozes* established in 1930, only Tziteli-Gora survived until the 1970s.

Because religion was considered ideologically incompatible with the Marxist state, a campaign to secularize the Georgian Jews was intensified in the mid 1920s. A network of schools, camps, and clubs was established to inculcate the youth with atheistic communism. During the purges of 1937–38, the most repressive period of Stalin's dictatorship, the authorities clamped down on Georgian-Jewish culture. *Chedarim* and *yeshivot* were liquidated. A number of leading rabbis and Zionists, accused of being "imperialist agents," were exiled to Siberia or thrown in jail and murdered without a trial.

In 1933, the Communist authorities, desiring to create a Soviet Georgian-Jewish culture along the lines of a Soviet-Yiddish culture, established the Historical and Ethnographic Museum of Georgian Jewry in Tbilisi. By 1941, this museum had managed to assemble over 4,000 books and pamphlets and hundreds of files of documents and photographs on the life of Georgian Jewry. The Communist authorities wanted to relegate the Georgian-Jewish culture and religion to the status of a cultural relic that needed to be preserved in a museum. To the Georgian Jews their religion was the fabric of their existence and not something to be placed in a glass case. During the Stalinist repression of the late 1940s the museum was shut down, the curator arrested, and the bulk of the material destroyed.

The Georgian Jews kept alive their collective Jewish identity throughout the period of Stalinist repression and beyond, more than did their Ashkenazi coreligionists in the former U.S.S.R. This is attributed to four broad factors: the community's fervent orthodoxy and religious Zionism; the tight-woven patriarchal nature of the Georgian-Jewish extended family; community solidarity and loyalty; and, last but not least, the tolerant, humane, and relaxed attitudes of the local Georgian authorities, who often nodded approvingly at underground Jewish communal and educational activity. The following is an example of their determination to preserve their Ebraeli identity.

In 1928 a fire broke out in the tightly clustered Jewish quarter in Kutaisi. Because the fire department did not arrive on the scene fast enough, scores of people burned to death, hundreds were injured, hundreds of homes burned, and more than 6,000 people were left homeless. Instead of trying to salvage their own possessions, the Jews, at great risk to themselves, rushed into the synagogue to retrieve the holy books and artifacts. A Georgian Red Cross mission arrived to set up a kitchen, but the Jews refused to touch the food unless their rabbis were allowed to render the food kosher. An argument broke out, and the Jews declared they would rather starve than eat nonkosher food. In the end, the Jewish side prevailed, and the rabbis were allowed to ritually slaughter the animals. Because a portion of the synagogue had been destroyed in the fire, the authorities decided that it was necessary to demolish the synagogue so as not to "endanger public safety." Their intention was to raze the synagogue to make room for a modern gymnasium. In an act of stubborn defiance the Jews lay down in front of the synagogue and vowed that their holy sanctuary would be destroyed only over their dead bodies. A delegation was sent to Moscow to get permission to restore the synagogue. After a year of intense lobbying, Moscow officials granted their request. The entire Jewish community donated money and energy, and the synagogue was restored.[15]

During the early 1950s, the period coinciding with the notorious Doctors' Plot and Stalin's paranoia about an anti-Soviet conspiracy of world Jewry, many Jews all over the Soviet Union, including Georgia, were rounded up and jailed. Prayerbooks and Judaic literature were confiscated and synagogues were closed. "The closure of synagogues was usually accompanied by plundering as well. Upon the clear instigation of local authorities, hired thugs would burst into synagogues, smash the premises, tear up books, damage and break valuable religious articles and throw them into the street."[16] However, when the authorities prepared to expropriate the synagogue in Kutaisi, the entire Jewish community, some 20,000 strong, organized a mass sit-in and vowed mass suicide. The authorities relented.

The following vignettes illustrate some of the unique folkways of the Georgian Jews, especially as they were practiced before the onset of Bolshevism in Transcaucasia.

In traditional Georgian-Jewish society the patriarchal family structure maintained and transmitted Jewish values and insulated its members from assimilation. As in the dominant culture, the social unit was the joint family. All the married brothers and their aged parents lived together in a house, with each married couple of the *didi-ojakhi* (joint family) maintaining a separate space or room in the house. Members of the family often numbered up to one hundred.

Each clan was led by the oldest male, whose authority was never questioned. He not only functioned in a supervisorial and judicial capacity, he was also the spiritual head of the clan.[17] The entire clan would eat together on the Sabbath and holidays. In recent times even Georgian-Jewish Communists observed the Sabbath. Most attended synagogue services and circumcised their children.[18]

Among the Ebraeli it was customary for the parents or relatives to arrange a match for their children. The family of the bride was interested not only in receiving the *gatzvila* (bride-price) from the prospective bridegroom, but also in the personality of the groom and the possible advantage of the union for the entire clan. The betrothal was consummated when the parents of the bride received a coin from the parents of the groom. After the bride-price was paid by the groom, the bride was regarded as his possession. The young couple did not actually see each other until the nuptial day.

A novel feature of the Georgian wedding was the role of the *dadiani*. When the procession reached the house of the parents of the groom, they were greeted by the *shoshbini*, the groom's best man, and the *dadiani*. The *dadiani* was chosen from among the middle-aged female relatives of the bride. To qualify as a *dadiani*, the woman had to be healthy and have healthy children. The *dadiani* represented the symbol of the future prolific life of the married couple. She was attired in a tall silk hat and offered to the newlyweds two cups, one with yogurt and the other with sugar and eggs. She gave the cup of yogurt to the bride, who would eat some of it and then smear the rest on the arch of the door. This was done to bring joy and happiness into the house. Afterwards, the *dadiani* offered to the bride and groom the cup containing sugar and eggs, saying to them: "May your life be fertile and sweet." The bride's female entourage would greet her with baskets of sweets, rice mixed with raisins, and loaves of *puani* (yeasted bread).

The actual wedding ceremony could take place at home or in the synagogue. The *shoshbini* and the *dadiani* stood beside the couple to guard against the shenanigans of the evil spirits. Among the Ebraeli the bridegroom's prayer shawl served as a *chuppah*. After reading the *ketubah* (marriage contract), the bridegroom would recite the Hebrew verse "If I Forget Thee, O Jerusalem," and sprinkle drops of wine on the floor with each word. All those present would try to taste the drops—as a guarantee of good luck. After smashing the glass on the floor, "a kind of contest was held between bride and groom, each trying to tread on the other's foot. It was believed that the one who won would be the ruler of the family."[19]

During the first week after the wedding, no one but the *dadiani* was permitted to visit the new bride. For seven days after the wedding the *shoshbini* would escort the groom to the synagogue. The groom was not permitted to be seen in public without his *shoshbini*. On the Sabbath after the wedding, the *shoshbini* would invite all the groom's relatives and friends to the synagogue. When the groom was called up to the Torah, the congregants would hurl raisins and candies at him. Wedding festivities usually lasted up to two weeks.

The belief in *batonabi* (evil spirits) attacking the woman in childbed and her newborn baby prevailed among Jews and Gentiles alike in Georgia.[20] *Devebi* (ogres), *k'ajebi* (goblins), and *sudi angeluzi* (ghosts) were feared and had to be appeased. *Shmatzui* or wise men were called upon to divine, tell fortunes, and write amulets. They were believed capable of psychically curing skin ailments and broken bones, and were expert in the use of herbs. *Kudiani*, or witches, were employed to cast spells against one's nemeses or to bring good luck. Amulets were worn on the body underneath the clothes, hidden in a baby's cradle or under the pillow of a woman who was giving birth, or hung from the wall. Amulets that came from the Holy Land were supposed to be especially effective.

During her pregnancy a woman was especially vulnerable to the pernicious influences of *batonabi*. To protect herself, she would always carry on her body an amulet containing special herbs, charcoals, and sulfur which was tied to a ribbon. On Erev Yom Kippur, in addition to the obligatory hen, two eggs were twirled over the head of a pregnant woman.

A birth always took place at the mother's parents' house. Her mother would care for her and her child for thirty days. When a woman was giving birth, no one was allowed to enter the house. The door and windows were locked up and covered with a thick cloth. At the time of birth, a candle was lit to expel the evil spirits. A *nali*, or horseshoe-shaped amulet, was hung on the wall, a dagger with a black handle was placed under the foot of the bed, and the Book of Psalms was placed on the side of the bed. If the birthing was difficult, they would call upon an old midwife who would throw three eggs on the wall and say: "With the same ease that these eggs were broken, you will bring a child into the world." The husband might be called upon to assist his wife. He would pour water into the pocket of his jacket and his wife would drink the water. The belief was that in this way he could pass his strength on to her. "The placenta [was] regarded as unclean and possessing supernatural powers, and therefore [was] buried in a place where no human being or animal could disturb or tread upon it."[21]

After giving birth, the mother was fed a special diet, which included dairy products but no meat for the entire year. After giving birth, the mother stayed in bed for a week. She was considered unclean for forty days after giving birth to a boy and sixty days after giving birth to a girl. After this period, she would go to the *mikvah* and then to the synagogue, circling it three times and kissing the walls. If she saw a dog, cat, or pig, she would have to wash a second time.

She would visit friends and relatives, and the hosts would serve her three nuts to increase her milk, three slices of bread so that her belly would swell up like yeast, and three glasses of wine so that the next baby would be as strong as wine.

Children's diseases such as measles, mumps, and chickenpox were a sign that the *batonabi* had come to dwell in the house. They had to be appeased to induce them to leave. Because, according to folk belief, the *batonabi* have a predilection for the color red, the room was decorated with red pieces of cloth. It was forbidden to enrage the *batonabi*. Anyone who entered the sick child's house asked the family members for forgiveness, but would never ask about the child's well-being. One never raised one's voice around a sick child. During the illness it was forbidden for family members to do laundry, slaughter chickens, or fry meat. Radishes and hot spices were also eschewed. It was an inauspicious time for family members to attend a wedding or a party. To placate the *batonabi*, an old woman called a *motzamluli* would come to the house of the sick child in the morning with flowers and water. Accompanying herself on bagpipes she would sing:

> Oh *batonabi*, you were sent by God
> Lord of the Roses
> In May the rose will bloom
> In June the wheat will ripen
> Oh *batonabi*, I beseech you to listen carefully
> In the house of the child's mother
> The Rose is blooming
> Lord of the Roses
> A golden cradle is standing
> Masters of the Roses
> Singing to him sleep, sleep
> Masters of the Roses
> Sleep, sleep, oh prince
> Masters of the Roses

The *motzamluli* would continue:

> I will sacrifice myself to you, oh *batonabi*
> I bring you a bouquet of cyclamens and roses
> Rise and stroll around the fields
> And the person that you have chosen to visit
> Leave him in our hands
> Go away, I will escort you to the door

Then motioning to the door she would sing:

> Here is the meadow, the cyclamens, the roses,
> the water, the granary
> I will sacrifice myself to you, oh *batonabi*.

If the *batonabi* were especially angry, the *motzamluli* would get down on her knees and ask the *batonabi* forgiveness and plead with them not to harm the sick child: "Instead of this child, please accept another live creature." A chick, lamb, or calf was sacrificed, and with a portion of the meat the *motzamluli* would circle the sick child's bed. At this point, if the child did not recover, the *motzamluli* would take colorful pieces of cloth, cakes, coins, nuts, colored eggs, flowers, and sweetmeats and cast them in a desolate place. This was designed to distract the *batonabi* or divert their attention. Friends and relatives who came to visit the child were obligated to bring a gift, such as a toy or candy. When the child recovered from the illness, he or she was given a bath in water mixed with sugar and flowers. But if the child died, they did not mourn in the house, for to do so would enrage the *batonabi*. They would leave the house singing and dancing.

Communal activities, profane as well as religious, invariably centered around the synagogue. The synagogue was headed by the *robi* (*chacham*) who fulfilled the role of religious leader, cantor, *mohel*, and ritual slaughterer. Before the Communist takeover of Georgia, some *robis* were trained in the seminaries in Lithuania, Turkey, and Jerusalem. Most *hakhamim* were not ordained and not very proficient in Talmud and *halakha*. Nevertheless, the *robi* was the ultimate authority, and his authority had a great impact on the whole life of the community.

With the arrival in the 1890s of Rabbi Avraham Halevy Khovoles, a *sheliach* of the renowned talmudist Rabbi Isaac Elchanan Specktor of Kovno, the Ashkenazi (Litvak) mode of pedagogy was instituted. Because the rabbi did not speak Georgian and the students did not understand Yiddish, his *shiurim* (talmudic discourses) were delivered in Hebrew. Despite opposition from some of the old guard *robis*, Khovoles not only established *chedarim* and *yeshivot* for young men but also brought in an educator to instruct girls in Hebrew. The Lubavitcher Chassidic movement also exerted considerable influence on the Georgian-Jewish community. Chabad rabbis began to carry on religious activities in the early 1920s and won many followers. Despite the danger involved, Chabad maintained a network of *chedarim* and the intrepid Chabad rabbis preached in the synagogues. Nevertheless, the overall level of learning and religious life of the great majority of Georgian Jewry was basic and unsophisticated.

The Georgian Jews are the only community in the former Soviet Union, besides the Bukharan Jews of Central Asia, who did not sustain significant losses during the Holocaust. The Nazi divisions pressing toward the oilfields of Baku, Azerbaijan, in the summer of 1942 never reached Georgia. Many Eastern European Jews fleeing Nazi-occupied territories found temporary asylum in Georgia. The encounter with Ashkenazi Jews did much to stimulate the national awareness of the isolated Georgian Jews.

The Ebraeli began to make *aliyah* in the mid-nineteenth century, and already by 1863 there was a Georgian-Jewish enclave in the Old City of Jerusalem. After the establishment of the State of Israel, many Ebraeli desired to make *aliyah*, but the Communist authorities refused to issue exit visas. After the Six Day War in 1967, the Georgian Jews spearheaded a nationalistic and Zionistic revival among Soviet Jewry by demanding to be allowed to leave. The strong Zionist commitment of Georgian Jewry was remarkable, considering that the Jews were relatively well-to-do in Georgia at this time, and were experiencing considerably less anti-Semitism than Jews anywhere else in the Soviet Union.

"It is a quirk of history," writes Leonard Schroeter, "that one of the most remote and least educated segments of Soviet Jewry should have captured the imagination of their fellow Jews and forced the government to some action. . . . "[22] On August 6, 1969 eighteen Georgian Jewish families addressed a letter to the United Nations Human Rights Commission, via the Dutch Embassy in Moscow, pleading for help in pressuring the Soviet authorities to allow emigration to Israel. This letter had a dramatic effect because it received wide publicity. Israeli Prime Minister Golda Meir tearfully read the letter aloud in the Knesset and described it as Zionism's most significant document. International pressure was exerted on the Soviet Union, and the Georgian families were granted permission to leave for Israel.[23] The process of a mass Georgian-Jewish *aliyah* was accelerated after a number of young Georgian Jews staged a sit-in demonstration in a central Moscow post office in 1970. As a result, thousands of Georgian Jews were given exit visas. These daring actions inspired the launching of the refusenik movement in other parts of the former U.S.S.R.

There were two groups of Georgian Jews affected by the authority's liberal emigration policy. The first people were blue-collar workers whom the government had no vested interest in retaining. The second group was made up of a hodgepodge of *luftmentchen* (people with no visible means of income), smugglers, and black ("free") marketeers, elements that Moscow prosecuted more aggressively than the non-Jewish population and was only too glad to be rid of because they were perceived to be undermining the strictures of the socialist state. During the various campaigns to root out economic crimes in the 1960s, only Jews were given the death penalty.[24]

The great preponderance of Georgian Jews who made *aliyah* in the 1960s and 1970s came from the smaller towns and villages. Few educated urbanites came during this period. Entire extended families and compatriots from the old hometown settled in Georgian enclaves in Ashdod, Ashkelon, and some smaller towns such as Kiryat Gat. In Israel the Ebraeli are referred to as Gruzinim. Considered hot-headed primitives, lawless and clannish, they were treated disdainfully by veteran Israelis because of the continuous involvement of a minority of Gruzinim in shady, underworld activities and group violence.[25] Gruzini criminality and hooliganism would become a "special police problem,"[26] and a popular expression among Israelis in the late 1970s had it that "the knife has passed from Moroccans to Georgians."[27]

For their part, the Gruzinim, most of whom came to Israel for religio-Zionist reasons, found many aspects of Israeli life alienating and undermining of their traditional way of life. They decried the immodesty of the modern Israeli woman, the disrespectful way that Israeli youngsters interact with adults and authority figures, and the fact that most Jews living in the Holy Land are *chilonim* (secularists) who don't eat kosher and who desecrate the Sabbath.[28]

During the civil strife in Georgia in the wake of the dismemberment of the former U.S.S.R. and the multiparty elections of 1990, many Jews once again resolved to leave their ancient adopted land. The organized Jewish community stood on the sidelines during the struggle engulfing President Zviad Gamsakurdia and his rivals before the former was ousted from power. Although generally opposed to Gamsakurdia and his dictatorial ways, the Jews were plainly worried about the consequences of appearing to take sides in a sharply polarized and repressive political climate. The volatile political situation, combined with a plummeting standard of living and skyrocketing crime, including kidnappings, is forcing many middle-class urban Georgian Jews to seek emigration abroad, and not necessarily only to Israel.

From the period marking the dissolution of the Soviet empire up to the present time (1999), some 15,000 Jews have emigrated from Georgia, a sizable number settling in the United States and Western Europe. For most of the Georgian Jews the world over, religion continues to play an important role in their lives. They continue to observe the religious laws, pray in the synagogue, and, unlike the Ashkenazi Jews of the former Soviet Union, have not married outside the faith in any significant number.

NOTES

1. Fitzroy Maclean, *To Caucasus, the End of All the Earth: An Illustrated Companion to the Caucasus and Transcaucasia* (Boston: Little, Brown, 1976), p. 11.

2. W. E. D. Allen, *A History of the Georgian People.* (London: K. Paul Trench, Trubner & Co., 1932), p. 3.

3. Darra Goldstein, *The Georgian Feast: The Vibrant Culture and Savory Food of the Republic of Georgia* (San Francisco: HarperCollins, 1993), p. xviii.

4. *A Short History of the Georgian Church* (London: Saunders, Otley and Co., 1836), p. 15.

5. K. Salia, "Outline of the History of Georgia," in *Georgia: An Introduction*, vol. 3, edited by Nino Salia (Paris: Bedi Kartlisa, 1975), p. 38.

6. David M. Lang, *The Last Years of the Georgian Monarchy 1658–1832* (New York: Columbia University Press, 1957), pp. 10–11.

7. Luigi Villari, *Fire and Sword in the Caucasus* (London: T. Fisher Unwin, 1906), p. 29.

8. According to Israeli researchers Wolf Moskovich and Gershon Ben-Oren, Ebraeli merchants and peddlers spoke an "argot" that incorporated many Hebrew, Aramaic, Persian, and Turkish words. In some places where the Ebraeli interacted with the Ashkenazim, Yiddish words and expressions were interjected in order to make the language incomprehensible to the non-Jewish population. See "The Hebrew-Aramaic and Georgian Components in the Spoken Language of Georgian Jews," *Proceedings of the Eighth World Congress of Jewish Studies* (Jerusalem: World Union of Jewish Studies, 1982), pp. 19–21.

9. *A Reconstruction, Using Anthropological Methods, of the Second Economy of Soviet Georgia* (unpublished dissertation, Middlesex Polytechnic, 1983), pp. 3–5.

10. Wendy Orent, *The Panther's Skin: The Politics of Identity Among the Georgian Jews in Israel* (unpublished dissertation, University of Michigan, 1986), pp. 61–62.

11. "The Long March of Georgian Jewry" *Jewish Observer and Middle East Review* 21:46 (17 November 1972), p. 19.

12. Michael Zand, "Georgia," *Encyclopaedia Judaica Yearbook 1988/89* (Jerusalem: Keter, 1989), p. 270.

13. Ibid., p. 271.

14. Ibid.

15. Bension Yakobishvili, "Georgian Jewish Culture," in *Jewish Culture in the Soviet Union*, edited by Z. Tartakover and A. Kolitz (Jerusalem, Cultural Department of the World Jewish Congress, 1973), p. 131; Mordechai Altshuler, "Georgian Jewish Culture Under the Soviet Regime," *Soviet Jewish Affairs* 5:2 (1975), p. 27.

16. Lily Baazova, et al., "Georgia: The Land and the Jews," *Ariel* 96 (1994), p. 23.

17. Alexander Grigolia, *Custom and Justice in the Caucasus: The Georgian Highlanders* (unpublished dissertation, University of Pennsylvania, 1939), pp. 60–62.

18. Benjamin Pinkus, *The Soviet Government and the Jews, 1948–67* (London: Cambridge University Press, 1984), p. 444.

19. Rachel Arbel and Lily Magel, *In the Land of the Golden Fleece: The Jews of Georgia: History and Culture* (Tel Aviv: Beth Hatfutsoth, 1992), pp. 121–22.

20. Folk beliefs relating to the Georgian Jewish lifecycle are liberally drawn from *In the Land of the Golden Fleece,* pp. 102–114, with permission from Rachel Arbel.

21. Grigolia, *Custom and Justice,* p. 96.

22. *The Last Exodus* (New York: Universe Books, 1974), p. 130.

23. For in-depth accounts of the Georgian-Jewish *samizdat* see Leonard Schroeter, "The Origins of the Georgian Aliya," *Midstream* 20:5 (May 1974), pp. 63–67; and Schroeter, *The Last Exodus,* esp. pp. 122–130. See also Mark Kipnis, "The Georgian National Movement: Problems and Trends," *Crossroads* (Autumn 1978), pp. 193–215.

24. Altman, *A Reconstruction,* pp. 3–14.

25. Gila Noam, Introduction to Yitzchak Elam, *Georgian Immigrants in Israel: Anthropological Observations* (Jerusalem: The Hebrew University, 1980), p. b; Ruth Seligman, "Israel's Georgian Jews: Combating the Stereotypes," *Hadassah Magazine,* 63:7 (March 1981), p. 9; Zvi Gitelman, *Political Resocialization of Soviet and American Immigrants* (New York: Praeger, 1982), pp. 159–162.

26. Menachem Amir, "Georgian Jews from the U.S.S.R.: Problems of Criminality and Adaptation to Israeli Society," *Crossroads* 14 (1985), p. 58. "They are portrayed as self-isolated and separated, violent, tough, cunning, with a strong penchant toward corruption, and as tending to operate as a tightly cohesive group in legitimate enterprises as well as in crime." See Menachim Amir, "Organized Crime and Organized Criminality Among Georgian Jews in Israel," in *Organized Crime: A Global Perspective,* edited by Robert J. Kelly (Totowa, N.J.: Rowman and Littlefield Publishers, 1986), pp. 173–74.

27. Yitzchak Elam, "Use of Force Among Moroccan and Georgian Immigrants to Israel," in *The Soviet Man in an Open Society,* edited by Tamar Horowitz (New York: University Press of America, 1989), pp. 323–47.

28. Wendy Orent, *The Panther's Skin,* p. 61.

Part VI

Three Mountain Jews of Daghestan
Credit: Yad Ben Zvi Archives

Samson Warriors, Bar Kochba's Heirs

BACKGROUND INFORMATION

The Daghestan Autonomous Republic of the Russian Federation is situated in the far eastern reaches of the Caucasian chain. It is bounded on the east by the Caspian Sea and on the north by the Kuma River. Daghestan, meaning "land of mountains" in Turkish, is one of the most ethnically heterogeneous countries in the world with thirty-two nationalities and a population estimated at one and three-quarters of a million. The republic's chief cities are its capital Makhachkala, Derbent, Kislyar, Izerbash, and Buynaksk. Some of the major ethnic groups inhabiting the highlands are the Avars, Darghins, Lakhs, and Lezghians. The Daghestanis are overwhelmingly Sunni Muslims of the Shafi'a school of jurisprudence. Most Daghestanis speak a Turkish dialect, although Arabic traditionally served as the important literary language.

"From antiquity," writes Theodore Shabad, "the Daghestani littoral of the Caspian Sea has furnished invasion routes for successive waves of migration from Asia to Europe. Segments of each migrating generation generally remained within the region and moved into the inaccessible mountains to escape the ravages of subsequent migration. As a result of this type of settlement the mountains have always had a denser population pattern than the coastal plain."[1]

In the third century C.E. Daghestan fell under Persian dominion. From the fourth century, an assortment of Turkish and Mongolian tribes from the Central Asiatic steppes continually overran Daghestan. By the time the Arabs penetrated the mountains in 642 C.E., there were religious communities of Zoroastrians, Jews, and Christians, in addition to the local animists. The establishment of the hegemony of Islam was a slow and difficult process. The eighth and early ninth centuries were a period of intense competition between the Arabs and the Jewish Khazars for control of this region.

The Mongol armies who conquered the Caucasus in the thirteenth century were composed primarily of Turkish soldiers who eventually settled in the region. It was their influence that made the most profound and lasting impact on Daghestani culture. For the next three centuries Daghestan became the object of intense rivalry between the Persians and the Ottoman Turks. Even though nominally subject to foreign rulers, the fierce, freedom-loving Daghestani tribespeople always retained an independent character.

With the Russian colonialization of the North Caucasus region beginning in 1820, the czar forced resettlement of the large populations of Daghestani and Chechen mountain peoples to the plains. He felt that in this way he could more easily control these heretofore unconquered mountain people. Hundreds of thousands of Daghestani Muslims fled to the Ottoman Empire. After the Communists came to power in Russia in 1917, the Caucasians carried out a wave of insurrections against their Bolshevik oppressors. Motivated by the rich oil and mineral deposits of the Caucasus, the Communist rulers ordered Red Army expeditions to squelch all resistance. This was done brutally. By the mid-1920s the entire Caucasus was finally taken over by the Communists.

The Daghestani tribespeople traditionally were engaged in animal husbandry, cultivating fields, and the handicrafts. In pre-czarist times Daghestani society was divided into principalities and ruled by feudal lords called *beks*. These principalities were based on voluntary alliances, not on formal structure of kinship or territorial claims.[2] Daghestani tribes were organized into strictly endogamous patriarchal clans, with cousin marriage being the preferred marriage pattern. The clans were comprised of extended families, with up to one hundred persons recognizing common ancestry. They lived together in one or more houses headed by the *baba* (patriarch and ultimate authority of the clan), who was the family representative to the outside world. Property was communally owned. When the patriarch died, each son set up an independent household with his own sons and grandchildren.

Like all inhabitants of the Caucasus, the Daghestani mountaineers were known as a fierce fighting people of great physical strength and endurance. They were superb horsemen who dressed in the Circassian mode of attire and habitually carried swords and pistols. "Boys are encouraged to develop into great warriors and robbers," writes Alexander Grigolia. "Robbery and raiding are looked upon by the North Caucasians not only as a licit occupation (as long as the victim is a stranger), but a very honorable one. Robbery is a . . . national virtue . . . [and] crime is glorified."[3]

The ancient tradition of *qan-alma* (vendetta) was practiced by all the mountain tribespeople of Daghestan, including the Jews. Life was considered precious, and blood was sacred. The mountaineers swore that he whose blood had been spilled must be avenged, and believed that the ghost of the victim restlessly hovered over the house of the living until it found peace. "Manslaughter," writes Czeslawa Kulesza, "was punished with a bloody revenge which sometimes implied full extermination of the family up to the seventh generation. Mothers were telling their children about the necessity to revenge their family's harms from their infancy. Sometimes when a whole family was destroyed, the revenge was taken over by friends."[4]

Because blood feuds could potentially last for generations, among different tribes a number of rituals evolved to halt the possible "Beirutization" of Caucasian society. According to anthropologist Sula Benet, "If a murderer desired reconciliation with the family of his victim, he could hide near their homestead until the appropriate moment and then run forward and put his mouth to the breast of the 'old woman' of the clan, thereby signaling his desire to become a milk relative and to end the hostilities. Then no one would be permitted to touch him, since milk relations were considered even stronger than blood relations. Marriages between the two warring clans could also bring about a truce. Thus, family solidarity both created the problem of the blood feud and provided for its solution."[5]

The people of the Caucasus are reputed to have the largest number of long-living people in the world. According to Benet, many Caucasian men and women live to the proverbial 120, and cases have been recorded of people as old as 135. This is attributed to a combination of factors: the hardy, fresh alpine mountain air, moderate intake of food and drink, sexual self-discipline and moderation, the skillful use of natural elixirs derived from hundreds of native nontoxic plant remedies, therapeutic hot mud and sea baths, and an overall *joie de vivre*.

Like other Caucasians, the Daghestanis are the most scrupulous observers of the laws of hospitality. A guest is considered sacred: When a Daghestani receives someone as his guest, the latter may entrust his life to his host's hands. They were and still are among the most deeply religious of all Islamic peoples, and constituted the least socially modern and least Sovietized of all the various Russified peoples of the former U.S.S.R.

THE MOUNTAIN JEWS OF DAGHESTAN

And we, the Tats
we, Samson warriors,
Bar Kochba's heirs . . .
we went into battles
and bitterly, heroically
struggled for our freedom.
—from *The Song of the Mountain Jews*

One of the most fascinating, but little-known, Jewish tribes is the so-called Mountain Jews of Daghestan. No one has been able to establish definitively the origins of this community. Living isolated in one of the most remote, impenetrable areas in the world for many centuries, they devolved into a fierce, illiterate, extremely superstitious people, similar to other mountain tribes in the region. They knew little of the Talmud and the customs that were universally accepted in normative Judaism. They did not even know of the existence of the Jews of Europe prior to the Russian conquest of North Caucasus in the early nineteenth century. Driven from their mountain enclaves (together with their Muslim compatriots) by the Russian colonizers, many settled along the coast in cities such as Makhachkala, Kuba, and Derbent. There they first encountered Ashkenazi Jews from the Pale of Settlement who had been given permission by the czarist government to settle in the area. Links soon were established with the major religious centers of Ashkenazi Jewry, and the religious life of the Mountain Jews was brought into greater uniformity with normative Jewry.

In dress and custom the Mountain Jews were hardly distinguishable from other Caucasian fighting peoples in the region. In contrast with their coreligionists in the Pale of Settlement, the Jews of Daghestan were traditionally a rural people who, despite their *dhimmi* status, were permitted to own land. And, in striking contrast to their brethren to the west, these sinewy, graceful, and elastic Jewish "Cossacks" were a fierce, bellicose tribe who would not hesitate for one moment to defend, by sword or the rifle, their family, religion, or personal dignity.

In addition to religious differences, the Mountain Jews were distinguishable from other Daghestanis by the language they spoke. The Jews did not employ the Turkish-based national tongue of their neighbors. They spoke among themselves a neo-Iranian dialect interspersed with Hebrew and Turkish loanwords. Judeo-Tat or Juhuri is written in Rashi script. As the language is based on Persian elements, Persia is the tribe's most likely geographical origin. Scholars speculate that the Mountain Jews originally migrated to the lowlands of southern Caucasia from Persia, where they had lived long enough to acquire local customs and the Tat dialect.

During the Middle Ages the Derbent region of Daghestan was known as Cufut-Dagh, or "Mountain of the Jews." This might indicate the aboriginality of the Jews in this region, and suggests that they were numerous at one time.[6] According to their own traditions, the Mountain Jews were led or pushed into this region by the conquering Assyrians or Babylonians. The fact that there were no *kohanim* or *leviyim* among them might affirm descent from the remnants of the Lost Ten Tribes of the Assyrian exile. However, real evidence of Jewish colonies in the Caucasus is traceable only to 80 B.C.E. when the Armenian king, Tigran the Great, invaded Palestine and brought back to the Caucasus a large number of his Jewish captives. The Talmud mentions the existence of a Jewish community in Derbent, and some prominent talmudic sages are known to have either come from or established *yeshivot* in Derbent and other cities in the North Caucasus.

It is possible that the Mountain Jews are descendants of Persian-Jewish soldiers who were stationed in the Caucasus by the Sasanian kings in the fifth or sixth century to protect the area from the onslaughts of the Huns and other nomadic invaders from the east.[7] Under the impact of the invading Turkic hordes, later generations of Jewish inhabitants of the Caucasian lowlands were forced to migrate even further north to Daghestan. Eldad Hadani, the Jewish traveler who visited this region in the late ninth century C.E., mentioned that the Jews of the Caucasian mountains lived harmoniously among neighbors who worshipped fire and married their mothers, daughters, and sisters.[8] According to an Arabic contemporary of Eldad, the Jews were ruled by their own "supreme ruler."[9] These sources, in addition to evidence that a Persian king transplanted 50,000 Caucasian-Jewish families to Persia in the fourth century, indicates that Judaism flourished in the Caucasus before the hegemony of Islam.

The Khazars, after settling in the Caucasus in the seventh century, played a dominant political role in the region for almost three hundred years. Some historians believe that the Jews of the Caucasus introduced Judaism into the kingdom of the Khazars in the eighth century. The Khazar period is considered the Golden Age of Caucasian Jewry. Jews fleeing persecution in Byzantium and the Islamic world found refuge there. After the Russian Vikings overran Khazaria in 969 C.E., and after its total annihilation by the Mongol armies around 1225 C.E., surviving Khazars and other Jews fled to the mountains of Daghestan. There, living under Muslim patronage, the Jews were subject to the *dhimmi* laws and were required to pay a poll tax to the Muslim tribal heads.

A thirteenth-century European eyewitness who traveled in the Caucasus wrote that Jews were numerous in Derbent.[10] Toward the latter part of the sixteenth century many Daghestani Jews descended from their mountain fortresses and established Jewish settlements in the lower valleys and coastal cities, especially in Derbent and Kuba. For a brief period the Jews experienced a cultural renaissance of sorts. Among their luminaries were Elisha ben Shmuel, a great poet and grammarian who wrote in Hebrew, and Gershon Lala ben Moshe Nagdi, a scholar who wrote a commentary on Maimonides' *Mishneh Torah*.

The deterioration of Mountain Jewish life in Daghestan coincides with the period of the early Russian intrusions into the region in the eighteenth century. The Jews suffered immeasurably because of the struggles between the Russians, Persians, Ottomans, and local Islamic rulers. They were also the victims of incessant brutalities meted out by Islamic fundamentalists. Entire Jewish villages along the coast were decimated, and many Jews were forcibly converted to Islam. The Persian conqueror Nadir Shah, despite being a friend to the Jews of Persia, laid to waste large portions of Transcaucasia and Daghestan and demolished the ancient Jewish settlement in Kolkat.

In 1820, under the influence of the fiercely puritanical *murid* fraternities (a Sufi revivalist movement), the bellicose North Caucasian mountaineers rose up in an epic struggle against their Russian oppressors. Shamyl, the national hero of the Islamic peoples of North Caucasia, after uniting the mountain tribes and engaging in *jihad* against the Russians, briefly established an independent state in Daghestan in 1830. He imposed strict observance of the *shariya* laws, but in violation of Koranic principles demanded the conversion of all the Mountain Jews. Fortunately for the Jews, the fanatical imam finally was defeated by massive Russian forces in 1859 and banished from the Caucasus. However, by that time much of traditional Daghestani-Jewish culture had been destroyed. It is believed that the Tat-speaking Muslims of Daghestan are the progeny of those Jews who were forcibly converted to Islam during the periodic outbursts of Islamic intolerance.[11]

Religious Zionist fervor took hold as early as 1840, when a trickle of Mountain Jews arrived in Palestine. By 1880 the colony was large enough to establish a *kollel* (the equivalent of a postgraduate school in talmudic studies) in Jerusalem. In 1907 Yaacov Yitzchaki, the Chief Rabbi of Derbent, made *aliyah*. Together with some fifty-six followers he founded a Mountain Jewish settlement that was later named after him.

In the formative period of czarist rule, the regime accorded the Mountain Jews the same treatment enjoyed by the other mountain peoples of the region, and the Jews jubilantly supported the Russians in their campaign to conquer the

region. Subsequently, because of intense pressure from the hostile Muslim population, as well as incipient czarist anti-Semitism, these rights were abrogated.
By the late nineteenth century the Mountain Jews were consigned to the same
pariah status as their coreligionists in the Pale of Settlement.

Because of their maltreatment at the hands of the czar and their Muslim
neighbors, a significant number of Mountain Jews supported the Bolsheviks
during the civil war of 1917. They formed a cavalry that fought alongside the
Red Army. In the aftermath of the conflict the Jews suffered heavy losses: Entire Jewish villages were wiped out and thousands of Mountain Jews were massacred by the reactionary White Guardists and Muslim nationalists. Thousands
of others fled to more remote mountain regions or found refuge among their
coreligionists in the Caspian Sea coastal towns. The animus harbored by the
Muslims toward the Jews did not diminish after the Russian Revolution. As late
as 1926 a blood libel against the Jews in Makhachkala resulted in a pogrom.[12]

After firmly establishing authority in the region, the Communist Party
came out with a strong anticlerical line and commenced to liquidate places of
worship and the religious schools. Secular schools and clubs for indoctrinating
the youth were established, with Russian as the language of instruction. The
Judeo-Tat script was changed from Hebrew to Latin and then to Cyrillic. A
modern Tat literature did flourish briefly in the 1930s, but died out with the
curtailment of the language after World War II. Under Stalin's policy of enforced collectivization of agriculture, the livelihoods of the mountain peoples
of Daghestan were wiped out, and the Jews began to move en masse from their
villages to the industrial centers of the Caucasus. Special *kolkhozes* (collective
farms) were established for the Mountain Jews in 1928, but these declined in
the late 1930s.

Although the moves to the cities quickened the disintegration of the clans,
the Mountain Jews nevertheless managed to resist assimilation more defiantly
than the more westernized, less observant Jews of the European Soviet Union.
This is attributed to the fact that the extended patriarchal family structure of
Daghestani society shielded its members from outside influences and faithfully
transmitted the religious traditions down through the generations. Instead of
the clans, a network of brotherhoods evolved, which maintained a tight tribal
connectedness. Religion remained triumphant even in the Communist ranks;
Mountain Jewish Communist Party officials, like their Muslim comrades, observed religious customs.

In those areas of the North Caucasus overrun by the Nazis, entire Jewish
villages were exterminated. According to researcher Gershon Ben-Oren, "There
is evidence that neighboring Gentiles, particularly the Balkars, protected Moun-

tain Jews from the Germans and unhesitatingly forfeited their lives in doing so; there were some, though (albeit a small number), who betrayed Jews to the occupiers."[13] During the Nazi occupation of Nalchik in 1942, hundreds of Mountain Jews were killed. After the Nazis withdrew from the city, many mass graves were discovered, holding, among other peoples, dozens of Mountain Jews. It was later discovered that they had been executed not by the Nazis but by the NKVD (Soviet secret police).[14] The Mountain Jews had served valiantly in the Red Army during World War II and one of them was handsomely decorated for planting the Soviet flag on the Reichstag in 1945.

After World War II, at the height of Stalin's madness, the anti-Jewish campaign in Daghestan was intensified. There was fear of a pogrom in 1960 after a local newspaper accused the Mountain Jews of using Muslim blood for ritual purposes.[15] Under Nikita Khruschev the repression was relaxed somewhat, and cultural and literary activities among the Mountain Jews revived slightly. After the Six Day War in 1967, the Mountain Jews, following the lead of their coreligionists in Georgia (but in a less clamorous manner so as not to antagonize their unsympathetic Muslim compatriots), demanded to be allowed to emigrate to Israel. In the late 1970s the Mountain Jews were victims of assault in several towns because of their struggle to leave for Israel. An estimated 10,000 made *aliyah* at that time.

With the disintegration of the Soviet empire, the extremely volatile Caucasus region has been a hotbed of Islamic insurgency. Many Mountain Jews who still live in Daghestan have been fleeing the conflicts. In the disputed territory of Nagorno-Karabakh during the early 1990s the Jews (Mountain and Ashkenazi) were unwittingly embroiled in the ferocious battles between Azeri Muslims and Armenian Christians. And in Chechnya, where a protracted guerrilla war against the Russians in 1994 resulted in the destruction of hundreds of towns and villages and took more than 100,000 lives, the pace of *aliyah* has also accelerated. An estimated 60,000 Mountain Jews are now settled in Israel, most in Be'er Sheva, Or Akiva, Sderot, and Ofakim in the Negev, and Acre in the North. There are probably less than 15,000 Mountain Jews left in the whole Caucasus as of 1999.

In pre-Communist times the Mountain Jews still practiced "the old ways," as illustrated by the following:

Usually a small minority of the population in the towns and villages of Daghestan, the Mountain Jews lived in their own special suburbs or in separate Jewish quarters. Typically their dwellings were mud huts plastered with dabs of cow dung mixed with straw. The better-off lived in two-story houses made from rough stone, the lower floor being used as a stable and storeroom and the upper floor containing the rooms for the family and guests. Houses were clustered together around a large single yard. Every mountain village or *aul* was encircled by a fortress that was surmounted by a fifty-to-sixty-foot stone tower. In case of attack, those not capable of defending themselves retreated to this tower (or hid deeper in the mountains).[16]

Village life centered around the clan and the village commune as the basic unit of society. Because of the alleged longevity of the people and early marriages, a clan could easily encompass four or even five generations, reaching seventy-five to 100 in number. The oldest male was the head of the family. When he died, the leadership was passed on to his oldest son. Each nuclear family consisted of a man and his wife, or wives, and children. If a man had more than one wife, each wife and her children occupied a separate hut.

Petty conflicts were usually ironed out by the arch-patriarch of the clan. If he could not resolve a matter, the case would be brought before the *nesi'a ha-edah* (community chieftains).[17] Before the Bolsheviks outlawed the practice in 1923,

[m]ortal revenge was carried out among the [Mountain Jews] with definite ceremonies and under the supervision of the elders of the village and the rabbi, who was responsible for the procedure. After a murder all the blood relatives of the murderer were notified that they would be abandoned to the revenge of the murdered man's family after three days. The relatives made use of these three days to withdraw to some stronghold and there defend themselves together against the attack of the hostile family. If the victim's relatives could take no revenge within the three days, the elders of the village and the rabbi then had to take a hand, according to the law, set a price on the murdered man's life and reconcile the families. The guilty family had to kiss the dust from the feet of their opponent at the scene of the reconciliation. The murderer himself was exiled for two years, then returned to the village, and to a certain extent as a substitute for the man he had killed, had to enter his family, where he was a favorite son of the house from then on.[18]

In pre-czarist times relations between Jews and Muslims in the *auls* of Daghestan and Azerbaijan were generally characterized by harmony and goodwill. Very often a young Jew and a Muslim pal would take an oath of blood-brotherhood. They would exchange daggers, then slit each other's left arm and suck blood from the wound. After this ceremony, they were considered brothers and treated as such. The new brother would be led to his new mother, who would give him of her breast as a symbol of admission into the family.[19]

Like other fighting peoples of the region, Mountain Jewish men dressed in the classic "Circassian" style. This consisted of an outer garment called a *tcherkeska*, which was made from homespun cloth. Silver-tipped cartridges and holders were sewn on both sides across the breast of the *tcherkeska*. A Mountain Jewish man also wore a *beshmet* (long white shirt buttoned up high, with a round stand-up collar). The leather belt was tight and supported the armature, which consisted of a powderhorn, a pistol, and a saber. The trousers were narrow, and the boots had no heels. A black *papak* (sheepskin cap) rounded out his attire. Weapons were worn even when praying in the synagogue. The dress of the women did not differ much from that of the men, except that the women wore a hair sack that was attached to the back of the head.

The Mountain Jews were originally farmers who cultivated their own land. Their main crops were rice, grapes, tobacco, grains, and a vine called *marena* from which madder (a red dye) was extracted. They also specialized in breeding silkworms and manufacturing silk. When driven off their lands, many turned to petty business trades and the handicrafts. In the latter occupations they established a fine reputation as tanners, jewelers, rug weavers, leather workers, and metal workers who specialized in making weapons. Under Communist rule only a fraction of the Mountain Jewish population remained farmers. A small number attended institutions of higher learning and turned to the professions.

Life in arch-patriarchal Daghestan was strictly controlled for Mountain Jewish women. All domestic chores were done by women, under supervision of the matriarch of the clan. In addition to cooking, cleaning, sewing family clothing, and caring for the young, women were burdened with the tasks of drawing water, hewing wood, and plowing fields.[20] They were as adept on horseback as their menfolk. Daughters were taught to dance and play an instrument in order to be able to entertain guests.

Children were married as young as ten, and matchmakers often were employed. Sometimes a suitor, with the help of his comrades, would abduct a bride from her parents' house. "If the girl's family learnt . . . about the kidnapping, it would try to get her back. At such times bloody scenes could happen but the girl was never returned to her parents. The pursuit and fight were arranged only to save the honor of the family. After [the] wedding, both families would usually come to terms again and they concluded an agreement on the payment for the girl *(kalym)*."[21] Weddings invariably took place in the wintertime. Festivities occurred at the bride's and groom's homes and lasted three or four days. During the processions to the couple's respective homes, the groom's *shoshbinim* (best men) galloped ahead on horseback firing pistol salutes in the air.

The notion that a man should remain unmarried was anathema to the Mountain Jews. Such a person was not considered to be a full-fledged member of the community. He was forbidden to carry weapons.[22]

According to the early-nineteenth-century missionary Jacob Samuel (who was a Jewish convert to Christianity), the Mountain Jews were in many ways pre-talmudic before they made contact with the Ashkenazim. They took the biblical injunction against seething a kid in its mother's milk (Exodus 23:19) literally and therefore had no compunctions about eating meat together with milk.[23] Being proto-Mosaic, they practiced Shabbat in an extremely austere manner; that is, by extinguishing the fires before sunset on Friday. They did not light *havdalah* candles.[24] The biblical passage in Leviticus 23:24 that concludes with "and ye shall afflict your souls" was rigidly interpreted to mean that children and animals also had to fast on Yom Kippur.[25]

> On the morning of the day of atonement, [Samuel observed] the males assemble together to afflict themselves with various penances, and give expression to their feelings in sighs, and lamentations, and groans. After about two hours spent in this discipline, they proceed to a well or cistern and draw water, pouring it on their heads and crying L'Adonai, L'Adonai. This occupies from two to three hours, when they cover themselves with dust and ashes, and return to the place of convocation, continuing their lamentations during the whole day. At sunset they proceed to the well or cistern, again draw water, and pour it on their heads three times crying, *kapir, kapir, kapir, forgiven! forgiven!* This finished, they dress in their best apparel, instruments of music strike up cheerful sounds, and running into each other's arms, embracing and kissing, they cry out *forgiven! forgiven!* They return to their families from whom they have been separated and the feast terminates in mirth and gladness.[26]

On the Sabbath, and Jewish holidays, the Mountain Jews would spend the day visiting their *hakhamim* (sages). The *hakhamim* would expound on the sacred texts and inform the people about the laws they were expected to observe. Before parting at sunset, the Mountain Jewish women would kiss the hem of the *hakham's* garment and the men would kiss his hands.[27] The Mountain Jews did not practice the *tashlich* ceremony (casting away sins into the sea) on Rosh Hashanah.[28] They did not make use of the *lulav* and *esrig* on Sukkot.[29] They celebrated the holiday of Shevuot for only one day (whereas Diaspora Jews observe two days).[30]

Generosity and hospitality are national institutions in the Caucasus. As one of the oldest inhabitants in the region and the people who brought monotheism to Caucasian soil, it may well have been the Jews who wove the biblical patriarch Abraham's practice of *hachnosat orchim* (welcoming guests) into the fabric of Daghestani culture. Every guest was treated as if he were personally sent by God. In every Jewish home a special room or hut covered with the finest carpets was set aside for guests. Every host would protect his guests with his life, and lavish on them the finest foods and spirits. The host and his family might forego eating meat in order to provide the guests with this luxury. Other villagers also would contribute provisions to serve the guest. Guests were entertained by the host's unmarried sons and daughters, who would sing and dance and play an assortment of instruments such as the *tar* (a plucked string instrument) and the *saz* (a long-necked fretted lute), while the young men engaged in choreographed sword or dagger dueling contests.

In the Jewish enclaves of Daghestan great emphasis was placed on developing the virtues of fierceness, courage, strength, loyalty, modesty, and independence of spirit. A father taught his son combat and the use of arms as soon as he was old enough to defend himself. The Mountain Jews were enthusiastic nature lovers and, like other peoples in the region, skilled horsemen and expert marksmen. When under attack, these Jewish musketeers would band together in a fighting force "all for one and one for all." If necessary, they were perfectly ready to sacrifice their lives for one another. They were a powerful people with soft hearts, passionately Jewish, and ready at any time to beat to a pulp those who would malign Judaism or harm a fellow Jew.

Also stressed in the Jewish (and the larger Daghestani) culture was the homage and deference due seniority of age, which found expression in a number of formal rules of etiquette. For example, one did not sit down until older people present were seated. One dismounted from horseback before addressing an older person. One offered one's horse to an elderly person who was going on foot to the same destination.[31]

In every town and hamlet the Jews established *battai chesed u'tzedakah* (houses of kindness and charity), a combination social service agency, hospital, and hospice, to help the poor, the sick, and the dying.[32] Individuals were sent to visit those in need of assistance. When someone was sick, a vigil was maintained until the person recovered. When a person was about to die, the entire community would come to his home to pay him homage. All the Jewish shops would close and work would come to a stop. Those gathered would ask forgiveness of the dying man, in case (God forbid) they had intentionally or inadvertently insulted him or hurt his feelings. They would beseech him to intercede on their behalf in the World to Come. They would try to assuage his fears by singing and playing various instruments, because they believed that music assisted the spirit in its migration from the body into the invisible world. When he was on the verge of expiring, those around him would recite the *Shema* (Hear O Israel) into his ears.

When a Mountain Jew died the women in the community would proceed to the dead person's home, wearing white clothing and yellow shoes. The dead person was laid on his face and the women would begin to howl, beating their breasts, scratching their skin, and tearing out their hair. They would so disfigure themselves that blood flowed from their faces. Oftentimes they would tear so hard at their hair that there were large gashes on their scalps from patches of missing hair. If a man died at the hands of avengers, they would not purify him or undress him, but would bury him with his weapons and let the Angel of Death have a reckoning with him.

The Mountain Jews believed that during the *shiva* period (seven days of mourning after death) the soul refuses to believe that it has just been separated from the body, and therefore still hovers over the house in which the person has just died. Acting on this belief, the Mountain Jews would light a candle and place a chair on the spot where the deathbed had been located. The candle was placed on a copper tray that in turn was placed on a stool. The tray symbolized the partition between the divine in heaven and man on earth. On each person's tomb was inscribed not only the name and date of death, but also the deceased's accomplishments.

Like their rugged, brawny, and simple brethren in Kurdistan whom they most resembled, the Mountain Jews placed little value on education as it is understood in normative (i.e., Ashkenazi, Sephardi, and Yemenite) Jewry. They believed that excessive study was destructive to faith, and by and large the Mountain Jews were illiterate. It was only after they had established contact with the Ashkenazim that the small number who could afford it sent their young men to Eastern Europe to wrack their brains in the sedentary atmosphere of the yeshiva. The general educational level of the Mountain Jews was very low, and the Torah knowledge of their *hakhamim* was generally limited. Derbent, which sometimes imported its *hakham bashis* (grand rabbis) from the Ottoman Empire, served as the spiritual center. On the local level the *hakham* functioned as *dayan, shochet, mohel,* and *melamed.* Beginning in the mid-nineteenth century, youngsters who showed ability were sent to study in *yeshivot* in Vilna, Warsaw, and Volozhin. Most arrived scholastically handicapped, in relation to the other students, and few actually attained ordination. But they returned to their villages with enough competence to qualify as *shochtim* (certified ritual slaughterers).

As in other societies where traditions are passed down orally, there were many talented musicians and wonderful storytellers among the Mountain Jews.

Their legends, poems, and folktales invariably featured great Jewish heroes and warriors from the Bible and from their own pantheon. Some of the more common themes of their lives and values dealt with bravery, intrepidity, the thrill of danger, love of weapons, and devotion to horses.

The Mountain Jews were graceful in their movements, and were excellent dancers until they were very old. On any festive occasion, but especially on holidays such as Chanukah and Purim, boys and men would join together for corral dancing, called *lezginka* in Tati. A small inner circle was composed of the tribal heads, and the outer circle included all the other men. In the center was the headman dancing *cossatzkah* style with a ceremonial artifact such as a Chanukah menorah or Torah scroll in his hand. Whenever the inner circle danced counterclockwise, the outer circle danced clockwise, and vice versa. The women would bring out sweets and place them directly into the dancers' mouths. Dancing might go on until the wee hours of the morning.[33]

Today among the Mountain Jewish youth in the Caucasus and in Israel, the religion is practiced *masorti* style—not Orthodox but traditional. The great majority still practice circumcision, traditional wedding rites, and say *kaddish* for the departed. In contrast with the Jews of Georgia, they do not meticulously observe Sabbath and the holidays, with the exception of the High Holy Days and Passover. Judeo-Tat is no longer spoken; they use the Russian language. However, their Jewish consciousness is very strong.

NOTES

1. *Geography of the U.S.S.R.* (New York: Columbia University Press, 1951), p. 231.

2. Shiri Akiner, *Islamic Peoples of the Soviet Union*, 2nd ed. (London: KPI, 1986), p. 124.

3. *Custom and Justice in the Caucasus* (unpublished dissertation, University of Pennsylvania, 1939), p. 148.

4. "Daily Life of the Caucasian Mountaineers in the Middle of the 19th Century," *Folia Caucasica* 2 (1987), pp. 64–65 and 544–45.

5. *How To Live To Be 100: The Lifestyles of the People of the Caucasus* (New York: Dial Press, 1976), p. 156. See also Human Relations Area Files, *The Caucasus* (New Haven: HRAF, 1956), p. 527.

6. R. Adighe, "Literature on Dagestan and Its People," *Caucasian Review* 4:1–5 (1957), p. 104.

7. Y. Brutzkas, "Di Geshichte fun di Berg Yiden oif Kavkaz," YIVO, *Historische Shriften* 2 (1937), p. 26; Chantal Lemercier-Quelquejay, "Islam and Identity in Azerbaijan," *Central Asian Survey* 3:2 (1984), p. 30.

8. Cited in Brutzkas, "*Di Geshichte,*" p. 28.

9. Ibid., p. 29.

10. Mordkhai Neishtat, "Mountain Jews," *Encyclopaedia Judaica*, vol. 12. (Jerusalem: Keter, 1973), p. 478.

11. "There are still villages," wrote Fannina Halle in 1946, "where the Mohammedan residents will display old Hebrew Bibles and claim with pride that their ancestors were Jews." See "The Caucasian Mountain Jews: An Ancient Tribe Under the Soviets," *Commentary* 4 (1946), p. 357.

12. An official memorandum submitted to the Soviet authorities by the Commission for the Rural Placement of Jews (KOMZET) investigating the causes of the 1926 pogrom concluded that the local Communist Party units not only did not protect but actually took an active part in the persecution of the Mountain Jews. For details of the memorandum see Solomon M. Schwarz, *The Jews in the Soviet Union* (Syracuse, N.Y.: Syracuse University Press, 1951), pp. 254–256.

13. Gershon Ben-Oren, "Mountain Jews," in *Azerbaijan: Mountain Jews, Urban Jews*, edited by Nina Benzoor (Haifa: Museum of Music and Ethnography, 1992), p. 152.

14. Rudolf Loewenthal, "The Judeo-Tats in the Caucasus," *Historia Judaica*, 14–15 (1952–53), pp. 77–78.

15. Joshua Rothenberg, "The Mountain Jews of Soviet Russia," *Jewish Frontier* (November 1967), p. 18.

16. Human Relations Area Files, *The Caucasus*, pp. 514–15.

17. Jacob Samuel, *The Remnant Found; or, The Place of Israel's Hiding Discovered* (London: J. Hatchard and Son, 1841), p. 103.

18. Essed-Bey, *Blood and Oil in the Orient* (London: Nash and Grayson Ltd., 1931), pp. 120–21. According to another version, if within three months the blood of the murderer was not avenged by the clan a truce was held and the murderer was sent into exile. After this period of exile he would return and was accepted as part of the victim's family. See Mardechai Altshuler, *The Jews of the Eastern Caucasus: The History of the "Mountain Jews" from the Beginning of the Nineteenth Century* (Jerusalem: Ben-Zvi Institute for the Study of Jewish Communities of the East—The Hebrew University of Jerusalem, 1990), p. 310.

19. Ibid., pp. 121–22.

20. John Abercromby, *A Trip Through the Eastern Caucasus* (London: Edward Stanford, 1889), p. 45.

21. Kulesza, "Daily Life," p. 59. See also Human Relations Area Files, *The Caucasus*, pp. 534–35.

22. Essed-Bey, *Blood and Oil*, p. 122.

23. Samuel, *The Remnant Found*, p. 89.

24. Ibid., p. 73.

25. Ibid., p. 58.

26. Ibid., p. 59.

27. Ibid., pp. 72–73.

28. Ibid., p. 57.

29. Ibid., p. 63.

30. Ibid., p. 55.

31. Human Relations Area Files, *The Caucasus*, p. 546.

32. The following ethnographic details are a free rendering translation of an 1895 description of the Mountain Jews by C. H. Braverman called "Minhag Hayehudim Hahurayim" ("Customs of the Mountain Jews"), found in Altshuler, *The Jews of the Eastern Caucasus*, p. 537.

33. Nissin Rosenthal, *Yiddish Leben in Ratten Farband* (Tel Aviv: Perets Farlag, 1971), pp. 319–20.

Part VII

Bukharan Elder Holding Lulav
Credit: Yad Ben Zvi Archives

The People with the
Blue-Stained Fingers

BACKGROUND INFORMATION

Central Asia is a colossal basin located on the northern foothills of the Pamir and Tien-Shan mountain ranges. It stretches from the Caspian Sea in the west to the Chinese border of Sinkiang in the east. Until 1991, this area was composed of five Islamic Soviet Socialist Republics: Uzbekistan, Kazakhstan, Turkmenistan, Kirghizstan, and Tadjikistan. In the aftermath of the breakup of the former U.S.S.R., only Tadjikistan has so far declined to join the other republics in the formation of the Commonwealth of Independent States.

With a population estimated at twenty million, Uzbekistan is the most densely populated of the former Central Asian Republics, and is also the most economically advanced. Known as the "Land of White Gold," Uzbekistan is today the world's third-largest cotton producing region, after the U.S.A. and China. The principal cities in Uzbekistan are Tashkent, Samarkand, and Bukhara. Tashkent, the largest city in Central Asia with a million-and-a-half residents, is the modern capital of Uzbekistan.

Variously referred to as the "cradle of the nations" and the "rubbish heap,"[1] Uzbekistan is peopled by more than a hundred different ethnic groups. The largest group, an estimated sixty-five percent of the population, are Uzbeks, a Turkish-Mongolian people who over the centuries have mixed extensively with the indigenous Tadjikis—also known as Sarts—an Aryan people of Persian origin. After the Uzbeks, the Tartars, Kazakhs, and unmixed Tadjikis make up the most significant minorities.

173

The national language is Uzbek, a Turkish dialect that has traditionally been spoken by the rural seminomadic and nomadic tribes, who make up about seventy percent of the population. Among the traders and urban people, the Tadjiki-Persian dialect was employed. Under Communist rule, Russian was imposed as the primary language in the urban schools and in the bureaucracy. With Uzbekistani independence from the former U.S.S.R. in 1991, the use of Russian has been discarded, and Uzbek again has become the official tongue.

Much of Central Asia is a vast expanse of searing desert. Civilizations were invariably built around oasis towns along the valleys of the two great rivers, the Oxus and the Jaxartes, and their tributaries. From remote antiquity Central Asia was the heart of the Silk Road and a staging post for camel caravans on their way from the Orient to the West. Its main crops were cotton and the mulberry tree, whose leaves fed the silkworms for the manufacture of silk. Central Asia contributed greatly to the manufacture of textiles and the production of dyes.

Crossing the desert was extremely dangerous. The fabled, walled Central Asian cities along the Silk Road—Bukhara, Samarkand, Merv, Khiva, and the oasis towns of the Fergana Valley—supplied the caravans with essential needs. They also provided protection from the elements and fierce bandit tribes. "The real key to success in the Central Asian caravan trade . . . were the diplomatic and military relations between the Chinese empire and the rulers of the Turkic and Mongolian nomad tribes which controlled crucial stretches of the routes."[2]

Life in a typical Central Asian city always centered around the colorful and lively bazaar. By the beginning of the seventeenth century the old caravan routes connecting Central Asia to the Occident began to decline. To some extent this was due to the brigands and highwaymen who made the roads extremely dangerous for travelers. But more significantly, it was due to the fact that China and Persia had shut themselves off from contact with the West, and more competitive sea routes were being developed via India. When the New World was discovered, "Europe got up, stretched, and faced itself in a different direction entirely for nearly five hundred years."[3]

A thriving civilization, Central Asia was subjected to frequent invasions by avaricious hordes from both east and west, but especially by waves of Turkish and Mongol nomads descending from the steppe regions. The documented history of Sogdiana, as Central Asia was known in antiquity, begins in the sixth century B.C.E., after its conquest by the Persian emperor Cyrus the Great. Sogdiana was part of the Persian-Achaemenid empire until conquered by Alexander the Great in 329 B.C.E., when it formed part of the Graeco-Bactrian state.

Sogdiana was overrun by the Huns (425 C.E.) and the Turkish Khagan (sixth century) before being conquered by the Arabs in the eighth century. After driving out the Turks, at least temporarily, the Omayyad caliphate imposed the Islamic religion and the Arabic script on the heterogeneous population.

Bukhara—described as the "glorious citadel of Arabian-Persian culture" and the "pillar of Islam" in the Omayyad and Abbasid (Arab), Samanid (Persian), and Karakhanid (Turkic) dynasties—developed into a major center of Muslim scholarship. It boasted hundreds of mosques and *medresses*, Islamic schools of higher education. Only Mecca and Medina are ranked as holier cities than Bukhara in the Islamic world. Bukhara is also the birthplace of Avicenna (980–1037), the greatest healer of the Middle Ages.

Around 1220 C.E. the Mongols erupted on the scene and demolished Bukhara, Samarkand, Khiva, and Merv. It is said that Genghis Khan was so infuriated by the resistance of the inhabitants that he would not rest until their blood reached his horse's knees. The Mongol conquest so rended asunder the old patterns of commerce and agriculture that it took almost two centuries for Central Asia to recover from the devastation. One of the components of Genghis Khan's Golden Horde was a conglomeration of nomadic Turkish tribes from northern Mongolia who became known as Uzbeks. The Uzbeks are believed to have taken their name from Khan Uzbek (1282–1342), the Mongol ruler who converted the Golden Horde to Islam. In the late fourteenth century the Uzbeks formed the core of the empire of Tamerlane. Under this mighty conqueror large cities were rebuilt along the Silk Route, commerce revived, and Bukhara and Samarkand, the "Jewel of Islam," were once again transformed into brilliant centers of scholarship and the arts.

After the death of Tamerlane, his empire came apart. Following a series of bloody civil wars, his territories in Central Asia were carved into the khanates of Khiva, Kokand, and Bukhara. Consolidated into a powerful force by Sheibani Khan in the first decade of the sixteenth century, the nomadic Uzbeks of Bukhara merged with the more sedentary Tadjikis (Sarts), the ancient Iranian peoples of this region, and made Bukhara City, the capital of the former emirate of the same name, their capital. The Holy City was made a forbidden zone from which all foreigners were rigorously excluded. After capturing Central Asia in 1740, Persia's great warrior Nadir Shah appointed a local feudal lord as the emir or governor of the province of Bukhara. Under the Manghit dynasty (1753–1920), Bukhara became a powerful theocracy governed by tyrannical emirs and a rapacious Islamic clergy. From being the "Athens" of Islamic culture that drew thousands of students from all parts of the world, Bukhara City degenerated to "a center of religious obscurantism and political reaction."[4]

Beginning in the early nineteenth century, Central Asia became the locus of the "Great Game," an imperial conflict of immense magnitude fought between Victorian England and a Czarist Russia, each frantically scurrying to control the riches of Asia and its biggest prize, India. In 1868 Central Asia was annexed by the Russians, and the emir of Bukhara became a vassal of the czar. A large portion of the emirate of Bukhara was incorporated into the newly created government of Russian Turkestan. Red Army troops deposed the emirate in September, 1920, and the territory became first the Turkestan ASSR and then, in 1924, the Uzbek Soviet Socialist Republic.

Well into the twentieth century many forms of infections, diseases, and epidemics festered in the urban areas of Central Asia due to the abysmally unsanitary conditions. Boils, tuberculosis, cataracts, filariasis, syphilis, and trachoma were rampant, as were outbreaks of leprosy, cholera, bubonic plague, dysentery, and *rishta*, a type of ulcer caused by drinking water from cisterns containing Guinea worms.

THE TADJIKI JEWS OF BUKHARA

Bukhara is different from any place that you and I know. It has
different light, different landscapes of sound and smell, a
different terrestrial geometry. The midday sky hangs higher,
shadows on a late autumn afternoon fetch farther. In every
direction the pitiless Central Asian steppe falls away to a more
distant horizon. Bukhara, it seems, might be at the center of the
world.

—Ted Levin and Otanazar Matyakubov, Bukhara:
Musical Crossroads of Asia (1991)

The guest is more important than the father of the family.
—popular Uzbek saying

The Tadjiki Jews are generically referred to as "Bukharans" because at the
time of the Russian conquest of Central Asia in the nineteenth century, the bulk
of the community was situated in the emirate of Bukhara. However, the Jews
traditionally referred to themselves as "Isroel" or "Yehudi." Before mass emigration to Israel and the United States in the early 1990s, the Jews of Uzbekistan
were concentrated in the cities of Samarkand, Tashkent, Bukhara, Khiva, and
the Fergana Valley towns of Kokand, Andijan, and Marghilan. A sizable Jewish
community was situated in Dushambe, the capital of Tadjikistan, and there were
small settlements in Ashkabad, the capital of Turkmenistan; in Frunze, the capital
of Kirghizstan; and in Alma Ata, the capital of the West Asian Republic of
Kazakhstan. These cities were situated along the Central Asian trade routes, and
some Jewish merchants settled permanently there. In this chapter, the main focus
of attention is given to the Jews of Uzbekistan, which was known in earlier periods as the Khanate of Bukhara and the Khanate of Turkestan.

Jews have been living in Central Asia since remote antiquity. Earliest theories ascribe the settlement of Jews in Central Asia to the Lost Ten Tribes taken
into captivity by Shalmanessar, King of Assyria, in 722 B.C.E. According to this
view, Samarkand is simply a twist of the word Samaria, from where the exiles
originated, and Bukhara is identified with the Habor of II Kings 17:6.[5] Palestinian Jews migrated eastward, possibly after the destruction of the First Temple,
and established themselves in this northern flank of the Persian-Achaemenid
Empire. Individuals and groups may have arrived after the conquests of Alexander
the Great, when commercial intercourse on the Silk Route was occurring to a

large degree between East and West. Additional waves of Jewish emigrants established themselves in the emporiums of the Kushan (circa 78 C.E.–225 C.E.) and Sasanian dynasties (225–650 C.E.) as merchants and middlemen of the cotton and silk trades and as specialists in the dyeing process.

The Jews of Central Asia were always easily identified by the blue stains on their hands. This dye was derived from the dried bodies of the female cochineal insect, which are mixed with indigo. The purplish-blue dye resulting from this process was supposed to have been made from a secret formula handed down from generation to generation. "The [Jewish] women," writes the early twentieth-century Orientalist William E. Curtis, " . . . are remarkably skillful weavers and produce the most exquisite velvets and brocades."[6] Jewish involvement in the dye-making process, Professor Menashe Har-El points out, may have been partly motivated by religious law, since before the codification of the Talmud (500 C.E.) the Jews were commanded to dye their *tallitim* (prayer shawls) in *tekhelet* (blue dye), extracted from a sea creature called *hilazon*.(*Hilazon* means "snail" in modern Hebrew.)[7] According to Jewish law, the *tzitzit* should have seven strands of white and one strand of blue. The *tzitzit* serve as a reminder of God's omnipresence. Over the centuries, knowledge of identifying *hilazon* and the process of deriving the blue dye was lost or forgotten by Jewry the world over, and *p'til tekhelet* was no longer worn.[8]

The suppression of the Jewish religion during the reigns of the Sasanian kings Yazdegerd and Firuz in the fifth century C.E. is believed to have caused a mass migration to Central Asia. Jewish merchants are known to have played a leading role in world trade in medieval times. By the ninth century the postmaster general of Baghdad, Ibn Khordadhbah, could describe the land and sea routes taken by Jewish traders, known as Radanites, from France and Morocco to China and India via Central Asia. [9] The famous Jewish traveler Benjamin of Tudela, who visited Samarkand around 1170 C.E., about a half-century before the Mongol massacres, claimed there were 50,000 Jews in that city, many of them learned and wealthy.[10] The earliest documentary evidence pertaining to Jewish settlement in Bukhara proper is derived from Ibn al-Fati, an Arab chronicler of the thirteenth century. He relates in his writings that in 1240 C.E. a fanatical Islamic fakir attempted to instigate a massacre against Christians and Jews.[11] "It is unlikely that any of the [Central Asian] cities had an unbroken record of viable Jewish communities," Professor Ira Sharkansky of The Hebrew University points out. "War, destruction, and slaughter swept across the region time and again in the wake of Alexander, of Genghis Khan, and of Tamerlane, and it would be surprising if the Jews escaped the common disaster. Each community may have fallen and risen several times, revitalized by new groups of Jewish migrants from elsewhere in the Middle East."[12]

The Jews of Bukhara City have many legends about the origins of their community. One such legend is that there was a khan whose wife could not conceive a child. Eager to have an heir, the khan consulted many doctors, but none could help him. Someone informed him of a Jewish doctor from Meshed who might be able to provide the queen with a cure. The Jewish doctor was brought in, and in little more than nine months the khan was blessed with a robust baby boy. The exhilarated monarch could not thank the Jew enough, and pleaded with him to come live in his kingdom, where he would be granted whatever his heart desired. But the physician, being a pious Jew, politely turned down the invitation because there were no Jews in Bukhara, and he could not pray without a *minyan*. The khan then offered to bring to Bukhara nine other Jews, who, together with the good doctor, formed the nucleus of the Jewish community there.[13]

If this story is true, the khanate's honeymoon with the Jews was an ephemeral affair. As *dhimmi* living in a Muslim land, the Jews of Bukhara were subjected to many restrictions. They were obliged to live in a special quarter called *makhalyah*, and forbidden to enter the city after sunset. They were compelled to pay burdensome taxes—and to add insult to injury were given a customary humiliating two slaps in the face upon payment.[14] They could not ride horses and camels, only asses, and they were prohibited from carrying weapons. They were forbidden to wear the type of silken sash called *takband* worn by the Muslims. Instead, they were required to girdle themselves with a skinny hempen cord. This way a Muslim could strangle the wearer if he believed the Jew was trying to cheat him.[15] They were forbidden to wear any sort of flowing garb or the *chalma* (turban). For head covering they were compelled to wear a black calico cap, called *telpaq*, that marked them as Jews. A miscreant caught wearing unsuitable attire was given a thrashing in the street by the mufti's police, or even hauled off to jail. If a Muslim hit a Jew, the Jew had to humbly submit. A Jew could seek no redress in a Muslim court. These restrictions were rigidly enforced, even though there was little real enmity among the Islamic people of Central Asia toward the Jews. Indeed, over time, the Jews were able to attain considerable wealth despite the institutional impediments.

With the reestablishment of the Jews in the khanate of Bukhara in the fourteenth century, which was a period of relative peace and tranquillity, the Jewish communities grew and prospered. A cultural elite that attained a degree of luxury and refinement was able to devote its leisure time to poetry and literature. The Bukharan Jews retained the Tadjiki language of their Persian roots but, like Jews in so many other parts of the world, they adopted a special dialect, called Judeo-Tadjik, that incorporated many words from Hebrew and Turkish and employed the letters of the sacred tongue. After the city of Samarkand was destroyed by Babi Mahemet Khan in 1598, the Jews fled to Bukhara City, strengthening the Jewish community there. There is a tradition among the Bukharan Jews that a segment of their community emigrated to China around this time and that this breakaway group soon ceased to have communications with the mother country.[16]

In the eighteenth and nineteenth centuries religious and political fanaticism grew more intense in the emirate of Bukhara. Predatory emirs waged savage wars against each other and plundered the downtrodden masses, Muslims as well as Jews. One infamous emir is said to have built a minaret out of the skulls of rebellious peasants his troops had beheaded.[17] During this epoch, Jews who were accused of a crime, such as selling wine to a Muslim, could avoid incarceration or the death penalty by abjuring their faith. Execution was carried out by means of beheading or throwing the condemned off the top of Kalan Tower in Bukhara City's town square. Those who converted when faced with this choice were derisively known as *chala* (imperfect ones), because the Muslims suspected them of remaining faithful to Judaism. In fact, these crypto-Jews played the Muslim game in public, usually intermarried among themselves (although some married Persian Shiite slaves), lived in a special quarter, but surreptitiously maintained contact with the Jewish community.[18]

In the oasis towns of Central Asia the social and business life of the city invariably centered around the marketplace. As an integral part of the bazaar, the Jews, grown portly, spent much of their leisure time sitting cross-legged in the *chaikhanas* (tea houses), puffing their *narghillas*, imbibing opium and cannabis, while being enthralled by the storytellers, vaudevillians, *bachchas* (dancing boys in drag), and the *shashmakama* ensembles who entertained the crowds with a repertoire of classical music and songs.[19] The Jews occupied a preeminent position as the most talented and distinguished of folk singers, instrumentalists, and dancers. Some were *khafises* (professional entertainers) who performed exclusively for the emir and his courtly retinue.[20]

As a result of affluence and assimilation, the Jews of Bukhara had, by the eighteenth century, become utterly ignorant and unobservant of Jewish laws. Links with Persian Jewry had been cut off after the rise of the xenophobic Safavid Shiites in the sixteenth century. The Bukharans possessed few teachers or holy books and had lost all knowledge of Hebrew. They still intoned a few prayers, which had been passed down from the ancestors, but in many ways their syna-

gogue services were hardly distinguishable from the Muslims'. They had completely forgotten *hilchat shechita* (laws pertaining to ritual slaughtering) and were
eating unkosher meat.[21]

Upon visiting Bukhara in 1793, Rabbi Joseph Maman al-Maghrebi, an
emissary from Safed, was perturbed by the deplorable spiritual condition in which
he found the Jews. Resolving to bring the Bukharan Jews back to the mainstream
of Judaism, he settled among them and married a local Jewish girl. He immediately sent away to Eastern Europe and Italy for holy books and ritual objects.
He imported Jewish scribes and renewed the contact of the Bukharan Jews with
world Jewry, but particularly with the scholarly "Litvak" Jews of Vilna. With
assistance from other *shelichim*, he was able to establish *yeshivot* and a rabbinical
seminary. In addition to exoteric works—Bible, Talmud, and Commentaries—
he introduced the studying of the *Zohar*. Because the Bukharans had mostly forgotten the Kurasani *nusach* (Central Asian rite) of their forebears and Rabbi
Maman mistakenly believed that they were descended from Spanish exiles like
himself, he "converted" them to the Sephardi *nusach*. In his thirty years of living
among the Bukharan Jews he instilled in them an appreciation of learning and
also a deep and abiding love of Zion. The Bukharan community received a spiritual boost from a number of other *hakhamim* who sojourned among them, and
from a wave of cypto-Jews who fled from Meshed. The Meshedi Jews emigrated
to Central Asia in 1839 to escape from a pogrom and forcible conversion to Islam.

Initially, the Russian annexation of Central Asia in 1865–68 resulted in
improved conditions for the Jews. Relations between Jews and Muslims had been
steadily deteriorating, and compared to the tyrannical emirs and their venal
henchmen, czarist rule seemed relatively benign. The Jews initially considered
the Russians to be a godsend. The Czar, not wishing to stir up a *jihad* against his
rule, allowed the Islamic community to function according to *shariya* law, and
he granted the emirs considerable autonomy in ruling Bukhara. Because the
Koranic laws were rigidly observed in the Holy City, the Jews residing there
were still subjected to the humiliating *dhimmi* laws. The relative freedoms accorded the Jews by the Czar led many Jews from Bukhara and other parts of
Central Asia to settle in Russian-controlled territories, especially in Tashkent,
the new capital of Russian Turkestan.

"The Civil War in the United States," writes Marat Akchurin, "had resulted in the sharp curtailment of cotton imports to Russia, which was now trying to find new resources of raw materials for its textile industry. The Russian
empire was aspiring to retrieve, as quickly as possible, some of the international
prestige that had been undermined by its defeat in the Crimean War of 1853–
56."[22] As subjects of the Czar, Jewish entrepreneurs were granted the same

freedom of movement and other rights accorded to Turkestan's Muslims. Not restricted to a Pale of Settlement or subjected to pogroms like their European brethren, the Turkestani Jews carried on a vigorous trade across the Russian empire. Their chief exports to Russia were cotton, silk, rugs, embroideries, indigo, rice, and dried fruits. In return, they imported from the mercantile power finished cotton products such as chintz, calico, brocades, hides, and iron goods. This activity was encouraged by the Czar because he needed their money and their enterprise.

Some Bukharan Jews became fabulously wealthy, possessing large tracts of land (mainly cotton, tobacco, and flax plantations) and orchards yielding pomegranates, apricots, and sesame seeds. They generally hired Muslim hands to work the land. A few Jews owned coal mines and oil mills.[23] In competition with the local Hindus, they functioned as bankers and moneylenders and, although regarded as an inferior race by their Muslim compatriots, were renowned for their honorable dealings.[24] Most Jews were small shopkeepers, who sold goods such as carpets, tobacco, snuff, teas, sesame seeds, dried fruit, and manufactured goods.

In their travels to the fairs of European Russia, the Bukharans encountered Ashkenazi Jewish civilization for the first time. As a result of interacting with Ashkenazi pietists, they reinforced and strengthened their own religious knowledge and were able to procure religious texts and artifacts lacking in Turkestan. Those who could afford it sent their young men to the great talmudic academies in Russian Poland and Lithuania. During this early period of czarist rule some Ashkenazi merchants and conscripts who were stationed in Tashkent settled in the capital. Some married local Bukharan girls, but for the most part, Ashkenazim and neo-Sephardim remained aloof from one another.

In a series of duplicitous acts, and in violation of previous agreements, the anti-Semitic czars pursued a policy of systematically curtailing many of the freedoms previously granted the Turkestani Jews. An *ukase* (decree) in 1889 legally distinguished the Jews from the Turkestani Muslims and rescinded the right of the Jews to own property. In 1900 Czar Nicholas II decreed that the Bukharan Jews' freedom of movement in European Russia be restricted to the Pale of Settlement established for Russian Jewry. After the aborted revolution of 1905, the Jews were falsely accused of stirring up the local Muslim population. In 1911 the Bukharan Jews' treaty rights were also infringed upon when they, too, were confined to a Pale of Settlement in Turkestan.

With the Communist revolution in 1917, which some Jews took part in and died for, all legal restrictions were lifted from the Turkestani Jews. Bukhara survived as a semi-independent emirate until 1920, when the emir was overthrown and fled to Afghanistan. Writes Joshua Kunitz, "The Emir, abandoning his hundred wives, but taking along his letter of credit on the English bank (fifty-four million gold rubles), fled from his capital. . . . To deflect popular resentment, the Emir incited the peasants to rob the Jews, who, he charged, had brought the Bolsheviks into the land. And, it is reported, to replenish his own depleted fortunes . . . he seized the wealthiest Jewish merchants in the region, decapitated them, and confiscated about three-quarters of a million dollars' worth of silver. The prettiest Jewish women he ordered seized and distributed among his followers."[25]

The aftermath of the Marxist revolution was initially both a blessing and a curse for Central Asian Jewry. On the one hand, the centuries-old institutionalized humiliations were swept away, and Jews could now attend universities and enter the professions. On the other hand, under Soviet collectivization, their industries and private property were expropriated, and the Jews, for the most part, were consigned to the status of déclassé. Deprived of their livelihoods, the Jews were coerced by the new regime to form agricultural *kolkhozes*—but attempts at making farmers of the Bukharan Jews invariably resulted in fiasco because they were the quintessential bourgeoisie: They had no aptitude or desire for agricultural work. The collapse of Bukharan Jewry's economic position gave impetus to a large migration to Palestine and Western Europe.

Actually, Bukharan Jews had begun to trickle into Palestine in the early nineteenth century at the urging of Rabbi Maman and other emissaries. These Jews came for purely religio-Zionistic reasons. In the 1830s they established a neighborhood in the Old City of Jerusalem known as the Rehovoth, but it came to be called more popularly the Bukharan Quarter. Subsequently, the Bukharan colony in Israel was augmented by waves of new immigrants, who left the old country during difficult times or for idealistic reasons. By 1897, the Central Asian Jews had established three synagogues, a Talmud Torah, and a yeshiva in the Bukharan Quarter. Prodigies from Bukhara were sent to study in the yeshiva in Jerusalem, and many would return to their birthplace as rabbis and educators. On the eve of the first World War, there were 1,500 Bukharan Jews residing in Jerusalem.[26]

The situation for Central Asian Jewry went from bad to worse in 1921, when the Bolsheviks adopted a policy of systematically suppressing Jewish cultural and spiritual life. In an attempt to Sovietize the local Jews, the Hebrew language was outlawed, the role of rabbis was severely curtailed, synagogues and Jewish schools were closed, and the Zionist movement was squelched. "The conversion of the Bukharan Jewish dialect to the Latin script," writes Professor Michael Zand, "was the first . . . Soviet experiment in forced assimilation.

Bukharan Jewish culture was used in this experiment and destroyed . . . because the Bukharan Jews, a small drop in the ocean of the non-Jewish population, appeared to the Soviet experts and administrators . . . an easy object of forcible accelerated de-ethnicization. Thus, Bukharan Jewish culture became the first culture in a spoken Jewish language to be condemned to destruction by the chiefs of the Soviet nationalities policy."[27]

The purges and liquidations taking place during the years of Stalin's "Great Terror" in the late 1930s also reached Central Asia. Most of the Bukharan Jewish leadership and cultural elite were rounded up, arrested, and in some cases eliminated. Many Jews were exiled to labor camps in Siberia and were never heard from again. Despite Communist repression, what held Bukharan Jewry together was a cohesive patriarchal family structure, clan solidarity, tight friendships, and a deep and abiding devotion to its religious heritage. There was no tolerance for intermarriage. Even Bukharan Jewish "historical materialists" and apparatchiks in the Communist Party attended Yom Kippur services and circumcised their sons.[28] Right under the collective noses of the KGB, children were taught to read Hebrew and the rudiments of Bible, and to pray.

During World War II over a million Jews (including the author's mother and grandfather), fleeing from the Nazi-occupied regions of Poland, Ukraine, and European Russia, found refuge in Uzbekistan. Many Jewish survivors from the labor camps in Siberia also settled there upon release. The majority of these Jews made Tashkent, the modern capital of Uzbekistan, their permanent home. Within twenty years after the onset of the war, the Jewish population of Uzbekistan (including Ashkenazim) almost doubled, from 51,000 to more than 94,000.[29]

Growing contacts between the Uzbekistani government and the Arab states after World War II exacerbated the enmity between the local Muslim population and the Jews. In the early 1960s a number of blood libel accusations led to violent outbursts against the Jews in Tashkent and Margelan. The pogrom that took place in Margelan in September 1961 was perpetrated after rumors spread that Jews had murdered a child because his blood was required for a Rosh Hashanah ritual. Roving bands of hooligans, with cooperation from the local militia, rampaged through the Jewish quarter, brutally assaulting Jews in the street and in their homes. The local police reportedly stood on the sidelines, or actively sided with the attackers. The Jews formed their own brigade and fought back. Only after six days of violent clashes did the authorities step in. Following protests from an American Jewish defense organization, an investigation was undertaken. The official explanation was that the child had been kidnapped by an Uzbek woman. "Her motive had been to hide from her husband the fact that she had undergone an abortion. The couple had separated during her pregnancy. When they were reunited several years later, she feared disclosure of the abortion. On a visit to Margelan she abducted Abdusatarov's child and presented him to her husband as her own." No punishment was ever meted out to the instigators of the violence, and not one of the police who aided and abetted them was dismissed from his post.[30]

It was not until after the Six Day War in 1967 that a mass migration of Bukharan Jews began to take place. Israel's astonishing success against its Arab enemies enhanced the Bukharan Jews' national awareness and pride, and many joined the ranks of the refuseniks who carried out demonstrations and clamored for the right to emigrate. From 1971 to 1985 an estimated quarter of the Tadjiki-Jewish population, some 17,000, were given exit visas. By 1987 there were an estimated 45,000 Bukharan Jews in Central Asia and 32,000 in Israel.

Coinciding with the disintegration of the former Soviet Union, there has been an increase in overtly anti-Semitic acts that has led to an acceleration of Bukharan emigration to Israel. In February 1990 some "unknown perpetrators" defaced and destroyed one hundred tombstones in a Jewish cemetery in Tashkent. Two months later a riot perpetrated by Islamic fundamentalists against Armenians and Jews in the city of Andijan, in the Fergana Valley of Uzbekistan, left more than forty families homeless. Panic-stricken, the vast majority of Jews in the valley emigrated to Israel. Subsequent hostilities in Dushambe, Tadjikistan, and other places have left the Jewish communities in Central Asia in a precarious and anxious state about their future. As of this writing (Summer 1999), there are probably fewer than 5,000 Bukharan Jews left in all of Central Asia. There are estimated to be 35,000 Bukharan Jews in New York. The overwhelming majority are settled in the Forest Hills section of Queens, and the rest reside in the Boro Park section of Brooklyn.

The rites de passage and daily cultural life of the Bukharan Jews in the pre-Soviet period are worth noting. For instance, as in other traditional Jewish communities in less developed societies, descent and kinship in Bukhara were derived patrilineally. The oldest male was the head of the extended family. Included in the extended family were the arch-patriarch's mother's sisters' children, his father's sisters' children, and his mother's brothers' children. Married sons remained members of the household until the death of the arch-patriarch. Households being large, it was common for fifty to one hundred members of a clan to eat together at the Shabbat or Yom Tov meal.

Under Islamic rule—that is, the period before Communist hegemony in Central Asia—the Jews were obliged to dress in public in such a way that they could be readily recognized as Jews. Like Turkestani Muslims, Jewish men shaved their heads, but left two thick *peot* hanging in a curl on either temple. The Jews were allowed to wear the national costume, a multicolored silken caftan called *djamo*, but were forbidden to wear a turban. In the Jewish quarter, in the comfort of their own homes, the Jews' appearance was in striking contrast with their persona in public. On the Sabbath and holidays, the men were gaily attired in hand-stitched yarmulkas of richly woven material and a special purple velvet *djamo* with a gold crown embroidered on the back.

Women were mostly confined to the home. When they did appear in public, they wore an artistically embroidered skullcap; a *parandja*, a silk knee-length robe with long false sleeves; and heavy stockings, over which was swathed a dazzling silk scarf called *duppi*. On the Sabbath and holidays they were attired in a mitre-like headdress that glittered with luxurious jewelry. Although not required by local Islamic law to wear the *chasband* (black horsehair veil worn by Muslim women), a Jewish woman would never dare to venture outdoors without one, lest she be subjected to insults and uncomplimentary remarks.

"The best streets [of Old Bukhara]," observed James Hutton, " barely exceed six feet in width, while the majority are not more than three or four feet. As almost everybody rides, the confusion arising from the crowd of camels, horses, and donkeys, jostling one another as they struggle through these narrow defiles, is both bewildering and disgusting."[31] Houses in the crowded and filthy Jewish quarter were built of mud and stone mixed with chopped straw, covered with plaster, and washed with calcimine. They were usually erected along a courtyard behind a gate or adobe wall. Each residence consisted of a series of rooms that opened onto the courtyard. The interiors were generally decorated with carpets and wall hangings of folk art. Meals were eaten with one's fingers, while sitting on cushions or rugs around a low table.

Standard breakfast fare included a form of bread boiled with milk and salt. Pony meat and a variety of dairy products derived from mare's milk, considered delicacies by other Central Asian peoples, were eschewed by the Jews. The main weekday dinner dish might consist of *shashlik*, small chunks of lamb, fat, onions, and spices fixed on a flat skewer and grilled on fire-blackened bricks. On the Sabbath a hearty rice dish called *plov* was served, consisting of mutton, carrots, onions, apricots, raisins, and almonds, with saffron giving the food its yellow and orange color. A variety of fish dishes were eaten at celebrations and during *shiva* (periods of mourning). Fish is symbolically connected with *gilgul neshamot,* or reincarnation of the soul of the deceased.[32]

In order to be able to distinguish each other's matrilineal genealogy, Bukharan Jews upon acquaintance would inquire about the other's *lakam*. The *lakam*, researcher Rebekah Mendelsohn explains, was a nickname which applied to the patrilineal descendants of the man for whom it was originally coined. The *lakam* labeled a person by a certain characteristic he possessed or by some incident in his life. Thus, a man who ate inordinate quantities of fish was called the Fish-eater. Another man who froze to death was always referred to afterwards as Frozen-death. A third man who had forty donkeys became known as Forty-donkeys. Other nicknames emphasized physical features, such as Tall One and Big Nose. These nicknames would "stick" with the patrilineal descendants of their original owners.[33]

Parents invariably arranged marriages. It was not uncommon for two pregnant mothers to contract a match between their children even before the future bride and groom were out of their respective wombs.[34] Generally, if a young man fancied a girl, he would never approach her directly, but would inform his mother of his interest. She in turn would discuss with her husband the girl's *yichut* (pedigree) and prospect as a choice for their son. Boys generally married in their mid teens, girls around the ages of ten to twelve. A girl was written off as an old maid if by her late teens she was still not married. Marriages between first cousins and also between uncles and nieces were quite frequent. Some Jewish men were polygamous, motivated by the desire to father many children, especially sons. Following talmudic precedence, marriages invariably took place on a Wednesday.

After the announcement of the engagement, three evenings were set aside for a formal gathering of the two families. Mendelsohn describes the wedding preliminaries:

> The families would congregate at the bride's home. . . . At the first meeting, called *kudobini*, the families would be formally introduced. At the second meeting, called *kalymboron*, the groom would pay the *kalym* [brideprice]. He would bring a case filled with gold or silver and place it on the table for the bride's family. The third meeting, usually the day before the wedding, was called *chinabandan*. . . . That meeting was highlighted by the application of ginger-colored henna to the tip of the boy's little finger and the girl's hand. . . . This procedure was accompanied by the music of a special player and singer, and a special pilaf was served to mark the occasion. . . . After the henna was applied to her hand, the girl was supposed to keep her hand closed that night while she slept. The paste would harden and in the morning it was cracked off and only a ginger-and-white design remained. This design stayed visible for about a month and was consid-

ered a mark of beauty. . . . The purpose of the preparation was to ward off any harm that might threaten the girl the night before her wedding. On her wedding day, in accordance with Jewish law, the bride-to-be went to the ritual bath to become purified from her menstrual uncleanliness. All the women of the *mishpacha* would attend her at the baths, and they would have a party there, drink *araq*, and eat sweets.

The wedding ceremony and reception were held at the bride's home. At the reception . . . a lavish feast was served, and often professional musicians were hired to play and accompany the singers and dancers. . . . After the festivities, the bride would be taken to the groom's house in a horse and cart. The horse and cart would be gaily decorated and musicians would accompany them through the streets. The groom was expected to come outside and carry his bride from the street to his room.

. . . The morning after the wedding, the "signs" of the bride's former virginity, i.e., the bedding, were a cause of rejoicing. To mark the occasion, the members of the family ate *nisalla*, a sweet made from sugar, rose water, and the whites of eggs. For the next seven nights, the groom's family were the hosts of the wedding guests. . . . Each night a different set of guests were entertained.[35]

Upon entering her new home, the bride was required to look at herself in the mirror. Her image in the mirror symbolized a life that would be "as bright and shining as a mirror."[36] The newly wedded woman was not permitted to visit her parents' house for one full year, or until the birth of a child, whichever came first. Her return visit to her parents' home was then marked by a great feast called *povokunon*.

Like their Uzbek neighbors, the Bukharan Jews, especially the womenfolk, were extremely superstitious. All kinds of precautions were taken to ward off the potential pernicious effects of *koz* (the evil eye) and *shaidim* (demons). Bukharan Jews believed that the night before the circumcision was a time when Lilith, an impersonator of the devil, would try to harm the child or snatch it away. Therefore, that evening a special *s'oodah* or dinner meal was held. This *s'oodah* was termed *brit Yitzchak* (Covenant of Isaac), and those in attendance recited the passage in the Torah that deals with Abraham's near sacrifice of Isaac.[37] As among other Jews of Persian origin, it was customary for Bukharan Jews to have a friend or member of the family stay up all night in the room with the child, reciting *tehillim* (psalms). The infant mortality rate being very high, Bukharan Jewish women who had experienced a loss would make a vow in order to protect a newborn child. Money was given to charity, and a lock of hair at the nape of the child's neck was left uncut. This lock was called *nizar*, a word derived from the Hebrew *nazir* (an abstinent, like the biblical Samson). Only when a child reached the age of ten or twelve would the lock be cut.[38]

Typically, a boy attended *cheder* until he was about ten or eleven. At that tender age he was considered mature enough to begin his apprenticeship as a merchant or artisan. If he came from a family of merchants, he would accompany his father or uncle to the workplace to observe the bargaining process. After five or six years of plying the trade, he was ready to assume full responsibility. An exceptional youngster who showed potential for talmudic brilliance was sent to the *yeshivot* in Lithuania.

When burying a loved one, the members of the family would circle the grave seven times and throw sacks of money to the four corners of the cemetery. This was done to confound the devil. If the devil did not find the grave, the Bukharan Jews believed, he would not be able to interfere when the deceased was judged in the afterworld. After the funeral the relatives and friends of the deceased would return to the dead person's house for a meal that opened with hardboiled eggs. They ate eggs because they are "a symbol of every little thing in the world and it comforts the people, reminding them that all is not lost and that life goes on."[39] During the *shiva* period, "a bonfire was lit outside the mourner's home. Female kin of the deceased, dressed in dark dresses and a black wraparound shawl, would circle around the fire singing the virtuous qualities of the deceased. They would sit on the floor, weep loudly, and tear at their hair."[40] The Bukharans had a tradition of eating fish during the entire first year of mourning, and during the entire week of each successive anniversary.[41]

Official political relations with the emir were carried on through the *kolontar*, a Jewish secular leader in the capacity of chief administrator, whose duty it was, together with the chief rabbi, to collect taxes and mediate between the government and the community. *Kolontars* were elected by the adult Jewish men in Bukhara and were assisted by *assakals*, who represented their respective Jewish quarters. The women of each quarter elected a *kayvani* whose function was to deal with conflict resolution and supervise the female aspects of religious ceremonies such as weddings, nuptial behavior, and wailing at burial services.[42]

The Chief Rabbi, or *molla-ye-kalan*, had many functions. In addition to his role as secular co-head, he served as spiritual leader and expositor of Torah, as cantor, ritual slaughterer, *cheder* teacher, and as master of ceremonies at all rites of passage. The most learned rabbis were oftentimes not homegrown, but sages and emissaries from Palestine and other talmudic centers in the Middle East and European Russia. In the late nineteenth century *shelichim* from the Chabad Chassidic movement were active among the Bukharan. As a result of these efforts, the Jewish religion was preserved in this community far more than among the Ashkenazi Jews in the Soviet empire, although even in Central Asia the attachment to Judaism has become severely eroded among today's younger generation.

NOTES

1. Y. Z., *From Moscow To Samarkand* (London: Leonard and Virginia Woolf, 1934), p. 113.

2. Johannes Kalter and Margarita Pavaloi, *Uzbekistan: Heirs to the Silk Road* (London: Thames and Hudson, 1997), p. 15.

3. Georgie Anne Geyer, *Waiting for Winter to End* (Washington, D. C.: Brassey's, 1994), p. 159.

4. Victor and Jennifer Louis, *The Complete Guide to the Soviet Union* (New York: St. Martin's Press, 1980), pp. 66–67.

5. Joseph Wolff, *Researches and Missionary Labours Among the Jews, Mohammedans, and Other Sects* (London, 1835), p. 191; David A. Law, *From Samaria to Samarkand* (Lanham, Md.: University Press of America, 1992), p. ii.

6. *Turkestan: The Heart of Asia* (London: Hodder and Stroughton, 1919), p. 172; See also Colin Thurbon, *The Lost Heart of Asia* (London: HarperCollins Publications, 1994), p. 98.

7. "Jews and the Great Silk Road," *Ariel* 8 (1991), p. 12.

8. According to the Talmud, substitute dyes can not be used to fulfill the mitzvah of *tekhelet*. The Talmud specifies that the dye has to be extracted from a live mollusk called *hilazon*. In his doctoral thesis on the subject of *tekhelet*, the future Chief Rabbi of Israel, Isaac Herzog, concluded that *hilazon* was *murex trunculus*. See Yaakov Glasser, Ari Segal, and Hillel Spielman, "Where the Sea Meets the Sky: Reinstituting Tekhelet," *Hamevaser*, 36:2 (1997), pp. 16–20.

9. *Jewish Travellers in the Middle Ages: 19 Firsthand Accounts*, edited and with an introduction by Elkan Nathan Adler (New York: Dover Publications, 1987), pp. 2–3.

10. Ibid., p. 53.

11. Walter Fischel, "The Leaders of the Jews of Bokhara," in *Jewish Leaders* (1750–1940), edited by Leo Jung (New York: Bloch, 1953), p. 535.

12. "Looking Out for Jews in Soviet Central Asia," *Forum-40* (Winter 1980–81), p. 118.

13. Abraham Emanuelson, *The Remnant of the Jews* (New York, 1929), pp. 43–44.

14. Itzak Ben-Zvi, *The Exiled and the Redeemed* (Philadelphia: Jewish Publication Society, 1961), p. 71.

15. Ole Olefson, *The Emir of Bokhara and His Country: Journeys and Studies in Bokhara* (Copenhagen: W. Heinemann, 1911), pp. 298–299; Joseph Wolff, *Researches*, p. 192.

16. Elkan N. Adler, *Jews in Many Lands* (Philadelphia: Jewish Publication Society, 1905), pp. 221–222.

17. Raymond A. Davies, *Soviet Asia: Democracy's First Line of Defense* (New York: The Dial Press, 1942), p. 136.

18. Joseph Wolff, *Researches*, p. 198.

19. Basil Blackwell in co-operation with the Crafts Council, *Ikats: Woven Silks from Central Asia* (Oxford: The Rau Collection, 1988), p. 11.

20. On the Central Asian Jewish musicians and entertainers see Theodore Levin, *The Hundred Thousand Fools of God* (Bloomington: Indiana University Press, 1996), chapters 2 and 7; and *Central Asia in Forest Hills, New York: Music of the Bukharan Jewish Ensemble Shashmaqam*, with notes by Ted Levin (Smithsonian/Folkways Recordings, produced in collaboration with the Ethnic Folk Arts Center, 1991).

21. Fischel, "Leaders," p. 539.

22. *Red Odyssey* (New York: HarperCollins Publishers, 1992), p. 337.

23. For a detailed analysis of Bukharan Jewish commercial operations in czarist times see Max Vekselman, "The Developement of Economic Activity of Bukharan Jews in Central Asia at the Turn of the 20th Century, *Shvut* (New Series) 1–2:17–18 (1995), pp. 63–79.

24. Curtis, *Turkestan*, p. 174.

25. *Dawn Over Samarkand* (New York: Covici, Friede Publishers, 1935), pp. 19–20.

26. Giora Pozailov, *The Aliyah of Bukharan Jews and Their Settlement in Eretz Israel Between 1868–1948* (Master's Thesis, Bar Ilan University, 1991), p. iii.

27. "Bukharan Jewish Culture Under Soviet Rule," *Soviet Jewish Affairs* 9:1 (1979), p. 22.

28. Boris Smolar, "Discovering the Jews of Bukhara," *Jewish Affairs* 29:4 (April 1974), p. 56.

29. David Sitton, *Sephardi Communities Today* (Jerusalem: Council of Sephardi and Oriental Communities, 1985), p. 193.

30. "Blood Libel," *Jews in Eastern Europe* 2:2 (May 1963), pp. 34–35.

31. James Hutton, *Central Asia: From the Aryan to the Cossack* (Nedeln, Liechtenstein: Kraus Reprint, 1977), p. 285.

32. Rebekah Z. Mendelsohn, *The Bukharan Jewish Community of New York City* (Master's Thesis, Columbia University, 1964), p. 69.

33. Ibid., pp. 75–76.

34. Ibid., p. 48.

35. Ibid., pp. 56–58.

36. Baruch Moshavi, *Customs and Folklore of 19th Century Bucharian Jews in Central Asia* (unpublished dissertation, Yeshiva University, 1974), p. viii (Ann Arbor, Mich.: University Microfilm).

37. Mendelsohn, *Bukharan*, p. 64.

38. Ibid., pp. 64–65.

39. Yu. I. Datkhayev, *The Bukharan Jews* (New York, n.p.-n.d.), p. 278.

40. Moshavi, *Customs*, p. ix.

41. Ibid., p. iv.

42. For a detailed description of the traditional religious and administrative structures of the Bukharan Jews see Michael Zand, "Bukharan Jews," in *Encyclopedia Iranica*, vol. 4 (London: Routledge and Keegan Paul, 1990), pp. 530–545.

Part VIII

Afghani Jewish Family, circa 1930
Credit: Reuven Kashani

A Remedy for the Evil Eye

BACKGROUND INFORMATION

Afghanistan is a mountainous, landlocked country in Central Asia, with Iran on its western and southern borders; the Central Asian Republics of Turkmenistan, Uzbekistan, and Tajikistan on the north; Pakistan to the east; and China, in the extreme northeast. With 252,000 square miles, Afghanistan is about the size of Texas. From 1931, during the reign of Sirdar Nadir Shah, up to the Soviet invasion in 1979, Afghanistan was a constitutional monarchy. Presently, Afghanistan is an Islamic theocracy, tightly controlled by the Taliban, and in a state of civil war. Its population is estimated at twenty million. The capital is Kabul. There are two official languages: Pashto, a language of the Iranian branch of the Indo-European language family, and Dari, or New Persian.

There are sixteen ethnic groups in Afghanistan, the two major groups being the Pathans (Pushtu), probably of mixed Turkish-Mongolian, Iranian, and Indian blood (although the Pathans think of themselves as true Aryans); and the Tadjiks, of Persian stock. There are many minority groups in Afghanistan. Only the Uzbeks (a Turkish-Mongolian people) and the Hazara (Mongols who arrived in Afghanistan with Genghis Khan and Tamerlane) have estimated populations of over a million.

Afghanistan is ninety-nine percent Muslim, an estimated four-fifths of whom are Hanafi Sunnis and the rest Shiite. In the 1930s Rosita Forbes described Afghanistan as "probably the most religious country in the world. Beggar and

Cabinet Minister are equally observant of the prayers and fasts enjoined by the Koran."[1] Islamic law has traditionally been very strictly observed, and the Muslim religious leaders have played an enormous role in keeping modern Western influences out of Afghanistan.

Waves of conquering armies—Persians, Greeks, Turks, Arabs, Mongols, Russians, and British—have tried to rule Afghanistan, with little lasting success. In 1979, the former U.S.S.R., renewing an old czarist ambition, invaded Afghanistan. But in a protracted war lasting almost a decade, the invading forces suffered a major defeat—as did all their predecessors. The proud Afghans, warriors by nature, have emerged from millenia of invasions and wars determined to preserve their independence. As a consequence of colonizing attempts, the Afghani rulers of the last two centuries avoided contact with the outside world. The traditional Afghani population consisted of nomadic tribes dwelling in tents. Intense tribal hostility leading to warfare has been common between and within many of these tribal groups to this very day.

Balkh, in the north, is referred to as the "Mother of Cities," because local tradition "asserts its antiquity beyond all other cities in the world."[2] According to this tradition, Balkh was founded by Cabul and Abul, or Cain and Abel. In medieval times Ghazni, in the north, was Afghanistan's greatest city and its capital. The gallant resistance made by the Afghans to stave off the Mongols brought a dreadful retribution and Ghazni was totally demolished in 1221 c.e. by Genghis Khan and his forces. During the period of Mongol conquest, Balkh became the capital and a major commercial center on the Silk Road from China to the West. Herat, today the second major city in Afghanistan, was a center of trade and a great seat of learning, especially during the Timurid period. Kabul, the present-day capital, is at least four thousand years old. In antiquity it was a major center for traders traveling east and west.

THE JEWS OF AFGHANISTAN

God knows on which knee the camel will squat.

—popular Pathan expression

Jews have been living in Afghanistan possibly since biblical times, but there is little information available on the Jewish community of antiquity. This is attributed to the fact that Jewish life, like so much of Afghani civilization in general, was virtually destroyed during the Mongol devastation in the thirteenth century, and there were few surviving records.

According to the *Tanach*, after the destruction of the Northern Kingdom (circa 722 B.C.E.), several of the tribes that made up the Lost Ten Tribes arrived in Gozan, which is believed by some to be the Hebrew pronunciation of the Afghani city of Ghazni. Added to these communities were Judeans brought there by their Babylonian captors. According to one authority, the "Arsathereth," mentioned by Ezra the Scribe as a refuge place for some of the Lost Ten Tribes, may refer to present-day Hazara.[3] Islamic legend has it that the Prophet Ezekiel settled in the Afghani city of Balkh.[4] In talmudic times the Jewish community of Afghanistan was under the jurisdiction of the yeshiva of Pumbedita in Babylonia, and contributed to its upkeep.[5] Whenever the Jewish ecclesiastic authorities in Babylonia wanted to rid themselves of schismatic and heretical types in their midst, they would permanently exile them to far-flung Afghanistan.[6] In the era of the tenth-century scholar Saadia Gaon, who waged a fierce campaign against the antirabbinic Karaite menace, Afghanistan was a hotbed of Karaism.

For many years rumors have abounded that the Pathan tribespeople, who in the late 1980s fought a *jihad* against the Soviet invaders, are of Jewish origin. "To speak of themselves as 'Bani Israil,' . . . is common," writes Edward Oliver, "and the grey-beards are fond of carrying history back to Ibrahim, I'sak and Yakub."[7] According to Henri Noach, "[e]tymologically 'Pathan' may derive from Piton, a grandson of Jonathan, the son of Saul," and "the Afghani royal family in particular trace[s] its ancestry to the tribe of Benjamin."[8] Pathan tribal chieftains, notably the Yosufzais and Durrani clans, claim that they are descended from Afghana, the son of Yirmiah, the son of Melik Talut (King Saul), and that at the time of the Babylonian captivity, in 586 B.C.E., the Afghana and Assaf tribes (Assaf being Afghana's younger brother) were driven by Buktanasar (Nebuchadnezzar) into the mountainous districts of Kohistan-i-Ghor, today known as Hazarajat, in central Afghanistan.[9] According to local tradition, they lived as Jews until the ninth year of Mohammed's mission, when an Afghani-Jewish convert to Islam named Khalil bin Walid, an emissary of Mohammed, sent a letter to his Israelite brothers in the mountains of Ghor, informing them of the appearance of the "Last Prophet of the Ages." A large percentage of the Jewish tribes converted to Islam. As a reward for fighting valiantly in the wars with the infidels, the title of Pathan (Rudder of the Faith) was conferred upon Qais, the leader of the Afghana tribes who was thirty-seventh in descent from King Saul.[10] "The gap of seventeen hundred years between Qais and his ancestor, King Saul," writes Syed Quddus, "is supposed to be filled in by thirty-six generations, which does not appeal to reason. The relationship of Qais with Adam and Abraham also cannot be established, the elements of space and time not tallying. The whole account of this theory is thus reduced to a legend pure and simple."[11]

Scholars searching for evidence of Jewish origins find hints in certain customs and practices of the Pathans. Eliyahu Avichayil, a contemporary Jerusalem rabbi and founder of Amishav (My People Returns), an organization dedicated to searching out lost Jewish communities around the world, claims that Pathan women wear amulets inscribed with the words *Shema Yisroel* and light candles on Friday before sundown.[12] A number of nineteenth- and early- twentieth-century European travelers and scholars were inclined to give credence to the belief that the Afghans were really Bani Israil based on the fact that there is a great likeness between the features of Afghans and Jews. They commented upon the "Hittite" noses and Semitic looks that made the two peoples virtually indistinguishable.[13] Other observers have pointed out other remarkable similarities. For instance, among their customs are circumcision on the eighth day, sidelocks and long beards, separation of meat and milk, lighting candles on Friday night and hiding them in a special basket, and the Passover-like practice of sacrificing animals. Underneath their outer clothing they wear a garment called *kafan* that looks like a tallit *kattan*.[14] The belief is that the Afghans at one time observed Jewish rituals but were forced to conceal their practices. Perhaps the Afghanis were forcibly converted to Islam at some point in the distant past. Nevertheless, according to Vartan Gregorian:

> there is no convincing evidence substantiating the theory of the Jewish origin of the Afghans. There is certainly no relationship between the Pashto and Hebrew languages; nor can reliance be placed on Afghan tribal genealogies, in which facts and chronology are often neglected in favor of legend. A plausible explanation of the origin of the Afghani tradition has been advanced by some modern writers, who hold that the Afghans may have desired to provide a common cultural and ethnic bond between themselves and other Pathan tribes in order to promote unity and to inculcate pride

in their alleged pre-Islamic monotheism—goals that could be achieved by accepting a common Biblical ancestry and grafting tribal genealogies onto the Islamic and Biblical traditions.[15]

Even if perchance the Afghans are descended from Jews, Afghanistan has always been a stronghold of Islam in Central Asia, and the Afghanis have traditionally harbored strong prejudices against the Jewish people.

Based on the meager information that has come down to us, we can surmise that Jewish culture flourished in Afghanistan before the arrival of Genghis Khan. The persecutions of the Jews in Persia by the Sasanian monarch Firuz in 490 C.E. scattered them all over Central Asia, including Afghanistan. Jews in medieval times capitalized on the fabulous wealth to be made in the trade centers of Balkh and Ghazni, along the Silk Route. In "The Book of Ways and Kingdoms," written around 815 C.E., Ibn Khordadbeh gives an account of Jewish caravan merchants known as Radanites, who spoke eight languages and traversed between France and China, using Balkh as one of the stopping-off points.[16] Benjamin of Tudela, who wandered over the greater part of the civilized world in the latter half of the twelfth century, estimated that there were 80,000 Jews in the city of Ghazni alone (although most authorities believe that this number is much too high).[17]

In the sixteenth century, Jewish life experienced a revival of sorts as the Jews assumed a prominent role in the commercial transactions carried out between Afghanistan, the Persian Gulf lands, and India. However, when the overland routes began to decline, so did the fortunes of the Jews in Afghanistan. Occupations became localized, and the Jewish communities in Afghanistan became isolated and economically and spiritually poverty-stricken.

It appears that in modern times there were two physiognomically distinct types of Jews in Afghanistan. One small group, almost indistinguishable from the Afghans by virtue of their tall slender bodies, long faces, and Mongoloid features, was possibly a remnant of those Jews who had survived Genghis Khan's invasion. These Jews spoke Pushtu and were concentrated in Herat.[18] The vast majority of Afghani Jews, however, were Bukharans or Persians Jews, such as the Meshedis who had fled the conversion decree in 1839. Most of these Jews settled in Herat, Kabul, and Maimana. In Kabul these newcomers settled among a small established community of Meshedi Jews who had been residing there since 1772, when Ahmed Shah Duranni transplanted some fifty Jewish families there to generate trade. These Jews spoke Tadjiki, a northern Persian dialect. By the middle of the nineteenth century there were an estimated 40,000 Jews living in Afghanistan.[19]

For a short period these Persian émigrés held an important economic position as traders between Afghanistan and Europe and Central Asia. However, after the deterioration of economic and social conditions in Afghanistan, and the incorporation of Central Asia into the Russian Empire, their economic role declined. There were pogroms in Maimana in 1876 and in Herat in 1879. Around this time the regime imposed on the Jewish community an exorbitant *harbieh* (war tax) in addition to the *jizya* (the poll tax paid by non-Islamic Peoples of the Scriptures), and forcibly drafted three hundred Jewish laborers for service in the armed forces. The Jewish conscripts were compelled to wear a black ribbon around their headdress to distinguish them from the rest of the Afghani population. Taking this as a foreboding sign of things to come, thousands of Afghani Jews fled to Persia, Central Asia, and the Ottoman Empire.

Following the 1917 Communist revolution in Russia, many Bukharan Jews, stigmatized as "bourgeois counterrevolutionaries," and having had their wealth expropriated, fled to Afghanistan to find haven there. Together with the Persian Jews, the Bukharans were instrumental in reviving, albeit briefly, what remained of Jewish life in Afghanistan. These Jews, together with the Indian minority in Afghanistan, monopolized certain trades, especially the manufacturing of sheepskin furs and carpets. Jews were also involved in manufacturing wine and *arak* (brandy made from anise seed). But since Muslims are forbidden to imbibe spirits, this illicit trade with the Muslim population was carried on surreptitiously.[20] With the exception of a handful of well-to-do merchants, most Afghani Jews were peddlers, small shopkeepers, and craftsmen who barely eked out a living. In 1927 there were an estimated sixty Jewish communities in Afghanistan, totaling only around 5,000 people.[21]

During the reign of the reform-minded Nadir Shah (1929–33), the feuding Afghani tribes were briefly reunited under a constitutional monarchy. The Jews were no longer obliged to live in the *mahalli yehudiyeh*, which was sealed off at night. Laws enacted in 1933 granted Jews equal rights. After Nadir Shah's assassination later that year, the political situation of the Jews rapidly deteriorated. By exploiting latter-day Pathan beliefs in their "pure Aryan" racial origins, and by presenting the Jews as a blight on Aryan civilization, the 1933 Nazi propaganda machine stirred up the Afghani masses against the Jews. A pogrom instigated by Shiite mobs broke out in Kabul, and the Jews were driven out of their homes and herded into a special makeshift quarter. Jews were banished from the small towns and border districts, and concentrated in Herat and Kabul. They were forbidden to leave the town of their residence without permission. Ostensibly, these harsh measures were taken to protect the Jews from being brutalized by their hostile neighbors, but obviously the government was responding to popular prejudice with its own form of persecution.

In the mid 1930s the government of Mohammed Zahir Shah introduced various monopolization measures that effectively eliminated Jewish merchants from carrying on independent trade as middlemen. Although Jewish emigration was illegal, their suddenly déclassé status forced many Jews to stealthily flee the country. Thousands found temporary asylum in Iran and India. Many more found haven in India during the great famine of 1944. They lived in Bombay in deplorable conditions before being transported to Israel in 1949–50. From 1951, when the emigration decree was annulled, up to the Six Day War in 1967, more than 4,000 Jews left Afghanistan. The overwhelming majority emigrated to Israel. The rest settled in Europe and the United States.

The Afghani Jews of the last century were very traditional and observant, but their spiritual level was not very high. Their education level was so low that they were obliged to import rabbis from as far away as North Africa and Eastern Europe. Each community was represented by a *kolontar*. The *kolontar* was elected by the patriarchs of the leading Jewish families and represented the community before the government. He was responsible for collecting the *jizya* from every male fifteen and older. A *chevra*, or communal council composed of the family heads, ran the internal affairs of the community. The *chevra* administered to the needy; adjudicated civil disputes; dealt with burials; and, when necessary, meted out corporal punishment for violators of Jewish laws.[22] Anyone refusing to comply with the decisions of the *chevra* was excommunicated from the community and denied entry to the synagogue.[23] The *chevra* avoided resorting to the local authorities because they mistrusted Islamic justice.[24]

Boys attended *cheder* and *midrash* until their mid teens, before entering the family occupation. As in most other Third World Jewish patriarchal societies, girls received no schooling whatsoever. Like their mothers, they rarely left the house. Their mothers taught them to knit and crochet, as well as other essential domestic skills. This constituted their entire education.

A Jewish woman or girl never went outdoors without wearing the *burqa*. This was a shapeless, loose, dark blue cotton garment that covered her from head to toe. There was only a small lacy inset over her eyes through which she could peer out. The color distinguished her from the Muslim woman, who wore a white *burqa*.[25] The men were attired in pajama-style trousers and a loose tunic of white cotton like the Muslims, but were distinguished from the latter by their black, dome-shaped karakul caps. According to local Jewish tradition, the color black symbolized mourning for the destruction of the Temple.[26]

The mores and folkways of the Afghani Jews were in many ways similar to those of their coreligionists in Persia, where the great majority originated. However, some of the customs and superstitions evolved out of a specifically Afghani milieu, and are therefore uniquely different from those of Jews elsewhere. For instance, as is a Jewish custom in many Muslim lands even today, the congregants removed their shoes before entering the synagogue. Inside, they sat cross-legged on the rugs and cushions. According to tradition, the men would sit along the walls of the synagogue, facing the raised platform from which the Torah scroll was read. From its outward appearance, a western Jew from any time period would hardly be able to distinguish the synagogue from an Islamic mosque.

On Tisha B'Ab, the solemn day commemorating the destruction of the two Temples, the Jews would sacrifice cattle and sheep, bought with money collected only from women, in the courtyard of the synagogue.[27] The eyes of the slaughtered animal were used as charms to ward off the evil spirits; the meat was distributed to the poor.[28] On Rosh Hashanah every family would slaughter a sheep in memory of the sacrifice of Isaac. A portion of this meat was given to the poor. Some of the blood was used to make a sign on the door, with fingers that had been dipped in the blood. Extremely pious individuals would also mark their foreheads with the blood.[29]

Scourging played an important role in the rites and rituals of the Afghani Jews. During the Passover *seder*, for example, when they came to the *Dayenu* verses, the Jews would lash one another with leeks to recall the Egyptian taskmasters' beating of the Jewish slaves.[30] On the day after Passover the men would go out into the fields and pluck green wheat stalks. Upon returning to the synagogue, they would strike one another with the stalks while wishing each other a Happy New Year.[31]

Every male over the age of thirteen, after undergoing ritual ablution on Erev Yom Kippur, would endure a ritual lashing to remind him of his sins and stir him to repentance. This ritual lashing, called *malkut*, was usually carried out in the women's gallery. *Malkut* consisted of a maximum thirty-nine lashings, which were administered with a whip made from cowhide and mule skin, while the penitent was standing with his hands tied to an overhead beam. Immediately afterwards, the penitent would contribute to charity and visit the *mikvah* a second time.[32]

The marriage age was around sixteen to eighteen for men. If by the age of fourteen a girl still wasn't married, she was considered an old maid and a source of great shame to her family. Although polygamy was permitted, because the Afghani Jews never submitted to the excommunication decree of the Ashkenazi talmudist Rabbeinu Gershom, it was rare among the Afghani Jews. It occurred almost exclusively among the well-to-do if the first wife had not given birth to a male.[33]

The groom's parents invariably chose their son's bride. In doing so, their primary criteria was the social and economic status of the prospective bride's parents. The groom's parents chose their son's bride without allowing him to express his feelings and wishes. The groom was not even permitted to see his betrothed, because she was required to remain veiled until the night before the wedding. The groom's family asked one of their female confidantes to conduct the marriage negotiations. If an agreement was reached, the bride's family signified their consent by sending the groom a chunk of sugar.[34] Two weeks later the bride's father invited his future in-laws and their relatives to a betrothal feast called *shirini khori*. A year or longer might elapse before the actual wedding took place, in order to enable the bride to prepare her trousseau.[35]

A day before the wedding the bride and groom were escorted separately to the *mikvah*. The evening before the wedding day was devoted to the ceremony of henna dyeing. Later that night, at the bride's home, the bridegroom had his first opportunity to see his bride without her veil on. *Shoshbinim* (best men) served him assorted sweets and entertained him. After the rabbi had dyed the palms of the groom's hands with henna, he was escorted home by his *shoshbinim*.[36]

On the afternoon of the wedding the *ketubah* (marriage contract) was drawn up and the young couple sat down to share their first meal together. At nightfall the wedding procession to the groom's house took place. Amidst much dancing and singing the bride was asked to sit down and grace the chairs placed by the invitees along the way. They handed her sweets and sprinkled her with rosewater.[37] A highlight of the wedding party occurred when the groom lightly placed his right foot on her right foot to symbolize his dominant position.[38] "A great bonfire was lit in the courtyard for the bride, and the bride and the young people would dance around it. Then a brightly painted sheep, decked out with roses and silk kerchiefs, was led out and slaughtered in her presence."[39] *Tallitim* (prayer shawls) served as a *chuppah* (canopy), and the guests held lighted candles during the ceremony. The lavish wedding festivity lasted for seven days and seven nights at the home of the bridegroom.

The infant mortality rate was very high, so a variety of magical potions and amulets, each of which had a specific purpose, were prescribed for a woman in labor. Erich Brauer, a Jewish anthropologist who visited the Afghani Jews in the 1940s, described the great lengths to which the Jews would go in order to keep the *shaidim* (evil spirits) at a distance from a mother who was about to give birth. Dr. Brauer described the practices and rituals surrounding childbirth as follows:

> The mother sits upon three stones during labor, and a sword is brought into the room. The newborn infant is drawn through the mouth of a wolfskin and for eight days is never laid down, but is held continuously in the arms of a specially qualified old woman. When this woman goes to bed, she passes the baby on to another woman. The infant is not fed by the mother for the first ten or eleven days. On the first two days the baby is given some water sweetened with sugar and a special kind of fruit, following which he or she is turned over to a wet-nurse. The mother's milk is drawn off during these ten days and poured out at some distance lest some woman should step over it and become infertile. In families which have lost several children, a mock marriage is arranged with a woman sixty or more in order to avert the Evil One's threat. In the same way, baby girls are "married" to old men.[40]

The circumcision ceremony took place in the synagogue. During the *millah* rite, Elijah's staff, a long wooden cane with an engraved silver handle, was removed from the *aron kodesh* (Holy Ark). The Afghani Jews believed that the old prophet, who is the patron saint of Jewish males, weary from his rounds of attending *brisot*, needs to lean on the staff. After the ceremony, the staff was taken to the child's home to protect him from the evil eye. Sick members of the community who drank the water used in rinsing the *mohel*'s implement were believed to become cured.[41] When a woman was ill, her son (if she had one) would bring a kettle filled with water to the House of Learning. He would pass the kettle around and the students would recite psalms over the kettle and expiate her malady with the "water of prayer."[42] When a member of the household became critically ill, the custom was to place a brick at the entrance of the house and draw squares with black coals. In each square they would place one raisin, one onion, some peanuts, and one penny. This was their way of appeasing the *shaidim*. No one dared pocket this coin because it was capable of transmitting the sick person's illness.[43]

Extremely superstitious like their Muslim neighbors, the Afghani Jews took numerous preventive measures to deal with potential misfortunes and accidents attributable to *shaidim* and ghosts. Charms, spells, and talismans were used to cure illness. Jewish ritualistic and sacramental objects were considered countermeasures against evil spirits. For example, knives were placed on top of jugs to keep ghosts from penetrating them.[44] The wax of candles used on Yom Kippur [45] and rainwater gathered on the seventh day of Passover were believed to have magical qualities as countermeasures to misfortunes and evil spirits.[46]

Every healthy Afghan Muslim is obligated to make *haj* to the holy city of Mecca at least once in his lifetime. Those who complete the journey are given the honorific title *haji*. In the same way, those elders of the Jewish community who fulfilled the mitzvah of *ohleh regel*—making pilgrimage to Eretz Israel—were bestowed with the appellation *haji*.[47]

Since 1948, more than 4,000 Afghani Jews have immigrated to Israel. In 1969 there were only an estimated 300 Jews left in Afghanistan. Prior to the Soviet invasion in 1979, there were only thirty Jews remaining, who still maintained a functioning synagogue in Kabul. As of summer 1999, there are no Jews living in Afghanistan. The largest concentration of Afghani Jews in the Diaspora today is located in the United States. There are an estimated 150 Afghani-Jewish families in New York, most of them concentrated in the borough of Queens. There are also tiny pockets of Afghani Jews in Bangkok, Hong Kong, Milan, and London.

NOTES

1. *Forbidden Road* (New York: E. P. Dutton, 1937), p. 38.

2. Frank Ross, ed., *Central Asia: Personal Narrative of General Josiah Harlan* (London: Luzac and Co., 1939), p. 28.

3. Edward E. Oliver, *Across the Border: or Pathan and Biloch* (Lahore: Al-Birini, 1972), p. 96.

4. Walter J. Fischel, "The Jews of Central Asia (Khorasan) in Medieval Hebrew and Islamic Literature," *Historia Judaica* 7 (1945), p. 37.

5. Clifford E. Bosworth, *The Ghaznavids: Their Empire in Afghanistan and Eastern Iran, 994–1040* (Edinburgh: Edinburgh University Press, 1963), p. 261.

6. Fischel, "The Jews of Central Asia," p. 32.

7. Oliver, *Across the Border*, p. 258.

8. "In Pursuit of the Lost Ten Tribes: An Odyssey to the East," *Forum* 61 (1988), pp. 42–43.

9. Itzhak Ben-Zvi, "Jewish Traditions Amongst Afghans and Pathans," *India and Israel* 5:7 (January 1953), p. 22.

10. On the myth of the Jewish origins of the Afghans see H. W. Bellew, *An Inquiry Into the Ethnography of Afghanistan* (Graz, Austria: Akademische Druck, 1973), pp. 20–21; Mounstuart Elphinstone, *An Account of the Kingdom of Cabul*, vol. 1, 3rd ed.,

with a new Introduction by Sir Olaf Caroe (London: Oxford University Press, 1972), pp. 206–209; Olaf Caroe, *The Pathans 550 B.C.–A.D. 1957* (Karachi: Oxford University, 1958), pp. 3–10; G. P. Tate, *The Kingdom of Afghanistan: A Historical Study* (Delhi: D. K. Publishing House, 1973), p. 10; Itzak Ben-Zvi, *The Exiled and the Redeemed* (Philadelphia: Jewish Publication Society, 1961), esp. pp. 180–91; and Oliver, *Across the Border*, pp. 96–101.

11. *The Pathans* (Lahore: Ferozson, 1987), p. 23.

12. *Wall Street Journal* (15 May 1991), p. 1; Yossi Klein Halevi, "In Search of the Ten Lost Tribes," *The Jerusalem Report* 1:35 (13 June 1991), p. 18.

13. See for examples, Alexander Burnes, *Travels into Bukhara* (London: Oxford University Press, 1973), p. 164; and S. K. H. Katrak, *Through Amanullah's Afghanistan: A Book of Travel* (Karachi: Sind Observer, 1929), p. 8.

14. See Abraham Ben Aghajan Hacohen's eyewitness account of the Afridi tribal customs in Itzhak Ben-Zvi, "Jewish Traditions," p. 25; Shalva Weil, "Pathan Puzzle," *The Jerusalem Post Magazine* (5 October 1979), p. 10; Al-Haj Khwaja Nazir Ahmad, *Jesus in Heaven On Earth* (Woking, England: The Working Muslim Mission and Literary Trust, 1952), pp. 289–337.

15. *The Emergence of Modern Afghanistan* (Palo Alto, Calif.: Stanford University, 1969), p. 27.

16. Elkin Adler, *Jewish Travelers in the Middle Ages: 19 Firsthand Accounts* (New York: Dover Publications, 1987), p. 3.

17. Hayyim J. Cohen, "Afghanistan," *Encyclopaedia Judaica*, vol. 2 (Jerusalem: Keter, 1973), p. 326.

18. S. Landshut, *Jewish Communities in the Moslem Countries of the Middle East: A Survey* (London: The Jewish Chronicle, 1950), pp. 69–70; *Jewish Chronicle* (9 October 1886), cited in *India and Israel* 5:7 (January 1953), p. 27.

19. Landshut, ibid., p. 68.

20. Ross, *Central Asia*, pp. 48–49.

21. Ben Zion D. Yehoshua-Raz, *From the Lost Tribes in Afghanistan to the Mashhad Jewish Converts of Iran* (Jerusalem: Mosad Byalik, 1992), p. 354.

22. Nehemiah Robinson, *Persia, Afghanistan, and Their Jewish Communities* (New York: Institute of Jewish Affairs, World Jewish Congress, 1953), p. 31; Joseph B. Schechtman, *On Wings of Eagles: The Plight, Exodus, and Homecoming of Oriental Jewry* (New York: Thomas Yoseloff, 1961), p. 257.

23. Robinson, ibid.

24. Schechtman, *On Wings*, p. 257; Ida Cowen, *Jews in Remote Corners of the World* (Englewood Cliffs, N.J.: Prentice Hall, 1971), p. 244.

25. Erich Brauer, "The Jews of Afghanistan: An Anthropological Report," *Jewish Social Studies* 4:2 (April 1942), p. 131.

26. Landshut, *Jewish Communities*, p. 70.

27. Robinson, *Persia*, p. 30.

28. Ibid.

29. Brauer, "The Jews of Afghanistan," p. 136.

30. Cowen, *Jews in Remote Corners*, p. 241.

31. Ibid., p. 242.

32. Brauer, "The Jews," p. 136 ; Zohar Negbi and Bracha Yaniv, *Afghanistan: The Synagogue and the Jewish Home* (Jerusalem: Center for Jewish Art—The Hebrew University, 1991), p. 31.

33. Brauer, ibid., p. 132.

34. Cowen, *Jews in Remote Corners*, p. 245.

35. Brauer, "The Jews," p. 128–29.

36. Ibid., pp. 129–30.

37. Ibid., p. 130.

38. Ibid., pp. 130–31.

39. Ibid., p. 131.

40. Ibid., p. 133.

41. Negbi and Yaniv, *Afghanistan*, pp. 34–35; Felice Maranz, "By the Staff of Elijah," *The Jerusalem Report*, 2:13 (16 January 1992), pp. 34–35.

42. Yehoshua-Raz, *From the Lost Tribes*, pp. 367–68.

43. Ibid., p. 368.

44. Otto Schnitzler, introduction to Reuven Kashani, *The Jews of Afghanistan* (Jerusalem: n.p., 1975), p. iv.

45. Ibid.

46. Brauer, "The Jews," p. 138.

47. Kashani, *The Jews*, p. 28.

Part IX

Malabari Jewish Children, Cochin, India
Credit: Judah Magnes Museum

Jewish Untouchables?

BACKGROUND INFORMATION

The Republic of India consists of twenty-five self-governing states and seven union territories, on a subcontinent about a third the size of the United States. With an estimated 800 million people, it is the second largest country in the world in population. New Delhi is its capital.

The Indians are mainly a rural people, with eighty percent of the population living in more than half a million villages. These villages vary in size from a couple of dozen people to several thousand, and are self-contained economic and social units existing in virtual isolation. Fourteen major languages and more than a thousand minor languages and dialects are spoken throughout India. Hindi is the official language of the country and English is a required language in the schools. Hinduism, Buddhism, Jainism, and Sikhism originated on this subcontinent. Hindus make up eighty-three percent of the population; Muslims constitute eleven percent; and the rest of the people are Sikhs, Jains, Buddhists, Farsis, Christians, and Jews.

Around 1700 B.C.E. the Aryans, an adventurous and belligerent pastoral people from somewhere in the northwest, conquered India and subjugated the natives, who were known as Harrapin (Dravidians). The Aryans were concentrated in the northern regions of India, and these people tended to be taller and have lighter skin color than the Indians in the south. In their new land, the Aryan conquerors synthesized elements of their own civilization with that of the indigenous people. They developed a pantheistic religion, called Brahmanism, embracing the eternal divine essence; a holy tongue called Sanskrit, and a social system called *varna* (class), in which distinct hereditary social classes are regulated in their social dealings with the others.

Writes Jacob Pandian: "Recent scholarship suggests that the institution of caste existed long before the Aryan speakers became part of that civilization. But because of the prevalence of racist theories of anthropology during the last two hundred years, many scholars assumed that racial tensions must have existed between the light-skinned Aryan speakers and dark-brown Dravidian speakers and, as a result, the caste system was imposed on the indigenous populations to safeguard or protect the racial purity of the Aryans. Modern scholarship suggests that the Aryans were assimilated into the preexisting caste-system of the Dravidian-speaking populations. It must be noted that physical features of skin color do not determine an individual's caste identity: People with light- and dark-brown skin color can be found in the same caste, just as diverse physical features can be found among members of an Indian family."[1] Pandian continues: "[T]here are no uniquely physical characteristics that can be identified as belonging to one caste. The Brahman who is black skinned . . . is not ranked as ritually impure or low because of his or her skin color. The untouchable is not given ritually pure or high status even when he or she has very light skin color. . . ."[2]

The full development of the rules regarding caste, a system of hierarchical organization, were formulated in the Code of Manu (circa 200 B.C.E.). This Code provided measures by which the small number of light-skinned conquerors could avoid being assimilated by the predominantly dark-skinned natives whom they considered inferior to themselves. The Bramaic system held that even the most casual contact with the lower castes polluted the higher caste. Intermarriage and eating together were forbidden to members of different castes. Breaking this law was punishable by social ostracism, and the loss of all rights and property. Caste membership was acquired by birth and remained determined for a person's entire life. Each caste was associated with a separate profession, trade, or occupation. It was forbidden for the members of one caste to do the work associated with another.

From the Aryan arrival up to Mahatma Gandhi's time, social stratification based on caste, language, and race was institutionalized. Transition from a lower caste to a higher caste was difficult, but could be achieved within a couple of generations by emulating Brahmanic practices of a regional dominant caste, such as eschewing alcohol or betrothing daughters at an extremely tender age. Invariably "members of the caste group that has moved up will have a revised history of the past that would exclude any reference to their former inferior status, and the lack of scholarly historiography was a functional component of rewriting the past."[3] Because of the rigidity of the caste system, life has changed remarkably little in India over the centuries.

Many of the virtuous principles identified with India, such as vegetarianism, religious tolerance, pacifism, and *ahimsa* (noninjury to living creatures), are attributed to the Mauryan Emperor Asoka, a convert to Buddhism who ascended the throne around 273 B.C.E. It was Asoka, the great unifier of India, who proclaimed, "All the roads lead to the same Godhead," and "All religions deserve reverence for one reason or another."

Arab armies brought the religion of Islam to India in the eighth century, and ruled large parts of Northern India from the twelfth to the eighteenth century. From around 1200 to 1750 a succession of nomadic Turkish-Mongolian tribes from the steppes of Central Asia invaded India. Tamerlane's devastation in the 1380s left Delhi a smoldering ruin, filled with the stench of rotting corpses. In 1526 Islamic Moguls from the Kush Mountains of Afghanistan conquered North India. During the reign of the Moguls, traders from Portugal and Spain began to arrive.

European powers were attracted to India's riches, and they competed for trading advantage. Each country tried to corner the market for the spices, cotton cloth, silk, indigo, and other goods that were in great demand in Europe. Portuguese trading posts established at Fort Cochin in 1500 were succeeded by the Dutch East India Company in 1663. During the seventeenth century the British East India Company established important trading posts and forts at Bombay, Calcutta, and Madras. In 1757 eventual control over all India was gained through British superior sea power in the Battle of Plassey. The British colonized India and exploited the country's natural resources and labor. Under British rule, India became the first Asiatic country to have a modern bureaucracy. Mahatma Gandhi and his followers, using a decades-long campaign of *satyagraha*, or nonviolent resistance, finally caused the British to withdraw from India in 1947. India thus became an independent country and is a full-fledged member of the United Nations

The following material focuses on Bombay and Cochin, where the two major Jewish communities are located:

Bombay, the capital of Maharashtra state, is the second-largest city in India, and it is the commercial, industrial, and financial center of the country. Once an island surrounded by malarial mud flats, it was passed on to the British by its Portuguese occupiers as a wedding dowry in 1661. Soon after the British takeover, Bombay developed into the "Gateway of India." The Konkan Coast, about twenty miles west of Bombay, is a lush area covered with palm and mango trees. Coconut and betelnut trees also abound. Rice, which grows extensively in the region, is the staple food.

Cochin is the largest city in Kerala State. This state, on the Malabar Coast, is a thin sliver of land at India's southwestern tip, about 250 miles long, wedged between the Arabian Sea and the Western Ghats. The Malabar Coast is about 600 miles south of Bombay. Kerala is one of India's smallest and densest states, created out of Travancore-Cochin and the Malabar Coast district of Madras State, in 1956. Its interior is tropical rain forest, and before they were hunted to near extinction abounded with tigers, black panthers, apes and herds of elephants, ibex, buffalo, and boar. Banana bushes, coconut, palm, cashew, and jackfruit and other tropical fruits are plentiful. From early antiquity this jungle paradise exported teas and spices, such as cinnamon, cloves, cardamom, lemongrass, and ginger. The most important export is Tellicherry pepper, called "black gold," for which the ancient traders—Phoenicians, Egyptians, Arabians, Greeks, and Romans—flocked to the ports at Cranganore and Poovar. The port cities of Kerala were major trading centers dating back to ancient times. The presence of centuries-old Christian, Muslim, and Jewish communities gives this part of southern India its cosmopolitan character. Referred to as the Venice of the East, Cochin has a surviving fort that is believed to be the oldest European settlement in India.

THE BENE ISRAEL OF BOMBAY

A woman who argues with her *teli* (oil-man) must sit in the dark.
A woman who marries a *teli* need never wash her hands with
water.

—popular Indian saying

According to ancient beliefs, the Bene Israel of Bombay have been living in India for more than two thousand years. Unlike Jews living in the Christian and Muslim world, they never experienced persecution because of their religious beliefs. India has a long tradition of being respectful to people of different faiths who have settled there, and the Jews were no exception. The tiny Bene Israel community was surrounded by tens of millions of Hindus and Muslims. Yet, throughout their history in India they managed to cling tenaciously to certain vestiges of the Jewish religion and were treated respectfully by their neighbors. Before their mass migration to Israel in the late 1940s and early 1950s, there were an estimated 30,000 Bene Israel in India. Today, almost fifty years after the *aliyah* to Israel, there are fewer than 5,000 Bene Israel left.

No one knows exactly how or when the community began to call itself Bene Israel. One hypothesis is that since the term "Jew" is offensive to Muslims, but the Koran speaks respectfully of the "Bene Israel," the Jews of the Konkan referred to themselves as Bene Israel so as to not antagonize Muslim conquerors. According to the nineteenth-century Bene Israel historian Kehimkar, "The hatred which the Mohammedans bear towards the name Yehudi (Jew) as may be seen from the Koran, is itself a ground for believing that our ancestors, through fear of being compelled to renounce their religion, or of losing their lives and property, thought it expedient to adopt the name less hated by the followers of Mohammed, viz. 'Bene-Israel' (children of Israel), which served both objects: the retention of their ancient name and faith, and the preservation of their lives and property."[4] Other scholars believe the name was conferred upon them by British colonial officers in the eighteenth century.

It is also not known exactly when the Jews arrived in India. Some historians think that they came during Solomonic times, or were a segment of the Lost Ten Tribes from Northern Israel that were driven into exile in 722 B.C.E. Their name might reflect the fact that they were from Israelite tribes, and not from the southern Kingdom of Judah. That is why, according to this view, they referred to themselves as Bene Israel. The nineteenth-century Jewish traveller I. J. Benjamin was convinced that the river Gozan, mentioned in the *Tanach*, is the Hebrew word for the Ganges.[5] Other historians contend that the Bene Israel came to India sometime in the first millenia of the Common Era, fleeing persecution in Babylonia or Persia; or perhaps they are the progeny of those primitive Bedouin Jewish tribes in the oasis settlements of southern Arabia, known as Banu Israil, who were expelled from the Hejaz after the hegemony of Islam in the seventh century.[6] It is also plausible that the medieval Jewish traders known as Radanites, who reached India from the overland highways across Bactria and the Oxus, made this tolerant land their permanent home.[7] The Bene Israel have their own fascinating account of how they settled in India.

According to Bene Israel legend, after the Greeks conquered Palestine in 332 B.C.E. life became extremely oppressive for the Jews. The situation became especially insufferable when, in the year 175 B.C.E., the Greek tyrant Antiochus Epiphenes tried to impose the Hellenistic religion on the Jews. This would eventually lead to the Maccabean revolt and the story of Chanukah. Almost immediately after the persecutions began, the Bene Israel say, a group of Jews from the Galilee managed to flee to Egypt. There, they boarded a ship probably sailing for Cheul, a major port city on the Maharashtra coast of west India. When they were within a couple of hundred yards off the port of Konkan, about fifteen miles from Cheul Creek, the ship ran aground and sank. Most of the people on board, together with all their possessions, including the Torah scrolls and prayer books, were lost. Out of all those on board, legend has it that seven men and seven women managed to swim ashore. After being given shelter by some kindhearted Hindus from Navgaon (a village twenty miles south of what would later become Bombay), the Jews found permanent abode on the Konkan Coast. The Bene Israel legend bears similarities to the neighboring Chitpavan Brahman legend concerning that group's arrival in the Konkan. That legend also features the arrival of seven shipwrecked couples.[8]

The Bene Israel were strongly influenced by the dominant cultures they lived among; in many respects their mores and folkways were intertwined with those of the Hindus and Muslims. This intertwining extended to their food, their manner and style of dress, and appearance. They spoke Marathi and their surnames were derived from the villages where their ancestors settled, but their given names were Indianized forms of biblical names, such as Musajee for Moses and Samajee for Samuel.

In traditional Bene Israel society, families lived in a joint household, like other Indians, and until fairly recent times, they practiced strict hereditary endogamy. This meant that when a son got married, he would bring his wife to live with him in his father's house. The *kulapa* (patriarch) would run the household, manage affairs, and settle arguments between members of the family. The wives of the sons would help their mother-in-law with the housework. Each person contributed to the welfare of the whole family. Bene Israel men sometimes practiced polygamy, which in Indian society was an indication of high social status and prestige. They were free to remarry if one of their spouses passed away. In emulation of, and deference to, Brahmanic custom, Bene Israel women very rarely remarried. It was common for children as young as three years old to get married. The betrothed children remained with their respective parents and did not live together until they reached adulthood, which in Indian society could be as young as ten.

Like other Indians, the Bene Israel loved to eat spicy food prepared with curry. Like many other low endogamous subcastes (*jatis*), they consumed meat and fish, but out of respect for orthodox Hinduism, which holds cattle to be sacred, and probably to raise their social status vis-à-vis the higher castes, they did not include beef in their diet.[9] Bene Israel women, like other Indian women, draped themselves with long, blazing wraparound silk dresses called *saris*. Bene Israel women adopted the custom of wearing rings and pendants in their noses and ears, and row upon row of glass bangles and gold and silver bracelets on wrist and ankle. But unlike Hindu women, Bene Israel women were never known to have worn the *tika*, the red or yellowish dot, on the forehead.[10] Hindu women wear the dot as a sign of good fortune. Bene Israel men wore the traditional white loincloth called *dhoti* and turbans, but were distinguished from non-Jewish men by their Orthodox-style *peot* (earlocks) and the absence of a *shendi* (a tuft on the crown of their heads). Such common higher caste Hindu practices as cremating the dead and *suttee*, the self-immolation of widows on the funeral pyres of their husbands, were anathema to the Bene Israel.

According to the *Manava Dharmashastra* (Manu's Brahmanic Code), it is sinful for a Hindu to work at pressing oil, because crushing oil-bearing seeds is considered destroying life.[11] The Jewish religion has a different attitude regarding what constitutes destroying life. For example, olive oil that they pressed themselves was included among the offerings that Jews donated to the Temple in Jerusalem on the holidays, and this was considered a great *mitzvah*. Pressing oil was a flourishing business in ancient Israel. Since most Hindus refused to do this sort of work, the Jews had no qualms about stepping in. They soon came to be known as *shenwar teli*, which in the local vernacular, Marathi, means "Saturday Oil Presser Caste," because they refrained from working on that day.

It is necessary to understand something about the Hindu religion in order to understand how the *shenwar teli* fit into the Indian caste system. For instance, Hindus believe in fate, which means that the course of a person's life is predetermined and cannot be changed. Hindus worship many different gods and a supreme being called Brahma. They also believe in reincarnation. By doing good deeds in this life, one creates good karma, which assures their return as a member of a higher caste. Hindu society was originally divided into four *varna*s, or castes, based on the kind of work the caste members performed. The highest caste were the priest-intellectuals called Brahmans. Below them were the warriors and rulers, known as Kshatriyas. They were followed by the Vaisyas, who were the merchant and landowning classes. The Shudras were a multitude of cultivators and laboring classes whose function was to meekly serve the three so-called twice-born castes. Each person's place in the caste system was unalterably fixed by birth. Over time, with changes in society, the caste system not only absorbed new occupations and new distinctions, but also streams of migrants and foreign invaders. The four basic divisions began to lose meaning as they were overtaken by thousands of different subcaste groups (*jatis*), many of them hoping to attain higher rank in their locales.

Members of the different castes never eat together and never intermarry. Every person is born into a caste, and he or she cannot leave the caste during this lifetime. Hindus believe that if people live a good life, then they will be reborn into a higher caste—but if they breach the rules of the caste they belong to, they will not only be banished from their family and community, but can expect to receive severe punishment in their future lives. Such people, Hindus believe, may come back in the next life as *panchjahanas* or Untouchables, the lowest-born of all castes. Hindus from the higher castes avoid contact with Untouchables. Higher caste Hindus must not touch them or anything they touch. Even being in the shadow of an Untouchable would make them unclean!

Although they were not considered to be an integral part of the Hindu caste system, Jews and other non-Hindu minorities, by virtue of the specific economic role they performed in local society, also formed bodies analogous to *jatis* (local or endogamous subcastes), and thereby were able to assimilate into the larger caste structure. At the same time, the religious separateness of the Jews and other religious castes was recognized as unique and respected, enabling these groups to retain their own autonomy. Since oil pressing was considered a particularly degrading *shudra*-like type of work (as compared with more respectable *shudra* occupations such as metal work or pottery, for example), Hindus of higher castes were especially careful to avoid making contact with the Bene Israel. For example, if a Bene Israel touched a plate that a higher caste person ate from, the plate was considered unclean and the higher caste Hindu would no longer be allowed to eat from that plate. For their part, the Bene Israel, fearing ritual pollution, shunned contact with the scavenging, carrion-eating castes, and avoided other castes who were reviled as the dregs of Hindu society.[12]

Under Jewish religious law, social differences based on caste and race are not recognized. In the Bible the Jews are referred to as a "nation of priests." This means that in the "eyes" of God, all Jews are considered equal. But the Bene Israel offspring of the shipwrecked survivors were isolated from the rest of world Jewry. They sacrificed animals, which may have been in keeping with the tradition of their ancestors in Temple times but just as likely was in emulation of the rituals of their Hindu neighbors. They appear to have forgotten the festivals of Shevuot and Sukkot, but did remember to refrain from work on the Sabbath, fasted on Yom Kippur, and celebrated a variant of Passover. They circumcised their male children on the eighth day, and recited the *Kriyat Shema* ("Hear O Israel God is One, God is One") when they were invited to each other's homes. But without possession of the Holy Writ, and with no knowledge whatsoever of talmudic developments, they could not follow most of the other commandments. Among the many things they forgot is that there is no such thing as a higher or lower caste among Jews. Living among the Hindus, they began to copy their neighbors' ways and developed a caste system of their own. *Gora*, or White Bene Israel, claimed to be the pure descendants of the seven surviving couples, while *kala*, or Black Bene Israel, were thought to be the offspring of Bene Israel and non-Jewish women, or from a divorced woman who had remarried. *Gora* treated *kala* like lower caste. Until the middle of the twentieth century, *gora* would not include *kala* in the prayer and *kiddush* services in the synagogue, or allow their children to marry *kala*. "Nevertheless," anthropologist Schifra Strizower reminds us, "*gora* and *kala* cannot legitimately be considered to have formed a full-fledged caste system. Relations between them were not conceived of as preordained or even as necessary."[13]

The Bene Israel carried on their traditional occupations in the towns and villages dotting the Konkan Coast. They processed seeds and nuts from coconuts, palm, sesame, neem, castor, mustard, and linseed—all derived from plants and trees that were either grown on their own land or were brought to them by other villagers who paid them for their services. The techniques for pressing oil were primitive in the extreme, but adequate for their limited production. A grindstone was propelled by one or two blindfolded bullocks harnessed to the apparatus, which went round and round in the mill. These processed oils were used as a cooking medium, for lighting lamps, for medical purposes, and as a body tonic. Some varieties of non-edible oils were used for burning in the lamps. The Bene Israel used coconut oil for Sabbath candle lighting.

As time went by, the illiterate Bene Israel's knowledge of Judaism faded under the twin pressures of Hindu surroundings and isolation from other Jews. They settled comfortably on their little farms in the mud and bamboo-hutted jungle villages of the Konkan Coast.[14] Surrounded by rice paddies and private orchards of plantain, mango, banyan, margosa, coconut, and palm trees, the Bene Israel enjoyed a reputation among their neighbors as hardworking, loyal, simple, and pious folks. There are many stories about the lives of the honorable and God-fearing Jewish men and women of the Konkan Coast. Here is one such tale.

Shlomo was a rich oil presser from the village of Tala who was blessed with much cattle and land. He was loved and respected by other Bene Israel, by his non-Jewish neighbors, and by the Hindu rulers of his area. But after the Muslims went to war against the Hindus, a false accusation was made to the Hindu rajah that Shlomo was conspiring with the Muslims against the Hindus. Shlomo was brought before the Hindu court in chains. He swore he was innocent of the charges, but to no avail. Shlomo was condemned to be trampled to death by an elephant. However, instead of killing him, the elephant gently picked him up and placed him on his back. The Hindu rajah, taking this as miraculous proof of Shlomo's innocence, gave him a permanent seat at the court as well as a large parcel of land.[15]

For many centuries the Bene Israel were unknown to other Jewish communities around the world. They were unknown even to Jews from other parts of India. It was only after a learned Jewish merchant named David Rahabi discovered them, while he was on a business trip to the Konkan Coast, that the Bene Israel first made contact with mainstream Jews. No one knows with certainty when Rahabi arrived, or where he came from. According to Bene Israel oral history, he came from Egypt around the year 1200 C.E., and he was believed to be the brother of the great Sephardi rabbi and philosopher Moses Maimonides. David Rahabi was reportedly a dealer in precious stones. In his writings, Maimonides mourned the drowning of his brother, whose ship had sunk in the Indian Ocean. The Bene Israel believed that this lends validity to their legend.[16] On the other hand, Maimonides may have known something about the Jews of Maharashtra. Probably basing his statement on anecdotal information, he commented on the Jews of India: "[They] know nothing of the Torah and of the laws nothing save the Sabbath and circumcision." He could not have been referring to the Jews of Malabar, since, as Shirley Isenberg points out, the Jews in that little principality had international trade connections and were therefore presumably in touch with the major centers of Jewish learning.[17] Some historians believe that Rahabi was a merchant with the East Indian Company, that he was from Cochin in the southern tip of India, and that he arrived in the Konkan in the mid eighteenth century.[18]

In the course of doing business in the town of Cheul, Rahabi would have

realized he had stumbled upon a peculiar lost tribe of Jews. It's possible he over-
heard them reciting a heavily accented version of the *Kriyat Shema* mantra they
intoned upon greeting each other. In order to be absolutely certain, the story
goes, he devised a test. He took a basket of two kinds of fish, one a kosher variety with fins and scales and another without fins and scales, and asked some
Bene Israel women to cook the fish for him. The Bene Israel women examined
both varieties and when they saw the one without scales and fins they profusely
apologized to Rahabi, saying that they could not cook that fish because it offended their religious sensibilities. This convinced him that they really were Jews.

Rahabi lived among the Bene Israel for two or three years before he was
murdered by a local village chieftain for reasons unknown. During this period
he taught the Bene Israel the rudiments of an up-to-date form of Judaism, i.e.,
the *mitzvot*, the Hebrew prayers, and the Jewish holy days. He appointed three
of his best students from the three leading Bene Israel families to serve as *kajis*.
This term is probably a variation of the Islamic word *cadi*, which is a combination of teacher and judge. These *kajis* would travel from village to village to teach
the toranic laws they had learned from Rahabi. They would settle communal
disputes and perform marriages and circumcisions. The position of *kaji* was eventually given formal recognition by the local tribal chieftains. The *kajis* served as
spiritual leaders of the Bene Israel community and the position was handed down
from father to son. This position became obsolete after the arrival of more
learned Jews from Cochin and Arabia in 1826.

Until the last decade of the eighteenth century the Bene Israel never possessed a synagogue. On the Sabbath day they abstained from work, and prayer
services took place at home. They would visit each other's homes to eat the
Sabbath meal, and before eating they would recite the *Shema* together. The *Shema*
was the only prayer they knew.

Darfalnichi San, which in Marathi means "Holiday of Closing of Doors,"
corresponds with Yom Kippur. On this day the Bene Israel sat "*sannyasin*-like"
fasting inside their homes with doors tightly shut. The day before they would
take a bath—first in warm, then in cold, water. They would eat a meal early in
the evening, and then fast for twenty-six hours until around 7 P.M. the following day. During their fast they avoided contact with all other people, and, like
Orthodox Jews in other parts of the world, they dressed entirely in white. They
believed that on this day all their sins were forgiven.[19] "By 'closing the doors'
on other castes," writes Shalva Weil, "they perpetuate the status of the absolute
purity of the Brahman. . . . In effect for one day in the year, the Bene Israel
'became' Brahmans, preserving the barriers between ideal values and hierarchical realities."[20] The day after *Darfalnichi San*, called *Shila San*, was both a

memorial service for the ancestors and a holiday of rejoicing. On this day they would distribute *tzedakah* (charity) among the poor and exchange gifts with their friends.[21]

A day resembling Passover was called *Anasi Dhakacha San*, or "Holiday of the Sealing Jar." A sealed jar of fermented liquor, which they abstained from drinking, was evidently substituted for *matzah* to commemorate the deliverance of their ancestors from Egyptian bondage.[22] No *sedarim* were ever conducted. In modern times the Bene Israel made *matzah* from rice rather than wheat. Having left Palestine in 175 B.C.E. (ten years before the Maccabean War and the re-dedication of the Temple), the Bene Israel were unaware of the festival of Chanukah. Before the arrival of David Rahabi the Bene Israel also knew nothing of the holidays of Shavuot and Sukkot and the four fasts of national mourning. Although the Bene Israel knew nothing of the holiday of Purim, they celebrated *Holi*, a Hindu festival that coincidentally takes place around the time of Purim, "when the Hindus light huge bonfires and dance around and shout and make weird noises."[23] The Bene Israel also adopted certain holidays from their Indian neighbors. For example, the Ramzan, a fast held throughout the Jewish month of Elul and derived from the Muslim fast of Ramadan.

Religious Jews pray only to God, but in oriental lands it is traditional to visit the grave of a great rabbi or saint and beseech the soul of the deceased pious one to plead on their behalf. Whenever evil things happen to Hindus, they pray to their local saints for help. During times of adversity, or after recovering from a serious illness, the Bene Israel, in emulation of their Hindu compatriots, also prayed to the Hindu gods and saints. They would burn incense and make sacrificial offerings at an altar. David Rahabi taught the Bene Israel that they must eschew Hindu polytheism and animism and pray directly to God, but if they wanted assistance from a saint, they could call upon the biblical prophet Elijah instead.[24] According to Shirley Isenberg, Jewish-Indian women were still "secretly offering petitionary prayers to idols of Hindu deities" as recently as the early nineteenth century.[25]

The Bene Israel had a special place in their hearts for Elijah the Prophet. According to Bene Israel legend, immediately after the shipwreck of their ancestors Elijah appeared at Navgaon and brought the half-dead seven couples back to life. Bene Israel believed that Elijah's footprints are visible on a rock at that location. Once a year they would make a pilgrimage to the rock to celebrate. The day that Elijah appeared to them and then ascended into heaven was an important holiday for the Bene Israel. On every occasion for thanksgiving, such as giving birth, a *malida* ceremony would take place at home commemorating the prophet as the harbinger of the Messiah. A *prasadam* or meal of *dudpak* (rice pudding) made with coconuts, raisins, nuts, and cardamom was eaten, together with a variety of seasonal fruit, rose water, and rice and wheat chapatis.

By Indian tradition a girl was betrothed at the age of nine or ten but didn't actually live permanently with her husband until she was about thirteen or fourteen. Bene Israel marriage ceremonies combined traditional Jewish *minhagim* with local color. Marriages were arranged by the parents. At the betrothal ceremony the bride's hands and feet were painted with henna, and haldi paste was applied to the hands and faces of relatives and friends. Before the wedding, relatives of the bride and groom sprinkled each other with rice water, adorned the bride's head with a garland of flowers or beads, and seated her on a chair beside a burning lamp and a container of rice. The groom's party entered with two complete sets of wedding finery, including *saris* and jewels, which were admired by all then presented to the bride. Sugar was then distributed to all the guests.

On the wedding day the groom, crowned with flowers, was led on horseback to the bride's parents' home. The marriage service took place in a booth. After the wedding, everyone went to the home of the bride for a wedding feast. When the bridal pair entered the home of the groom the next day, a brother or sister of the groom stood in the doorway and extracted a solemn promise from the blushing pair to give one of their children in marriage to one of his or her own children.

The night after the wedding a celebration called *varat* took place at the home of the bridegroom's parents. Surrounded by well-wishers, the bride, wearing a veil, and the groom, sitting directly across the table from her, fed each other a sweet rice dish to symbolize a sweet and harmonious married life together.

A custom observed by Bene Israel women and similarly practiced by Jews in parts of Central Asia was the "Nazarite Vow." A woman who for many years had difficulty giving birth to a male child would make a vow that if she were given a son, she would raise him as a *nazir*. For the first six years after the birth of the child, no razor was permitted to touch his head. On his seventh birthday, a special haircutting ceremony was celebrated in the synagogue with magnificent pomp and splendor. The youngster, in elegant garments and mounted on a pony, together with friends and relatives on horseback, marched through the streets leading to the synagogue, accompanied by musicians playing fife and drums. In the synagogue the child was seated in a special chair, where each of the guests was given the honor of snipping off a strand of his hair. The bobbed hair was weighed and, according to the vow, its weight in gold or silver was donated to *tzedakah*. The hair itself was thrown into the sea.[26]

In order to understand the reasons the Jews left the villages of the Konkan Coast for the modern city of Bombay, some twenty miles away, it is necessary to understand British colonial policy in India. Like other Europeans before them, the British initially came to India as travelers and merchants. Beginning in the latter decades of the sixteenth century they established trading posts that became settlements and eventually grew into colonies. Being the mightiest imperial power in the world in the eighteenth century, the British succeeded in driving from India their major European rivals, the Dutch and the Portuguese. During this period India was split into small kingdoms, some Hindu and some Muslim. The British skillfully pitted the different groups against each other. The absence of a strong central ruler in India enabled the British to gain control of more and more territory and to set up their own government. By 1858 the whole Indian subcontinent had become officially part of the British Empire.

The first British trading post in India was founded in 1611, and was run by the East India Company. At first, the Company's factories were located in Surat, a seaport in West India. In the middle of the eighteenth century the main factory was transferred to Bombay. This made the city a major trading center, which also served as a British fort. The British extended equal opportunities to all Indians, but especially to minorities who were neither Hindu nor Muslim. A continuous stream of Bene Israel youths abandoned "their somnolent hollows in the creeks and crags of Kolaba District"[27] to take advantage of these opportunities by joining the British forces in greater proportion than the rest of the population. Among the early Bene Israel recruits who gained great distinction, both as a Jew and as a military man, was Samuel Ezekiel Divekar.

Divekar had enlisted in the East India Company as a twenty-year-old in 1750. Eventually he rose through the ranks and became a commandant. During the second British war with the Muslims of Mysore (1780–84), Divekar was captured and brought before Tippoo, the Sultan of Mysore. Tippoo had a reputation as a cruel tyrant and fanatical Muslim. He always gave his prisoners of war a choice: conversion to Islam or death by the sword. When Tippoo asked Divekar what his religion was, he replied, "I am a Bene Israel." Fortunately for Divekar, Tippoo's mother was sitting nearby. Interrupting her son, she pleaded with the Sultan to spare Samuel's life, for the Koran speaks well of the Israelites and she had never seen an Israelite before. In gratitude to the Almighty, Divekar in 1796 built the first synagogue in Bombay. The synagogue was originally called Mogen David, but was later renamed Sha'ar Ha-rachamim (Gates of Mercy).

By the mid nineteenth century, an estimated twenty percent of Bene Israel men served in East India Company battalions. At the time of the so-called Indian Mutiny of 1857 the Bene Israel made up about fifty percent of the officer strength of the Bombay Native Infantry.[28] They established a reputation as loyal and intrepid soldiers fighting for the British not only in India, but also in the

British wars of annexation against Burma, Afghanistan, Persia, Aden, and in the Horn of Africa. Because of this military reputation, the British recruited the Bene Israel to fill positions in the Bombay civilian bureaucracy. The Bene Israel were effectively eliminated from military service only after the British instituted a policy of assigning officer ranking on a percentage basis of the enlistment from each caste. The Bene Israel were too small a group to form a designated unit.

The Bene Israel took advantage of many other opportunities offered them by the British. Many found employment and settled in other parts of India such as Poona, Delhi, Calcutta, Ahmedabad, Thana, and Karachi. They attended British schools, learned English, and the better educated entered white-collar positions in education, administration, and medicine. So many Bene Israel entered government service that they came to be known as a "clerk caste." In striking contrast with the higher caste Hindu women who, because of societal inhibitions, were universally illiterate and forbidden to work outside the home, Bene Israel women attended schools of higher education and established themselves admirably in teaching and nursing.

After David Rahabi, other teachers helped the Bene Israel become more traditional Jews. In 1826 a small group of Jews from Cochin arrived in Bombay. The Cochinis, like the Bene Israel, were drawn to Bombay by the job opportunities available there. They had never lost contact with world Jewry and were well versed in Jewish law and lore. They opened Hebrew schools where Bene Israel children could learn Sephardic traditions and to read and write Hebrew. The Cochin Jews also translated the Bible in the synagogue on the Sabbath and on the holidays and served as teachers, cantors, and circumcisers.

Paradoxically, an even greater religious influence on the Bene Israel came from Western Christian missionaries who were very active in India during the early nineteenth century. Many Bene Israel youngsters attended missionary schools established by the Reverend John Wilson of the Church of Scotland, and attained degrees that gave them entry into the professions. The missionaries translated the Bible and other Hebrew classical writings into Marathi. They placed great emphasis on the Hebrew language in the curriculum and, for the first time, any Bene Israel who could read his native language could now have access to the Jewish literary heritage. Whenever the missionaries argued with the Bene Israel in order to try to convert them, the Bene Israel would say, "We realize we still don't know everything about our religion and we cannot answer all your questions. If you want answers to these questions, our learned rabbis elsewhere can answer them. Go ask them."[29] Only three Bene Israel were known to have converted to Christianity, and two of these later returned to Judaism.[30]

As early as 1730 small groups of Jews fleeing persecution in Aleppo, Syria began to settle in the English fort-dominated townships of Surat and Bombay. These were followed by some Jews from Baghdad who also settled in Surat to engage in trade, but not long afterward most returned to their mother country. Jews from Arabia did not really begin to make their impact on Indian society, and particularly on Indian-Jewish communal affairs, until the arrival of David Sassoon (1792–1864). He was the scion of five generations of Baghdadi *nasiim* (princes) and the victim of an extortionist Ottoman pasha. David Sassoon found asylum in Bombay with his large family and entourage in 1833. Because of the fabulous wealth they accumulated from trade in indigo, opium, precious stones, and textiles, the Sassoons became known as the "Rothschilds of the East." Internationally, they and their associates—and their rivals the Ezras, Gubbays, Ezekiels, Kadoories, Eliases, and other Arabian-Jewish merchant princes—established a great empire that eventually branched out to Rangoon, Hong Kong, Singapore, Shanghai, and other places. In Bombay, Poona, Madras, and Calcutta, the Sassoons pioneered in banking and industry, especially cotton textile mills. They employed, in addition to others, Cochin Jews and Bene Israel. They erected educational and philanthropic institutions such as hospitals, museums, and libraries. The Sassoons also established printing presses. Hoping to find greater freedom and higher income, coreligionists from Iraq and other parts of the Middle East migrated to India to work for the Jewish merchant princes of the Orient. By 1864 there were almost 3,000 Arabian Jews in India. By 1941 their totals had increased to almost twice that number. These Jews rarely adopted an Indian language as their mother tongue. They stuck with Arabic, but later switched to English. Since the majority had come from the city of Baghdad (which is also where they sought the spiritual and halakhic guidance of their *hakhamim*), all Arab-speaking Jews were generically referred to as Baghdadis.

When the Baghdadis first came to India, they got along amicably with the Bene Israel. They prayed in the Bene Israel synagogues and buried their dead in the Bene Israel cemeteries. However, by 1864 the Baghdadis had built their own synagogue and did not want to be associated with the Bene Israel. They had become more successful and modern than the Bene Israel. And the fact that they had whiter skins and dressed and acted like Europeans made it easier for them to imitate, and be accepted by, the British. Staking out their claim to a higher social and ritual position, the Baghdadi "Brahmans" began to think of themselves as "ancestrally pure Jews" and acted prejudicially against their darker-skinned brethren. They accused the Bene Israel of not being "pure" Jews because they worshipped idols, and alleged that Bene Israel men had married Hindu women without properly converting them, so that their offspring were not fully Jewish. Since there were no authentic records to help the Bene Israel throw light on their obscure history, they defended themselves against this charge by arguing that they had always made a clear distinction between the descendants of such mixed marriages, or *kala*, and the pure Bene Israel, or *gora*. This argument would not have been convincing even to nonprejudicial outsiders since objective students of the scene observed that in fact some *gora* were darker skinned than *kala*.[31] What's more, according to the Bene Israel scholar Rebecca Reuben, writing in 1913, the *kala* could all be traced back to one Gentile ancestor three or four generations before her time.[32] These were obviously specious and futile arguments on the part of low-status natives who felt under attack and defensive. It was not in the vested interests of the more privileged Baghdadis to make a distinction between *gora* and *kala*. They required all the Bene Israel who attended services in their synagogues to sit in the back benches and would not count them in *minyan*. Rabbinical emissaries from the Land of Israel who periodically visited the Jewish communities in India during the nineteenth century oftentimes castigated the Baghdadis for maligning the integrity of the Bene Israel. One Ashkenazi rabbi went so far as to state that "whoever is against those who are not 'white' has no share in the World to Come."[33] This and other statements on behalf of the Bene Israel from rabbis around the world, including the Sephardi Chief Rabbi of England, Moses Gaster, did nothing to sway the Baghdadis.

Only with the rise of Mahatma Gandhi, the great Hindu leader who peacefully brought an end to English domination of India, and who officially abolished the caste system in the late 1940s, did the bickering among different Jewish groups begin to subside. By that time the State of Israel was being formed. The Baghdadis, who were perceived as being closely identified with the British, headed for the West—primarily England, Canada, and the United States—and the majority of Bene Israel, very nationalistically Indian, but also religious, left their beloved country with great ambivalence to build a better life in Israel.[34]

The Bene Israel were never very poor. But, unlike the Baghdadis, few if any ever became fabulously rich. Urban Bene Israel were mostly drawn to government service or became soldiers, nurses, teachers, peddlers, farmers, and carpenters. Some attended universities and became doctors, lawyers, and administrators. But considering their insignificant numbers in terms of the overall population, the number of prominent personalities the Bene Israel community contributed to India is amazing. They produced a number of politicians, two of the most outstanding being Dr. Ezekiel Moses, mayor of Bombay (1937–38), and Shalom Bapuji Israel, Prime Minister of Janjira State, also in the 1930s. Among the highest echelon military officers there are Benjamin Samson, who rose through the navy ranks to become a rear admiral, and his brother Reuben Samson, who became a major general in the army. In addition to the above prominent figures, the Bene Israel community has produced a Nobel laureate for poetry in Nissim Ezekiel, two beauty queens in Esther Abraham and Fleur Ezekiel, an accomplished sitar player in David Satamkar. They have contributed a considerable number of screen idols and directors to the Indian stage and film industry, two of the most beloved being the dramatist Joseph David and the matinee idol Ruby Mayers, described by one writer as "the most popular, beautiful and the brightest film actress in the Indian film world."[35]

When Mahatma Gandhi embarked on his long fasts to protest the British occupation of his country, a Bene Israel doctor named Abraham Solomon Erulkar was often at his side, tending to his medical needs. Erulkar was president of the Medical Council of India in the 1940s. In this capacity he was instrumental in providing temporary visas to many Eastern and Central European Jews who fled from the Nazis before and during World War II. He also assisted in granting medical licenses to German-Jewish doctors so that they would be allowed to practice medicine while living in India.

With the creation of the State of Israel, the Bene Israel, motivated by both economics and idealism, emigrated to Israel. Most settled in development towns like Beersheva, Dimona, Lod, and Kiryat Sh'moneh. Others were attracted to *kibbutzim* and *moshavim*. In 1951 a group of 150 Bene Israel living in Israel, perceiving themselves to be victims of racial and religious prejudice, went on a hunger strike. After a campaign of nonviolent resistance as taught by Gandhi, they were repatriated to India by the Jewish Agency. Back in India they found themselves without jobs or housing and soon pleaded to be allowed to return to Israel. The Israeli government was reluctant to pay for the second trip, but after receiving letters of repentance the Jewish state relented.

For many centuries the Bene Israel had been regarded as Jews in India and treated tolerantly, but soon after arriving in the Jewish state they were being denied equal rights from, of all people, other Jews. Local rabbis were asking for directives from the Chief Rabbinical Council in Jerusalem on how to minister to the Bene Israel. These rabbis were apprehensive about performing marriage ceremonies between Bene Israel and members of other Jewish communities because of the persistent fear that they were not "pure" Jews. The fear was that the Bene Israel did not conduct marriage and divorce in accordance with halakha. Consequently, their legal right to marry according to Jewish law was in question. These rabbis were particularly concerned because there were among them incestuous marriages. They were also concerned about the nonpractice by the Bene Israel of the *chalitza* ceremony (Deuteronomy 25:5–10), the release of a childless widow from the religious obligation to marry her deceased husband's brother "that his name may not be blotted out in Israel." The *chalitza* ceremony symbolizes the formal severance of the bond between the widow and her deceased husband's family and absolution of contempt for him "that doth not build up his brother's house." It is enacted before a rabbinical court of five persons. Halakhicly, the nonperformance of this ceremony could render marriage by the widow bigamous and adulterous, and her offspring *mamzairim* (bastards). Some rabbis even suggested that by a rabbinic procedure the Bene Israel should be converted first to Islam or Christianity and then formally reconverted to Judaism. A decision was finally reached in 1962. The rabbinate concluded that marriage with the Bene Israel was halakhicly permitted, but it was the responsibility of rabbis functioning as marriage registrars to investigate the female lineage, plus all divorces that might have taken place among the ancestors of the Bene Israel party to a mixed marriage "as far back as possible."[36]

The Bene Israel community in Israel was stunned by this ruling. Their reputation tainted with the presumption of *mamzairut* (bastardy), thousands of Bene Israel took to the streets, staging a series of vigorous protests at the headquarters of the Jewish Agency and the Chief Rabbinate in Jerusalem. They were joined in their hunger and sit-in strikes by leading figures of the Israeli political left. This projected a poor public relations image for Israel as being a country practicing color prejudice. After international outcry, the Israeli parliament passed a resolution affirming the Bene Israel as Jews in all respects, and with the same rights and privileges as other Israeli citizens.[37]

There are an estimated 40,000 Bene Israel worldwide, of which more than 30,000 live in Israel. With the great majority of Bene Israel settled abroad, Jewish life in India today is moribund. Those who remain still strongly identify with Judaism and the State of Israel, and their synagogues are still their primary social, cultural, and religious centers. But many Bene Israel synagogues are boarded up for lack of congregants. There are no rabbis in India, although there are a few *mohelim*, *shochtim*, and *chazanim*. The overwhelming majority of Bene Israel today are lower middle class, mostly employed in white-collar government jobs. Of the 5,000 Bene Israel remaining in India, 4,000 reside in Greater Bombay. The other thousand are located in Ikane, Poona, and the Raigad district.

THE MALABARIS AND PARADESIS OF COCHIN

> Shadowed by mountains clad in luxuriant vegetation on one side,
> bathed by gentle blue seas lapping golden beaches on the other,
> the paddy fields fed by scores of streams and backwaters, Kerala
> seems almost paradisal. Perhaps that picture of Eden was the
> reason that the great religions of the world first sought Indian
> shores here.
>
> —S. Muthiah, *The Splendour of South India (1992)*

> If you have a new religion to impart to the world nowhere will
> you find a more promising seedbed than in Kerala.
>
> —John Keay, *Into India (1973)*

> The Jewish community of India has rendered and continued to
> render notable services in many fields. It has contributed men of
> distinction to business and industry, to the civil service and the
> armed forces, and to the world of scholarship.
>
> —Prime Minister Indira Gandhi on the 400th anniversary
> of the Paradesi Synagogue, in Cochin, 1968

In contrast with the Bene Israel of Bombay, the quality of Judaism of the ancient Jewish community in southern India has never been questioned. Though far removed from the major centers of Jewish learning, the Jews of the Malabar Coast did not exist in complete isolation. Over the centuries they were visited frequently by Jewish merchants who traveled to India to engage in spice and incense trading, and by itinerant *hakhamin*. Their numbers were periodically augmented by Jews seeking asylum in southern India from persecution in the Christian and Muslim worlds. These newcomers provided their coreligionists with Holy Books and kept them up-to-date on Jewish matters. Also in contrast with the Bene Israel, the Jews of the Malabar Coast were always considered high caste. While there have been other Jewish autonomous zones in the postexilic period, the nearly millennium-long independent principality that existed on the Malabar Coast, where the Jews were ruled by a succession of Jewish chieftains, is a unique and extraordinary occurrence in the Diasporic experience.

The Jewish connection with southern India is very old. There were many migrations of Jews to this region throughout the centuries. Malabar has always been one of the world's leading producers of spices, especially pepper. The Jews

who settled there found the political and business atmosphere extremely tolerant. Allowed to live in peace and practice their religion unhindered, the Jewish
community thrived and "played a role far out of proportion to its numbers."[38]
Many became merchants in the spice, incense, and other trades, and grew fabulously wealthy.

In I Kings 10:22 we are told that King Solomon, in a joint venture with
Hiram the Phoenician, opened a trade route from the southern Israelite port
of Ezion-geber (near modern Eilat) through the Gulf of Aqaba to the Red Sea.
Expert Phoenician shipwrights helped to construct the vessels ("Ships of
Tarshish") that were manned by mixed crews of Phoenician and Israelite sailors. Among the various places these flat-bottomed cargo ships sailed was the
fabulous gold-producing land of Ophir. The roundtrip trading voyage took three
years, and these merchants brought back rich cargoes of gold, almug (sandal-
wood), precious stones, ivory, apes, and peacocks. Today no one knows exactly where Ophir is located. Some historians speculate that since India traditionally had an abundance of these commodities, then Ophir must be India. The
Hebrew word for peacocks—*tukiym*—is derived from the old Tamil word *takoi*,
showing specifically that it was from South India that Solomon's traders brought
peacocks.[39] "It is very plausibly conjectured," writes Krishna Chaitanya, "that
the teak from the forests of Kerala was used by Solomon in the building of the
Temple. . . . "[40] According to ancient beliefs, King Solomon's ships berthed at
the coastal village of Poovar, south of Trivandram, the present-day capital of
Kerala. Seduced by this tropical paradise, some of these Jewish merchants and
sailors may have established a colony and settled there permanently.[41] The Hindu
rajahs of this region undoubtedly had heard of King Solomon. An ancient wedding song of the Christians of Malabar says that Habban, an Indian-Jewish merchant, was sent to Palestine by a rajah to fetch an architect who could construct
a temple even more beautiful than King Solomon's.

There are strong oral traditions among the Malabari Jews that they are
descended from the tribes who were carried away into captivity by the Assyrians
in 722 B.C.E., by the Babylonians in 586 B.C.E., and after the disasters inflicted
on Palestine by the Romans in 70 and 135 C.E. It is possible that Jews arrived
together with other merchants from the Roman Empire in the first century B.C.E.,
after the Greek mariner Hippalus discovered how to exploit monsoon winds to
cross the Indian Ocean from Arabia in about forty days.

Malabar is the earliest seat of Christianity in India. John Keay points out
that "southern India is one of the few places outside Palestine where Christianity arrived before it became identified with Rome."[42] According to local Christian belief, Saint Thomas, one of the original Twelve Apostles, landed on Malankara

near Cranganore in 52 C.E. He hoped to spread the Gospel among the Jews of India. This would indicate that the Jewish community was well-known and sizable enough for him to make this long, arduous journey worthwhile. As is customary among Jews, the guest received a *kabbalat panim* (reception) at the harbor, in this case from a Jewish girl playing a flute. According to legend, Saint Thomas did not fare well among the Jews. He converted only forty who, together with a much larger number of Brahman proselytes, formed the nucleus of the Syrian Christian Church of South India.[43]

A Roman merchant vessel that sailed regularly on the Red Sea from Arabia to Ceylon and southern India is reported to have found a Jewish colony in Malabar in the second century C.E. Moses de Paiva, a Dutch Jew who visited Cochin in 1686, asserted that in 370 C.E., 70,000 to 80,000 Jews arrived on the Malabar coast from Majorca. The Cochin Jews explained to him that their forefathers had been taken into captivity on this island after the destruction of the Second Temple by the Roman Emperor Titus.

Still other Malabari Jews have a long-standing belief that some of their ancestors came to India via Yemen.[44] This theory is supported by the fact that the two *edot* share many similar *minhagim* (rites), and that there is a strong physical resemblance between the Cochinis and the Yemenites. Some historians place the time of arrival of the Jews at the shores of Malabar in the era of the persecutions that took place in the Persian Empire under King Firuz (457–484 C.E.). Because of a charge that two Magians, members of the priestly class of the Zoroastrian religion, were murdered by the Jews of Isfahan, one-half of the Jewish population of that city was put to death. Jewish children were taken away by force, to be raised as fire worshippers.[45] Those Isfahani Jews who were able, fled to Arabia and India.

Among the prominent Jews of antiquity who are believed to have settled in India were Rabbi Samuel, a Levite from Jerusalem, and his son Rabbi Judah Levita. They are said to have brought with them from Majorca the silver trumpets that were used to announce the Jubilee. In biblical times the Jubilee (*yovel*) was a Jewish holiday celebrated every fiftieth year. During the Jubilee, lands that had been sold were supposed to be returned to ancestral ownership and slaves were to be set free. Local legend has it that these trumpets were saved when the Second Temple was destroyed. They were said to have been in the possession of the Malabari Jewish community until around 1150 C.E., when they were smashed in a vicious squabble between Levites and non-Levites. It was customary for the Levites to sound the trumpets to announce the approach of the Shabbat, but one week they were late in doing so. As the sun was about to set and the trumpets hadn't sounded, some non-Levites got impatient and blew the trumpets. This made the Levites so furious that they smashed the trumpets.

The Jewish influence on South Indian culture must have been more than nominal. There was a talmudic sage in the fourth century named Rabbi Judah who was originally a Hindu from Malabar who converted to Judaism. Eventually, he journeyed to Babylonia to study at the great *yeshivot* there. Concerned about having kosher food available on his long voyage, the Talmud informs us, Rabbi Judah stocked up on an ample supply of salted chicken.[46]

Whatever the time of their arrival in South India, the Jews found safe haven in the city of Cranganore (called Shingly by the Jews), a major international trading center on the Malabar Coast. The monarchs of the region, a Kshatriya dynasty known as the Cheras, were famous for their piety, benevolence, and hospitality to foreigners. In this highly tolerant religious and political atmosphere provided by the Malabar rulers, the enterprising Jewish immigrants contributed greatly to expanding commerce and trade along the coast of southwest India, and between India and other countries.

Because of the Jews' contribution to Malabaran society, their honest business practices, their prowess on the battlefield, and their long-standing loyalty to the throne, one Chera emperor, Bhaskara Ravi Varma II, expressed his indebtedness to them by presenting the leader of the Jewish community of Cranganore, Joseph Rabban, with a set of large copper plates engraved with a charter of royal privileges the Jews could enjoy. These celebrated copper plates are inscribed in the archaic Tamil language and none of the scholars who have studied them have been able to give an authoritative translation of the date of presentation or of the text. Traditional belief among the Jews of Malabar has it that this magnificent and epoch-making document was presented in 379 C.E., or nine years after their arrival from Majorca. Heinrich Graetz was of the opinion that the presentation was made in 490 C.E. to refugees originally from intolerant Persia.[47] Some scholars ascribe the plates to the eighth century, and others believe this event took place sometime between 974 and 1020.[48] In any event, this charter stated that Rabban and his fellow Jews could have a pocket principality of their own in Cranganore, called Anjuvannam, with Joseph Rabban as sovereign prince.[49]

Some historians describe Anjuvannam as a small independent kingdom with Joseph Rabban as its first king. However, according to Benjamin J. Israel, "[I]f the terms of the grant are studied, it does not amount to more than the conferment of the kind of feudatory privileges which Indian rulers were wont to bestow on their nobles, falling far short of sovereignty, somewhat resembling the rights belonging to feudal barons in medieval Europe."[50] Still other scholars consider Anjuvannam to have been merely a corporation or a trade guild within the town.[51]

Among the seventy-two privileges granted the Jews of Anjuvannam were freedom from taxation and the right to own the land "so long as the world and moon exist." They were given the right to use a palanquin, carry an umbrella, and bear arms—rights that were the prerogative of the ruling class. They were allowed to ride horses and elephants, a privilege generally denied Jews in all parts of Africa and Asia. These famous copper plates, considered the "Magna Carta" of Kerala Jewry, can be found today in the Paradesi Synagogue in Cochin. How the copper plates given to Joseph Rabban by the emperor ended up in the Paradesi synagogue is a mystery no historian has been able to solve. The Black Jews accused the White Jews of stealing the plates from them, as they considered Rabban to have been one of them.

The principality of Anjuvannam—or Shingly—existed for more than three hundred years. Anjuvannam is only twenty-seven square miles and is believed to have had a population of about 20,000.[52] Nissim, the fourteenth-century rabbi who visited Anjuvannam, may have been indulging in poetic license when he wrote:

> I traveled from Spain—
> I had heard of the city of Shingly—
> I longed to see an Israel King,
> Him I saw with my own eyes.

Then a tragic event took place that resulted in the destruction of the principality. This disaster occurred when the line of Joseph Rabban died out in 1341. A violent dispute over the leadership of Anjuvannam broke out between two brothers of a noble family indirectly descended from Rabban. The younger brother, Joseph Azar, in league with the Rajah of Cochin, succeeded in murdering some of his elder brother's adjutants. Under the Hindu law of succession, the eldest brother always inherits the throne. This attempt at breaching custom infuriated the neighboring princes. Their troops attacked Joseph Azar and his supporters. Many Jews were killed, and Anjuvannam was destroyed.

According to legend, Joseph Azar escaped by swimming across the river from Cranganore to Cochin with his wife on his back. The unlikely element in this legend, Barbara Johnson Hudson notes, is the fact that it is a twenty-mile swim, and the river is infested with crocodiles.[53] However, he did arrive. After establishing a Jewish colony in Cochin, Azar built the Cochangadi synagogue in 1344. He was followed soon after by his elder brother and his brother's followers. A greatly diminished Jewish community continued to survive in Shingly until 1524, when its remnants moved to Cochin. This second wave of settlers established a synagogue known as Kadavambhagam.

Since many Jews were heavily involved in commerce, they had to move to Cochin for another reason. In the early 1340s a heavy flood silted up the entrance to the port of Cranganore and formed an enormous natural harbor in Cochin twenty miles to the south. Cochin supplanted Cranganore as a great trading center.

The Jews attained a high degree of prosperity in their new home. They performed important services for the Cochin rajahs as advisors and moneylenders, and as diplomats helping to settle political and commercial disputes. They fought courageously in the rajahs' army, but refused to fight on the Sabbath, which limited their effectiveness. One benevolent rajah granted the Jews some land next to his palace. This neighborhood, under the walls of a fort in the southern end of the Mattancheri district, became—and is still known as—Jew Town. The rajah granted the Jews complete religious and cultural autonomy. He appointed a Jewish headman called *mudalier*, who exercised civil-criminal jurisdiction over the community. The rajah reserved for himself the right to try capital offenses. This was a not a hereditary title but was conferred on those Jewish magnates who had great influence with the rajah. With the advent of British rule in Cochin in 1796, the position of *mudalier* was terminated.

With the exception of one massacre, perpetrated by Muslims against Jews in the sixteenth century primarily for economic reasons, the two religious groups got on remarkably well. Lamentably, the same could not be said about relations between the various Jewish groups in Cochin. On a microcosmic level, Jewish life in South India reflected the Hindu social structure and, as in Bombay, the Jews of the Malabar Coast became victims of the Indian caste system. The acrimony among the various Jewish quasi-castes sometimes resulted in physical violence.

"It is a fair rule," writes George Woodcock, "in considering Indian castes from a historical point of view to assume that the lowest represent the oldest inhabitants of the country, and the highest the most recent comers."[54] In Cochin the major division was between the so-called Black Jews, or Malabaris, who claimed to be the original settlers on the Malabar Coast, and the White Jews, or Paradesis (which means "foreigners" in Malayalam, the local tongue). The Paradesis came from places as diverse as Spain, Syria, Egypt, England, and Germany but also claimed to be the "true" original settlers. These two *jatis* (endogamous subcastes) were in turn subdivided on the basis of pure Jewishness and those who were descended from the slaves of Jews. The Whites had their *meshachrarim* (emancipated slaves) who were the offspring of freed slaves and converts to Judaism. The *meshachrarim* were referred to as the "Brown Jews." The pedigreed Blacks, known as *myuchasim* in Hebrew, made a clear distinction between themselves and the *aynum-myuchasim* (non-pedigreed), the Blacks' equivalent of *meshachrarim*. The masters of the half-breed Brown Jews considered them to be of a higher caste than the Black Jews. "[The] reference groups [of the Paradesis] were their high-status Hindu neighbors, whose conduct they could see and some of whose standards they wanted to emulate in order to maintain a respectable position among them".[55]

For Christians, Muslims, and Jews alike, writes David G. Mandelbaum, "the social structure of Kerala Hinduism was the matrix for their own social organization. Though their respective scriptures decreed that all who kept the faith were ritual equals, that idea was challenged by the hierarchical perspective of the Hindus around them, who took rigid stratification and the radiation of pollution to be axiomatic. So if the devotees of these imported egalitarian religions were to be taken as worthy, respectable people by the majority in the region, they too had to demonstrate their relative purity, at least by keeping the more polluted of their own faith at a suitable social distance."[56]

The Whites demonstrated their relative purity by regarding the Blacks as being of low caste—the offspring of their own converted slaves. This behavior is consistent with foundation myths of high-ranking Hindus in the region. The Black Jews, in turn, questioned the White's notions of superiority and treated them as a bunch of Johnnies-come-lately who were lax in their religious observances. The Black Jews, notes Mandelbaum, "did not abjure caste discriminations, but like most aspiring *jatis* only denied their own inferiority and insisted that they merited a higher rank in the local caste order. In their case, the higher rank was that of ritual equality with the White Jews."[57] Blacks and Whites lived in separate quarters, did not intermarry or dine together, prayed in separate synagogues, and were buried in separate cemeteries.

Nowhere in his diary does the famous Sephardi traveler Benjamin of Tudela mention encountering "White" Jews when he visited Malabar in 1167. After describing the Jews as devout and learned, he informs us that "the inhabitants are all black and the Jews also." Most of the White Jews were believed to be Sephardim and conversos from Spain and Portugal who drifted to Cochin after the expulsion of 1492, or maybe earlier. From the fifteenth to the eighteenth century, Jews from places as varied as Palestine, Iraq, Yemen, Germany, Holland, and Poland also trickled in. All were attracted by the favorable economic opportunities connected with the trade in spices and precious stones. These fairer-skinned Jews were at first on good terms with the

Malabari Jews and very likely married among their leading families. However, with the appearance of the extremely bigoted Portuguese conquerors in the sixteenth century, and later with the arrival of the British—and the association of skin color with the theory of the superiority of the white races over the dark—the lighter-skinned Jews began to separate themselves from their darker-skinned brethren. Favored by the rajahs because they were better connected internationally and had a greater command of the languages spoken by the European traders, the Paradesis eventually supplanted the Malabaris as the dominant Jewish group in South India. Left open to the Malabari Jews were the local *shudra*-like occupations: shopkeeping, small trading, the crafts (especially ship building), and farm labor.

Like Jews in other parts of the world who have yellow, black, or white pigmentation, the skin color of the Malabari Jews could be attributed primarily to intermarriage with the native population. In traditional Jewish law, a child born of a Jewish mother or a woman who converts to Judaism is a Jew irrespective of the color of his or her skin. In this regard it is also important to remember the oft-repeated empirical observation of Rabbi Ishmael (*Mishnah Negaim* 2:1), who informs us that the most perfect example of a Jewish type is "like boxwood, neither black nor white, but of some intermediate shade." Those Jews who have lived in the Middle East since biblical times, such as the Jews of Yemen, Iraq, Kurdistan, and Persia, are probably most representative of this Semitic-Jewish color type.

The term "Black Jews," Harry Simonoff observed, is, of course "a misnomer, since they are no darker than their brown-complexioned Hindu neighbors."[58] It may have been due in part to "Spanish arrogance,"[59] but just as likely to the fact that the high caste Paradesis, imitating the local (Nambudiri) Brahmans' attitude toward the dark-skinned, snub-nosed, low caste Dravidians, contemptuously stigmatized the Malabaris as *dasyus* (black people). "South India is more bigoted and reactionary than North India," L. S. S. O'Malley informs us, ". . . and the doctrine of untouchability is carried to lengths unknown in the north."[60] Another objective outsider, a Lithuanian rabbi named David D'Beth Hillel, who lived in Cochin for four months in 1828–29, observed of the Malabaris that "though called Black Jews, they are of somewhat darker complexion than the White Jews, yet they are not of the color of the natives of the country or of persons descended from Indian slaves." While pointing out that there were no *kohanim* or *leviyim* among them (although there may well have been at one time), D'Beth Hillel was inclined to believe and accept the Malabaris' view of themselves as being descended from the Jews of the first captivity.[61] In fact, by the early nineteenth century the line of *kohanim* on the Paradesi side was about to become extinct. The Paradesis had to induce a visiting Baghdadi *kohen*, and subsequently his son, to remain in Cochin.[62]

Slavery was practiced in Cochin until 1854, and both Malabari and Paradesi communities had their share of slaves. According to Jewish law, when a Jew purchases a slave, he must treat him or her with dignity and respect. For example, he must provide sustenance for his slave before he himself is allowed to eat and drink. In some ways, a slave had the same religious obligations as a Jew. For example, a male slave was circumcised and was forbidden to work on the Sabbath and holidays. A slave who was freed could choose to return to his or her original religion or become a Jew. If an ex-slave chose to be a Jew, he or she "enters the Jewish fold with all the rights, privileges, duties, and responsibilities of a full Jew."[63] The only thing that is required of the former slave is to undergo *tevillah*, immersion in a ritual bath. The emancipated slave is then free to marry genuine Jews. In contrast to Jewish law, but out of respect for caste, the former masters continued to treat the offspring of their manumitted slaves as untouchables. They refused to grant their slaves formal certificates of manumission. Katz and Goldberg explain: "In order to preserve their self-identity and their coveted high caste status definitions of Jewish 'substance' or 'blood' they went several steps further. Not only were the Cochinites concerned about a mother's substance, but the purity of a father's substance as well. Marriage and sexual relations were, therefore, of paramount concern, because if the Jewish blood of a couple was considered 'tainted,' the partners and offspring of that union were no longer recognized as 'proper' Jews by the Jewish community."[64]

Responding to a query of the White Jews, the great rabbinical authority the Radbaz (Rabbi David ibn Zimri, Chief Rabbi of Alexandria, circa 1540) permitted marriage between "pure" Jews and those who were not genuine and original Jews or former slaves, since, if they had undergone *tevillah*, they became Jews beyond any question. Over the centuries rabbis from around the world again and again condemned the Paradesis for defying rabbinic teaching. They castigated the Paradesis for their scornful attitude toward the *meshachrarim* and toward the Malabaris. They even threatened to impose the dreaded *chairim* (excommunication decree) if the Paradesis did not mend their ways. But these protests invariably fell on deaf ears.

The Jewish "untouchables" or "Browns" attached to the White community had restricted rights in the synagogue. They could pray in the synagogue, but were forbidden to sit on the benches. They could only sit on the floor near the back door of the synagogue, and were denied the right to get married in the synagogue. They could not even receive burial rites in the Whites' cemetery.

In 1845 the *meshachrarim*, unable to bear the abuse of the Whites any longer, moved from Jew Town to the British Fort Cochin, where they built their own synagogue and cemetery. For many years they prospered. However, a plague broke out in Fort Cochin and they were forced to return to Jew Town. This time they could enter the Whites' synagogue only upon paying a stiff fee. Even more humiliating, at the conclusion of the Yom Kippur service they were obligated to kiss the hands of their former masters.

This problem of Jewish caste persisted until 1932. In that year one courageous *meshachrar*, Abraham Barak Salem, an attorney and disciple of Mahatma Gandhi, threatened *satyagraha* (nonviolent resistance) in the synagogue on Yom Kippur if the Whites did not give up their un-Jewish practices. Fed up with the smug, callous attitude of their elders, some younger members of the White community joined Salem in his threatened action. This brought the White community to its knees. From then on, the *meshachrarim* were provided with seats, were called up to the Torah on the Sabbath, and could be buried in the White Jews' cemetery (although in a separate area).

The increasing European demand for spices, especially pepper, led the leading European powers to acquire trading posts in India. The Portuguese (1498–1663) were the first Europeans to occupy India. After bringing the dominant sovereign of South India, the Zamorin (sultan) of Kozhikode, temporarily to his knees, Portuguese soldiers under the command of the explorer-navigator Vasco da Gama invaded the dominions of the Cochin rajah. Initially, the rajah of Cochin received the Portuguese with open arms because the latter had dealt a military blow to his belligerent arch-rival, the Zamorin and his Mapilah (Muslim) allies. Reverting to their policy of treachery and opportunism, the Portuguese then turned their cannons on Cochin. The helpless rajah was forced to make outrageous trade concessions and become a vassal of the Portuguese. The Portuguese, backed by a fleet of warships, monopolized the spice trade along the western India littoral. To perpetuate enmity among the warring kingdoms, and especially to undermine the influence of the relentless Zamorin of Calicut, they granted the lesser chieftains, including the Cochin rajahs, a degree of independence.

The century-and-a-half of Portuguese rule is considered the most bitter chapter in the history of the Jews of South India. Zealous bearers of the Cross, the Portuguese introduced European forms of religious intolerance to the Indian subcontinent. They treated the Jews of Cochin contemptuously and imposed all kinds of cruel restrictions on them, including arbitrary taxes. In 1504 Portuguese soldiers captured Cranganore and plundered both Jewish and Muslim properties. In 1513 the fanatical Portuguese brought the Inquisition to Goa, a coastal town some 300 miles north of Cochin. Alphonso de Albuquerque, Governor of Portuguese possessions in India, in a letter to the king of Portugal, reported that there were large numbers of Spanish and Portuguese Jews in India. He inquired of His Majesty whether he had permission to exterminate them one by one. Fortunately, the Portuguese king did not consent to this.

It is claimed that there were 80,000 Jews in Cranganore in 1524 when jealous Muslims, allied with the Zamorin of Calicut and competing with the Jews for the monopoly of the pepper trade, slew many Jews, burned down their houses and synagogues, and drove many out of town. The Jewish community of Shingly never recovered from this debacle. Of the remnant that survived, some fled to the nearby town of Chendamangalam, where a small colony existed until the early 1950s. Others settled in Parur, Mala, Ernekulam, and the Mattancheri section of Cochin. In 1565 the remaining Jews of Cranganore were attacked once again, this time by the Portuguese. As in the past, the Jews fled to Cochin, where they placed themselves under the direct protection of the benevolent Cochin rajah. The rajah granted them some land adjoining the grounds of his own palace and political as well as economic privileges. The magnificent Paradesi synagogue was built on this land three years later.

Before being driven out of the Malabar Coast by the Dutch in 1663, the Portuguese committed many atrocities against the Jews. In 1662 the Dutch made an attempt to capture Cochin from the Portuguese. The Jews, who treated the Dutch as saviors, openly provided them with assistance. They paid dearly for it: The Dutch expedition did not succeed, and the infuriated Portuguese wreaked vengeance on the Jews. They overran Jew Town in Cochin, sacking houses and damaging the synagogue. All the original documents relating to the ancient Jewish community of Malabar are believed to have been destroyed in the carnage. The Jews were forced to flee to the hills and valleys of the interior. The rajah of Cochin, who protected the Jews and granted them a site in the very vicinity of his palace, was scornfully referred to by a contemporary Portuguese historian as the "King of the Jews." The Jews returned in 1663 when the Dutch, on their second invasion, captured all the Portuguese forts on the Malabar Coast, including Cochin.

Under Dutch domination (1663–1795) the Jews once again lived happily and prospered. The Dutch were tolerant and did not interfere in religious matters. They allowed the Jews to repair their synagogues and build new ones. They helped revive Cochin Jewry's role in international trade and ended their cultural and religious isolation from the Jews of the West. The Jews, in turn, were of great service to the Dutch as intermediaries to the Cochin rajahs and as international agents, trade negotiators, diplomats, "court Jews," bankers, and financiers. The greatest of the Jewish merchants was Ezekiel Rahabi (1694–1771), from the Paradesi community.

The son of immigrants hailing from Aleppo, Syria, Rahabi was a merchant, agent, banker, diplomat, and community leader all rolled into one. In the service of the Dutch East Indies Company, Rahabi traded in spices, linen, cotton, rice, dyes, wax, lumber, and other items. He constructed huge warehouses and transportation facilities. Together with other South Indian Jewish merchants, he built enormous ships that transported goods to many parts of Asia and the Middle East. Many of these ships had Hebrew names like Rachel, Daniel, Isaac, Jerusalem, and Ashkelon, and were manned by Jewish captains.

A humanitarian and ecumenicist, his house in Jew Town was a meeting place for local rulers, visiting dignitaries, and diplomats. When the authorities of the Mar Thomite community (Syrian Christians in India) wanted to bring Cochin a bishop from Iraq in 1747, it was Rahabi who dispatched a ship to fetch him and advanced a considerable sum of money to cover the entourage's travel expenses.[65]

In the aftermath of the Portuguese devastation, Malabaran Jewish culture was at a very low ebb. It was only after the Dutch conquered southern India that the isolated and traumatized Jewish community was able to reestablish contact with their coreligionists overseas. At the behest of the Portuguese Jewish community in Amsterdam, a delegation of Sephardim arrived in Cochin in 1686. "The impact of this visit on the Cochin Jewish community was unprecedented," writes Walter J. Fischel. "They had a distinguished visitor from across the ocean from their own coreligionists . . . whose presence bore testimony that they in Cochin were not forgotten, that their state was an object of interest and solicitude to their brethren."[66] The Dutch Jews brought with them Torah scrolls, updated religious literature, and religious articles such as *mezuzot* and *tefillin*, which they generously donated to the community. Additional *sefurim* and religious artifacts were later sent to Cochin, purchased with monies that the Paradesi merchant David Rahabi (Ezekiel Rahabi's father) put at the disposal of the Dutch Jews. From this point on, the Jews of Malabar were in regular contact with their brethren in Holland, and their *minhagim* more or less conformed with those of the Portuguese Sephardim.

The British (1795–1948) succeeded the Dutch as rulers of South India. The period of British domination marks a gradual decline in the fortunes of the White Jews of Cochin. Although the Jews suffered no persecutions or restrictions under the British, or the successive rajahs of Cochin, they became an impoverished community for a number of reasons. Unlike the Dutch, who used the Jews as middlemen in their dealings with the Rajahs and Indian society, the British handled all the commercial transactions themselves. Under the British, the centers of trade shifted to other parts of India, such as Surat, Calcutta, and Bombay. Many Jews from the Malabar Coast were attracted to the economic opportunities these new industrial centers provided.

Another reason for the decline of the Cochin community is attributable to the White Jews themselves. The descendants of immigrant families like Rahabi were not as hardworking, dynamic, or ambitious as their fathers and grandfathers had been. They made little effort to expand the family enterprises, preferring the fruit of other peoples' labors. They lived mostly off the family inheritance, which eventually dwindled.[67] By the mid nineteenth century the White Jewish community of Cochin was a mere shell of its former self. There was so much inbreeding among the Paradesis that by the middle of the twentieth century almost fourteen percent of their population was classified as mentally defective.[68]

Wherever the Jews lived in the Diaspora, they developed their own pidgin tongue. For example, in Eastern Europe the Jews combined mostly German and Hebrew to create Yiddish; in Spain and the Ottoman Empire, a Jewish dialect—Ladino—was formed from Spanish and Hebrew. On the Malabar coast of South India, the Jews spoke a mixture of Malayalam and Hebrew, with a sprinkling of Tamil, Spanish, Dutch, and English thrown in.

Before the abolition of the caste system among Jews, the Malabaris and Paradesis prayed in separate synagogues. Neither community ever possessed ordained rabbis. The religious leader was one who was recognized as the most erudite and pious man in the community. The White Jews, who were always a small minority of the Jewish population, prayed in the Paradesi synagogue. This synagogue, built in 1568 by Spanish Jews, has often been called the "Taj Mahal of the Indian Jews." The floors of the sanctuary were composed of 1,115 blue and white ceramic tiles, each with a different design, imported from China and presented to the congregation by the rajah of Cochin in 1762. The exterior of the synagogue was considerably embellished in the mid eighteenth century with the addition of a three-story clock tower donated by Ezekiel Rahabi. In 1968, on the 400th anniversary celebration of the synagogue, Prime Minister Indira Gandhi headed the delegation of dignitaries who came to honor the small synagogue. A special stamp was issued by the Indian post office, showing a picture of the synagogue.

In the late nineteenth century, the Rev. J. H. Lord observed that the Black Jews still made use of the privileges granted in the copper plate charter, whose transfer from the Black Jewish community to the Paradesi synagogue has never been explained. These privileges involved the following practices described by Rev. Lord:

> The Black Jews still carry a silk umbrella, and light lamps at day-time when proceeding to their synagogue on the eighth day after the birth of their sons. They spread a cloth on the ground, and place ornaments of leaves across the road on occasions when their brides and bridegrooms go to get married, and use then *cadanans* (mortars which are charged with gunpowder, and fired), and trumpets. After the wedding is over, four silk sunshades, each supported on four poles, are borne, with lamps burning in front, as the bridal party goes home. The Black Jews say that the White Jews use none of these, and never have done so. The White Jews aver that they were accustomed formerly to use such privileges, but have discontinued them.[69]

The Paradesis did indeed have customs that stressed their lineage to Joseph Rabban and the principality of Anjuvannam. A gold chain, worn over the left shoulder and across the right hip by the Paradesi groom at his wedding, was supposed to represent the "reign of Joseph Rabban."

Rabbi David D'Beth Hillel observed in the early nineteenth century that the Malabaris were more devoutly Jewish and knowledgeable of Jewish laws and traditions than the Paradesis.[70] The Black Jews had seven synagogues in Cochin and the nearby towns. The oldest of these, Kadavambhagam, founded in 1539, fell into disuse in the 1950s after the congregation migrated en masse to Israel. (In 1992 this synagogue was carefully dismantled and brought to Israel to be reconstructed for permanent display at the Israel Museum in Jerusalem.) Ruby Daniel, a Cochin Jew, in a recently published autobiography, recounts the following anecdote about the Kadavambhagam synagogue:

> A space was kept open between the Kadavumbagan [*sic*] synagogue and the river. In the days before cars or trains the maharajah of Cochin used to travel by boat from his palace at the northern end of Jewtown. In order to travel south, he would pass by this site. Whenever he was about to pass by, the Jews . . . were always informed ahead of time. They would then open the doors of the synagogue and they would open the doors of the *heykhal*—the ark where the Torah scrolls are kept. The Maharajah's boat would stop at the synagogue landing and he would stand up and then prostrate himself toward the synagogue.[71]

Many miracles were attributed to the Kadavambhagam synagogue, and the edifice was revered by Jews and Gentiles alike.

The Jews of Cochin had many unusual holiday *minhagim*, a few of which will be cited here. On the Shabbat and Yom Tov it was the custom to read the weekly Torah portion from the mezzanine of the synagogue. On Passover, the *ma nishtanah* (Four Questions) were asked not by the youngest member at the *seder* table, as is customary everywhere else, but always by the father. A piece of the *afikomen* was preserved for the entire year. When traveling by sea, the *afikomen* was carried along because it was believed to be "efficacious in calming stormy waters."[72]

There was a unique Shevuot custom among the Jews of Cochin of solemnly reciting aloud in the synagogue all of the 613 commandments. *Sukkot* were constructed from *cadjan* leaves (dried leaves of coconut palms). On Simchat Torah the Cochin Jews had a tradition of laying a red carpet around the outside of the synagogue and parading the Torah scrolls around the building seven times. A favorite Purim custom, writes Ida Cowen, "was to have two wooden figures, elaborately clothed, swatting each other until one was in fragments. The broken form represented Haman, the victorious one—Mordechai."[73] To preserve the memory that their ancestors were driven out of Cranganore, the Jews of Cochin kept the custom of never spending the night there. If for some reason a Jew found him or herself in Cranganore late in the day, he or she would hurry to leave before sunset.[74]

Before their mass migration to Israel in 1948, there were an estimated 2,700 Jews in Kerala, of whom 2,500 were Malabaris and 200 were Paradesis. Although most of the Malabaris were poor, that was not the reason they emigrated to Israel. Neither did they come, like most other immigrants to Israel, because of persecution in the old country, since none had existed there for almost 400 years. They came solely because they believed fervently in the religio-Zionist dream.

Upon arriving at Lod Airport the "Jews from the jungles" were sprayed with DDT by an immigrant absorption staff "which referred to them simply as 'blacks,' [and] regarded them as people without culture or identity."[75] Many were suffering from elephantiasis, a mosquito-borne disease that occurs in people who live in tropical climates. It is called elephantiasis because the legs swell up to the point where they look like an elephant's legs. Israeli health officials were concerned that the disease was contagious. On a doctor's recommendation, the Indians were settled in cool and dry regions in Israel. Many settled in *moshavim*, of which the most successful are Nevatim near Be'er Sheva, K'far Yuval in the Upper Galilee, and Mesilat Zion near Jerusalem. The Cochinis are said to have helped pioneer the raising of hothouse flowers (especially gladiolas) in the Negev. According to Dr. Shalva Weil, they are prosperous and "have become a symbol of success in the Israeli ethnic mosaic."[76]

As of this date (1999), there are no more than twenty Jews left in Cochin. These are mostly elderly people from the Paradesi community who have chosen to remain. The last *minyan* was held in 1987. The tiny community is described as being like one big family today. Cochin's Jew Town—now minus its Jews—is one of the city's major tourist attractions.

NOTES

1. *The Making of India and Indian Traditions* (Englewood Cliffs, N.J.: Prentice Hall, 1995), pp. 67–68.

2. Ibid., p. 113.

3. Ibid., p. 72.

4. Haeem S. Kehimkar, *The History of the Bene Israel of Bombay* (Tel Aviv: Dayag Press Ltd., 1937), pp. 74–75.

5. *Eight Years in Asia and Africa, from 1846–1855* (Hanover, 1863), p. 145.

6. H. G. Reissner, "The Ummi Prophet and the Banu Israil of the Qur'an," *The Muslim World* 39 (1949), pp. 276–81; Shirley B. Isenberg, *India's Bene Israel: A Comprehensive Inquiry and Sourcebook* (Berkeley: Judah L. Magnes Museum, 1988), p. 7.

7. Isenberg, *India's Bene Israel*, p. 20. See Ibn Khordadbeh description of the Radanite traders in Elkan N. Adler, *Jewish Travelers of the Middle Ages: 19 Firsthand Accounts* (New York: Dover, 1987), pp. 2–3.

8. Kehimkar, *The History*, p. 14; Shellim Samuel, *A Treatise of the Origin and Early History of the Ben-Israel of Maharashtra State* (Bombay: Iyer and Iyer, 1963), p. 7.

9. There were Bene Israel from the Konkan villages who after making *aliyah* in the 1950s were shocked to find that Orthodox Jews in Israel were eating beef. These illiterate Bene Israel were convinced that beef was considered *treif* (not kosher) in the Torah.

10. Rebecca Reuben, *The Bene Israel of Bombay* (Cambridge: Cambridge University Press, 1913), p. 6.

11. J. H. Hutton, *Caste in India: Its Nature, Function, and Origins*, 4th ed. (London: Oxford University Press, 1963), p. 89.

12. Kehimkar, *The History*, p. 93.

13. Schifra Strizower, "The Bene Israel and the Jewish People," *Salo Wittmayer Baron Jubilee Volume* (New York: Columbia University Press, 1977), p. 872.

14. This region was later designated as the Kolaba District of the Maharashtra State by the British.

15. Cited in Shirley Isenberg, *India's Bene Israel*, p. 27.

16. Schifra Strizower maintains that the Bene Israel knew nothing about Maimonides' writings before the onset of the twentieth century. See *The Children of Israel: The Bene Israel of Bombay* (New York: Schocken, 1971), p. 35.

17. *India's Bene Israel*, p. 23.

18. Strizower, "The Bene Israel and the Jewish People," p. 866.

19. Kehimkar, *The History*, p. 18.

20. "Yom Kippur: The Festival of Closing the Doors," in *Between Benares and Jerusalem: Comparative Studies in Judaism and Hinduism*, edited by Hananya Goodman (Albany: State University of New York, 1994), p. 98.

21. Kehimkar, *The History*, p. 18.

22. Ibid., p. 21.

23. Reuben, *The Bene Israel*, pp. 8–9.

24. Ibid., p. 13.

25. "The Bene Israel Villagers of Kolaba District, " in *Studies of Indian Jewish Identity*, edited by Nathan Katz (New Delhi: Manohar Publishers and Distributors, 1995), p. 90; See also Joan Roland, *Jews in British India: Identity in a Colonial Era* (Hanover, N.H.: University Press of New England, 1989), p. 38.

26. Kehimkar, *The History*, pp. 27–28.

27. I. A. Ezekiel, "Martial Traditions of the Bene-Israel Community," *India and Israel* (February 1949), p. 18.

28. Ibid.; Benjamin J. Israel, *The Bene Israel of India: Some Studies* (New York: Apt Books Inc., 1984), p. 18. According to Joan Roland, these percentages cannot be confirmed. See *Jews in British India*, p. 22.

29. Kehimkar, *The History*, p. 181; Benjamin J. Israel, *Religious Evolution among the Bene Israel of India Since 1750* (Bombay, 1963), pp. 10–11.

30. Shirley Isenberg, "Paradoxical Outcome of Meeting of Bene Israel and Christian Missionaries," in *Jews in India,* edited by Thomas A. Timberg (New York: Advent Books, 1986), p. 354.

31. Strizower, *The Bene Israel of Bombay*, p. 27.

32. Reuben, *The Bene Israel*, pp. 7–8.

33. Abraham Ya'ari, *Sheluhei Erez Yisra'el: Toldot ha-Shelihut Meha-arets la-Golah me-Churban Bayit Sheni Ad ha-Meah ha-Tesha Esrah* (Jerusalem: Mosad ha-Rav Kook, 1951), p. 134.

34. Many Bene Israel who had been employed by the Sassoons found themselves out of work with the closing down of the Bombay mills. On the early Bene Israel *aliyah* see Joan Roland, *Jews in British India*, pp. 247–253.

35. "The Jews and the Indian Film Industry," *Israel and India* (1967), pp. 9–18. According to Jacob Pandian, Bene Israel actresses were at a premium because of their relatively light-skinned features. See *The Making of India*, p. 110.

36. Walter J. Fischel and Naftali Bar-Giora, "Bene Israel," *Encyclopaedia Judaica*, vol. 4 (Jerusalem: Keter, 1971) pp. 496–497; Strizower, *The Children of Israel*, pp. 95–96. On the marriage and divorce customs of the Bene Israel in India see Kehimkar, *The History*, esp. pp. 106–110.

37. T. V. Parasuram, *India's Jewish Heritage* (New Delhi: Sagar Publications, 1982), pp. 88–89.

38. Ibid., p. ix.

39. K. P. P. Menon, *History of Kerala*, vol. 1 (New Delhi: Asian Educational Service, 1982), pp. 297–98.

40. *Kerala* (New Delhi: National Book Trust, 1972), p. 6.

41. Some historians identify Ophir with Supara, an ancient port near Bombay.

42. *Into India* (New York: Charles Scribner's Sons, 1973), p. 69.

43. On the legend of St. Thomas in India, see George M. Rae, *The Syrian Church in India* (London and Edinburgh: William Blackwood and Sons, 1892), pp. 39–61.

44. L. K. Ananta Krishna Iyer, *The Cochin Tribes and Castes*, vol. 2 (Madras: Government of Cochin, and London: Luzac & Co., 1909–12), p. xx.

45. Cecil Roth, *A Short History of the Jewish People*, revised and enlarged illustrated edition (London: Hartmore House, 1969), p. 122.

46. Cited by Parasuram, *India's Jewish Heritage*, p. 7.

47. Heinrich Graetz, *History of the Jews*, vol. 2 (Philadelphia : Jewish Publication Society, 1893), pp. 628–30.

48. For detailed analyses of the various translations of the copper plates see A. Galletti, et al., *The Dutch in Malabar* (Madras: Government Press, 1911), pp. 192–98; Edgar Thurston, *Castes and Tribes*, vol. 2:C to J (Madras: Government Press, 1909), pp. 469–77; Nathan Katz and Ellen S. Goldberg, *The Last Jews of Cochin: Jewish Identity in Hindu India* (Columbia, S.C.: University of South Carolina Press, 1993), pp. 42–46.

49. Anjuvannam literally means "five castes,"and the Jews were considered one of five classes of artisans in Kerala. According to R. Champakalakshmi, "Anjuvannam seems to have referred to Jewish traders who came to the west coast and acquired settlements." See "The Medieval South Indian Guilds: Their Role in Trade and Urbanization," in *Society and Ideology in India: Essays in Honor of Professor R. S. Sharman*, edited by D. N. Jha (New Delhi: Munshira Manoharlal Publishers, 1996), p. 62.

50. *The Jews of India* (New Delhi: Centre for Jewish and Interfaith Studies, 1982), pp. 41–42.

51. M. G. S. Narayanan, *Cultural Symbiosis in Kerala* (Trivandrum, India: Kerala Historical Society, 1972), p. 29.

52. Prem Doss Yehudi, *The Shingli Hebrews* (Trivandrum, India: Sachethana, 1989), p. 23.

53. *Shingli or Jewish Cranganore in the Traditions of the Cochin Jews of India* (Masters' thesis, Smith College, 1975), p. 88.

54. George Woodcock, *Kerala: A Portrait of the Malabar Coast* (London: Faber and Faber, 1967), p. 58.

55. David G. Mandelbaum, "Social Stratification Among the Jews of Cochin in India and in Israel," in *Jews in India*, edited by Thomas A. Timberg (New York: Advent Books, 1986), p. 101.

56. Ibid., p. 100.

57. Ibid., p. 108.

58. *Under Strange Skies* (New York: Philosophical Library, 1953), p. 190.

59. Ibid., p. 191.

60. *Indian Caste Customs* (Cambridge: Cambridge University Press, 1932), p. 22. In Kerala the pariah castes were supposed to be not only untouchable, but unapproachable and unseeable as well. They were required to maintain specified distances between themselves and the various higher castes. They were not allowed to walk on public roads and were obligated to bang a gong to warn approaching Brahmans. See E. M. S. Namboodiripad, *Kerala: Yesterday, Today, and Tomorrow* (Calcutta: National Book Agency, 1967), p. 47.

61. Walter J. Fischel, *Unknown Jews in Unknown Lands: The Travels of Rabbi D'Beth Hillel (1824–32)* (New York: Ktav, 1973), p. 114.

62. Schifra Strizower, *Exotic Jewish Communities*, pp. 107–108; Nathan Katz and Ellen S. Goldberg, "Jewish 'Apartheid' and a Jewish Gandhi," *Jewish Social Studies* vol. L:3–4 (Summer–Fall 1988/1993), p. 158; Nathan Katz and Ellen S. Goldberg, "The Sephardi Diaspora in Cochin, India," *Jewish Political Studies Review* 5:3–4 (Fall 1993), pp. 113–14.

63. Louis Rabinowitz, *Far East Mission* (Johannesburg: Eagle Press, 1952), p. 111.

64. Katz and Goldberg, "Jewish 'Apartheid'", p. 150.

65. For a detailed account of the life and activities of Ezekiel Rahabi see Walter J. Fischel, "The Contribution of the Cochin Jews to South Indian and Jewish Civilization," *Commemoration Volume*, edited by S. S. Koder, et al. (Cochin: Kerala Historical Association, 1971), pp. 14–66; and Walter J. Fischel, "Cochin in Jewish History: Prolegamena to a History of the Jews in India," *Proceedings of the American Academy for Jewish Research* 30 (1962), esp. pp. 41–59.

66. Fischel, "The Contribution," p. 49.

67. David G. Mandelbaum, "The Jewish Way of Life in Cochin," *Jewish Social Studies* 1 (October 1939), p. 439.

68. Strizower, *Exotic Jewish Communities*, p. 119.

69. Henry J. Lord, *The Jews in India and the Far East* (Westport, Conn.: Greenwood Press Reprint, 1976), p. 89.

70. Fischel, *Unknown Jews*, p. 114.

71. Ruby Daniel and Barbara Johnson, *Ruby of Cochin: An Indian Jewish Woman Remembers* (Philadelphia: Jewish Publication Society, 1995), p. 129.

72. Ida Cowen, *Jews in Remote Corners of the World* (Englewood Cliffs, N.J., 1971), p. 206.

73. Ibid., p. 205.

74. S. S. Koder, "The Jews of Malabar" *India and Israel* (10 May 1951), p. 31.

75. Shimon Lev, "From Cochin to Nevatim" *Eretz Magazine* (Autumn 1992), p. 29

76. "Malabar to Moshav," *The Jerusalem Post Magazine* (31 August 1984), p. 9.

Part X

Chinese Jewesses at the K'aifeng Conference, 1919
Credit: Chinese Jews by William Charles White

The "Blue-Turbaned Muslims"

BACKGROUND INFORMATION

Today, with more than 1.2 billion inhabitants, China is the most populous country in the world. After the Russian Federation and Canada, it is the third largest in area. Most Chinese call themselves Han, after the Han dynasty that ruled China from 206 B.C.E. to 228 C.E. An estimated ninety-four percent of the population is Han. The remaining six percent of the population belong to more than fifty-five minority groups, each with their own language and culture. There are an estimated fifty million Muslims in China.

Chinese civilization has more than 3,000 years of continuous recorded history, the longest of any country in the world. Until 1911, China was ruled by emperors throughout a succession of dynasties. For more than two millennia China was cut off from the rest of the world by the Great Wall, which is 1,700 miles long. It was built by the Ch'in regime in the third century B.C.E. to keep out invaders from the north and prevent China from making contact with the "barbaric" outside world. Around the thirteenth century, after Genghis Khan's conquest of China, the Great Wall ceased to serve this purpose. Today the Great Wall is primarily a tourist attraction, although China's contact and relationship with other countries is still limited.

Trade routes along the old Silk Road were reopened around 138 B.C.E. after the successful Chinese campaigns against the Hsiung-Hu nomadic tribes of the north. Camel teams working in relays first carried silk, iron, and hides, and later porcelain, across Central Asia, India, and the Roman Empire. These were exchanged for precious stones, glass, amber, textiles, and other commodities from the West. By the T'ang period (618–907 C.E.) commerce was booming, and this contributed to the growth of a large merchant class. As a result, the army and bureaucracy were greatly expanded. By the ninth century a brisk trade with Muslim merchants from Arabia and Persia was taking place in Canton and along the southern coast of China. It is believed that Muslim and Jewish middle-men introduced cotton from India into China during the Song dynasty (960–1279 C.E.). "[T]he spirit of intellectual curiosity and tolerance which marked the age encouraged a sympathetic attitude to religious and artistic ideas of for-eign origin. . . . The T'ang court welcomed foreigners, took a keen interest in alien customs and religions, and extended a friendly welcome . . . to travelers from Western regions."[1]

On the other hand, disdain for the barbarians was constantly reinforced by encounters between the Han Chinese and the Jurchen (Turkish and Mongo-lian) invaders. Despite this, the invaders who stayed, and settled down, inter-married with Han women. Instead of conquering, or being conquered, they were assimilated. Eventually they converted to Chinese ways so thoroughly that over time they became almost indistinguishable from the people who were native to the regions where they had been absorbed.

Under the great Mongol conqueror Kublai Khan, China enjoyed its most brilliant spell of prosperity. The Mongols, or Yuan as they are known in China, appear to have been adept in managing subject peoples, and tended to be toler-ant of all the subject religions in their realm. They availed themselves of the services of many subject peoples and were willing to learn from them. Many of the best and brightest of Yuan advisors and ministers were drawn from Chinese minorities such as Tibetans, Uighurs, and Central Asian Muslims. Even Euro-pean travellers and explorers filled these positions. Marco Polo is a familiar example of those advisors.

By the late eighteenth century, China was visited by explorers, traders, and missionaries from Portugal, Holland, England, France, and Spain. In the nineteenth century, seafaring captains from America also took an active part in exploiting the resources and markets of the East. This imperialism forced the warring Chinese factions to pull together. From 1839 to 1911 a series of wars and grassroots rebellions against imperialistic intrusions—the Opium Wars (1839–42; 1856–60), the Taiping Rebellion (1850–64), and the Boxer Rebel-lion (1900–01)—resulted in humiliating defeats for China and its dismember-ment by foreign powers.

By 1911 the dinosaurish Manchu dynasty had been discredited by revolutionary forces. Rebellions broke out in all the provinces. The Chinese Empire collapsed and was supplanted by a Chinese Republic. After years of civil war, the People's Republic of China was proclaimed by the Communists in 1949. The former Nationalist government fled to the island of Formosa, which they took over and later renamed Taiwan.

Henan province in south-central China is considered the cradle of Chinese civilization. Situated on the Yellow River, whose Chinese name translates as "China's Sorrow," Henan perennially suffered from floodings that destroyed everything. Kaifeng is a historic city in Henan Province, about 470 miles from the capital, Beijing. During the Song period, Kaifeng was the imperial capital of China and a major point on the Silk Route from the West. In this epoch Kaifeng was the grandest city in China—if not the whole world. A census taken in 1105 estimated there were 260,000 households in Kaifeng. In addition to being a major trade center, Kaifeng served as an intellectual and artistic center. After the Jurchen nomads sacked Kaifeng in 1127, the Song court fled southward to Hangzhou and Kaifeng never regained its imperial splendor.

For over 2,000 years Confucianism has shaped Chinese life. Confucius (551–479 B.C.E.), one of China's greatest philosophers, emphasized the importance of ethical relations and the dignity of man. Confucianist concepts were primarily practical methods for the ordering of life. Society is based on kinship structure. In human relations everybody should behave according to correct norms. Fundamental to the social order are the Five Relationships: between ruler and subject, father and son, husband and wife, older brother and younger brother, and mentor and protégé. According to Confucius, human nature is best manifested in love between parents and children. Social order and political harmony are best manifested when moral harmony exists. When a person is respectful to his parents, he can be expected to be loyal to his ruler, loving toward his wife, kind to his brother, and faithful to his friends. In short, "Confucianism maintained the importance of tradition, of obedience to authority, of rites and etiquette in the regulation of daily life, and of a rational benevolent existence."[2] Every Chinese owed absolute obedience to the emperor. The empire was perceived as a gigantic family in which the emperor was the benevolent father and the subjects were his children. The emperor was regarded as the "Son of Heaven." As such, he was considered both king and high priest, and the link between heaven and earth.

There was no country in the world where learning and scholarship were held in greater honor than in Old China. In theory, education was open for all without any class distinction. On the pyramid of power, just beneath the Imperial family, were the scholar-officials or mandarins who ran the empire. In the sixth century C.E. a system of civil service examinations was introduced for recruits wishing to work in the government bureaucracy. These rigorous examinations, based mainly on memorized texts, tested the applicant's mastery of Confucianist canon. The mandarins, as Confucianist scholars are called by Westerners, enjoyed great prestige and many privileges.

In Chinese society the highest status was given to the scholar-bureaucrats, who were seen as the transmitters of the ancient heritage and the personification of Chinese virtues. These were followed by the farmers, who fed the nation, and the artisans, who processed what the farmers produced. Merchants, regarded as outright exploiters who made profits from other peoples' labor, were down toward the bottom rung of the social scale. Somewhere in between the merchants and the social pariahs—i.e., slaves, prostitutes, and jesters—was the soldier class. Because their function was to kill and destroy, the military profession was considered uncouth and loathsome to the Chinese.[3]

Ancestor worship is the oldest and most widespread of Chinese religious practices. It was the heart of Chinese faith. The Chinese believed that the spirit of a dead person could control the welfare of the rest of the family still living. Offerings were made to the ancestors, who, according to ancient belief, watched over their descendants as guardians and benefactors.

THE JEWS OF KAIFENG, CHINA

> Those who attempt to represent God by images or pictures do
> but vainly occupy themselves with empty forms. Those who
> honor and obey the sacred writings know the meaning of all
> things; and eternal reason and the sacred writings mutually
> sustain each other in testifying whence men derived their being.
> All those who profess this religion aim at the practice of goodness
> and avoid the commission of vice.
>
> —excerpt from the Stone Inscription of 1489,
> outlining Chinese-Jewish monotheism.

No one knows exactly when the Jews first set foot in China. According to the Chinese Jews' own records, their ancestors arrived as far back as the period of the Zhou dynasty, or sometime between 1056 B.C.E. and 256 B.C.E. The Jews probably migrated to China in several streams at various dates, but historians believe with great certainty that they have been living continuously in China since the ninth century C.E. The Jewish population was at its peak during the Ming dynasty (1368–1644), though never amounting to more than 4,000. It is remarkable that until the nineteenth century those Jews who lived in Kaifeng were able to withstand assimilation into the vastly greater Han and Muslim populations. Numerous sources mention the existence of Jewish settlements at Hangchow, Ningbo, Canton, Beijing, and other places, but these communities disappeared without leaving a trace. The general belief is that most of these communities eventually assimilated into the Confucian milieu or converted to Islam.

Contrary to the experience of Jews the world over—the experience in India being the only other exception—there is no documentary evidence to indicate that Chinese Jews were ever victimized, as Jews, by institutional racism or systematic religious intolerance. Perhaps with the exception of the Qing (Manchu) dynasty (eighteenth century), when all non-Han people in China were made to feel like aliens, the Jews always had the same civil and political rights that were accorded everyone else, and they were never subjected to restrictive legislation. The Jews of China knew nothing about the Spanish Inquisition, the Chemielnitzsky pogroms, and other iniquities perpetrated against their fellow Jews all over the globe. For many centuries they maintained their separate existence in China and withstood the power of absorption and assimilation. In their heyday they produced a thriving religious and communal life and maintained numerous synagogues.

To understand China's treatment of its Jews one needs to understand the traditional Chinese attitude toward foreigners who came to live in their midst. Generally, the Chinese rulers tended to be disdainful toward non-Chinese, especially the "barbarians" who repeatedly invaded the country. At the same time, they viewed religious and racial differences with a broad-minded tolerance. China had no established religion, and religious beliefs were left to family and individual conscience. Emperors might have a predilection for one particular religion, but no Chinese emperor ever compelled his subjects to follow his example. The difference between Chinese and "barbarian" was cultural, rather than racial or religious. Any foreigners who accepted Chinese culture were considered Chinese, regardless of their creed or ethnic background. All civilized peoples were welcome on China's shores, and different religions were regarded as acceptable as long as they "did not threaten either the supreme authority of the state over the lives of its subjects, or the established patterns of public morality."[4]

The Chinese, S. M. Perlmann reminds us, "believe that the best way to conquer an enemy is to make a friend of him. . . . China has always granted equal freedom and equal rights to everyone regardless of nationality or faith, and she has succeeded in converting into patriotic Chinese the adopted strangers who came to her shores."[5] In an environment that cultivated tolerance, or at very worst courteous indifference, the Jews—though minuscule in number—flourished, and were able to assume positions of leadership out of proportion to their numbers. During their Golden Age, from approximately the thirteenth to the eighteenth century, they produced what might be called a Sino-Judaic culture. Chinese Jews studied Confucian philosophy and took part in Confucian rites. Their synagogues looked like pagoda temples, and they offered kosher sacrifices to their ancestors. Numerous Jews rose to become provincial governors, ministers of state, school supervisors, high-ranking army officers, and police chiefs.

The most important source of information about the origin, history, and culture of the Kaifeng *kehillah* (community) are three stone stelae (tablets) with carved Chinese characters that stood outside the old pagoda synagogue in Kaifeng until the mid nineteenth century. The three inscriptions, dated 1489, 1512, and 1663, offer three different dates for the time of the arrival of the Jews in China. The inscription of 1489 implies that the ancestors of the Kaifeng community settled in that city during the period of the Song dynasty, or sometime between 960 and 1126 C.E. The religion is said to have come from T'ien-chu or West Country, which scholars translate variously as India or Persia. We are informed that seventy families arrived, bringing a tribute of precious cotton cloth, and asked permission of the emperor to settle in his land and practice their religion unhindered.

The stele inscription of 1489 states that the synagogue in Kaifeng was originally constructed in 1163, during the Jin dynasty. From that year until its demolition in 1849, the synagogue was repeatedly damaged by flood and fire, and several times repaired and enlarged. The synagogue was rebuilt for the first time in 1279 during the reign of Kublai Khan, and the names of fourteen rabbis are given. The stone inscription of 1489 had been erected to commemorate the reconstruction of the synagogal compound after the devastation caused by the deluge of the Yellow River in 1461. The damage was so severe that only the foundations remained. Torah scrolls were procured from the Jewish communities in Ningbo and Ningzhia. The stele of 1489 points to the year 1421 when the emperor gave the physician Yen Cheng a gift of incense and permission to rebuild the synagogue. Yen Cheng was permitted to change his family name to Zhao and was designated a Major of the Embroidered Robe Bodyguard. The year 1421 is considered by scholars to be the turning point for the acceptance of the Jews in China.

Confucianist-influenced cultural modes, alien to Judaism, were incorporated into the architecture, the ambiance, and the actual worship in the synagogue. The synagogue, called the Temple of Purity and Truth, was built pagoda style. As sketched by the Jesuit Father Jean Domenge in 1722, it consisted of a portico with a double row of four columns and a three tiered roof. The synagogue compound, measuring 350 to 400 feet by 150 feet, consisted of four separate courts and various edifices for ritual ablution, residence, worship, and work.[6] Upon entering the temple, the congregants were obliged to remove their shoes and enter the *mikvah* chamber. After the ritual ablution, each congregant changed into holiday attire and covered his head with a blue *kippah* (skullcap).

The interior architectural design was modeled after the Jerusalem Temple. In front of the entrance to the inner sanctum stood two huge statues of lions on pedestals. Behind the statues were two large vases with flowers. The ritual of *gid anusheh* (removing the sciatic nerve of a slaughtered animal) was performed in the synagogue courtyard. The sanctuary proper was located in the center, an edifice sixty feet by forty feet, built along the lines of a Persian *mikdash*.

Chinese Jews practiced the traditional form of Judaism, with slight modifications. They fervently believed in Jehovah, whom they called August Heaven, studied Torah, circumcised their boys, eschewed nonkosher foods, affixed *mezuzot* to their doorposts, and strictly observed the Sabbath and the Jewish holidays. On Yom Kippur, the tablet dated 1663 states, " . . . .they close their doors and meditate all day. They neither eat nor drink, but cultivate their innate goodness."

In 1512 additional textual material was engraved on the reverse side of the stele of 1489, to memorialize the Jews living in other cities of the Middle Kingdom. The inscription plainly states that the Jewish religion was brought to China during the reign of the Han emperor Ming Di, who ruled from 58 to 76 C.E. The stele of 1663 had the Jews arriving in China as far back as the Zhou dynasty, or 1122–256 B.C.E. Historians have discounted this more ancient dating as a protective maneuver by its non-Jewish author to convince the Han that the Jews had inhabited the Middle Kingdom for so long that they were dyed-in-the-wool Chinese. The stele of 1663 recounted the major events in Kaifeng Jewry's history: the deluge of 1642 that destroyed the temple and wiped out most of the Jewish population, the rescue of the Jewish holy books, and the rebuilding of the temple in 1653. These events will be elaborated upon later in the chapter. The stone inscription of 1663 is not extant—though, fortunately, rubbings of its text have survived. Although a stone inscription of 1679 still exists and the date is still decipherable, its surface is largely disfigured. A Jewish scholar who examined the stelae in the early 1980s has described them as being "badly eroded . . . [and] possibly beyond restoration."[7]

What seems clear from the stone inscriptions is that the Jews did not arrive directly from Palestine, but via other countries in which they stopped. It is also obvious that they did not enter China only once, in a single group, but must have arrived both individually and in groups over a time span that has to be measured in centuries. Some historians believe that if the Jews came to China fleeing persecution, they must have come in family groups, and did not begin to intermarry with their hosts in appreciable numbers for some time. On the other hand, if they arrived essentially as traders or adventurers, then the men must have greatly outnumbered the women. In that case, the Jewish men were able to retain their identity only because, although they intermarried almost from the start, they were careful to hand down their Jewish loyalties to the children they fathered. Jewish men preferred to marry the monotheistic Muslims rather than the Buddhists and pagans, and converted their women to Judaism. In China, women married into the husband's clan and contact with the father's clan became minimal. Because Jewish women would have been permanently lost to the Jewish people in this way, they were forbidden to marry non-Jews.

It has still not been firmly established whether the Jews came to China via the Red Sea, or the Persian Gulf via India, or overland from Persia through Afghanistan and Central Asia. Perhaps both routes were used at different times. If they reached the ports of China by sea, they followed China's extensive river system to such important trading centers as Beijing, Nanking, Hangzhou, and Kaifeng. The Jews are not known to have spread beyond the big trading port cities of China.

There are many theories concerning the origins of the Chinese Jews. Some of these theories seem farfetched, if not outright absurd. Others are highly speculative and totally without foundation. Still others seem logical but cannot be substantiated. Many books and articles on Sino-Judaica have been written, elaborating on a gamut of origin theories. In this short space only the more tenable theories will be discussed, starting with the school that ascribes a Persian origin for Chinese Jewry.

The Canadian Anglican bishop William White, who lived in Kaifeng for many years and authored a three-volume text on the Chinese Jews in the 1940s, stressed the fact that the Hebrew writings of the Kaifeng community contained letters of the Persian alphabet and many Persian words, which would point to a long sojourn of the ancestral community in Persia.[8] The outstanding Australian Sino-Judaic scholar Donald Leslie, while not entirely ruling out a Babylonian origin, says essentially the same thing: While language evidence "cannot be conclusive alone . . . their use of spoken Persian and written Judeo-Persian . . . weigh heavily in favour of a Persian rather than an Indian or Yemenite origin.[9] The early twentieth century Canadian Protestant minister Allen Godbey was of the opinion that the Chinese Jews came from Persia because their synagogue resembled the *mikdash* (temple) style interior found in Persian lands.[10] Jesuit missionaries in eighteenth-century China also concluded that "West Country" was Persia and that they must have come by way of Khorasan and Bukhara, by land.[11] This view was corroborated by the nineteenth-century Anglo-Jewish traveler Elkin Adler, who believed that the Jews of Kaifeng were originally from Khorasan. According to Adler, the rubrics in the Kaifeng liturgy were in the Bukharan-Persian dialect. Khorasan was historically the "gateway to China." The Jews traveled via Merv, which "commanded the great roads from Khiva to Herat and Bukhara to Meshed, and is thus at the crossway of the caravan routes to Persia, Afghanistan, India, China, and Turkestan."[12] There is a long-held belief among the Jews of Central Asia, originally from Persia themselves, that their ancestors were expelled from Bukhara by Jagatai, Genghis Khan's successor. Some migrated to China and soon ceased to have communications with the mother country.[13]

The Jews are said to have come from T'ien-Chu, or West Country, which usually means India to the Chinese. Some authorities take this literally and suggest that the Jews came by sea from Cochin or overland from northwest India. Perhaps they were, as Berthold Laufer speculated, Indian Jews who had emigrated from Persia.[14] Modern Chinese scholar Pan Guandan offers several theories, one of which ascribes an Indian origin to the Chinese Jews. He accepts the Bene Israel of Bombay's traditional view of their own Indian origin. According to this view, the Jews fled Judea around 175 C.E. at the outset of Seleucid repression (and before the Maccabean revolt) and sailed to the Konkan Coast of India via Alexandria. They remained there for eleven hundred years until the middle or end of the eleventh century, when some of them sailed for China and settled in Kaifeng.[15] The Kaifeng Jews, like the Bene Israel of Bombay, "had not even a shadow of such a holiday [as Chanukah]."[16]

Some scholars believe that it was not persecution but commercial gain that brought the Jews to China. According to Samuel Krinsky, as far back as early Achaemenid times (fifth century B.C.E.), skilled Jewish artisans engaged in producing luxury items such as glass vessels "depart[ed] from Babylonia and established themselves at the core of the Chinese empire in order to serve this developing, lucrative market for their ware."[17]

L. Carrington Goodrich believes that since the Jews (together with Arabs) arrived in Kaifeng with "western cloth"—cotton—they probably came from India.[18] Cotton was not yet current in China. According to Pan Guandan, it is also possible that the Jews may have come from Ceylon, since that country had a sizable Jewish colony in the ninth and tenth centuries.[19] (The Jews of Ceylon are believed to have originally come from southern India.)[20] Sydney Shapiro, translator and editor of an important work on the Chinese Jews that was written from the perspective of Chinese scholars, has creatively synthesized the arrival theories of the Jews to China in this way:

135 A.D. Defeat by the Romans of the Bar Cochba revolt. Jews are expelled from Jerusalem. It was at this point that the large-scale Diaspora . . . began. Over the next five hundred years thousands of Jews migrated into Persia and Arabia. Part of these continued north into Afghanistan, Balkh, Samarkand and Bokhara in Central Asia, all on the old Silk Road. Some, probably around the seventh century, moved overland from there into northwest China, also known as Chinese Turkestan, where they settled, though not in large numbers. A few advanced further into north China. Another part of the Jews in Persia and Arabia migrated south into India, settling mainly in southwestern ports along the Arabian Sea. Some of them became merchants and traveled to China on Arab, Persian or Chinese vessels during T'ang and Song (seventh to thirteenth centuries), and settled in seaports on China's southeast coast.[21]

This theory is feasible because it is known that the various "barbaric" Turkish and Mongolian tribes, who had acted as a barrier against free intercourse between Persia and China, were completely subdued when the T'ang came to power in 618 C.E. Foreign trade flourished. There is evidence of foreign religions, such as Nestorian Christians, Zoroastrians, Manicheans, and, later, Muslims and Jews entering the country during this epoch. Arab and Persian merchants were found in sizable numbers in China. They established colonies, a number of which ultimately grew to considerable size. By the ninth century, the trade carried on between the West and China was handled mainly by Muslim entrepreneurs. Commerce was transacted not only via the well-traveled Silk Road, but also via sea routes. Merchant vessels sailed from the Persian Gulf ports, skirted India and Sumatra, and then landed their goods at Canton, Chu'an, Hangchow, and other Chinese coastal cities.

Sharing in this trade, though on a lesser scale, were polyglot Jewish merchants, known as Radanites, who, the ninth-century Persian Postmaster General Ibn Khordadbeh informs us,

> traveled from West to East, from East to West, partly on land, partly by sea. They transport from the West eunuchs, female slaves, silk, castor, marten . . . and swords. They take ship from Firanga (France) . . . and make for Farama (Pelusium). There they load their goods on the backs of camels and go by land to al-Kolzum (Suez). . . . They embark in the East Sea and sail from al-Kolzum to al-Jar (port of Medina) and Jedda (port of Mecca), then they go to Sind, India and China. On their return from China they bring back musk, aloes, camphor, cinnamon, and other products of the Eastern countries to al-Kolzom, and bring them to Farama, where they again embark on the Western Sea. . . . Sometimes these Jew merchants, when embarking in the land of the Franks . . . make for Antioch . . . thence by land to al-Jabia. . . . There they embark on the Euphrates and reach Baghdad, whence they sail down the Tigris to al-Obolla. From al-Obolla they sail for Oman, Sind, Hind, and China.
>
> These different journeys can also be made by land. The merchants that start from Spain or France go to Sus al-Aksa (Morocco) and then to Tangier, whence they walk to Afrikia (Kairouan) and the capital of Egypt. Thence they go to al-Ramla, visit Damascus, al-Kufa, Baghdad, and Basrah . . . cross Ahwaz, Fars, Kirman, Sind, Hind, and arrive at China. Sometimes, also, they take the route behind Rome, and, passing through the country of the Slavs, arrive at Khamlij, the capital of the Khozars. They

embark on the Jorjan Sea, arrive at Balkh, betake themselves from there across the Oxus, and continue their journey toward [the yurts of] Toghoz-ghor, and from there to China.[22]

In the Middle Ages, during periods of Christian-Muslim animosity, when many trade routes were blocked, the Jews were best equipped to carry on trade between Asia to Europe.[23] According to the Chinese scholar Zhang Xing Lang, "When the Mongols invaded southern Europe, Russia and Poland, and their legions penetrated Germany, Hungary and Austria, they captured many Jews and brought them back to China. . . . "[24]

By far the most important and desired commodity China had to offer was silk. This was in such great demand in the Mediterranean world that it was said a pound of silk was worth a pound of gold. Silk was the principal commodity going westward in exchange for gold, silver, glass, amber, and precious stones. "It stands to reason," writes Salo Baron, "that some Jews, particularly from Egypt, took part in that trade."[25] Presumably, these Chinese commodities were sold for a high price in the bazaars of Cairo and Alexandria.

The earliest unquestioned record that indicates the presence of Jews in China is dated from the eighth century C.E., or T'ang times. There was evidence discovered in 1902 by the Anglo-Jewish archaeological surveyor and traveller Marc Aurel Stein consisting of 200,000 ancient manuscripts in the Caves of a Thousand Buddhas, located in Tun-Huang on the edge of the Gobi desert.[26] Archaeologists' dates for the manuscripts range from the fourth to the eleventh century. Among the items Stein found in a chamber in the caves, which had been sealed up for nearly a thousand years, was a leaf of paper bearing a *selicha* (Hebrew penitential prayer) composed of passages from *Tehillim* (Psalms) and *Neviim* (Prophets). In 1908, a letter written in Judeo-Persian was discovered in Chinese Turkestan. The writer was addressing himself to a fellow Jew in Tabaristan, or west Persia. He was expressing hope that the latter might help him unload a flock of mangy sheep. The probable date of the letter was around 718 C.E.

By the eighth century C.E. the Jews were sufficiently numerous in China for the emperor to have appointed a special officer to supervise them. The Arab writer Abu-Zaid al-Sirafi (circa 916 C.E.) mentioned that Jews were among the 120,000 foreigners who were slaughtered in Canton by the rebel Banshu in 877–78 C.E.[27] They were massacred presumably because they were wealthy. The Venetian traveler Marco Polo (1254–1324) reported that the Jews of China were sufficiently numerous in his day to assert a political influence on the court of Kublai Khan. He observed that Jews, Muslims, and Christians debated the merits of their respective religions at the khan's court.[28]

Thirteenth-century Chinese archives in Hangchow show that the officials on the local sugar board were all wealthy Muslims and Jews. Apparently they were caught tampering with the weights, and were punished by the authorities. The Spanish-Jewish traveller Suleyman of Andalusia recorded that he found Jewish communities in all the major Chinese cities and that he conversed with them in Hebrew.[29] A frustrated Andrew Perugia, Bishop of Quanzhou in the fourteenth century, wrote to his superiors in Rome that he had failed in his attempts to convert any Jews.[30] In 1346 the Arab envoy Ibn Batuta referred to the existence of Jewish, Christian, and Turkish communities in Hangchow. He remarked that "these are numerous . . . [t]heir streets are well disposed, [and] their great men are exceedingly wealthy."[31] The Jesuit missionary Alvarez Semmedo, writing in 1642, reported that Jews were living in four Chinese cities and were highly esteemed by their fellow citizens.[32]

During the Song dynasty (960–1126 C.E.) seventy Jewish families, led by their headman, were invited by the Song Emperor to live in his capital. Querying the Jews about the fundamental tenets of their religion, the emperor found little in the Jewish Ten Commandments that was incompatible with the basic tenets of Confucianism. To prove "their amenability to the discipline of Chinese civilization,"[33] it was necessary for the Jews to present gifts to the emperor. As a representation of a costly gift, the Jews presented the emperor with a tribute of cotton cloth. The gift of cotton points to an Indian origin for Kaifeng's Jews, because the cotton plant was not yet cultivated in China and was highly appreciated there. The Emperor said: "You have come to our Central Plain. Preserve your ancestral customs and settle in Bianliang (Kaifeng)."

In traditional Chinese culture the most basic social and religious institution was the family unit. The oldest male in the family was the patriarch, the center of authority and respect. Leadership normally passed down to the oldest son. In both traditional Chinese and Jewish culture, age was held in great esteem. Large families were glorified, and often three or four generations lived together.

Marriages in China were brokered. The choice of partners was never left to the groom and bride; they had no say in the matter. When a young man reached the age of sixteen, his father or older brother sought the services of a matchmaker, who would seek to arrange a marriage. Girls younger than fourteen were forbidden to marry. The matchmaker tried to select a mate who would be compatible. Among the Han Chinese, a man could have only one legal wife, but he could take as many concubines as he wished and could afford to support. If his wife failed to provide him with a son, the husband would be strongly pressed by his parents and even his wife to take a concubine. Jews and Muslims were known to practice polygamy. The Jewish mandarin Zhao Ying Zou was listed in the Codex as having two wives; Zhang Mei, which means Zhang the Handsome, had at least six wives. Persons with the same surname could not marry because they were considered relatives.

Respectable Jewish menfolk, like their Han compatriots, were generally clean-shaven. After the Manchurian conquest in 1644, Chinese men had to shave their heads and wear pigtails as a sign of subjugation and submission. Military men traditionally wore long sidewhiskers and a goatee, as it was a sign of virility to have a vigorous growth of hair. Children's heads were shaved, leaving only a small tuft on top of the head.

While Confucius conceded that women were human beings, he considered them of a lower state than men: "It is a law of nature that women should be kept under the control of men."[34] With few exceptions, women in China were provided with no education whatsoever. A woman was taught to be completely submissive to her husband. When a man and his wife had to appear together in public, the woman customarily walked ten paces behind.[35] Widow chastity was an ideal, and therefore widows were not permitted to remarry. Foot binding was widely practiced among the Chinese upper classes from Song times onward. The binding process began when a girl was between five and eight. Bound feet were considered not only erotic but the mark of affluence and good breeding. Photos taken of the Kaifeng Jews in the late nineteenth and early twentieth centuries reveal that the women were subjected to the same terribly painful and crippling practices as their Han Chinese sisters.

Infanticide of baby girls was practiced wholesale by all classes of Han Chinese society. Boys were considered a valuable addition to the family, because they would grow up to labor for the family and keep up the sacrifices to the ancestors. Girls were considered an economic liability. A daughter impoverished the family. She was an additional mouth to feed, and after marriage she moved out of the house. Because of their great poverty, many Han Chinese families sold their daughters as slaves, or as wives and concubines. In very stressful times they sold their female children to the Jews, who adopted them and brought them up in the Jewish faith. The Han strain in Kaifeng Jewry must have been considerable, because over the centuries the Jews became more or less indistinguishable from the larger society.

The Jews of Kaifeng referred to themselves as I-su-lo-yeh (Israel). Like their Muslim neighbors, they established separate quarters within the city and voluntarily lived apart from the Han Chinese. And like Jews in other traditional settings, they preferred to settle their disputes in their own religious courts, except when a serious crime was committed against a Chinese. In the seventeenth century, Jesuit missionaries in China inform us, the Saracens (Muslims) were "always looked upon as outsiders."[36] The Jews, considered to be merely a subgroup within the vastly larger Muslim community, were probably perceived likewise. They did not figure often in the early Chinese records. The Han Chinese often had difficulty distinguishing the Jews from their Muslim neighbors. This is understandable, since both groups were Caucasoid peoples who originated in Central Asia, lived in secluded quarters, and maintained their own graveyards. They wore more or less the same dress in public and eschewed eating pork, cats, and dogs. They performed the "deplorable" act of circumcision on their males, and practiced polygamy when it was permitted. Still, there were a number of cultural nuances that made it relatively easy for local Han to distinguish between a Jew and a Muslim. Among Jews it is customary to extract the *gid anusheh* (sciatic nerve) from the animals they slaughter. This tradition is based on the Genesis story of Jacob wrestling with the angel. To commemorate the fact that the angel wrenched Jacob's hip at the socket, the Jews do not eat the sinews near the sciatic nerve. Because of this peculiar custom, the Han Chinese were in the habit of referring to the Jews as *Tiao Chin Chiao*, or "The religion that plucks out the sinew." An alternate designation for the Jews was *Lan Mao Hui Hui*, or the "Blue-turbaned Muslims," because they were invariably attired in blue headgear in public, whereas the Muslims tended to wear white.

Kaifeng Jewry spoke the local Han dialect. Originally, many of them were probably proficient in Hebrew and Aramaic. In the early centuries of their arrival, New Persian, the lingua franca of Central Asia, was probably spoken in their everyday lives. Notations and explanatory comments in the synagogue texts were written in Judeo-Persian.

Unlike Jews in the Muslim and Christian world, the Jews of Kaifeng were never persecuted or confined to specific occupations. There were among them farmers, silk breeders, artisans, shopkeepers, and manufacturers. Some were merchants involved in importing and exporting goods from India and Persia. The better-educated entered the civil service and attained the rank of mandarin. Some of these Jewish mandarins occupied important positions in the government bureaucracy. Many Jews were attracted to military careers. Twice, in 1329 and 1355, the Jews were summoned to Beijing to bolster the Mongol Imperial Army.

The Kaifeng Jews prayed three times a day, but the congregants wore no *tallaitim* or *tefillin*. Their Torah readings were divided into fifty-three *parshiot* (chapters) instead of fifty-four, which would indicate a Persian origin for the *kehillah*. Also like the Persian Jews, they counted the Hebrew alphabet as being twenty-seven letters rather than twenty-two. However, the Torah was encased in a Yemenite fashion. This might indicate an Indian origin, since the Malabari Jews had a strong belief that they originally came to India from Yemen. Perhaps a compromise regarding the practice of various *minhagim* was ironed out by the disparate (and contentious?) groups in the community, not unlike the "Ritual of Kaffa" in fifteenth-century Crimea (see part 4, "On the Russian Riviera"). No quotations in the holy books were derived from the *Gemurah* portion of the Talmud, but the *kehillah* did possess various *mishnaic* excerpts, which were included in the text of their prayer books. The Jews awaited the Messiah, but did not expect him to come for another 10,000 years.

The Jews of Kaifeng borrowed Chinese Muslim titles to denote their religious leadership. There were three kinds of office-bearers: *wusida*, *man-la*, and *andula*. The *wusida*, a variation of the Persian term *ustad*, or Chief Rabbi, was the hereditary spiritual head of the community. He exercised jurisdiction over the *kehillah* and was responsible to the Chinese authorities for his flock. The *man-la*, or *mullah*, was one who was well versed in the Hebrew Scripture, exhorted others to lead a good life, and served the role of the synagogue functionary. The *andula* has been translated by some scholars to mean the *shochet*/sinew extractor, and by others to mean the superintendent or *shamash*.

During the prayer service the congregation faced westward, toward Jerusalem, but did not wear *tallaitim*. The rabbi wore a blue headdress and blue shoes and had a red satin umbrella held over him during the reading of the Torah. The *ba'al koreh* (reader) removed the *Ta-king* (Torah) from the ark and placed it on a magnificent pulpit with an embroidered cushion called the "Throne of Moses." When reading from the Torah, the barefooted *ba'al koreh* would cover his face with a transparent cotton veil in memory of Moses, who had covered his face with a veil when he came down from Mount Sinai and presented the Torah to the Children of Israel. Standing next to him was a prompter, and some paces away a *man-la* stood to correct the prompter just in case he misread the text.

In front of the Throne of Moses there was a long stand for candles, incense pots, and other ritual items. Incense was burned in honor of the ancestors, but without the Chinese-style pagan images. Above this chair loomed a great tablet with gold Chinese letters proclaiming "Long Live the Emperor." Obeisance to the emperor was required by law. But so that no one forgot who reigned supreme, the Chinese Jews added Hebrew characters, which the non-Jews could not understand, above the proclamation. This was the *Shema*, Judaism's eternal affirmation of the unity and uniqueness of the Supreme Ruler. The emperor was "the son of heaven," but "August Heaven" or "The Formless One," as the Jewish God is variously referred to by Kaifeng Jewry, was the highest of all. The tablet of the emperor was covered up or removed during *tefillah*, the prayer service, and there were no images or tablets in the synagogue other than the suspended scrolls referring to the articles of faith. The sanctuary possessed a Holy of Holies, a separate compartment where no one but the *wusida* could enter. This special chamber was where the *sefer torahs* were located.

Connected to the synagogue was a chamber called the Hall of the Holy Patriarchs, in which incense sticks were kept burning in ceremonial bowls, in honor of the *avot* (forefathers of the Jewish people). Offerings of meat and seasonal fruits and vegetables were made at different times of the year by the Jews in memory of their forebears.

The Kaifeng Jews always stressed that they were only honoring their ancestors, not worshipping them. Following Confucian custom, Chinese Jewry preserved the memory of their fathers with religious reverence by inscribing tablets with their names. These inscriptions drew parallels between the basic tenets of Confucianism and Judaism, and they show how both follow the *tao* in their emphasis on moral conduct. "Moses is discovered to have thought out the *Chung-yung* or the Golden Mean of Confucius,"[37] and over and over again attempts were made by the Jews to show that there was nothing in the Torah that was not in conformity with Confucianist canon. The Jews of Kaifeng adopted the feudal Three Duty Relationships and Five Cardinal Virtues, even employing the lexicon of Confucianist cosmology to describe their own spiritual values. This was stated in forceful terms in order to allay the suspicion that Judaism did not esteem the virtues inherent in Confucianist philosophy. In the inscription of 1489 on the stele we are told:

> Our religion and Confucianism differ only in minor details. In mind and deed both respect Heaven's Way, venerate ancestors, are loyal to sovereigns and ministers, and are filial to parents. Both call for harmony with wives and children, respect for rank, and for making friends. In short, nothing less than the Five Relationships.

The economic and political position of the Chinese Jews was greatly enhanced during the lenient and tolerant period of Mongol rule (1272–1368). The Mongols did not trust the educated classes of Han Chinese with bureaucratic powers, and instead employed various minorities, such as Tibetans, Uighurs, Muslims, and Jews, in official positions. Investment brokering, tax farming, foreign trade, and the highest government positions were reserved for non-Chinese. Kublai Khan's reign was marked by tolerance for rival religions and by economic privileges for members of favored religious groups, which included Jews. The practices of ritual slaughtering and levirate marriage outraged the

Mongols' sense of propriety and therefore were banned. Although they included the Jews, these edicts were directed primarily at the Han and the Muslims.

The establishment of the Mings, who overthrew the Mongols in 1368, may have had short-term repercussions in the Jewish communities because the Jews had rallied behind the Mongols. It is known that by 1461, when the synagogue was deluged by the overflow of the Yellow River, the leader of the Kaifeng community obtained permission from the provincial treasurer to rebuild the synagogue. This would indicate either that there was a marked improvement in their circumstances or that there had never been a decline.

Matteo Ricci (1552–1610) was an Italian Jesuit missionary stationed in Beijing who was instrumental in establishing the first Christian presence in China since Mongol times. In June 1605, Father Ricci was visited in Beijing by Ai Tian, an elderly gentleman from Kaifeng. Ai Tian was a district magistrate who had passed the provincial-level exams and had come to Beijing to take the examinations for the *jin shih* degree (Achieved Scholar or doctorate). He had read a report about some Europeans who, like himself, practiced a monotheistic religion, yet were not Muslims. Never having heard of Christianity, Ai Tian concluded that the foreigner was a follower of the Mosaic Laws, like himself. Ai Tian introduced himself as a fellow believer who had come to pay his respects. Father Ricci led him into the chapel. On the wall was a painting of the Madonna with the infant Jesus and John the Baptist. Nearby was another painting representing four of the Apostles. Ricci knelt down before the paintings, and the visitor immediately followed suit. "We in China do reverence our ancestors," Ai Tian proclaimed, and, pointing to the painting of the Virgin Mary, said, "This must be Rebecca with her sons Jacob and Esau. As to the other painting—why make obeisance to only four sons of Jacob? Were there not twelve?" Ricci, supposing him to mean the twelve Apostles, nodded in agreement. Then it suddenly dawned on the Jesuit that he might be carrying on a miscommunication with a Chinese Jew. Upon closer examination, Ricci observed that although the man was dressed like a Chinese mandarin, he did not look typically Chinese. Inquiring further, he learned that Ai Tian was indeed a Chinese Jew.

Ai Tian told Ricci that many other Jewish communities had existed in China for many centuries, but only the Jewish community in Kaifeng still survived, although in greatly diminished numbers. He stated that in Kaifeng there were ten or twelve families of Jews, and they possessed a synagogue that had recently been renovated. In the synagogue was preserved a Torah scroll that was about four or five hundred years old. When shown a Bible in Hebrew, Ai Tian confessed his inability to read it, although he recognized the characters. Because of his Chinese studies, Ai Tian told Ricci, he had neglected Jewish learning, and he was chastised by the rabbi of his community.

Two years later, in 1607, Ricci sent two Chinese Catholic converts to Kaifeng with a letter to the rabbi. The letter stated that the Jesuit mission in Beijing had all the texts of the Hebrew Bible and also the New Testament. Ricci conveyed the message that the Messiah had already come to redeem the people more than 1,600 years ago. The rabbi could not agree on this point, because the Messiah was not supposed to come for another 10,000 years. Old and ailing, he was worried that he would die without leaving a worthy successor. Because of Ricci's reputation in China as a sage and an honorable man, he was willing to pass on the rabbinate to the Jesuit Father on condition that he promise to give up eating pork. Ricci politely declined. Ten years later, when Ricci's journal was published in Europe, the western world first gained knowledge of China's Jewish community.

When the Catholic Church fathers first arrived in China, they came with the intention of converting pagans to Christianity. Having discovered the existence of a long-established Jewish colony in China, they wanted to understand how the Jewish community had modified a number of its ancient traditions and practices to make them compatible with Chinese beliefs, and attempted to determine what compromises were most necessary to gain converts.[38] For example, they wanted to know if aspects of Confucianism constituted "reverence" as opposed to "worship," and which aspects could be in no wise inimical with Catholic doctrines. Known as the Rites Controversy, the Catholic missionaries sought to utilize Sino-Judaic guidelines laid down by Chinese *halakhists* over the centuries for determining how tolerant it could afford to be with regard to those vestiges of Confucianism that the Chinese converts were carrying over with them to Christianity.

The Jesuits of the China mission who encountered the Jews were feverish in their desire to study their holy texts. They hoped to prove that there was some kind of international Jewish conspiracy at work to conceal the Truth: that earlier Jews had accepted Jesus as Christ but that after the emergence of Christianity, rabbis the world over deliberately expunged the vital passages. If, as it was believed, Kaifeng's Jewish community was ancient and its Torah scrolls originals, then surely they would find the uncensored material. But try as they might, the Jesuits found nothing to substantiate their allegations.

In his work *The Hope of Israel* (1650), Rabbi Manasseh ben Israel, of Amsterdam, claimed that certain Asian Jews, fleeing from the oncoming Mongol forces, crossed into the New World, thereby becoming the very first arrivals in that part of the globe. Those Mongols who, continuing the pursuit across the "Sea of Anian" on a land bridge, set foot slightly afterwards in the Americas, became the red-skinned people whom Europeans chose to call the Indians. The first Americans then were Asiatic Jews, according to Manasseh. The presence of the Lost Ten Tribes in the remote Far East and the New World was used by Manasseh ben Israel as an argument for convincing the Lord of the Exchequer, Oliver Cromwell, that it was the British Isles (from which the Jews had been expelled in 1279) that was the only remaining one of the four corners of the earth where, according to the biblical prediction, the Redeemer would gather together the Jewish remnant and then usher in the Messianic age. Manasseh ben Israel did not succeed.[39]

(Interestingly, neither did Sir James Harrington, an English scholar and admirer of Cromwell. Harrington propounded a scheme for solving the Irish as well as the Jewish "problem." In his work *Oceana* (to paraphrase Louis Hyman), he preached the return of the Jews to the soil as in biblical times and advocated the colonization of Ireland with Jews who would be attracted by the promise of religious and civil freedoms and the opportunity of living together. He proposed that parts of Ireland should be leased to Jews, allowing them religious autonomy so they would come from all over the planet. It is fortunate that Harrington's plan died in the printing.[40] It seems preposterous to imagine that Chinese or, for that matter, Ethiopian, Yemenite, or Moroccan Jewish farmers in Ireland could have served the British effectively as a replacement peasantry.)

In 1642 the city of Kaifeng was besieged by the Tartar rebel Li Tzu Zheng, who had rebelled against the ruling Ming prince and proclaimed himself emperor of the confederate Shun dynasty.

> Li first attacked the city in 1641 but retired after a few months . . . possibly because Kaifeng, with its fifty-foot walls, higher and stronger even than those of Peking, and its extensive outer fortifications, was too heavily defended. Returning in 1642, he laid siege to the city in the hope of starving it into submission. But at the end of nine months, in spite of a famine during which human flesh was sold openly in the markets at a price slightly higher than that of pork, while it was considered patriotic to throw the bodies of the dead into the streets to save others from starvation, Kaifeng was still holding out.[41]

Toward the end of the siege rice was sold at the price of pearls.[42] To save the city from falling into rebel hands, the Imperial forces breached the dikes of the Yellow River twice. The Yellow River was said to have flooded more savagely than at any other time in its history. "The destruction was so terrible, it is said that over a million people were drowned in the waters that stood as high as twenty feet."[43] Only seven clans, or an estimated 200 of the 500 Kaifeng Jewish families, managed to get across to the safe side of the river. The synagogue was swept away, and with it twenty-six volumes of *sefurim* (holy books) of various sorts and most of the Torah scrolls.

Two young Jews, Gao Hsien and Li Zh'eng, braved the raging waters and managed to retrieve ten of the scrolls and various scriptures that had sunk beneath the waves. Fragments from several salvaged Torahs, waterlogged and badly damaged, were dried out and patched together into one complete Torah scroll. Twelve other scrolls were gradually restored to make thirteen in all. There is a record of a synagogue at Ningbo sending a Torah scroll to the Kaifeng *kehillah*. The Kaifeng temple was rebuilt under the supervision of the Jewish mandarin Zhao Ying-zheng.

During their Golden Age, Kaifeng's Jews were held in great honor in China. There were among them provincial governors, judges, school superintendents, army officers, and landed gentry. The reverse side of the 1663 inscription includes twenty Confucian degree holders, fourteen military officers, and four official physicians. Considering that at its very peak the community probably never totaled more than 4,000 men, women, and children, this makes their status and achievements far out of proportion to the rest of the population of China.

Undoubtedly, the outstanding Jewish personality of Kaifeng is the above-mentioned Zhao Ying-zheng, whose Hebrew name was Moshe ben Avrom (1619–57). Ying-zheng is the only known Jewish mandarin with a *jin shih* degree, the equivalent of a doctorate that he won at the relatively young age of twenty-eight. The highlights of his curriculum vitae read like this: Secretary, Board of Punishment; County Magistrate, Henan Province; Department Head, Henan Flood Prevention Board; Assistant Governor, Fukian Province. Additionally, he gained popular acclaim for efficiently exterminating a gang of bandits in Fujien province, settling long-pending criminal cases, and establishing schools for the common people. Zhao Ying-dou, Ying-zheng's brother, was *kung-sheng* (Elevated Man), or master's-degree-level mandarin, who became County Magistrate of Henan Province.[44]

In 1653, Zhao's mother died. Zhao returned to Kaifeng to sit *shiva* and fulfill the obligatory two years and seven months of mourning, which is Chinese custom. During this interlude he got energetically involved in Jewish communal affairs. A competent Hebraist, he assisted the rabbi in the collation of the Torah scrolls recovered from the flood of 1642. With his brother Ying-dou, he helped excavate the foundations of the synagogue. Not only did Ying-zheng direct the rebuilding of the synagogue, he also personally underwrote the cost of building three additional sections at the rear hall of the synagogue. Ying-zheng wrote a tome called *The Vicissitudes of the Holy Scripture* and Ying-dou authored a work called *Preface to Clarifying the Law*. Nothing is left of either book.

One wonders at the breadth of the Zhao brothers' (and other Jewish Confucianists') Judaic scholarship. Training for the grueling civil service exams began in school at the tender age of eight, or even younger. Students who studied for the exams had little incentive to learn anything besides the Four Books and Five Classics on which they were going to be examined. To pass the civil service exams required encyclopedic knowledge and also the memorization of entire books by heart. Students were known to study twenty hours a day for the exams.[45] Needless to say, there was woefully little time or energy left to concentrate on anything else. The estimated one percent of the candidates who passed the district exams were granted the baccalaureate-level degree of *sheng-yuan* or Budding Genius and were qualified to take the provincial exams. Only an estimated one percent of those who took the provincial exams passed. These candidates were conferred the title of *kung-shen* (*chu-jne*) or Elevated Man, which qualified them to go to the capital to take final exams. The estimated one percent of the Elevated Men who passed these exams were conferred the degree of *jin shih* or Achieved Scholar. These doctoral-level mandarins were awarded the highest-level jobs in the Chinese bureaucracy.[46]

For Chinese Jewry's best and brightest, taking the civil service exams would have required seriously compromising some fundamental Jewish tenets. Upon arriving in the capital, every candidate was obliged to worship the God of Literature and offer sacrifices to Confucius in the Confucian Temple. This smacked of paganism, of the deification of a human being. The Jews honored Confucius, writes Salo Baron, "but Jewish leadership elsewhere would undoubtedly have taken umbrage at the formal sacrifices and banquets staged in honor of a pagan religious teacher. Yet this is exactly what the Kaifeng Jews did in tribute to Confucius, even if they somewhat modified these ceremonies so that they would not conflict with their own laws."[47] According to the Jesuit Father Gozani, these modifications entailed excluding the offering of swine flesh and only making very low bows and prostrations.[48]

No specific time or single event can be identified as the factor that marked the beginning of the end for the Jewish community of Kaifeng. There were a number of occurrences that contributed to this demise.

First there was the gradual loss of outside contacts that were necessary to nourish their cultural heritage. Over the centuries the Chinese Jews are believed to have become completely isolated from their coreligionists in the outside world, with perhaps the sole exception of Persian Jewry. Traditionally, their coreligionists in Persia supplied the Jews with enough resources to perpetuate Jewish culture. During the Ming period it was the stated policy of the emperors to prohibit the movement of their subjects to and from other lands and, at the same time, to keep as many foreigners as possible out of China. The later Ming period coincides with the rise of the fanatical Safavid Shiite dynasts in Persia. By the late sixteenth century Persian Jewry was itself effectively cut off from the major centers of Jewish learning. It is highly unlikely that the now ill-treated Jews of Persia, themselves rendered impoverished and unlettered, could have continued to render knowledgeable assistance to their brethren in China, even if there was some degree of contact between the two communities.

A second possible reason for the demise of Kaifeng Jewry was the deluge and floods of 1642. The loss of so many lives and of the bulk of their library may have started their downhill course. Even those Chinese Jews who remained faithful to the religion retained less and less of the practices. And even the most learned had difficulty reading the holy texts fluently in Hebrew. Centuries would pass before there would be renewed contact with the outside world, but by then it was much too late. By the mid nineteenth century, Chinese Jewry had lapsed into abject ignorance and poverty.

A third reason for the decline is that the intelligentsia of the community took to studying Chinese rather than Hebrew literature. They concentrated on Chinese studies so they could take the official examinations, which would lead to well-paying jobs in the civil service. As was pointed out earlier, to pass the civil service exams entailed many years of poring over the classical Chinese texts. This rigorous study left little time to concentrate on Jewish subjects, and therefore the Jewish Confucianists tended to be ignorant of Jewish scholarship.

To discourage nepotism and favoritism, those Confucianists who held military or civil service positions were oftentimes required to leave the milieu in which they were born and raised and resettle with their families in new surroundings.[49] They were continually shifted from place to place and might be assigned to districts that were hundreds, if not thousands, of miles from home. Kaifeng's Jewish elite were thus compelled to move to other parts of the country where they and their children had no contact whatsoever with other Jews, and so they ended up losing all ties to Judaism.

Finally, affluence and assimilation contributed heavily to the deterioration of Sino-Judaic culture. The Jews adopted Chinese customs for birth, marriages, and funerals. In the course of time, Chinese Judaism became heavily diluted with Buddhist, Taoist, Confucianist, and Islamic concepts. Ethnic consciousness among the more prominent Jews dimmed, and this in turn influenced the entire Jewish community. "The last rabbi of the community died around 1800, but long before that time the cultural decline had become so pronounced that the remnants of Chinese Jewry had become shockingly ignorant of their own heritage."[50]

The Jesuit priests who visited Kaifeng in the eighteenth century found a Jewish colony that was rapidly declining. When Father Jean-Paul Gozani visited Kaifeng in 1704, there existed only eight clans bearing seven names and comprising a thousand people. The Jews had married Han women and adopted Chinese names. Only a few could still read the Torah and the prayer services in Hebrew. However, they still eschewed pork, practiced circumcision, and observed the Sabbath and the Festivals. Two decades later, the French Jesuit Jean Domenge visited the Kaifeng *kehillah* and immortalized the synagogue with his elaborate sketches of the architecture of the temple. He drew a sketch of a skullcapped *ba'al koreh* with pigtail, reading from a Torah encased in Yemenite fashion.

In 1724 the Qings (Manchus), fearing the impact on Chinese culture made by foreigners, and particularly missionaries, outlawed proselytizing. Foreigners were removed from inland cities and settled in Canton. There were numerous Hui (Muslim) rebellions in the eighteenth and nineteenth centuries that were harshly suppressed, and anti-Muslim feeling became intense. Because the Jews lived in close proximity to and were generally identified with the Hui, they too were despised by the Han Chinese. As a result, many Jews chose not to profess their adherence to Judaism openly. Though the Jews petitioned the emperor for aid in rebuilding the synagogue, assistance was never forthcoming.

The Opium Wars, fought between the British, who wanted to monopolize the opium trade, and the Chinese, who vehemently opposed it, resulted in a series of humiliating defeats for the Chinese. Under the terms of the Treaty of Nanjing (1842), the British wrested numerous economic, political, and military concessions from the enfeebled Middle Kingdom. Among the concessions the hapless Chinese were forced to make was a guarantee that foreigners had a right to come freely to China. Soon after the Chinese ban against Christian proselytizing was lifted, many European missionary groups were stirred into action.

Around this time the British consul in Jerusalem, James Finn, a member of the London Society for Promoting Christianity among Jews, interested himself in the Kaifeng Jews. Finn never visited Kaifeng, but based his first study of the Chinese Jews on the writings of the Jesuit Fathers of the previous two centuries. In his later work, entitled "The Orphan Colony of Jews in China," published in 1872, he gave the text of a letter in Hebrew and English he had written to the Jews of Kaifeng in 1844. This letter was sent to the British consul of the island of Amoy, who translated and forwarded the letter to the Jews of Kaifeng. The reply to his letter was not received until twenty years later. "Daily, with tears in our eyes," it read, "we call on the Holy Name. If we could but again procure Ministers and put our house of prayer in order, our religion would have a firm support."[51]

In the late 1840s, natural disasters struck China repeatedly. A tremendous inundation of the Yellow River in 1849 caused awful devastation and demolished the synagogue. Many of those whose homes had been destroyed emigrated to neighboring provinces. As a result of the Taiping mass evacuation and relocation in 1857, the Jews, together with the rest of the population of Kaifeng, were dispersed all over the country. The remnant that remained was left spiritually and materially poverty-stricken. "This flood, coupled with the rebellion, broke them up so completely that the new generation was raised in utter ignorance of everything connected with their religion and history."[52]

The first successful attempt to re-establish contact with the Jews of Kaifeng was undertaken in 1850. The British diplomat James Finn's studies on the Chinese Jews had come to the attention of Dr. George Smith, the Anglican bishop of Hong Kong. At the suggestion of Dr. W. H. Medhurst, a missionary of the Society for the Promotion of Christianity among Jews, based in Shanghai, two Chinese Christian converts were despatched to inquire about the circumstances of the orphan colony. The Chinese missionaries left Shanghai in November 1850 and after a journey of twenty-five days and seven hundred miles sailed into Kaifeng. With the assistance of a Chinese Jewish conspirator, the missionaries absconded with, among other thing, eight Hebrew texts they had pilfered from the shabby remains of the synagogue. They returned to Kaifeng a year later, and this time sojourned for a couple of months. They purchased six Torah scrolls and some forty small manuscripts, and were accompanied back to Shanghai by two Kaifeng Jews, who stayed a few months at the London Society's mission there.

The Chinese Protestant missionaries reported that the surviving three hundred Jews lived in abject ignorance and misery. The Jews told them that they were considered "foreigners," along with the Muslims and others whose ancestors had come to China from abroad. When food or other provisions were rationed, those perceived as foreigners were lowest in priority. News of the Kaifeng Jewish community attracted worldwide attention.

In 1852, American Jewish societies were organized, first in New York and then in New Orleans, to aid isolated Jewish communities, including the Kaifeng orphan colony in China. By the time the societies were ready to send help, their activities were interrupted by the Civil War. In 1865, the Chief Rabbi of England, Nathan Marcus Adler, wrote to the director of the Sassoon banking house in Shanghai, suggesting that two Kaifeng Jews be brought there and educated so as to enable them to return to Kaifeng and take up positions as Jewish educators in the community. Two young men were indeed chosen but, to everyone's dismay, they became homesick before completing their studies and returned to Kaifeng.

The first Westerner to go to Kaifeng since the Jesuit Gaubil's visit in 1724 was the American Protestant missionary Dr. W. A. P. Martin. He arrived in 1866, and to his dismay found that the remnants of the Jewish community were so demoralized and impoverished in the aftermath of the Taiping Rebellion that they were forced to sell the remains of their synagogue compound, brick by brick, in order to bring in cash for basic necessities. Only the stone tablets of 1489 and 1512 were still standing. Martin was told that the last rabbi had passed away about a half-century earlier and not one individual could read or speak Hebrew. The Jews seriously considered displaying their holy books in the marketplace in the hope of attracting the attention of wandering Jews who might be able to explain the texts. Martin observed that the Jews were rapidly assimilating among the Muslim and "heathenish" communities, and in physical appearance and dress were indistinguishable from their neighbors.[53]

The first Jew from the outside world to visit the Kaifeng community was the Austrian merchant J. L. Liebermann in 1867. He made a survey of the Jewish quarter and found a colony of between four hundred and five hundred Jews living in poverty and squalor. Among other things, he was informed that the Jews no longer observed the Sabbath.[54]

The Boxer Rebellion (1898), a grassroots antiforeign movement that culminated in an uprising against Westerners and the murder of thousands of Christians in China, exacerbated problems for the Kaifeng Jews. Perceived as outsiders and fearing for their lives, many Jews felt compelled to hide their ancestry.

The Jewish community of Shanghai had on several occasions organized itself to try to rehabilitate the Jewish orphan colony in Kaifeng. In 1900, the Shanghai Society for the Rescue of the Chinese Jews was formed with the specific intention of building a synagogue and school in Kaifeng. Although this organization continued to exist until the mid 1920s, the more pressing problem of assisting the survivors of the pogroms in Eastern Europe supplanted the issue of Kaifeng's Jews. An invitation was extended to the Jews of Kaifeng to come to Shanghai, where they would be provided with employment, but only eight people came. Disappointed that the Shanghai Jews could not assist their community to rebuild their synagogue, six of the eight Kaifeng Jews returned home. Only one elderly man, Li Ching-sheng, and his twelve year old son, Li Tsung-mai, chose to stay in Shanghai. The senior Li died shortly after their arrival. Although his son was circumcised and adopted by a Shanghai Jewish family, he turned out to be indifferent to Judaism. After World War II, he returned to Kaifeng and died there in 1948.

In 1908, the Canadian Anglican Bishop William White arrived in China to establish a mission in Kaifeng. White lived in Kaifeng for twenty-five years, and during that time he took an active interest in the welfare of the Jewish orphan colony. By the time of his arrival, all that remained of the synagogue was a foul pool. The Jews, in their extreme need, had dug up the very topsoil and sold it. In 1919, Bishop White bought the synagogue site and the two remaining stone stelae, promising to return them if the Jews ever resumed practicing their religion. The synagogue grounds were eventually converted into a YMCA. White held a series of meetings with the Kaifeng Jews to try to reorganize and reeducate them, but his efforts were fruitless.

David Brown, publisher of a journal called the "American Hebrew," visited the Kaifeng Jewish community in 1932. He made the following observation: "They know they are Jews, but know nothing of their Judaism. They realize they are Chinese, completely assimilated, yet many retain pride in the knowledge that they spring from an ancient people who are different from the other Chinese in Kaifeng."[55] The Jews requested that Brown help educate their children so that they could learn about their heritage. No assistance was ever forthcoming.

After occupying Kaifeng during World War II, the Japanese, concerned that the Jews might pose a threat to the security of their forces, sought to compile a list of all the Jews in conquered territories. According to one elderly Kaifeng Jewish informant, who was interviewed by Dr. Irene Shur in 1987, the Japanese conducted a house-to-house search for Jews but could not find any. This was attributed to the fact that their neighbors would not betray them.[56] Two Japanese officials who visited the Jews—and whom the Jews feared were sent to persecute them—in fact wrote sympathetic reports about them.

Very little is known about the Kaifeng Jewish community from the establishment of Communism in China through the Cultural Revolution and the downfall of the Gang of Four in 1976. The Czech Sinologue, Timoteus Pokora, who visited Kaifeng in 1957, observed Jews attending Muslim and Buddhist services. The Jews were no longer concentrated in their special section, but were living all over the city. Those Jews he interviewed perceived their Jewishness strictly as a nationality.[57]

According to Rabbi Anton Laytner, editor of *Points East: A Publication of the Sino-Judaic Institute*, who has visited Kaifeng in recent times, there are at least 2,000 people in Kaifeng who can claim Jewishness based on their holding one of six distinctive Kaifeng Jewish surnames.[58] The Jews are scattered in many different localities—in Beijing, Shanghai, Nanjing, Zhengdu, Kuanming, Xian, Lanzhou, and Loyang. According to Professor Jin Xiao-Jing, there are also pockets of Jews in Shansi, Kansu, Jinghai, Sinkiang, Szechuan, Yunnan, Kiansu, Chekiang, and Yangzhou.[59] The Communist regime granted the identified Jews quasi-official standing as a racial group different from the Han, but did not recognize them as a national minority. The Kaifeng Jews display pride in their past by writing *Youtai* (Jew) on all certificates of registry in the space allotted for nationality. "Others have registered as members of the officially recognized Muslim minority because they do not eat pork."[60] Correspondent Michael Parks reported in 1982 that the Jews working in government were given official leave on Rosh Hashanah and Yom Kippur.[61]

Some vestiges of Jewish observance are still practiced by the Chinese Jews, albeit in greatly distorted form. Melbourne "Age" Peking correspondent Tony Walker interviewed a middle-aged Kaifeng Jew who ate pork but plucked out the sinew. He recalled that at certain times of the year his family baked bread without salt.[62] According to Anton Laytner, "many of the older generation have memories of their parents and grandparents observing quasi-Jewish customs, as do they themselves in some cases. Passover is the major festival. . . . Matza was and is eaten, and some recall the smearing of rooster or lamb blood—or cinnabar and water—on the doorposts of the houses as late as the 1930s."[63] The Anglo-Jewish businesswoman Phyllis Horal interviewed a retired business administrator who remembered his father smearing chicken blood on the doorpost of his house at the time of the Chinese Spring Festival "so that the Angel of Death would pass us by."[64] Dr. Shur similarly reported having interviewed a Kaifeng Jew who recalled that his father would dab chicken blood on the top edge of their gate during the Chinese New Year.[65]

There is a great desire among today's younger generation of Chinese Jews to learn more about their past. During the Cultural Revolution family records, photographs, and other mementos were destroyed by either rampaging Red Guards or the families themselves. However, since the Chinese Jews, like all other Chinese, trace their descent patrilineally, writes Stanford University professor Wendy Abraham, "this . . . raises problems for other Jews who define Judaism matrilineally, according to Halacha. By this criteria Chinese Jews are not 'really' Jewish and haven't been for hundreds of years."[66]

Still, today the main street where the Jews of Kaifeng once lived is called the Lane of the Teaching Scriptures. Some of the former Jews who have remained have created a museum to preserve the remnants of their culture. At the present time a synagogue/cultural center/memorial hall is being built on the site of the ancient synagogue. There is also talk of getting permission from the authorities to restore the ancient cemetery. The Chinese Jews, writes Dr. Shur, "feel a close kinship to Jews throughout the world and look forward to meeting those who visit Kaifeng."[67]

NOTES

1. Cited in Howard D. Smith, *Chinese Religions* (London: Weidenfeld and Nicholson, 1968), p. 148.

2. *China*, by the editors of Time-Life Books (Amsterdam: Time-Life Books, 1984), p.68.

3. Dun J. Li, *The Ageless Chinese: A History* (New York: Charles Scribner's Sons, 1965), p. 354.

4. Smith, *Chinese Religions*, p. 162.

5. *The History of the Jews in China* (1913 text), reprinted in *Studies of the Chinese Jews: Selections from Journals East and West*, edited by Hyman Kublin (New York: Paragon Book Reprint Corp., 1971), pp. 156–57.

6. Edward Isaac Ezra, "Chinese Jews," *The East of Asia Magazine* 1 (1902), p. 281.

7. Betsy Gidwitz, "From Moses to Mao: When a Jew Visits China," *Moment* 6:10 (November 1981), p. 35.

8. *Chinese Jews*, vol. 3 (Toronto: University of Toronto Press, 1942), pp. 9–10.

9. "Persia or Yemen? The Origin of the Kaifeng Jews," *Irano-Judaica* (1982), p. 106.

10. *The Lost Tribes A Myth—Suggestions Towards Rewriting Hebrew History* (Durhah, N. Carolina: Duke University Press, 1930), p. 411.

11. Godbey, ibid., p. 399; Arthur Sopher, *Chinese Jews* (Tel Aviv, 1961), p. 2.

12. *Jews in Many Lands* (Philadelphia: The Jewish Publication Society, 1905), pp. 213–214.

13. Ibid., pp. 221–22; Joseph Wolff, *Researches and Missionary Labours Among the Jews, Mohammedans, and Other Sects* (London: n.p., 1835), p. 192.

14. "A Chinese-Hebrew Manuscript: A New Source for the History of the Chinese Jews," *American Journal of Semitic Languages and Literature* 46 (April 1930), reprinted in Kublin, ed., *Studies of the Chinese Jews*, p. 164.

15. "Jews in Ancient China—A Historical Survey, 1953, Revised 1983," in *Jews in Old China: Studies by Chinese Scholars,* translated, compiled, and edited by Sidney Shapiro (New York: Hippocrene Books, 1984), pp. 76–78, 92.

16. Pan Guandan, "Jews in Ancient China," p. 90.

17. *The Glassmakers: A Jewish Odyssey* (New York: Hippocrene Books, 1991), p. 267.

18. *A Short History of the Chinese People*, 3rd ed. (New York: Harper and Brothers Publishers, 1959), pp. 134, 151.

19. Pan Guandan, "Jews in Ancient China," p. 84. See also H. G. Reissner, "The Jews in Medieval Ceylon," *Israel and India,* 4:3 (September 1951), pp. 22–25.

20. "South India was both on the transit trade and terminal trade from West Asia to China, through Sri Lanka and South-East Asia." See R. Champakalakshmi, "The Medieval South Indian Guilds: Their Role in Trade and Urbanization," in *Society and Ideology in India: Essays in Honor of Professor R. S. Sharma*, edited by D. N. Jha (New Delhi: Munshira Manoharlal Publishers, 1996), p. 89.

21. Shapiro, *Jews in Old China*, p. x

22. Excerpt from the "Book of Ways and Kingdom" found in *Jewish Travelers in the Middle Ages: 19 Firsthand Accounts*, edited and with an introduction by Elkan Nathan Adler (New York: Dover Publications, 1987), pp. 2–3.

23. Krinsky, *The Glassmakers*, p. 260.

24. "Contact Between Ancient China and the Jews," in Shapiro, *Jews in Old China*, p. 10.

25. *A Social and Religious History of the Jews*, vol. 18: *The Ottoman Empire, Persia, Ethiopia, India, and China*, 2nd ed. (New York: Columbia University Press, 1983), p. 417.

26. On Aurel Stein and the discovery of the Caves of a Thousand Buddhas see Wilfrid Blunt, *The Golden Road to Samarkand* (New York: Viking Press, 1973), esp. pp. 235–54.

27. Cited in Donald Leslie, *The Survival of the Chinese Jews* (Leiden: E. J. Brill, 1972), p. 7–8.

28. *The Travels of Marco Polo,* Marsden's translation, edited by Thomas Wright (London: H. Bohn, 1854), p. 166.

29. Cited in L. Rabinowitz, *Jewish Merchant Adventurers* (London: Edward Goldston, 1948), p. 72.

30. Cited in Leslie, *Survival*, p. 15.

31. *The Travels of Ibn Batuta*. Samuel Lee's translation (London: J. Murray, 1829), p. 217.

32. Ezra, "Chinese Jews," p. 280

33. Michael Lowe, *Imperial China: The Historical Background to the Modern Age* (New York: Frederick A. Praeger, 1966), p. 249.

34. James W. Bashford, *China: An Interpretation* (New York: The Abingdon Press, 1916), p. 128.

35. Li, *The Ageless Chinese*, p. 363. Similarly among ultra-Orthodox Ashkenazim, the woman traditionally walked behind her husband.

36. Matteo Ricci, cited in Albert Chan, *The Glory and Fall of the Ming Dynasty* (Tulsa: University of Oklahoma, 1982), p. 118.

37. Edward H. Parker, *China and Religion* (New York: E. P. Dutton, 1905), p. 170.

38. For a detailed discussion of the Rites Controversy see Michael Pollak, *Mandarins, Jews, and Missionaries* (Philadelphia: Jewish Publication Society, 1980), esp. pp. 77–99.

39. For critical analyses of seventeenth-century Western Christianity vis-à-vis the Kaifeng *kehillah*, and Manasseh ben Israel's motives for exploiting the discovery of the Chinese Jews to aid world Jewry, see Michael Pollak, "The Revelation of a Jewish Presence in Seventeenth-Century China: Its Impact on Western Messianic Thought" (study presented at the symposium "Jewish Diasporas in China: Comparative and Historical Perspectives," John K. Fairbank Center for Asian Research, Harvard University, 16–18 August 1992) pp. 1–27; Ismar Schorsch, "From Messianism to Realpolitik: Menassah ben Israel and the Readmission of the Jews to England," *Proceedings of the American Academy for Jewish Research* 45 (1978), pp. 187–208; Richard H. Popkin, "Jewish Messianism and Christian Millenarianism." In *Culture and Politics from Puritanism to the Enlightenment*, edited by Edward Zagorin (Berkeley: University of California Press, 1980), pp. 67–90.

40. Louis Hyman, *The Jews of Ireland: From Earliest Times to the Year 1910* (Shannon, Ireland: Irish University Press, 1972), pp. 11–12.

41. Peter Lum, *The Purple Barrier: The Story of the Great Wall of China* (London: Robert Hale Ltd., 1960), p. 158.

42. Chan, *The Glory*, p. 312.

43. J. MacGowan, *The Imperial History of China*, 2nd ed. (Shanghai, 1906), p. 513.

44. For detailed biographical sketches of the Zhao brothers see Donald Leslie, "The K'aifeng Jew Chao Ying-Ch'eng and His Family," reprinted in Kublin, ed., *Studies of the Chinese Jews*, pp. 103–137.

45. Harold H. Sunoo, *China of Confucius: A Critical Interpretation* (Virginia Beach, Va.: Heritage Research House, 1985), pp. 96–97.

46. K. S. Tom, *Echoes From Old China* (Honolulu: Hawaii Chinese History Center, 1989), pp. 139–142.

47. Baron, *A Social and Religious History*, p. 424.

48. Ibid.

49. Harold E. Gorst, *China* (London: Sands and Co., 1899), p. 141.

50. Meyer Passow, *Exotic and Vanished Jewish Tribes* (Tel Aviv: WIZO, 1974), p. 21.

51. "The Orphan Colony of Jews," cited in White, *Chinese Jews*, vol. 1, p. 86.

52. Ezra, "Chinese Jews," p. 294.

53. "A Visit to the Jews in Hunan," cited in White, *Chinese Jews*, vol. 1, p. 184–87.

54. Ezra, "Chinese Jews, p. 291.

55. "Through the Eyes of an American Jew" (articles from the American Hebrew and Jewish Tribune, January to March 1933), cited in White, *Chinese Jews*, vol. 1, pp. 150–64. See also Pollak, *Mandarins*, pp. 230–34.

56. "A Chinese Puzzle: Who are the Jews of Kaifeng?" *Jewish Monthly* 101:7 (March 1987), p. 18.

57. Pollak, *Mandarins*, p. 248.

58. "When East Meets West: A Ground-Breaking Conference Studies Jewish Diasporas in China," *Points East: A Publication of the Sino-Judaic Institute* 7:3 (October 1992), p. 9.

59. Cited in Chan Sui-jeung, *Monographs of the Jewish Historical Society of Hong Kong*, vol. 2. (Hong Kong: Jewish Chronicle, 1986), p. 52.

60. *London Jewish Chronicle* (18 June 1993), p. 20.

61. *Los Angeles Times* (23 November 1982), p. 14.

62. "China's Lost Jews," *World Press Review* (July 1982), p. 62.

63. Laytner, "When East Meets West," p. 9.

64. "Sweet and Sour History," *London Jewish Chronicle Magazine* (6 December 1991), p. 30.

65. Shur, "Chinese Puzzle," p. 18.

66. "A Chinese Jewish Identity," *Hadassah Magazine* 69:1 (August-September 1987), p. 21. See also Laytner, "When East Meets West," p. 9. Chan Sui-jeung erroneously asserts that Kaifeng's Jews trace their ancestry through the maternal side. See *Monographs*, p. 47.

67. Shur, "Chinese Puzzle," p. 19.

Part XI

Tomb of Rebi Shlomo of the Snake, Ourika, Morocco
Credit: Keren T. Friedman

Mellah, Medinah, Marabouts, *and* Mahia

BACKGROUND INFORMATION

The Kingdom of Morocco is located in the northwest corner of Africa, only twelve miles from Europe across the Strait of Gibraltar. Morocco is bounded on the north and west by the Mediterranean, on the east and southeast by Algeria, and on the south by the Sahara Desert. The population of Morocco is estimated at twenty-eight million, two-thirds of whom are Arab and one-third Berber, with very small French and Spanish minorities. The modern capital is Rabat. The mother tongue of the majority is Arabic, and the majority of the population belongs to the Maliki sect of Sunni Islam.

The Atlas Mountains are named for the titan Atlas, who in Greek mythology was ordered by the supreme deities to hold the heavens on his shoulders. The Atlas is a vast mountain chain in the fertile interior of Morocco. It is twelve hundred miles long, extending through the three countries of the Maghreb—Morocco, Tunisia, and Algeria—and separating the Mediterranean basin from the Sahara Desert. The Atlas Mountains include the High Atlas range, which rises to over 13,000 feet in the southwest; the Middle Atlas, which branches off from the High Atlas in a northeasterly direction; and the Anti-Atlas, the foothills between the High Atlas and the Sahara Desert.

Despite its geographic proximity to Europe, Morocco remained feudalistic and remarkably unaffected by Western civilization until the arrival of the French just before World War I. Morocco's great isolation is to a large extent attributed to her harsh reaction to European imperialism. For more than a thousand years Morocco was an Islamic theocracy ruled by a succession of sultanic dynasties, many of them tyrannical. The sultan's authority was oftentimes weak and extended barely beyond the confines of his capital. Real political power was concentrated in the hands of the *kaids*, or barons, of each locality. Morocco's political and economic instability was due to the fact that the *kaids* were continuously at war with each other. Added to Moroccan society's ills were the perennial problems of epidemics, famines, and natural disasters that periodically decimated the population.

The Atlas Mountains are inhabited in part by two groups of Berber tribespeople. One group lives in tents, is nomadic, and supports itself by animal husbandry. The other consists of farmers who live in isolated, fortified mountain villages where they cultivate terraced gardens that yield an abundance of Mediterranean fruits and cereals. Neither group has much contact with the Arabs of the towns and cities in the lowlands. Berber villages or *qsars* are usually walled and are built so that they back against mountain slopes or are located on tops of cliffs. Each *qsar* is an economic unit whose members cooperate closely and share resources.

The Berbers, the indigenous people of North Africa, are believed to be a Caucasian people related to the ancient Iberians of Spain. Their migration into Morocco began toward the end of the second millennium B.C.E. In 684 C.E., crusading Muslims from the Arabian peninsula raided Morocco and established an Islamic society whose culture and language were Arabic. These Arabs married Berber women of the lowland towns and established themselves as a political elite. The first great Islamic dynasty in Morocco was founded in 788 C.E. by Idris I, a descendant of the Prophet Mohammed. The "pure" Berber groups living in the hinterland converted to Islam only after putting up a ferocious resistance that lasted for almost three centuries. But even after being subjugated and living in mountain fastnesses, they managed to continue resisting Arab political control. Ostensibly orthodox Muslims, the Berbers retained strong Judaized and pagan beliefs from the pre-Arabic period and evolved their own peculiar form of North African Islamism.

Traditional Berber tribal politics in the Atlas Mountains was democratic to the extent that all male adults of the tribe chose the tribal lord and had input in all matters relating to war and justice. All the various castes in Berber society, including the black Islamic slaves known as Haratin, could participate in the *djemaa* (tribal council). In most areas of the Atlas, only the Jews, who had spurned the Prophet, were excluded from tribal affairs.

Writes Henrik de Leeuw:

What has tended to mold [the Berbers'] character more than anything else is that they have been reared in a world of barren peaks, where fertile valleys are scarce and not productive enough to feed even those in their vicinity, with the result that, before the extension of French authority, raid followed raid, villages were burned and sacked, men were tortured and murdered, and women were raped. Here, too, blood feuds between whole families raged. Tribe fought tribe, village against village, and even household against household. No wonder the average life span of a Berber at one time was judged to be thirty-five.[1]

The Atlas Mountains traditionally served as a refuge area for dissident religious and political groups too inaccessible to subdue. For many centuries these mountain fastnesses were inhabited by fierce Berber tribes whose belligerence permitted no stranger to approach this area. Berber tribes were constantly at war with each other and with the central government. Because the Berbers are a tribal people whose sole loyalty is to family and clan, the central government in the lowlands (*bled el-maghzen*) oftentimes found it impossible to impose its rule on the hinterlands (*bled essiba*). Obedience to the sultan was little more than nominal, even during those rare periods when the central government was strong.[2] The Atlas Mountains could not be safely penetrated by foreigners until after World War I, when the French authorities brought the entire country under control. Until 1933 the Berbers were essentially a people without central authority.

Some Berber tribes in the Atlas Mountains have a long-standing belief that they are descended from Canaanites who fled a wrathful Joshua bin Nun. Others claim descent from the four sons of Goliath who fled Gaza after their father's debacle at the hands of King David. Historians assert that around 1000 B.C.E., the period corresponding with King David's reign, the Barbary Coast of North Africa was settled by seafaring Phoenicians, a Canaanite people who spoke a Semitic dialect called Punic. Several centuries later, traders from Carthage established trading posts on the coastline of Morocco. They in turn were followed during the next thousand years by Romans, Vandals, and Byzantines, none of whom were able to penetrate deeply into Morocco. Many Berber tribes retreated to the mountains, from which they were able to stage frequent attacks on enemy outposts.

Worship of Muslim saints known as *marabout*s is pervasive in North Africa. *Marabout*s are mystics and miracle workers endowed with *baraka*, or divine grace. They wander through the countryside healing the sick and employing charms and talismans to ward off evil spirits. Believers worship at the tombs of the *marabouts*, for they believe that even after death the holy ones can cure them. The great Islamic *marabouts* were venerated by the Jews as well as by the Arabs and Berbers.

In March 1912 the sultan of Morocco signed the historic Treaty of Fez, which made Morocco a protectorate of France and greatly reduced the sultan's authority. After a three-year campaign of political and guerrilla warfare against the French, Morocco attained independence in 1956 and has been a constitutional monarchy since 1962.

THE JUDEO-BERBERS OF THE
ATLAS MOUNTAINS OF MOROCCO

In some seasons the gardens . . . are so productive that oranges
are absolutely of no value except it be for pelting the Jews.
                    —Arthur Leared, *Marocco and the Moors (1891)*

A Berber sleeps until 10 A.M. to avoid seeing a Jew in front of
him before breakfast.
                                    —popular Moroccan saying

Morocco was once the home of the largest Jewish community in the
Muslim world, and over the centuries produced many outstanding rabbis and
sages, some of whom had a strong mystical bent. Before the successive waves of
mass migrations to Israel and the West that began after 1948, there were an
estimated 260,000 Jews in this North African kingdom. They were spread out
over the length and breadth of the country, but lived predominantly in the major
urban areas: Casablanca, Fez, Meknes, Marrakech, Tetuan, and Sefrou. Today
there are only an estimated 12,000 Jews left in Morocco.

The Moroccan Jewish community formed three distinct social classes.
The upper crust of Moroccan Jewish society were the *migarashim*, exiles from
Spain who arrived after the pogroms of 1391 and the expulsion of 1492. These
Sephardim, writes Michael Laskier, "lived mostly in the north . . . were most
receptive to European ideas, and their manners and customs differed from
those of the rest of the Jewish population. They practiced monogamy [and]
their segment of the population presented the prime candidates for banking
and trade. . . . "[3]

Of the *toshavim*, or original inhabitants, there were two types. One type
were the Judeo-Arabs, Middle Eastern Jews who may have followed the armies
of Islam—or they may have arrived even earlier, fleeing the Visigoth invaders
of the Iberian peninsula. Either way, they lived in an Arab milieu in the interior
of the country and in the coastal towns. The second type of *toshavim* were the
Judeo-Berbers, also known as *Pilichtim* because they claimed descent from émigré
Palestinians of ancient times. However, they may have been part-Berbers who
were converted to Judaism.[4] These Judeo-Berbers lived in the rural areas, in
the Sous plains beyond the Atlantic, in the rugged arc of Rif Mountains to the
north, and in the Atlas Mountain range in the south. In the latter region the Jews
spoke the language of the Chleuh Berbers called Tashilhait as well as other re-

gional Berber dialects and Arabic. So as not to be understood by their Muslim neighbors, the Jews in some areas resorted to a pidgin Berber that drew heavily from Hebrew, Aramaic, and Arabic. In their physical features and many of their customs they were indistinguishable from their Berber compatriots. Until the nineteenth century the three Jewish groups in Morocco maintained their own unique customs and had little social intercourse with one another.[5]

Since the *migarashim* and the Judeo-Arab communities come under the rubric of Sephardi culture, the ancient, isolated, and little-known Berber Jews from the lofty Atlas Mountain region will be the primary focus in this chapter. However, before delving exclusively into the subject of the Atlas Mountain Jews, a thumbnail sketch of the larger Moroccan Jewish experience will be useful in providing context.

The history of the Jews of Morocco is marked by cycles of turbulence and relative tranquility, which varied from period to period and from locality to locality. The French traveler Emile Lemoigne, who visited Morocco in the 1920s, made the following observation:

> Here perhaps even more than elsewhere the Jewish race [*sic*] has for centuries had to endure martyrdom. Hated by all, humbled, subjected to a veritable and odious bondage, it was always the first victim of the political upheavals which periodically convulsed the country. Pillaged, despoiled, living in a state of perpetual alarm in the midst of a degradation imposed by its masters, it nevertheless was able to bear all the evils which beset it without losing the quality of intelligence and industry.[6]

Islamic enmity toward the Jews had its basis in two primary factors: religious fanaticism, and envy of Jewish wealth. Moroccan Sunnism, like Yemenite and Persian Shiism, Norman Stillman informs us, has always interpreted "in the most literal sense" the Koranic injunction to humble the nonbeliever.[7] All kinds of restrictions were imposed on the Jews to remind them of their second-class status. For example, the Jews were not allowed to leave the ghetto after sunset, they could wear only dark colors, and when they passed a mosque they had to walk barefoot. As *dhimmi*, the Jews were obligated to pay a heavy tribute or *jizya* to the Muslim sovereign, who in turn was obligated to guarantee the Jews' protection. Inspired and stirred up by the fanatical *marabouts*, *cherifs* (princes who claimed descent from Mohammed), and local Islamic religious leaders, the Muslim population at times came to harbor intense feelings of hostility and rancor toward the Jews.

Especially during periods of political instability, it was common for the Muslim masses to violate Koranic injunctions against physically harming the *dhimmi*. In these stormy times they would often vent their rage at an unpopular sultan by lashing out at the Jews. Since the sultan was the official protector of the Jews, the antidynastic outbursts directed at them were oftentimes really a ploy to expose the sultan's own weakness. But even the heavily fortressed *mellah*s (Jewish ghettos) guarded by Islamic sentinels could not shield the Jews from whimsical sultans, rapacious pashas, and the frenzied mobs who would periodically ransack the ghetto and massacre the inmates.

The word *mellah* means "salt" in Arabic. No one is certain how the ghettos acquired this appellation. An apocryphal view holds that a *mellah* was the place where Jewish butchers were compelled to pickle the heads of the sultan's enemies for public display above the gates of the towns, as a warning to potential offenders. The first *mellah* was established in Fez in 1438 after a massacre was perpetrated against the Jews, who were accused of placing wine in the mosques. The sultan transferred the entire Jewish community to a location near the site of *Wadi al Mellah* (Salt Stream). Subsequently, Jewish communities all over Morocco were removed from the *medinah*s to the special Jewish quarter in the city, adjoining the *casbah*. "The new Jewish quarter . . . became the prototype of the Moroccan ghetto," writes Jane Gerber. "The name was soon applied, along with Juderia or Juiverie, to all the ghettos of Morocco."[8] Jews were ghettoized to ostracize them as well as protect them.

The typical urban *mellah* was an overcrowded, stench-filled enclave with tumbledown hovels, narrow lanes, and untidy shops. "Yet to the Jewish confines you must turn," writes Ben Assher in *A Nomad in Morocco*, "would you survey the worst conditions—horrible haunt of an unhappy population living like animals in mud-made dens. Half of the persons here ensconced seem semi-blind, and for distressing sights of poverty and body's woe, let me commend you to these hovel homes."[9]

Conditions went from very bad to terrible in the mid nineteenth century, when Jews from the mountain regions began to descend on the urban *mellah*s for economic opportunities and caused the *mellah*s to swell to overflowing. It was not unusual to find ten to fifteen families crowded into one tiny dwelling with the crudest of sanitation. Alcoholism and prostitution among Jews was rampant, and there was a very high incidence of infant mortality.[10] Ragged, dirty children played in the garbage heaps that cluttered the streets, and they became afflicted with trachoma, tuberculosis, and other ghetto diseases. Even the wealthier Jews lived in this unhygienic squalor.[11]

As in so many other places in the Middle East and Central Asia, the Jews made an imprint on North African civilization many centuries before the Arabs arrived. When, exactly, Jews began to settle in the southern mountain regions of Morocco is not certain. Leo Africanus, a sixteenth-century European traveler, wrote that in the fifteenth century there were tribes in several places in the Atlas Mountains who still owned land and claimed descent from the warriors of King David.[12] Belief has it that in Solomonic times Jewish merchants ventured forth on Phoenician ships to purchase gold in ancient Rabat. Perhaps a few Jews may have reached Morocco's shores after the destruction of the First Temple, but most historians believe that they began to arrive in substantial numbers only after Julius Caesar conquered North Africa in 146 B.C.E. Twelve ships with Jewish political prisoners are said to have arrived from Palestine after the destruction of the Second Temple by the armies of Vespasian and Titus, circa 70 C.E. The Jews were spread out not only in the coastal towns, but also inland, in the mountains and the desert oases. Their influence spread among the pagan Berber population so that by the sixth century many Berber tribes had converted to Judaism. In some cases entire Berber tribes in the Atlas Mountains became Judaized.

Under the pre-Christian Romans, and later the Vandals, the Jews of Morocco lived in a state of considerable prosperity as merchants and craftsmen. In the sixth century many Spanish Jews emigrated to Morocco to escape Visigothic persecution. When the Byzantines under General Belisarius conquered the country in 533 C.E., the social and economic position of the Moroccan Jews in the plains deteriorated. However, the bellicose Berber tribes in the interior were unaffected by events in the lowlands. When Arab armies invaded North Africa in 642 C.E. and penetrated into the Atlas Mountains in 667 C.E., Jews and Berbers fighting side by side were briefly able to withstand the Arab onslaughts. According to legend, the unifying force was a valiant Jew queen from the Atlas Mountains named Kahina Dahiyah Bint Thabitah ibn Tifan.

This remarkable woman is known by the cognomen El Kahina, and she is believed to have been descended from a Jewish priestly caste. According to the great Arab historian Ibn Khaldoon, the Arab general Hassan ibn al-Numan had destroyed Carthage in a surprise attack and then turned his attention to the most intransigent force in the region: namely, the armies of the Jewish warrior-queen of the Jerava Berber tribes. In the ensuing battle the Arabs were stunningly routed. During the next five years the Berbers enjoyed a respite and El Kahina, we are told, ruled over her kingdom with justice and wisdom. Around 693 C.E. the Arabs attacked a second time, with a much larger force.[13] The queen and her troops went into hiding and resorted to guerrilla tactics against the vastly superior enemy numbers. Like Bar Kochba, the Jewish hero in the revolt against the Romans some 500 years earlier, El Kahina went down fighting with sword in hand. So that the Arabs should not enjoy the fruits of their conquest, the Jerava burned all their possessions. When she was finally captured, El Kahina's head was chopped off and sent back to the Arab caliph in Baghdad.[14] The Arab victory over the Jewish queen squelched the last attempt by the Berbers to establish their own independent state. Many of the pagan Berber tribes were forcibly converted to Islam, and it is believed that some of the Judaized tribes voluntarily converted as well. Islam now ruled supreme all over North Africa.

In the early centuries of Idrisid (Arab) rule, the Jews enjoyed tolerable security despite being handicapped by the *dhimmi* laws. The heyday of Moroccan Jewry coincides with the Jewish renaissance in Spain, and the former was culturally and spiritually intertwined with its coreligionists to the north. Scholarship flourished, and the city of Fez attracted students from all over the world to its rabbinical academies. Then, with the rise of the fanatical Almohades sect that originated in the Atlas Mountains (1146–1269), this felicitous and creative epoch of Jewish life in Morocco came to an end.

Under the Almohades tyrants, the Jews were given the choice of emigration or conversion. Many found haven in the Christian kingdoms of Spain. Those Jews who resisted were put to the sword. Those who chose to remain were converted to Islam, though most secretly adhered to Judaism. As neo-Muslims, they were treated suspiciously and subjected to all kinds of humiliations. For example, they were forced to wear a grotesque looking cap with flaps down to the ears, called the *qalansuwa*. Moses Maimonides wrote a famous epistle to the Jews of North Africa in 1173 asking the communal heads to launch a collection for the purpose of ransoming captives and admonishing the Jews to remain firm under the storm. The climate became somewhat more tolerant under later Almohades rulers, but not until the Merinids (1269–1465), nomadic Berbers from the south who supplanted the Almohades, did the Jews openly return to their faith.

The Jewish community in Morocco was greatly increased by the influx of exiles from Spain in 1492 and Portugal in 1496. Offered hospitality by the sultan, thousands of Sephardim settled in the large, coastal cities in the north. Held in contempt for not being sufficiently Orthodox in their faith, and feared as commercial rivals who had superior business acumen, a domineering style, and greater influence, the new arrivals, many of them former conversos, were treated by the *toshavim* with hostility and envy. Separating themselves from the other Jews in the *mellah,* the *migarashim* spoke Haketia, a "bastard Spanish mixed with Hebrew [and] Arabic,"[15] maintained separate *minhagim* (rites), and treated the *toshavim* as low-caste. "The natives," writes Isadore Epstein, "were forbidden to partake of their bread, meat, or wine; visit their sick; initiate their children into the Abrahamic covenant; to join them in any religious service; and to remain within the Synagogue whilst their services were proceeding within the adjoining room, the Bet-Medrish. . . . The privileges in regard to regal taxes granted to the emigrants only tended to aggravate the matter, and were not conducive to communal harmony and peace."[16] The *migarashim* were especially disdainful toward the mountain Jews, whom they referred to in a derogatory manner as *chleuh* (a generic term for the Berber tribes in the western High Atlas) or *forasteros* (strangers), and whom they considered to be a race apart.[17]

"Soon after their arrival from Spain," writes Rom Landau, "quite a few of the Sephardim became converts to Islam, and local gossip has it that a considerable number of the more distinguished Arab families in Fez and Rabat descend from these converts."[18] Eventually the *toshavim* in the larger cities were incorporated into the Sephardi milieu. The Sephardim contributed multilingual businessmen with international connections who were masters of finance and shrewd diplomats. By virtue of "their cultural and intellectual attainments [they also] provided North African Jewry with a new type of learned and enlightened spiritual leader who helped raise the Barbary Jew from the deep morass of ignorance they had waded for several centuries. . . ."[19]

According to French anthropologist Pierre Flamand, as late as 1949 there were 155 Jewish settlements located in towns and villages throughout the Atlas Mountain region.[20] In these towns and large villages they were confined to their own separate quarters; in the rural districts they lived in unfortified hamlets, or clusters of hamlets, adjoining the Berber villages. Jewish enclaves were undefended, since Jews in these parts, with some exceptions, did not participate in the tribal wars. In some villages the Jewish population might consist of no more than a half-dozen families. Houses were built of stone or baked mud mixed with straw, and some reached several stories high. These edifices were usually surrounded by gardens and orchards. In some places the Jews lived in dugouts or caves. Like the Atlas Mountain Muslims, the Jews lived in patriarchal extended families, with each nuclear family occupying a room in a house or living in an adjoining house around a shared courtyard. Each extended family comprised all the descendants of a common ancestor. The courtyard was where the communal cooking was done.

In the pre-French protectorate period the mountains and remote desert oases of Morocco, called the *bled essiba* or "land of dissidence," were areas where the authority of the sultan could not penetrate. The Jews in these places lived in a feudalistic environment entirely dependent on the mercy of the tribal lords called *sayed*s. Being itinerant peddlers, the Jews moved around by donkey or on foot from one Berber village to the next, sometimes living for considerable periods among the various Berber tribes they visited. A mode of relationship called *dehiba* evolved in which a Jewish serf was obligated to make a gesture of submission to the *sayed* or some private Berber patron by slaughtering a sheep or ox at the gates of the patron's castle in return for direct protection. Thereafter, any injury inflicted against a Jew was "avenged by the protecting Berber as though it had been committed against a member of his own family."[21] As David Hart points out in his study of the Ait Waryaghar tribes of the Rif Mountains, "The keynote of Jewish behavior was that of safety in humility; conversely, for a powerful man to have 'his own' Jew was considered a sign of prestige. Because the Jews stood entirely outside the political system, and because their occupational services were much in demand, to kill or even molest a Jew was an infinitely worse offense than to kill a fellow tribesman, for a Jew's protector would show absolutely no mercy to the killer."[22]

Relegated to the lowest rung of the Atlas Mountain social totem pole, the Jews were little more than chattels who could be bought and sold at the whim of their *sayed*s. Everything a Jew owned theoretically belonged to his master. A Jew who desired to marry was forced to ransom his future wife from his prospective father-in-law's overlord, whose permission he needed to marry the girl. He could carry on commerce in the countryside unrestricted, but he had no other freedom of movement and needed permission from his overlord to travel.[23] The Jew was so indispensable to the prosperity of the region that while he was away, his family was held hostage by the lord in order to guarantee his return. "Should violence break out, everything the Jew earns is snatched from him; his children are taken away; finally, he himself is put on the market and sold at auction. Or else his house is pillaged and destroyed, and he and his family chased away."[24]

In addition to *dehiba*, Jews who traveled extensively around the Berber villages were obligated to pay an exorbitant highway tax (*zattata*) to the local tribal chieftains. This tribute was another form of protection from murder and theft.[25] In spite of the protections provided them, Jews were constantly attacked by highwaymen and every journey was a perilous undertaking.

As occurred among the Jews of Yemen, Persia, and in the *shtetlech* in Eastern Europe, the relentless institutionalized persecution had a cowing and demoralizing effect on the Jews of the Moroccan *bled essiba*. "Centuries of this oppression have naturally had a deleterious effect on the characters of the victims, who are cringing cowardly creatures, never daring to answer back and seldom even standing erect—a people demanding the utmost pity."[26] On the other hand, Nahum Slouschz, who visited the area in the 1910s, painted a pic-

ture of the Jews that is quite different. He observed that in certain areas of the
Atlas Mountains there were warrior tribes of Jews who were splendid swords-
men and horsemen, and hard drinkers:

> The Jews form an important part of the population of the Atlas. In cer-
> tain villages, they form a third and in others even a majority of the popu-
> lation. They are very courageous, traveling fearlessly through the most
> dangerous regions and maintaining relations with all the surrounding
> tribes. No one knows the country or its people better than they. . . . Some
> of them travel about as healers, a cross between sorcerers and tellers of
> tales, working on the imagination of the natives, who are all illiterate.
> . . . The Jews of the Atlas are, on the whole, a healthy and vigorous
> lot. . . . But they are treated with contempt by their neighbors. The
> meanest and most insignificant negro treats a Jew as though he were an
> outcast."[27]

Atlas Mountain Jews served their own and other Berber mountain communities as artisans and minor traders. As craftsmen, they had a virtual monopoly
in embroideries, making jewelry, tanning, shoemaking, and carpentry. Jewish
women assisted their husbands by performing those tasks that could be carried
out at home. Peddlers usually traveled on donkeys in twos and threes and set
up makeshift camps in the local bazaar. Some went door to door hawking a wide
assortment of domestic items, such as clothing, jewelry, crockery, hides, food-
stuffs, and herbal cures. The Jewish peddlers would stay in one place for about
a month and then move on to the next village. They would buy or barter a variety of items in one town and sell them in the next. Some Jews engaged in
commerce and moneylending, while others were pawnbrokers. In some localities the Jews worked as farm laborers, and although Jews in the Atlas Mountains were forbidden to own land, exceptions did occur. A Jewish specialty was
distilling *mahia* for illegal sale to the Muslims. Mahia is an aniseed or fennel-
flavored brandy made from grapes, pomegranates, figs, or dates. It was also made
from water in which honeycombs had been boiled.

Many craftsmen traveled from *suq* to *suq* practicing their profession. Itinerant peddlers would leave their families behind for months at a time, returning home only for the major holidays or to replenish their supplies. Lawrence
Rosen has pointed out that the Berbers preferred to do business with the Jews
rather than with the Arabs, so as not to jeopardize their independence.[28]

Because the local rabbis were often not very erudite themselves, major
halakhic responsa and spiritual guidance was drawn from the rabbinate of the

larger cities of the region, primarily Marrakech. Additionally, rabbis and emissaries from Palestine would periodically visit the region, and as a result there was a heavy kabbalistic and messianic flavor to the mountaineers' Judaism.

As in many other places in the far-flung parts of the Diaspora, the lives of the Jews of the Atlas Mountains were bound up with all sorts of ancient beliefs and superstitions that were drawn from the local Berber and Arab population and became an essential part of their existence. For instance, most Moroccans, Jews as well as Muslims, believe in *jinnis*, a race of spirit beings whose supernatural powers can be used for good as well as evil, but mostly for evil. *Jinnis* were believed to have been created from fire and predate man, but they can transform themselves into human or animal form and influence human affairs. They are invisible, and though they possess no bodies, they can consume many foods. They especially savor blood. *Jinnis* live underground or suspended in the air, and form their own tribes and nations, each with their own sultan. Most Moroccans have a morbid fear of *jinnis*, because they are capable of causing pain and accidents. Consequently, a whole assortment of incantations, charms, symbols, and number forms were devised as precautions against them.[29] Islamic *jinnis* are called *muminin* (believers) and are white, green, and yellow; whereas Jewish *jinnis* are referred to as *jnun sebti yin*, or Saturday *jinnis*, and are always black. Muslim *jinnis* attack people on Fridays; Jewish *jinnis* attack on the Sabbath. Muslims believe that the Jewish *jinnis* are especially malicious during the scorching summer heat.[30] According to Westermarck, a Muslim who wants to summon a Jewish *jinni* for the purpose of practicing witchcraft

> does all kinds of disgusting things. He eats his own excrement, and dirties his clothes with them; drinks his own urine if thirsty, and sprinkles his clothes with it . . . makes an ablution with his urine, and prays with his face turned in the wrong direction, that is, not towards Mecca. He writes on the paper the name of the *jenn* . . . burns the paper together with some coriander seed, and in burning it recites the name of the *jenn* and some passages from the Koran with the word Allah and other holy words exchanged for *sitan*; and continues this recitation until the *jenn* comes.[31]

The Jews of Morocco referred to the *jinnis* by the talmudic name *shaidim*. They believed that every Jew has a *shaid* counterpart who is capable of causing him or her sudden illness or misfortune. To ward off the pernicious powers of the *shaidim*, angels were invoked with the assistance of the Kabbalah. Further, to protect against injury or the evil eye, special prayers were intoned, magical potions were employed, and charms and amulets scribbled with excerpts from the *Zohar* were worn on the body.

Like Jews everywhere else in North Africa, the Atlas mountaineers made frequent pilgrimages, individually and collectively, to the tombs of *marabouts* (*tzaddikim*). The Jewish *marabout* might be from a particular region and venerated only by the locals of that area who knew of his or her good works. Or perhaps he might be a well-known rabbi or emissary from Palestine or from other parts of Morocco and North Africa who attained a reputation as a charismatic, pious, and learned man. Virtually every Jewish community in Morocco had its own patron saint. A few of the *marabouts* were women. Multitudes would flock to a *marabout*'s *kouba* (tomb) on the anniversary of his or her death and on Jewish holidays, especially Lag B'Omer. Those in a more distressed state, such as barren women and the sick, would ritualistically kiss the walls and the ground of the sanctuary or dab their foreheads with ashes from the fire that was kept going all night, and pray to the saint to intercede with the Almighty on their behalf. They might leave a bottled drink in the sanctuary so that it would absorb the holiness of the place, and later this liquid would be rubbed on an ailing organ or drunk as a catharsis.[32] Candles were lit, animals were slaughtered, and *tzedakah* (charity) was distributed. A *hilula*, or sacred festivity of eating and drinking, singing, and dancing, would take place inside or near the tomb "in a frivolous picnic-like atmosphere" that might last for several days.[33]

The Moroccan Jewish custom of venerating saints was influenced only in part by the Arab and Berber milieu. Marvin Lowenthal reminds us that

> [t]he Jews may have borrowed their pirates from the Moors, but *zaddikim* and *geburim* (saints and heroes) they have venerated since Biblical days. Pilgrimages to the tombs of Biblical, Talmudic, and latter-day saints have always had their vogue, no less among European than Oriental Jews. It is certain that Yehiel of Paris, Judah He-Hasid of Regensburg, and the Baal Shem would be annoyed by any theory of Moslem origin. Even the *baraka* exuded by the tombs is no Moorish invention. "And it came to pass, as they were burying a man, behold they spied a band of Moabites, and they cast the man into the tomb of Elisha, and as soon as the man touched the bones of Elisha, he revived and stood upon his feet." (II Kings, 13:21)[34]

Israeli anthropologist Shlomo Deshen (in summing up the findings of Norman Stillman) compares and contrasts the concept of the Moroccan *tzaddik* with that of the Islamic *marabout*. "In both cases the element of personality and ancestry are salient to the believer. But in contrast to the *marabout*, the *tzaddik* causes fewer miracles in his lifetime, his physical appearance is not considered as power laden . . . and he does not usually become legendary in his lifetime."[35] Some Jewish saints were recognized as possessing *baraka* by the Muslims and were considered holy men worthy of veneration. Whereas Muslims were permitted to make pilgrimage to the *koubas* of the *tzaddikim*, Jews were forbidden from entering the sanctuaries of the Islamic holy men in many places in Morocco, including the Atlas Mountains.

Despite their reverence for individual Jewish saints, there was institutionalized contempt for the Jews among Morocco's Muslims. During times of drought the Jews were rounded up in the market and commanded to pray for rain. The belief was that Allah would readily grant the prayers of the Jews because they smelled so terrible; He would therefore send down rain in torrents in order to get rid of their smell.[36] It was axiomatic among the believers that a prayer said in the house of a Jew would never reach Allah's ears. Should a Jew cross the threshold of a believer, the angels would desert the place for forty days.[37] A Muslim who made pilgrimage to Mecca might lose his divine grace if he exposed himself to the look of a Jew. If a woman desired to domesticate her husband, "she procures some urine of a Jew and a piece of liver of a sheep or goat and boils it with oil; by partaking of this mixture he will become timid like a Jew or a sheep or a goat."[38] As late as 1950, Rom Landau in his travelogue writes that he "noticed repeatedly that when an uneducated Arab or Berber had to use the word 'Yehud' (Jew), he first apologized, as though he were going to use an unclean or vulgar expression."[39]

In some places in the Atlas Mountains the *dhimmi* regulations pertaining to attire were not as heavily enforced as they were in the lowlands, and for the most part the Jews in these areas were dressed indistinguishably from the Muslims. Jewish men wore a long, loose-fitting shirt over which they wore a black hooded cloak called *jalabiya*. In many regions the Jews were obligated to wear a special black skullcap and black slippers. In some areas, however, what distinguished Jewish men from their Gentile neighbors were dangling earlocks, a tuft of hair in the center of the head, and a pair of gold earrings. The tuft, tradition has it, was worn to commemorate the destruction of the Holy Temple. The gold earrings kept alive the memory that their ancestors did not believe in paying homage to an idol, since one group of Jews would not melt down their jewelry for the construction of the Golden Calf.[40]

Jewish women were dressed exactly like their Muslim counterparts. They wore a single sheet of woven cloth wound round their bodies, with the ends meeting over the breast where they were held together by silver clasps of exquisite but simple design. Rectangular silk kerchiefs were wrapped over their heads and around their necks. They wore huge earrings of gold and silver fili-gree. Their necks and legs were adorned with gold bangles, and on their arms they wore bracelets, usually set with stones. Married women were veiled so that the public could never see their faces. On the Sabbath and holidays, Berber women would paint their fingers, eyebrows, and noses with henna. As tattoo-ing is considered a form of defiling one's body and therefore sinful, this custom was eschewed by Jewish women. The following vignettes illustrate what is known of the Atlas Mountain Jews' daily lives in the pre-*aliyah* period.

In the Atlas Mountains the *slas* (synagogues) were simple structures, with one tiny room, usually made of mud and painted in local colors. In some places the synagogues were painted white with blue doors; in other places they were painted red. The Moroccan synagogue, Marvin Lowenthal observed, is "the oldest purely Jewish model that survives. And its antiquity may redeem its un-deniable ugliness and squalor. . . . If a [rabbi] were felt to be inordinately spiri-tual, a genuine *baraka* to his followers, he was presented a house which was there-upon converted into his synagogue."[41]

The pedagogical system was quite backward, and the great majority of Jewish mountaineers were functionally illiterate. At the age of five or six, boys attended *kuttab* (*cheder*). There they were taught to read the *Chumash* and the *siddur*, but the meaning of the words was not always explained or understood. The teachers, who oftentimes were barely literate themselves, tended to be harsh disciplinarians who resorted to a cane or strap without much hesitation. The rare youngster who showed promise of becoming a *talmud hakham* might be sent to a yeshiva in Marrakech or another large Jewish community in the lowlands if his parents had the means. Although girls received no formal education whatso-ever, they were taught by their mothers to memorize entire prayers of consid-erable length.

Marriages were generally arranged by a matchmaker, usually a friend or relative of the young man. The age of fifteen to twenty was considered suitable for boys; girls might be as young as five or six.[42] Sometimes the disparity in age was much more extreme. Occasionally a vibrant youthful girl would be mar-ried to a decrepit-looking man of fifty or sixty.[43] It was fairly common for uncles to marry nieces and for men to marry their paternal aunts.[44] Polygamy was permitted, but not prevalent. If the parents of the bride consented to giving their daughter's hand, the groom's mother would consummate the agreement by giving the girl a present of jewelry. To ensure that the child would be a male, a pregnant woman would swallow the testicles of a goat dipped in honey.[45] Be-cause the *jinnis* are capable of bringing disaster on joyous occasions, women would make trilling noises called *you-you*s at the birth of newborn child. *You-you*s were supposed to have the effect of frightening the *jinni*s away.

Everyday meals were served in a common dish that was placed on the ground. Everyone squatted on the ground around the dish and scooped up morsels with the first three fingers of the right hand. The food was formed into a lump and tossed into the mouth, the serving hand not being allowed to touch the mouth. The most common native dishes were *couscous*, granulated macaroni cooked with pieces of meat; *harcra*, spicy lentil soup; *pastella*, pigeon pie stuffed with eggs and seasoned with parsley, onion, and aromatic herbs; *mechoui*, lamb either oven roasted or grilled and prepared with a hot herbal paste; saffron-honey chicken; and mutton cooked slowly in honey, with raisins and almonds and a variety of ground seeds and spices. Ox brains and testicles were also delicacies. On the Shabbat, *skhina*, the Moroccan version of *cholent*, was served. *Skhina* is made from layers of meat, potatoes, chick peas, cereal grains, hard-boiled eggs, and spices. Favorite beverages were almond milk and mint tea. As a gesture of appreciation and enjoyment, belching and licking one's fingers in abandoned pleasure were considered good manners.

An especially festive occasion for the Atlas Mountain (and all Moroccan) Jews was the celebration of *maimuna* on the day after Pesach. On this day the Jews dressed in their most lavish finery and made merry in the streets. No one is sure of the exact origins of the word *maimuna*. Some say the word is derived from the name of Maimonides' father, who sojourned in Fez for a time. Others hold that the word *maimuna* is a local variation of the word *emunah*, or belief in the Coming of the Messiah and the Redemption of Israel, a major theme of the Passover story. The *maimuna* may be reminiscent of the festivals of biblical times when pilgrimages would be made to Jerusalem.

In the eighteenth and nineteenth centuries, fleeing the incessant anarchy and pillage that was wreaking havoc on the *bled essiba*, entire Jewish communities in the Atlas Mountains gradually migrated to the urban centers of Morocco. "The penetration of European political and economic influence into the larger towns and the presence of consulates and legations . . . offered the Jewish migrants a safer refuge from political instability and economic uncertainty."[46] Under the French Protectorate (1912–56) the Jews' *dhimmi* status was abolished and they were no longer obligated to pay the *jizya*. The Jews were given freedom of expression and movement, and they were no longer forced to live within the confines of the *mellah*. Nevertheless, the mass influx of Jews from the interior and the mountains into the Jewish quarters of Fez, Marrakech, Meknes, Sefrou, Casablanca, and other *mellah*s turned these places into virtual slums. Alcoholism, drug addiction, prostitution, and infectious diseases scourged the Jewish population.

In 1942 there were only about 30,000 Berber Jews in the mountain regions and in the desert. There were estimated to be about 75,000 to 80,000 Berber Jews in all of Morocco in the 1940s. *The Encyclopaedia Judaica* has estimated that there were perhaps 10,000 Jews in the Atlas Mountains alone in 1948.[47] The messianic fervor that gripped the pious Jewish masses of Morocco after the founding of the State of Israel touched off a spontaneous mass *aliyah* among the Jews in the remote mountain regions. By the end of the 1960s, all of them had left.

In Israel, writes Harvey Goldberg, "[the Atlas Mountain Jews] became a symbol of the extreme variety and 'exoticness' of the mass immigration of that period."[48] Most had arrived in Israel with little more than the clothing on their backs. Stigmatized with rest of the Moroccan *olim* (immigrants) by Israeli officials as "temperamental, aggressive, and primitive,"[49] most Atlas Mountain Jews were settled first in *ma'abarot* (tent compounds) and then crammed in temporary housing in development towns. Many eventually found part-time work as farm laborers and tree planters in kibbutzim and *moshavim*. Whole villages of the Atlas Mountains were transplanted in the Taanach region, the hills of the Galilee, and the Lachish region. "They were pioneers of flowers for export," writes Laible Hoffmitz. "They . . . .made an invaluable contribution to the development of Israeli agriculture. . . . With the sweat of their brows they made these places bloom."[50]

NOTES

1. Henrik de Leeuw, *Crossroads of the Mediterranean* (Garden City, N.Y.: Hanover, 1954), p. 221.

2. For a concise and useful discussion of the conflict between the *bled el-maghzen* and the *bled essiba*, see Jane Gerber, *Jewish Society in Fez, 1450–1700* (Leiden: E. J. Brill, 1980), pp. 6–13.

3. *North African Jewry in the Twentieth Century* (New York: New York University Press, 1994), p. 15.

4. Bernard G. Hoffman, *The Structure of Traditional Moroccan Rural Society* (The Hague: Mouton, 1967), pp. 37–38. Some scholars such as H. Z. Hirschberg and Harvey Goldberg have presented a more skeptical view of the phenomenon of Judaized Berbers. According to Goldberg, the evidence that many of the tribes of North Africa "had ac-

cepted a form of Judaism in the pre-Islamic period and that consequently, many of today's North African Jews are the descendants of Berbers . . . is thin, and this should alert us to possible ideological overtones that may be involved. The thesis of the Judaizing Berbers clearly emphasizes the antiquity of Jews in the region (which is historically documented), and perhaps (this is speculation), in the colonial situation, hinted at the association of the Jews with the French, who tried to woo the loyalty of 'the Berbers' in an attempt to separate them from the urban Arab Muslims." See "The Mellahs of Southern Morocco: Report of a Survey." *The Maghreb Review* 8:3–4 (1983), p. 61. See also H. Z. Hirschberg, "The Problem of the Judaized Berbers," *Journal of African History* 4:3 (1963), pp. 313–339.

5. Michael M. Laskier, *The Alliance Israelite Universelle in Morocco and the Jewish Communities of Morocco 1862–1962* (Albany: State University of New York Press, 1983), pp. 20–21.

6. *Le Maroc; Le Pays et son Histoire* (Paris: Editions Notre Domaine Colonial, 1928), p. 73. (French)

7. "The Moroccan Jewish Experience: A Revisionist View," *The Jerusalem Quarterly* 9 (Fall 1978), p. 118.

8. Gerber, *Jewish Society*, p. 19.

9. (London: H. F. and G. Witherby, 1930), p. 166.

10. Walter B. Harris, *Tafilet: The Narrative of a Journey of Exploration in the Atlas Mountains and the Oases of the North-west Sahara* (Edinburgh and London: William Blackwood and Sons, 1895), pp. 45–46.

11. Pierre Loti, *Morocco* (New York: Frederick A. Stokes, 1914), pp. 234–243 and 288–89; Pierre Loti, *Into Morocco* (Chicago: Rand, McNally, 1892), pp. 310, 315. Arthur Leared, *Morocco and the Moors* (New York: Sampson, Low, 1891), pp. 173–74.

12. Cited in Joseph L. Williams, *Hebrewisms of West Africa* (New York: The Dial Press, 1931), p. 208; and Robert Montagne, *The Berbers: Their Social and Political Organization* (London: Frank Cass, 1973), pp. 9–10.

13. It is known that some Jews accompanied these Arab invaders to Morocco. The city of Meknes is believed to have been settled by Jewish soldiers who served in the Arab legions around this time.

14. William Spenser, *The Land and People of Tunisia* (Philadelphia: Lippincott, 1967), pp. 55–56. According to another legend she preferred "to die only as a queen . . . and fell gloriously by her own sword." See Henrik de Leeuw, *Crossroads of the Mediterranean* (Garden City, N.Y.: Hanover House, 1954), pp. 97–98. For a critical view of Ibn Khaldoon's account see Norman Roth, "The Kahina: Legendary Material in the Accounts of the 'Jewish Berber Queen.'" *The Maghreb Review* 7:5–6 (1982), pp. 122–25.

15. Rom Landau, *Moroccan Drama, 1950–55* (London: Robert Hale, 1956), p. 28.

16. *Studies in the Communal Life of the Jews of Spain* (New York: Hermon Press, 1968), p. 15.

17. Walter B. Harris, *Morocco That Was* (Boston: Small, Maynard Co., 1921), pp. 308–11; Hoffman, *The Structure*, pp. 37–38.

18. Landau, *Moroccan Drama*, p. 30. See also Ralph de Toledano, "The Jews of Morocco," *Midstream,* 38:1 (January 1992), p. 25.

19. Epstein, *Studies*, p. 17.

20. Cited in Dorothy Willner, *Nation-Building and Community in Israel* (Princeton, New Jersey: Princeton University Press, 1969), p. 255.

21. Harris, *Tafilet*, pp. 98, 173; See also Joseph Thomson, *Travels in the Atlas and Southern Morocco: A Narrative of Exploration* (New York: Longmans, Green and Co., 1889), pp. 251–52; Nahum Slouschz, *Travels in North Africa* (Philadelphia: Jewish Publication Society, 1927), p. 477; Lawrence Rosen, *Bargaining for Reality* (Chicago: University of Chicago Press, 1984), p. 153.

22. *The Aith Waryaghar of the Moroccan Rif: An Ethnography and History* (Tucson: University of Arizona Press, 1976), pp. 279–80.

23. Montagne, *The Berbers*, p. 45.

24. Andre Chouraqui, *Between East and West* (New York: Atheneum, 1973), pp. 93–96. See also Slouschz, *Travels*, p. 483.

25. Clifford Geertz, "Suq: The Bazaar Economy in Sefrou," in *Meaning and Order in Moroccan Society: Three Essays in Cultural Analysis,* edited by Clifford Geertz, et al. (Cambridge: Cambridge University Press, 1979), pp. 137–38.

26. "Morocco." *The Jewish Encyclopedia*, vol. 9 (New York: Funk and Wagnall, 1905), p. 28.

27. *Travels*, pp. 466–68. Henrik de Leeuw mentions a bellicose tribe of Jews in the Glaoui Atlas Mountain region. See *Crossroads of the Mediterranean*, p. 157.

28. *Bargaining for Reality: The Construction of Social Relations in a Muslim Community* (Chicago: University of Chicago Press, 1984), pp. 152–53.

29. David M. Hart, *The Ait Atta of Southern Morocco: Daily Life and Recent History* (Cambridge: Menas Press, 1984), pp. 108–13.

30. Edward Westermarck, *Ritual and Belief in Morocco*, vol. 1 (London: MacMillan and Co., 1926), p. 296.

31. Ibid., p. 360.

32. Yoram Bilu, "Dreams and Wishes of the Saint," in *Judaism: Viewed from Within and from Without*, edited by Harvey Goldberg (Albany: State University of New York Press, 1986), p. 291.

33. Yoram Bilu, "Personal Motivation and Social Meaning in the Revival of Hagiolatric Traditions Among Moroccan Jews in Israel," in *Tradition, Innovation, Con-*

flict: Jewishness and Judaism in Contemporary Israel, edited by Zvi Sobel and Benjamin Beit-Hallahmi (Albany: State University of New York Press, 1991), p. 49.

34. Marvin Lowenthal, *A World Passed By: Scenes and Memories of Jewish Civilization in Europe and North Africa* (New York: Harper and Bros. Publishers, 1933), p. 400.

35. *The Mellah Society* (Chicago: University of Chicago Press, 1989), p. 84. See also Norman Stillman, "Saddiq and Marabout in Morocco," in *The Sephardi and Oriental Jewish Tradition*, edited by Issacher Ben-Ami (Jerusalem: Magnes Press, The Hebrew University, 1982), pp. 489–500; Issachar Ben-Ami, "Saint Veneration Among North African Jews," *Jewish Folklore and Ethnology* 5:2 (1993), pp. 78–83. On the role of the *marabout* in Berber Muslim culture see Michael Brett and Elizabeth Fentress, *The Berbers* (Oxford: Blackwell Publishers, 1997), esp. pp. 142–49.

36. John Windus, *A Journey to Mequinez: The Residence of the Present Emperor of Fez and Morocco* (London: J. Tonson, 1725), p. 62; Budgett Meakin, *The Moors: A Comprehensive Description* (London: Sonnenschein, 1902), p. 446; G. Montbard, *Among the Moors: Sketches of Oriental Life* (New York: Charles Scribner, 1894), p. 15.

37. Westermarck, *Ritual and Belief*, vol. 1, p. 229.

38. Ibid., vol. 2, p. 301.

39. *Invitation to Morocco* (London: Faber and Faber, 1950), p. 210.

40. Moshe Dluznowsky, "Moroccan Jews: Impressions," *Jewish Frontier* 22:9 (244) (September 1955), p. 28. Yedida Stillman points out that from Genesis 25:4 we know that the Israelites in Bible times wore earrings. See "The Evil Eye in Morocco," *Folklore Research Center Studies*, vol. 1, edited by Dov Noy and Issachar Ben-Ami (Jerusalem: Magnes Press, The Hebrew University, 1970), p. 86.

41. Lowenthal, *A World Passed By*, p. 397.

42. Eugene Aubin, *Morocco of To-day* (London: J. M. Dent and Co., 1906), p. 292; Willner, *Nation-Building*, pp. 261–62.

43. W. F. Ainsworth, ed., *All Round the World: An Illustrated Record of Voyages, Travels, and Adventures in All Parts of the World*, vol. 1 (London and Glasgow: William Collins, Sons, and Co., 1894), p. 349.

44. Milton Jacobs, *A Study of Cultural Stability and Change: The Moroccan Jewess* (Washington, D.C.: Catholic University of America, 1956), p. 16. Niece marriage is permissible by Jewish law.

45. Ibid., p. 22.

46. Michael Laskier, "Aspects of Change: The Jewish Communities of Morocco's Bled," in *Communaites Juive des Marges Sahariennes du Magreb*, edited by Michel Abitbol (Jerusalem: Institut Ben-Zvi, 1982), p. 332.

47. David Corcos and Hayyim J. Cohen, "Atlas," *Encyclopaedia Judaica*, vol. 3 (Jerusalem: Keter, 1973), p. 827.

48. "The Mellahs of Southern Morocco" *The Maghreb Review* 8:3–4 (1983), p. 62.

49. Eliezer Ben-Rafael, "The Changing Experience, Power, and Prestige of Ethnic Groups in Israel: The Case of the Moroccans," *Israel, State and Society 1948–88* 5 (1989), p. 48.

50. "North African Jewry in Israel," *Viewpoints* 9:3 (Spring–Summer 1976), p. 31.

Part XII

Jewish Cave Dwellers of Libya
Credit: Yad Ben Zvi Archives

Cave Rabbis? Cave Synagogues?

BACKGROUND INFORMATION

In the mythological origins of Libya, a story is told about the gardens of the Hesperides. They were located in the vicinity of Cyrenaica. The golden apples that grew in the garden were guarded by nymphs, with the aid of a dragon. Gaea gave these apples to Hera as a wedding gift, and fetching some of these apples was one of the labors of Hercules. Nearby, in the extreme western part of Africa, was situated the River Lethe, in Hades, whose water was the "water of forgetfulness."

Most modern-day Libyans are a mixture of Berber and Arab stock. They are a Sunni Muslim tribal group who speak an Arabic that has Hamitic or Afro-Asian roots. The Libyans have traditionally been a tribal people; egalitarian; intensely loyal to family, village, and community; who recognize no government but their tribal chiefs. For most of their history they have managed to remain largely independent of domination. Invasions by Egyptians, Phoenicians, Greeks, Romans, Byzantines, Vandals, Spaniards, and Ottomans had no lasting impact on Berber culture. Only the two major Arab invasions (in the seventh century from the Arabian Peninsula, and from Egypt in the twelfth century) had an indelible impact on Libyan Berber civilization. The Berber tribes fiercely resisted the Arab assaults, but in Cyrenaica they were eventually subdued and absorbed by the latter. In Tripolitania many Berber tribes, some of them "Judaized," fled to the edge of the Sahara Desert or to the more easily defended mountains. There they dug caves and subsisted by hunting and grazing herds of sheep and goats. Only in these regions did the racial composition of the Berbers remain relatively unadulterated.

The Spaniards conquered Tripoli in 1510, demolished the houses, and expelled the inhabitants. Tripolitania came under Ottoman control in 1551, and from that time until 1911 this region was ruled directly or indirectly by the Porte. For an interim period, 1711–1835, local Janissaries known as the Karamanlis seized power and unified the country by extending their control over Fezzan and Cyrenaica. This period of Karamanli ascendancy coincided with the era of the "Barbary Pirates," whose booty filled the coffers of the local *beys* (regents). In 1835 the Ottomans deposed the last of the Karamanlis and reestablished direct rule. Seeking a place under the African sun, the Italians occupied Libya following the collapse of the Ottoman regime in 1911. Led by a Bedouin religious movement known as the Sannusi Order, the Libyan masses put up a fierce resistance against the Italians. Libya became pacified only after Mussolini's brutal campaign of suppression in 1923.

Libyan soldiers fought courageously against Rommel's troops in the desert battles of World War II. The Italian fascists were driven out in 1943, and Tripolitania was placed under British Military Administration after the war. In 1949 the United Nations resolved that the three territories of Libya should be constituted as a single independent state. Following the unification of Libya in 1951, the British placed the Cyrenaica Sannusi tribal chieftain Idris on the throne. He was proclaimed constitutional monarch of the independent Kingdom of Libya. On September 1, 1969 Libya was declared a revolutionary republic by Colonel Moammar Khadhafi.

The Great Socialist People's Libyan Arab Jamahiriya ("People's Power") lies on the Mediterranean Sea, surrounded on the east by Egypt; on the west by Algeria and Tunisia; and in the south by Niger, Chad, and the Sudan. It is more than twice the size of Texas, with a population of about five million. Prior to independence from Great Britain in 1951, Libya was divided into three autonomous regions: Tripolitania, Cyrenaica, and Fezzan. Most of the inhabitant have always lived in Tripolitania, in the northwestern province. Tripoli, its chief port, is the capital of Libya.

Libya is characterized by burning deserts and a shortage of water. Only about three percent of the land mass is cultivable. Before dictator Moammar Khadhafi's modernization programs, which began in 1969, one in five Libyans suffered from eye diseases, and one in ten was completely blind. Diseases such as trachoma, tuberculosis, and eczema were also widespread. More than any other people in the world, Libyan Jews suffer from an affliction known as

Creutzfeld-Jakob disease. This is a rapidly progressive mental illness that is believed to be caused by the practice among Libyan Jews of eating lightly cooked sheep brains that are infected with a lethal virus similar to that which causes Mad Cow Disease.

In the early twentieth century, Cyrenaica was considered as a possible national homeland for Jews. With the blessing of the Ottomans, the Jewish Territorial Organization set up a special commission in Cyrenaica to study this proposal. The commission concluded that the inadequate water supply made this impossible for a large population.[1]

THE JEWS OF LIBYA: MERCHANTS
AND CAVERN DWELLERS

> Sleep in the beds of Christians
> But don't eat their food.
> Eat the food of the Jews
> But don't sleep in their beds.
> —Berber proverb

Jews may have first arrived in Libya during King Solomon's time, when Phoenician sailors founded trading posts along Libya's shores, or possibly after the destruction of the Temple in 586 B.C.E. Josephus claims that the first arrival of Jews in Libya took place during the reign of the Greek emperor Ptolemy I, around 320 B.C.E., when Jewish military guards were transferred from Egypt to the Cyrenean Pentapolis (modern-day Benghazi) to strengthen his regime there. These Jews enjoyed equal rights with the other inhabitants, who were primarily Greek settlers, and they were a privileged group governed by their own local authorities. With many more Jews arriving from Palestine during the persecutions of Antiochus Epiphenes, around 175 B.C.E., these military colonies gradually developed into civilian towns. The Libyan Jewish community prospered and contributed liberally to the upkeep of the Temple in Jerusalem. By the first century of the Common Era, Cyrenia—the Libya of antiquity, which included Egypt—possessed the largest Jewish community in the Diaspora. Recent historians estimate their numbers to have been around one million.[2]

The political climate changed radically for the worse, for Libyan Jewry, after the destruction of Jerusalem in 70 C.E. by the Roman emperor Titus. One of Titus's generals brought some 30,000 Jewish captives to Cyrenia. In 73 C.E., Libyan Jewry attempted to avenge the loss of Jewish independence in Palestine when, under the leadership of the Zealot Jonathan the Weaver, the poorer elements of the Jewish population of Cyrenia began to arm themselves and prepare for insurrection. The Zealots were a radical political and religious sect who openly opposed Roman rule in Palestine. The richer Jews of Cyrenia, wishing to maintain their comfort and status quo, informed the Roman governor of Jonathan's intentions. The governor promptly captured and killed thousands of Jonathan's followers. When Jonathan was brought before the governor in chains, knowing who had betrayed him, he took revenge by telling the governor that the rich Jews had financially supported his cause. The Roman governor was delighted to hear this allegation and used it as an excuse to put 3,000 rich Jews to death and confiscate their property. He had Jonathan the Weaver tortured and buried alive.[3]

A second, and even larger, mass revolt broke out in North Africa in 115 C.E. during the reign of the Roman emperor Trajan. This rebellion had even more tragic results for the Jews. It was led by Lukuas, whom the Romans referred to as the "King of the Jews," because he wanted to establish a Jewish kingdom in North Africa. The fact that Rabbi Akiva journeyed to this region around this time attests to the messianic character of the movement.[4] The fighting started in Alexandria, Egypt, where there was much hostility between the Jews and their Hellenistic neighbors, and it soon spread to the rest of Egypt and Cyrenia. At first, the Jews had the upper hand and massacred many thousands of Greeks and Romans. The Roman emperor sent in a war fleet under the command of Marcius Turbo and, after much fighting, almost the entire Jewish population of Cyrenia was annihilated.[5] Only small groups of Jews remained in the interior of the country. Others who survived fled to the mountains and took refuge in caves, which became their permanent homes.

Very little is known about the Jewish community of Libya-Cyrenia during the following three centuries. In the fourth century C.E., after Christianity became the adopted religion of the Eastern Roman empire, the Jews were persecuted and forbidden to practice their religion. The situation brightened for the Jews after the Vandals subdued Tripoli, around 455 C.E. The Vandals were an east German tribe who practiced a heretical form of Christianity called Arianism. In Europe they had once been relentlessly persecuted by their Byzantine (Roman Catholic) masters; now they were a mighty power conquering lands occupied by the Byzantines—Gaul, Spain, and North Africa. The Jews, who had assisted the Vandals in driving out the Byzantines from Libya, were once again permitted to worship openly. Some historians believe that during this period the Jewish influence in Libya was widespread, and that many Berber tribes chose to convert to Judaism.[6]

The Jews paid dearly for their support of the Vandals when, in 533 C.E., the Byzantines, under General Belisarius, reconquered North Africa. During the reign of the intolerant emperor Justinian, the Jewish religion was outlawed and many synagogues were converted to churches.

When the Arab crusaders invaded Libya in 670 C.E., tribes of pagan Berbers, Christians, and Jews joined forces in defense of their territory. This coalition attacked the Arab-held plains and was overwhelmed. The survivors quickly retreated into the wild mountains and the trackless desert where they carried on ferocious guerrilla warfare against the Arab invaders. After almost a century of struggle, the Berbers were finally subdued and forcibly converted to the Islamic faith. Some Christians managed to flee to the Byzantine Empire. The majority of the Jewish population in Tripoli and other cities also fled. Of those who remained behind, some survived by embracing Islam, and others saved themselves by taking refuge in the Berber cave villages of Messallata and Derna, in the mountains of Tripolitania.[7] It was around this time in Tripolitania that a Jewish queen named Fanana is supposed to have ruled over a Berber tribe called the Ureshfani.

Interestingly, many Berber tribespeople of the Tripolitanian hinterland today have a traditional belief that they came originally from Palestine. According to the early-twentieth-century Franco-Jewish scholar-traveler Nahum Slouschz, one tribe, the Ibn Novairi, believed they were descendants of the Philistines who fled from King David. Another tribe, the Mozabites, claim descent from Ammon and Moab, and since they look upon themselves as brothers of the Israelites, they have tended to be well-disposed toward them. There were numerous Islamic tribes in Libya who claimed direct descent from Jews, but as a result of either persecution or indifference they deserted their historical faith. Three such tribes living in Tripolitania were the Ureshfani, the Brami, and the Ghariani. The Berber Muslims referred to these three tribes as Yehudi or Jews.[8]

Attracted by a more stable and tolerant Muslim regime, many Jews from other parts of the Mediterranean began to arrive in Libya. As *dhimmi* (protected People of the Scriptures), the Jews of Libya lived in relative peace and security and were thus able to thrive. "During the middle ages," writes Slouschz, "the Jews were able . . . to maintain commercial relations with every part of the desert as far as the Sudan. . . . Since the whole trade between the Sahara and the Christian Mediterranean was in their hands, the Jewish merchants of Tripoli strove continually to ensure the security of the routes leading to the rich Sudan. . . ."[9]

Because they were *dhimmi*, the Jews were obligated to pay the special head tax called *jizya*. They had to wear distinctive clothing and were forbidden to engage in occupations that would place them in a position of authority over Muslims. But it was only under the Almohades, a fanatical Berber dynasty ruling North Africa in the twelfth and thirteenth centuries, that the Jews of Libya endured physical persecution as well as religious bigotry.

From the twelfth century until the 1800s, the Jews of Libya were forced to perform the most humiliating and repugnant tasks in society. The most horrible of these tasks was that of public executioner. Whenever a man was condemned to death, guards would be sent out into the street to stop the first Jew they met and force him to chop off the condemned man's head. This was usually a cruel, lingering death because the Jew, not being a professional executioner, oftentimes didn't decapitate on the first or second stroke. When he finally did succeed, his task was only half completed; he was then made to carry the head to the main gate of the town and place it on a spike.[10]

In the rural areas of Tripolitania there evolved a moral code among the Berber tribes that obliged a Berber *saheb* (lord) to protect a Jew who was dependent upon him. It was a disgrace for a Berber tribal lord not to come to the defense of his Jewish servant. There were times when tribes went to battle in matters concerning a Jew. The Jews were considered to be the property of the Berber *saheb*, who could sell his Jewish subjects to another *saheb* or pass them down to his children as an inheritance.[11]

After the anti-Jewish massacres in Catholic Spain in 1391, many Sephardim found a haven in Libya. At the time of the expulsion of the Jews from Iberia in 1492 and 1497 there were some eight hundred Jewish families living in Tripoli. When the Spaniards captured Tripoli in 1510, they persecuted the Jews mercilessly. Many Jews were killed, imprisoned, or sold as slaves. Some fled to the secure mountains of Djebel Gharian in Tripolitania, where they took refuge in caves. These caves became their permanent dwellings. Some Jews who lived in the Gharian caves as recently as 1950 had a traditional belief that they were descended from refugees who settled in this region during Spanish domination.

In the late 1540s a great Moroccan rabbi named Shimon Ben Labi stopped in Tripoli while on his way to making a pilgrimage to Palestine. Although the port city was now under control of the Knights of Malta and the political situation of the Jews had become less oppressive, Rabbi Ben Labi found that life under the Spanish tyrants had taken a heavy toll on the tiny Jewish community. Struck by their miserable plight and their great ignorance in religious observance and learning, Rabbi Ben Labi abandoned his trip to Palestine and instead took up the position of Chief Rabbi of Tripoli. Ben Labi single-handedly revived the spiritual life of Libyan Jewry. During his lifetime Tripoli became an outstanding center of talmudic and kabbalistic learning. One unusual *minhag* he instituted was the reading aloud of the *Shemonai Esrai* portion of the Friday evening prayer service. According to one source, this highly "unorthodox" way of reciting these prayers "is attributed to the need to educate the sixteenth-century Jews by enabling them to hear the prayer read properly out loud."[12]

With the Ottoman Turkish conquest of Libya in 1551, the Jews once again enjoyed relative peace and prosperity. As in other lands ruled by the Ottomans, the Jews in their *hara*s (Jewish quarters) were governed by their own independent religious authorities in a system called *millet*. The community was led by a chief rabbi known as the *hakham bashi* and by a chieftain called *kaid* in Turkish. The *kaid* was appointed by the Libyan government to represent the Jewish community. He collected taxes, maintained law and order, and could impose fines. Under the corrupt Ottoman *pashas* it was often necessary for the Jewish community to pay off crooked officials with large sums of *baksheesh*.

There were three occasions when the survival of the Jewish community in Libya was in jeopardy. The first crisis occurred in 1588, when there was an uprising of Islamic militants against the Ottomans in Tripolitania. Many Jews were forcibly converted to Islam at that time, but as soon as the rebellion was crushed, the Jews returned to their ancestral faith.

The second crisis took place in Tripoli in 1705. That year the *bey* (regent) of Tunis, Ibrahim Sherif, was waging war with the Ottomans. He laid siege to Tripoli and threatened to wipe out the entire population, but a plague broke out among his troops and his soldiers were forced to retreat. The rabbis saw God's hand in this miraculous turn of events and established a special festival of thanksgiving. They called it Purim Sherif, to distinguish it from the Purim celebrated by all of world Jewry.

The third crisis occurred under the rule of a local Libyan dynasty called the Karamanlis (1711–1835), a period when Libya was only marginally under the control of the Ottomans. In 1793 a buccaneer named Burghel and his henchmen took possession of Tripoli and drove out the Karamanli governor. As a result of these violent changes, the Jews were exposed to many cruelties. After a two-year siege, the Karamanlis recaptured the city. The anniversary of this date was celebrated in Tripoli by the Jews as Purim Burghel. In 1835 the Ottomans established direct rule over Libya, and the Jews were given the same civil rights—at least under the law—as that of other subjects of the Empire.

Until the late nineteenth century international trade in Libya was largely in Jewish hands, especially the trade links between Europe and the Sahara. One occupation that the Jews dominated was the trade in ostrich feathers. Whole families were invoived in cleaning and dyeing the feathers.[13] Other Jews dealt in gold dust, ivory, silk, and spices. Before its abolition in the late nineteenth century, some Jews were also involved in the lucrative African slave trade. During the Ottoman period, the Jews were middlemen in the business of ransoming Christians who had been captured by the Turks.[14] Some Jews even rose to high positions as diplomats and financiers. Most, however, were paupers who eked out their livelihoods as smiths, furniture makers, and embroiderers.

Since working with metals is considered dishonorable among Muslims, the Jews always monopolized this trade in Libya. Most Jews earned their living as blacksmiths, goldsmiths, and silversmiths; or by making farm implements, weapons, and jewelry for their Muslim neighbors. Money was virtually unknown in Libya until the Italians arrived in the period immediately prior to World War

I. The Jews exchanged their created products and services for natural products such as raw materials, and for food supplies during harvest time. There were special *suqs* (markets) in the cities in which Jews had a virtual monopoly, e.g., in goldsmithing, silk manufacture, or spices. Many Jews peddled an assortment of wares all over the desert and the hinterland.

There was no love lost between Muslim and Jew in Libya. The Jew was constantly made to feel inferior to the Muslim—yet the Muslim was obliged to tolerate the Jew because he could not do without his services. The Jew provided the Muslim man with virtually all his tools, instruments, and weapons, and the Muslim woman with all her household utensils, ornaments, and jewelry. Jewish craftsmen had a long-standing reputation for making superior products, and Jewish merchants and peddlers had a reputation for honesty and integrity.

Four centuries of Ottoman rule in Libya came to an end in 1911 when the Italians annexed the country. For the next quarter of a century Jewish life in Libya flourished as never before. The estimated 20,000 Jews in the coastal capital alone (twenty percent of the total population) boasted more than forty synagogues. *Dhimmi* laws were abolished, and the Jews were given equal rights with the Muslims. To improve their political and economic standing, many Libyan Jews became proficient in Italian. In addition to the Arabic and a Magrebian-accented Judeo-Arabic that they spoke among themselves, their mastery of Italian served them well in the capacity of agents and translators for the Italians vis-à-vis the Arab population. The Jewish community of Italy also assisted the Jewish community of Libya in many ways, especially in helping to upgrade and modernize Jewish educational institutions.

Like other Jews of North Africa, the Jews of Libya never accepted the excommunication decree of the tenth-century Ashkenazi talmudist Rabbeinu Gershom in regard to polygamy. Sephardim from Italy would often go to Libya to take a second wife if their first wife could not conceive after ten years of marriage.

After the Italian fascist occupation of Libya in 1938, the Jews once again endured many hardships. Anti-Semitic laws were introduced. For instance, Jewish youngsters were compelled to attend fascist schools and Jewish shopkeepers were forced to keep their businesses open on the Shabbat. Jews who broke these laws were publicly flogged.

When the Nazis stormed Tripoli in 1942, some Jews once again fled to the caves of Djebel Gharian. Those less fortunate—a great majority—were rounded up and sent to local labor camps, where they were forced to lay the rail link between Egypt and Libya. These tracks were regularly bombed by the

British air force. The Jews of the city of Benghazi, the second-largest Jewish community in Libya, sustained the greatest losses. Most of the Jewish community was transported to the Giado concentration camp 150 miles south of Tripoli, where hundreds died from starvation or disease. During the British bombing of Tripoli many Jews found temporary shelter among their cave-dwelling brethren in the Tripolitanian hinterland.[15]

British forces liberated Libya in January 1943, and Jewish soldiers of the Eighth Army were the first to enter Tripoli. With the conclusion of World War II, Jewish life in Libya briefly returned to normal. However, late in 1945, disaster struck again, and from this disaster the Jewish community never recovered. On November 4th and 5th of that year vicious anti-Jewish pogroms by local Arabs broke out in Tripoli and a number of villages, leaving a sizable percentage of the Jewish community in a state of utter destitution. Violent demonstrations against Jews in Egypt on the twenty-eighth anniversary of the Balfour Declaration were reported on Libyan radio, and the following day rioting against the Jews broke out in Libya. At the same time, rumors were being spread that an Islamic religious leader had been attacked by Jews in Tripoli, and that Jews in Palestine were murdering Muslims praying in a mosque in Jerusalem. The British Military Administration stood on the sidelines for the first couple of days before declaring a curfew.[16]

The precarious existence of Jewish life in Libya became even more precarious in 1948. That year another pogrom took place in Tripoli, only this time the Jews were better prepared to defend themselves. Some Tunisian volunteer soldiers, on their way to join the Arab forces during Israel's War of Independence, arrived in Tripoli. Again, no one knows exactly how the riot started or by whom: Some historians believe that the Tunisian soldiers stirred up the population to attack the Jews; others claim that it was a bunch of young Jewish toughs who started the melee by jeering the Tunisians when they marched past the Jewish quarter.[17] Jewish losses were significant, but not as great as they had been in 1945.

Libya was no longer a land where Jews could live harmoniously with their neighbors. For this reason, the Israeli government evacuated some 29,000 Libyan Jews without opposition from the pro-West Libyan monarchy of the time. This evacuation, by air and by sea, took place between 1949 and 1952, and included the entire community of cave dwellers from Djebel Gharian. Most settled in Natanya and the Tel Aviv suburb of Bat Yam, as well as on a number of *moshavim*. An estimated 6,000 Jews, mostly from the wealthier classes, chose to remain in Libya.

Libya became an independent country in 1951 by a vote of the General Assembly of the United Nations (Israel's vote was cast in favor of independence for Libya). In spite of the fact that the constitution guaranteed equality for all its citizens, Jews were not permitted to vote or hold elective office or to be employed by the government. A brutal pogrom took place in Tripoli during the Six Day War in 1967. After the seizure of power by the extreme militant Colonel Moammar Khadhafi in 1969, and the confiscation of Jewish property soon afterwards, the remaining Jews fled to other parts of the world, most of them coming to the United States and Europe. There are no Jews left in Libya today.

No one knows exactly when the Jews first settled in the Libyan caves. In the mountains of Morocco and Algeria and in the region of Tripolitania in Libya there existed tribes of Jews who for many centuries lived in underground caves. To escape hostile attention, they excavated underground caverns for their homes and synagogues. Only their cemeteries were placed on the surface. Jewish cave-dwelling communities in Libya may date back even before 70 C.E., when the Jewish historian Josephus wrote about them. However, it can be said with a great degree of certainty that there was continuous Jewish settlement in the Djebel Gharian region since at least the Almohades period (twelfth century). In 1510, when the Spaniards invaded Tripoli, a sizable percentage of the Jewish community fled to Tajura, a coastal village east of Tripoli, and to Djebel Gharian, sixty miles south of the coast. The Jews of the caves of Djebel Gharian had Sephardic traditions from Mediterranean lands.

Although almost nothing is known of the details of daily life for the ancient cave-dwelling communities, there is enough documentation from the mid nineteenth century on to reasonably reconstruct what these underground communities may have been like.

The Djebel Gharian region forms part of the Western Mountains and is located on the southern border of Tripolitania. In the early part of the twentieth century it contained approximately one hundred underground villages. Jewish cave villages were separate but located near Muslim cave villages. Most of the Muslims were involved in herding sheep and goats or in raising grains and fruits.

The Jews of Djebel Gharian settled in three cave villages: Tigranna, Ben Abbas, and Tagsot.[18] Of these, only Tigranna remained inhabited until the transfer of the entire community of 550 people to Israel in 1951. Actually, the Jewish inhabitants of Tigranna originally lived in the village of Jehisha. One elderly former cave dweller explained to Israeli anthropology professor Harvey Goldberg in the early 1970s that hostile Muslim neighbors used to sneak around while no one was watching and put frogs in the pots of the Jews while their Shabbat meal was cooking in the courtyard. It became very difficult for the Jews to eat an uncontaminated hot meal on the Shabbat. This last assault on their religious integrity convinced the Jews that it was no longer possible to live amicably with their Muslim neighbors, so they moved to Tigranna.[19] During an outbreak of the plague in 1837, many of the inhabitants of Ben Abbas perished. The survivors left the village for Tripoli, with only four families remaining behind in the mountains.

The cave villages of Djebel Gharian are set on a high plateau covered with olive, fig, palm, and other Mediterranean fruit trees.[20] The clay soil was soft because the region received an ample amount of rainfall each year. In anthropological terms, the Gharian caves conform to the grand-court type of architecture.[21] Cave dwellings were dug thirty to forty feet deep underground with the doors bolted into the hillside. Hilly terrain and lush undergrowth helped to conceal the cave entrances from marauding bandits. Anyone going into or coming out of the underground caverns had to traverse a long, winding tunnel. The tunnel was made narrow so that people were forced to proceed single file. This prevented invaders from overwhelming the cave dwellers by a mass attack. People entering the narrow shaft came first to the stable, then the storage area and workshop. This layout was designed for safety's sake, so that intruders would encounter the animals first and the disturbed animals would raise an alarm, thus warning the inhabitants.[22] The dwelling areas were located in the most secure place, farthest from the hillside entryway, and they surrounded a courtyard that was open to the sky.

Each subterranean village consisted of six to eight cave pits, or dwellings, branching out from the courtyard "like spokes on a wheel."[23] Each dwelling or apartment had several rooms and housed a nuclear family. Dwelling areas were designed and located so that they received light, sunshine, and fresh air from the courtyard skylight. The floors and walls of the cave apartments were covered with carpets. The rooms were illuminated at night by silver oil lamps.[24] Ethel Braun gives us an early-twentieth-century description of the interior of one cave apartment:

> The room is really a cave scooped out in the earth, the only light coming from the doorway. As my eyes grow accustomed to the gloom, I can see the ceiling just above my head, almost touching me. Rows of preserved fruit tins, sardine boxes, old bananas, Indian corn, and whatnot are strung across it as ornaments, a 'fantasia' of decoration. All round the walls are other tins, boxes of native construction, strings of shells, a few Soudanese

ornaments, dish-covers, pots and pans. Several holes had been scooped out of the sides of the walls to serve as receptacles for garments or food-stuffs, and there are two old stools—otherwise the room is bare of furni-ture. There are other rooms, all much the same, all opening out into the courtyard.[25]

As a sign of mourning for the destroyed Temple in Jerusalem, one corner of the wall of a Jew's dwelling place was always painted black.

Water was obtained from a cistern located in the center of the courtyard. Also branching off from the central courtyard was the *sla* (synagogue and *kutab* or *cheder*). There were at least three such underground villages that held up to a dozen separate family units in each. These family units consisted of all the generations living together—children, parents, grandparents, and even great-grandparents.

Travelers who visited the Jewish cave-dwelling communities in the early twentieth century observed that the inhabitants tended to be taller and healthier than those in the cities.[26] This may be partially explained by the fact that the region had the highest average rainfalls in Tripolitania, which nourished their crops. The surrounding fruit trees contributed to the cave dwellers' health by providing an abundance of olives, dates, figs, pomegranates, grapes and citrus fruits, peaches, and almonds. The caverns remained agreeably cool in summer and warm in winter. This protection from extremes of temperature and weather also may have contributed to the cave dwellers' well-being.[27]

The Jews of Djebel Gharian may have been superstitious and backward by the standards of sophisticated urban people. However, most of the men were literate enough to read the prayers, although they would not have been well versed in Scriptures. Their children attended *sla* (*cheder*) and some of their rab-bis were scholars and worldly-wise. Some of their *hakhamim* were imported from Jerba and other centers of rabbinic learning in North Africa. As everywhere else in Jewish North Africa, saint worship was very common in the Libyan country-side. Deeply venerated by Berber and Jew alike were the holy tombs of the *marabouts* and *shadarim* (*shelichim*, or emissaries from Palestine) who either died or were killed by brigands on their missions across the hinterland Jewish com-munities. Their tombs became a site of worship later on.

Sometimes [writes Nahum Slouschz] travelers who come across the dead body of a holy man carry it to the nearest Jewish house, and point out to the faithful the spot where they found it. And the Jews bury the body there, placing a white stone over it, and sometimes they rear a whole mauso-

leum on the spot. The dead rabbi is now a Jewish *marabut*. The tomb becomes a center of pilgrimage for the poor, who light oil lamps by the tomb
to invoke the aid of the saint, and for the sick, who flock thither praying
for a miraculous cure—even for the Mussulmans.

And then legends begin to gather around the grave of the saint; miracles and prophecies and fulfillments are told of; strange figures are seen
to steal at night from the tomb. After a generation the exact date of the
rabbi's death is forgotten; old legends and new legends mingle about his
name, and the *marabut* becomes a prophet of old, a spirit which dominates
the whole region. Awed into belief, the Arabs and Berbers . . . begin in
their turn to honor the rabbi's grave, and jealous that so holy a place should
belong to the Jews, they take advantage of their greater numbers to drive
the Jews away and appropriate the sanctuary. Often they build a mosque
about the tomb, still keeping the Jewish name of the saint. And often his
name is forgotten, and he becomes a Sidi Mohammed. . . . I know of
no greater sorrow, of no anguish more acute than that of the Jews of
Africa, when the saint who has been their guiding spirit . . . is taken from
them by the Mohammedans. And so tenacious is the hold which the dead
have over the living, that often entire Jewish villages have gone over to
Islamism, simply because their dead saint has been seized by the Mussulmans, and, as Jews, they would no longer be permitted to come to him
on a pilgrimage.[28]

The leader of the cave-dwelling Jewish communities was a *sheikh*, who
was the senior member of the community, and usually the most worldly and
the wealthiest.[29] He was appointed by the *bey* of the Gharian and served as the
intermediary between the Jewish community and the regional government. The
Jewish community was dependent upon him to represent its interests. It was
his duty to collect both government and Jewish communal taxes, the latter from
the sale of religious honors and from the *gabila*, a tax paid by the customer for
a ritually slaughtered animal.[30] The *sheikh* was not obligated to pay taxes himself. He also collected funds to support schools and teachers and for the upkeep
of the synagogue.

The *sheikh* had the power to decree corporal punishment for a transgression of religious practices. For example, if a Jewish adult—anyone over thirteen—was known to be avoiding prayer services in the synagogue, the *sheikh*
would direct his assistant to haul the offender into the synagogue. Here, the
assistant would remove the offender's shirt and mete out *malkut* (bastinado).

This consisted of up to thirty-nine lashes, depending on the offender's tolerance for physical punishment.

The Djebel Gharian region's Muslim authorities permitted the Jews to own land, which was used for grazing herds of goats and sheep and cultivating orchards and fields of grain. Land and flocks owned by Jews were tended by Muslims, who were paid a portion of the profit. The Jewish landowners fulfilled the biblical commandment of *leket* (gleanings), meaning that the remaining grain from a reaped field was to be collected by the poor in that region, Muslim as well as Jew. [31]

Many of the underground dwellers earned their living as shopkeepers, craftsmen, weavers, tinkers, and itinerant peddlers. Jewish smiths made agricultural tools, housewares, and weapons for the Muslims. In addition to domestic chores, such as grinding corn, drawing water, and chopping wood, Jewish women contributed to the family coffers by working as weavers or by cleaning grains after they were harvested. Crafts were bartered for crops at harvest time. During a drought or crop failure, Jewish craftsmen were the first to suffer. Jews in the rural areas were allowed to own land, and in some cases physically worked the field themselves. Where Jews owned flocks of livestock some were shepherds, but more commonly their flocks were tended by Muslims. [32]

As *dhimmi*, the Jews of Gharian were forbidden to wear bright-colored clothes. They dressed in black-hooded cloaks called *barracan*s (a garment that resembles a Roman toga). It had wide trousers like the Berber Bedouins', but with black garters around the knee. The Jews' turbans had to be black or blue, which were colors the Muslims avoided; red was the color worn by Muslims. Both Arabs and Jews shaved their heads, leaving just a clump of hair on the top of the skull. For the Arabs, this was to enable an angel to carry them to Heaven; for the Jews, this was as a reminder of the destruction of the Holy Temple.

"According to some European sources," writes Rachel Simon, "in the countryside, and especially in the Tripolitanian mountain (in Yefren and Gharyan) Jewish women were almost equal to men . . . they mingled freely with men, sat side by side with them, ate with their husbands, and young girls were unveiled."[33] Jewish women wore a one-piece shawl that was draped around the body. They tended to be heavily bedecked with engraved earrings, bracelets, and necklaces. The motif of the engravings was usually a *menorah* or a *Mogen David*. These metal ornaments were supposed to protect them from the evil eye.

The Jews of Djebel Gharian had certain Passover customs (or lack thereof) that were in contrast to Jewish communities everywhere else. Even though the Haggadah explicitly states, "Let all who are hungry come and eat," the Jewish cave dwellers would close the entrances of their dwellings on the *seder* nights and not accept guests. This behavior is attributed to the marrano existence the Jews were forced to endure, stemming from either the Almohades period or after Spanish conquest of Libya in the early sixteenth century. In either case, it was originally due to a fear of informers revealing that they were practicing their historical faith.[34]

In the cave regions of Gharian, the Jews used to celebrate a third day of Shevuot, unlike traditional Jews anywhere else in the world, who observe only two days. It was instituted by them in memory of Moses, who struck a rock that miraculously gushed forth water in the desert.[35]

According to the great Spanish-Jewish sage Moses Maimonides, the highest form of *tzedakah* (charity) is practiced when the donor has no idea to whom his gift is going and the recipient doesn't know the source. In Djebel Gharian, *tzedakah* was distributed in the following way: At the Thursday market the leaders of the community would approach other Jews to request that they donate money to help the poorer members of the community celebrate the Shabbat. These funds would then be discreetly distributed to avoid embarrassing the poor people.[36]

The Feast of Roses, or Engagement Day, was celebrated the day after Passover by all the Jewish communities of Libya. In Djebel Gharian girls would dress up in their finest clothing, gather around a well, and wait for young men to make their choices. A suitor would declare himself by throwing a rose to the girl he fancied. If she returned it, the boy would send his mother to the girl's house to discuss possible marriage. If she did not return the rose, things might get a little prickly. "Each person has a Mohammedan friend who stands by his side to help him against a fellow Jew who may oppose him," Mordechai Hacohen informs us. "If a youth desires a certain maiden, but her father refuses to give her to him, then the youth's Mohammedan friend intervenes in the affair so that the youth gets the maiden against her father's wishes."[37]

Since the cave dwellers' peddling occupations required many to be gone from the community for long periods, marriage ceremonies invariably took place on Jewish holidays, especially on Sukkot. The latter holiday was an especially good time because it coincided with the postharvest period when their Muslim clients could remunerate the Jews in kind for products and services provided.[38] The evening on which the bride was led from her father's dwelling to her husband's dwelling was called *lilet a-rahla* (the Night of the Journey). Prior to her departure, the bride had to swallow seven twisted cotton wicks dipped in olive oil.[39] She was covered with a veil and walked slowly, accompanied by two girl-friends. There was much chanting and dancing along the pathways until the bride arrived at the groom's place. Before entering the threshold of her betrothed, the bride would take a chicken egg out of her bosom and throw it against the wall, symbolizing the destruction of the Temple in Jerusalem.[40]

It was the custom that after the birth of a male child two eggs would be tossed against the ceiling.[41] After the circumcision in the synagogue, the father of the infant would be wrapped in his tallit (prayer shawl) until the newborn urinated. He would then invite the congregation to a toast of licorice brandy and a feast of lamb and *bazin*.[42] *Bazin* is the national dish of Libya, consisting of barley meal, olive oil, and pepper, and it is crumpled and eaten with the fingers.

During the savage pogrom of 1945, the Jewish communities in the Tripolitanian hinterland survived relatively unscathed. "Communal relations in Gharian," former cave-dwelling informants told Harvey Goldberg,

> were maintained with the help of ceremonial action. Local Muslim no-
> tables told the leaders of the Jewish community to hold a kind of "open
> house" in which food and drinks were lavishly served to all comers. For
> twenty-four consecutive hours Muslim and Jewish guests came in and
> out of the house of the Jewish sheikh. People reiterated pat phrases such
> as "we are brothers," "we have lived together for thousands of years,"
> "your father is our father," and "each man has his own religion." All of
> these statements, in contrast to the riot situation, celebrate[d] the same-
> ness of Jew and Muslim, and de-emphasize[d] the distinctions between
> the communities.[43]

In 1950–51 the cave-dwelling Jews of Djebel Gharian made *aliyah* to Israel together with the other Libyan Jews. They settled in the lush orange-growing region of the Sharon, north of Tel Aviv, where they established a *moshav* called Porat. Many of the former cave dwellers still reside in Porat today—in modern housing.

NOTES

1. Gwynn Williams, *Green Mountain* (London: Faber and Faber, 1963), pp. 39–40.

2. H. Z. Hirschberg, *A History of the Jews of North Africa,* vol. 1: *From Antiquity to the Sixteenth Century* (Leiden: E. J. Brill, 1974), p. 27.

3. Ibid., p. 28; Andre Chouraqui, *Between East and West: A History of the Jews of North Africa* (New York: Atheneum, 1973), p. 11; John M. G. Barclay, *Jews in the Mediterranean Diaspora: From Alexander to Trajan* (Edinburgh: T&T Clark, 1996), pp. 239–42.

4. Hirschberg, ibid., p. 31.

5. Ibid., p. 29. For details of the uprising see Joseph M. Modrzejewski, *The Jews of Egypt: From Ramsees II to Emperor Hadrian* (Princeton, N.J.: Princeton University Press, 1995), pp. 198–205; Shimon Applebaum, *Jews and Greeks in Ancient Cyrene* (Leiden: E. J. Brill, 1979), esp. ch. 6 and 7; and A. Kasher, "Some Comments on the Jewish Uprising in Egypt in the Time of Trajan," *Journal of Jewish Studies* 27:2 (Autumn 1976), pp. 147–58.

6. Sydney Mendelssohn, *The Jews of Africa: Especially in the Sixteenth and Seventeenth Centuries* (London: Keegan Paul, 1920), p. 64.

7. Ibid., p. 59.

8. Nahum Slouschz, *Travels in North Africa* (Philadelphia: The Jewish Publication Society, 1927), p. 109–11.

9. Ibid., p. 104.

10. Nina Epton, *Oasis Kingdom: The Libyan Story* (New York: Roy Publishers, 1951), p. 43.

11. Harvey E. Goldberg, *Jewish Life in Muslim Libya: Rivals and Relatives* (Chicago and London: The University of Chicago Press, 1990), p. 39.

12. Harvey E. Goldberg, and Claudio G. Segre, "Holding on to Both Ends: Religious Continuity and Change in the Libyan Jewish Community, 1860–1949," *Maghreb Review* 14:3–4 (1989), p. 168.

13. Slouschz, *Travels*, p. 7.

14. Ibid., p. 8.

15. Harvey E. Goldberg, *Cave Dwellers and Citrus Growers: A Jewish Community in Libya and Israel* (Cambridge: Cambridge University Press, 1972), p. 20.

16. For detailed accounts of the riot, see Harvey E. Goldberg, *Jewish Life*, ch. 7; and Renzo De Felice, *Jews in an Arab Land: Libya 1835–1970* (Austin: University of Texas, 1985), ch. 7.

17. S. Landshut, *Jewish Communities in the Muslim Countries of the Middle East: A Survey* (London: The Jewish Chronicle, 1950), p. 91.

18. For firsthand descriptions of Jewish life in the caves see Slouschz, *The Jews*, esp. pp. 115–47; D. Kleinlerer, "Cave Dwellers of North Africa," *The Jewish Tribune* 4:22 (31 May 1929), pp. 1 and 4; and Lawrence Resner, *Eternal Stranger: the Plight of the Modern Jew from Baghdad to Casablanca* (Garden City, N.Y.: Doubleday, 1951), pp. 105–109.

19. Goldberg, *Cave Dwellers*, p. 38.

20. For a detailed description of the physical geography of Tripolitania see David J. Mattingly, *Tripolitania* (Ann Arbor: University of Michigan Press, 1994), pp. 9–14.

21. H. T. Norris, "Cave Habitations and Granaries in Tripolitania and Tunisia, *Man* (Old Series) 53, 125 (June 1953), p. 82.

22. Miriam Nick, "The Jewish Cave Dwellers of North Africa," *Museum Haaretz*, Bulletin no. 9 (June 1967), pp. 106–107.

23. Norris, "Cave Habitations," p. 82.

24. Resner, *Eternal Stranger*, p. 107.

25. *The New Tripoli, And What I Saw in the Hinterland.* (London: T. Fish, 1914), pp. 238–39.

26. Kleinlerer, "Cave Dwellers," p. 4.

27. Paul W. Copeland, *The Land and People of Libya* (Philadelphia: Lippincott, 1967), p. 79; Anthony Thwaite, *The Deserts of Hesperides* (London: Secker and Warburg, 1989), pp. 92–93.

28. Slouschz, *The Jews*, pp. 101–102.

29. For a discussion of the role of the Jewish *sheikh* see Harvey E. Goldberg, "From Sheikh to Mazkir: Structural Continuity and Organizational Change in the Leadership of a Tripolitanian Jewish Community," *Folklore Research Center Studies* 1 (1970), pp. 29–41.

30. Goldberg, *Cave Dwellers*, p. 33.

31. Ibid., p. 17.

32. Ibid., p. 262.

33. Rachel Simon, *Change Within Tradition Among Jewish Women in Libya* (Seattle: University of Washington Press, 1992), p. 29.

34. Slouschz, *The Jews*, p. 237; Yishak Sabban, "The Customs of Libyan Jews," *The Sephardic Scholar*, Series 3 (1977–78), p. 91.

35. Mendelssohn, *The Jews*, p. 67.

36. Goldberg, *Cave Dwellers*, p. 33.

37. Harvey E. Goldberg, ed., *The Book of Mordechai: A Study of the Jews of Libya* (Philadelphia: Institute for the Study of Human Issues, 1980), p. 140.

38. Ibid., p. 125.

39. Harvey E. Goldberg, "The Jewish Wedding in Tripolitania: A Study in Cultural Sources," *Maghreb Review*, 3:9 (1978), p. 2.

40. Goldberg, *Book of Mordechai*, p. 124.

41. Nick, "Jewish Cave Dwellers," p. 108.

42. Goldberg, *Book of Mordechai*, p. 121.

43. Goldberg, *Jewish Life*, p. 121.

Part XIII

Jewish Bride, from the Island of Djerba, Tunisia
Adorned with gold jewelry and her hands dyed in
special patterns with henna, she prepares for the
traditional fourteen-day wedding celebration.
Credit: Keren T. Friedman

From the Land of the Lotus Eaters

BACKGROUND INFORMATION

The Arab Republic of Tunisia lies on the Mediterranean coast, squeezed between Algeria on the west and Libya on the east. It is equal in size to the state of Missouri. Tunisia's total population is estimated at nine million. Along with Morocco and Algeria, it forms the Berber-influenced part of North Africa known as the Maghreb, which means "west" in Arabic. Formerly a French colony, Tunisia has been a constitutional republic since 1956. The capital is Tunis and the official language is Arabic, with French widely spoken as a second language.

According to local Berber tradition, the Canaanites, who were driven out of Palestine by Joshua, settled in Tunisia. These Canaanites, who came to be known as Phoenicians, later built the great city of Carthage, near the site of modern Tunis. Carthage, "Mistress of the Sea," was destroyed by Rome in 146 B.C.E. In time, and in turn, other conquerors followed: Vandals, fifth century C.E.; Byzantines, sixth century; Arabs, seventh century; Spaniards and Ottomans, sixteenth century; and French, nineteenth century. The Arab component of Tunisian society was introduced twice, during the conquests of the seventh century C.E. and after the Almohades invasion in the twelfth century. Because there were no mountain lairs in Tunisia to retreat to—as, for example, in Morocco, where the Berber people put up fierce resistance against the invaders— the Tunisian Berbers quickly embraced the Muslims' religion and culture and intermarried with them.

Jerba is a small island lying just off the southeast coast of Tunisia, in the gulf of Gabes. Its population is estimated at 70,000. Jerba was immortalized in Homer's epic poem "The Odyssey." Jerba was said to be the land of the lotus-eaters that enchanted Ulysses and his sailors when they joyously ate the fruit of the lotus. In reality, the lotus plant has never been known to grow on this arid, semidesert island.[1]

In Phoenician times Jerba was known as Meninx, and was a great trading center since antiquity for the production of purple dye. Its economy since Roman times was based mainly on the growing of olives. Throughout the centuries Jerba has served as an island haven for people fleeing religious and political persecution. In the sixteenth century the island became an issue in the struggle between Spain and the Ottomans for mastery of the Mediterranean. Jerba finally came under Turkish rule in 1631.

Whereas the people on the Tunisian mainland are a mixture of Berber and Arab stock, those of the island are almost entirely of unmixed Berber stock. Due to great isolation and much inbreeding, the Jerbans evolved into a distinctive racial type.[2] On Jerba, half the population still speaks the Berber tongue. The Jerban Berbers belong to the Kharidjite sect of Sunni Islam in which a Jewish element is very distinct. In sharp contrast with the mainland, Jerban society has until very recent times been nominally impacted by Western trends. Today it is a favorite beach resort for European youth.

THE JEWS OF JERBA, TUNISIA

> The further south in Tunisia, the further back in time one goes,
> till history fades into legend and legend into mythology.
>
>   —John Anthony, *About Tunisia* (1961)

> Lured by the soothing sound of flowing water you enter the
> world of the date palm. The scent of Jasmine follows you in
> every direction.
>
>   —Keren T. Friedman, *The Rabbi with the*
> *Long White Beard* (1973)

Judeo-African tradition ascribes the earliest settlement of Jews on Jerba to Davidic and Solomonic times, as well as during the Babylonian captivity in 586 B.C.E. in the Punic-Carthaginian age. These communities were augmented by subsequent arrivals of Jews after the destruction of the Second Temple in 70 C.E., when 30,000 Jewish slaves were settled throughout Carthage by the Roman emperor Titus.[3] Spanish refugees, fleeing persecution by the Visigothic kings, increased the population in the seventh century. In the seventeenth century Southern European Sephardic merchants known as Granas also settled in Tunisia.

Throughout the centuries—the period of Almohades rule being an exception—the Jews of Tunisia have lived under relatively tolerant conditions. During the centuries of foreign aggression the Jews lived in separate quarters called *hara*s and managed to retain their own identity and way of life. Although *dhimmi* (subject People of the Scriptures), they were given much latitude and controlled much of the trade and commerce of the country. Tunisian Jews flourished as international merchants, interpreters, diplomats, and government officials.

During the age of the enlightened Aghlabid emirs (tenth and eleventh centuries) Kairouan, the capital of Ifriquiya (Tunisia), was transformed into a great center of Islamic and Jewish learning. Kairouan supplanted Babylonia as one of the preeminent spiritual centers of Jewish life, producing a preponderance of outstanding rabbis, scholars, and *naggidim* (princes). The Jewish community of Ifriquiya experienced great adversity during the periods of the Almohades and Spanish conquests. With emancipation after the onset of French rule in 1881, even greater opportunities opened up for the Jews, and a secularization process began to set in. As late as 1945 there were an estimated 100,000

Jews in Tunisia, half of whom lived in the capital, Tunis. The other largest Jewish communities on the mainland were concentrated in Sfax and Sousse. Since the creation of the State of Israel and Tunisian independence, their numbers have steadily declined. Most have emigrated to France, while smaller numbers have settled in Israel and the United States. Today there are fewer than 3,000 Jews left in all of Tunisia.

Since the Jews of the Tunisian mainland are predominantly Sephardim, heavily influenced by the Spanish exiles, they are outside the purview of this book. Of greater interest here is the ancient Jewish enclave on the island of Jerba. Described by the noted anthropologist Clifford Geertz as "a capital of dug-in provincial culture,"[4] Jerba is the only example we have left of Jewish "*shtetl*" life in North Africa.

The Jews of Jerba were considered to be the most pious and traditional of Tunisian Jewry, and they developed a reputation for producing great rabbis who wrote prodigious, scholarly tomes. Unlike the Jews of the mainland, the Jerban Jews (like their Muslim neighbors) made little contact with the French colonialists, and therefore until very recent times knew very little of Western ways. The Jews of Jerba, led by their rabbis, stubbornly resisted any attempts to introduce secular education and modern fashions into the community.

Like the Eastern European Chassidim and the Yemenites in their respective milieus, the Jews of Jerba had little social intercourse with the non-Jewish population. They lived in their separate villages and did not utilize the local Arabic script. Their Arabic was so heavily laden with Hebrew words that the Jerban-Jewish dialect was incomprehensible to the local Berber population. "Whatever their early history," notes Anthony Sylvester, "they appear to be Jews by racial origin, not converted natives of Djerba. The reason for this, adduced by scholars, is that the Jews have long heads and aquiline noses while the rest of the Djerban people are mostly brachycephallic.[5] At its height before 1948 the Jewish community was estimated at 4,500. The thousand or so Jews who still live on the island to this day still preserve many ancient traditions while continuing to live in a rabbinic theocracy.[6]

According to the oldest local beliefs, the Jerban Jews go back to Davidic times. Joab ben Tzeruya, King David's general, is said to have pursued the Philistine enemy all the way to the island.[7] Ancient tales tell us that the earliest Jerban Jews are the progeny of a tribe of *kohanim* (priests) who fled from Jerusalem after the destruction of the Temple by Titus in 70 C.E. Another viewpoint ascribes the arrival of these priests even earlier, to the First Temple period after the Babylonian devastation in 586 B.C.E. In any event, they are said to have salvaged a stone with Hebrew inscriptions and a door from the Temple. Although these relics are nowhere to be seen, some of the residents believed they were incorporated into the foundations of the El Ghriba Synagogue.

Throughout the centuries Jerba was off-limits to Levites, who had considered making the island their permanent home. Legend has it that when Ezra requested the ingathering of the exiles, few Levites accepted the invitation. Because of a great dearth of priestly assistants, he entreated the Levites of Jerba to respond to his call, but his earnest request fell on deaf ears. Bitterly disappointed, Ezra cursed the Jerban Levites, and within a year they all died. Consequently, the sages on the island decreed that all visiting Levites must remove themselves from the island before one year passed.[8]

The original Jewish communities were augmented by some Jewish "draft dodgers" in North Africa who found asylum on the island, circa 790 C.E. After the imam Idris proclaimed Mauritania independent of the caliphate of Baghdad, many of the Ubaid Allah Jewish tribe were recruited into the imam's army. However, when they realized they would be pitted against fellow Jews who were under the command of the caliph of Baghdad, the Ubaid Allah tribe refused to serve. In retaliation, the imam attacked them and dealt them a serious blow. Among other things, he decreed that the Jews would have to pay an exorbitant poll tax and would be obligated to provide the imams' harem with a yearly quota of Jewish virgins. Rather than accede to the tyrant's demands, the tribe fled en masse to the island of Jerba.[9]

More Jews arrived in Jerba from other parts of North Africa during the intolerant Almohades rule (twelfth and thirteenth centuries), and after the expulsion from Spain in 1492. In the nineteenth century a small group of Jews, mostly merchants from Italy, settled in the village of Hara Kebira. These latter were more Westernized and did not mix with the native Jews, whom they perceived as retrograde and unenlightened. The rift between the newcomers and the indigenous Jews on the island in many ways mirrored the split that had developed within the Jewish community in Tunis a century earlier. In the mainland capital, a schism occurred between the Touansa, or native Jews, and the Grana, eighteenth-century arrivals from Italy. The two communities were polarized by acute differences in custom, culture, and economic status, the Grana being far more affluent and Westernized.[10]

The two Jewish villages in Jerba are five miles apart in distance and are located in the desert area outside the town limits. Hara Kebira, "The Big Village," is located near the market town of Houmt Souk. Hara Sghira, "The Little Village," seven kilometers to the south, is the site of El Ghriba, the "Marvelous Synagogue." In former times Hara Sghira was inhabited exclusively by a clan of *kohanim* (priests) who tended to keep themselves apart from the other Jews on the island. In commemoration of the destruction of the Temple, instrumental music was banned at Hara Sghira. Even the presence of musical instruments was not tolerated.

El Ghriba is perhaps the oldest synagogue in continuous existence in the world. It is a sacred place to Muslims as well as Jews. The synagogue is called El Ghriba or "the Stranger" after a legendary Jewish girl who arrived out of nowhere. The townspeople revered her as a *marabout* (saint) for the miracles she performed. The walls of the synagogue are adorned with magnificent tiles, Byzantine columns, a carved wooden pulpit, and exquisite silver work. The floors are covered with straw mats. The synagogue has two chambers: the sanctuary where the congregants pray, and the *kodesh kadashim* or Holy of Holies. Shoes are removed when entering the *kodesh kadashim* in the chamber where the Torah scrolls are kept. At one time the *kodesh kadashim* contained some hundred Torah scrolls. According to Nahum Slouschz, none of these Torah scrolls date back earlier than seventeenth century. Slouschz, a French professor who visited Jerba in the early 1900s, was told by his informants that as soon as the rollers of the Torah scrolls were worn out, it was the custom to bury the *sefer torah* with the body of a saintly man.[11]

Jerban Jewish men sit cross-legged or lie on their backs while praying. They dress in long cloaks with burnooses (hoods) and wear black bands around their knee-length pantaloons to signify their mourning for the destruction of the Temple. This, more than any other feature, distinguishes the Jews from the rest of the population.

El Ghriba drew pilgrims from all over North Africa. The pious, the lame, the poverty-stricken, the barren, and the diseased all converged with supplications for healing. They would also bring with them money for charitable donations. People would come all year round, but especially for Yom Kippur and for the spring festival of Lag B'Omer. On Lag B'Omer the Jews commemorated the founding of the synagogue by the refugee priests and also the appearance of the mystery girl who performed miracles. The highlight of the event was the Procession of the Menorah, when thousands of the faithful paraded in and around the synagogue carrying an enormous silver candelabrum. Girls desiring to get married left a raw egg on the spot where the miracle-making girl's dead body is supposed to have been found.

Many of the *minhagim* (customs) of the Jews of Jerba are ancient and not found in Jewish communities elsewhere. Their traditions were often interspersed with the folkways and superstitions of the Berber Muslim natives. Every Friday before the onset of the Shabbat it was customary for the Jewish women of Jerba to visit the graves of their relatives and lament over them. To announce the onset of the Sabbath, a ram's horn was blown. During the Kol Nidre service on Yom Kippur the worshippers sought to intensify their atonement by standing barefoot on hard chickpeas.[12] The Passover *charoset* left over from the *seder* was pasted on the side of the doorway to ward off evil spirits.[13] On Shevuot young girls wore cookie necklaces shaped to represent key objects in the holiday story: for example, tablet shapes to symbolize the Torah; a ladder to recall Moses climbing Mt. Sinai; and hand and finger shapes denoting hands reaching for the Torah.

Like their Muslim neighbors, Jewish women wore the Hand of Fatima charms called *hamsa* to protect them against the evil eye. They wore necklaces of colored stones and fish teeth to ward off diseases. Paintings of fish adorned the entrance of the house and the walls of Jewish homes to bring good luck, productivity, and fertility. Doors were painted blue because blue was considered an auspicious color.

Marriages were traditionally arranged by the parents soon after their children's birth. Usually couples were actually married when barely into their teens. It was quite common to marry within one's family. For instance, uncles frequently married nieces. Polygamy was permitted, and some rich men had as many as four wives. The bride did not meet the groom until the night of the wedding. During the engagement period the in-laws exchanged couscous dishes on *Erev Shabbat*.[14]

In the old days fat was beautiful in Tunisia (and everywhere else in North Africa), a sign of vibrant health and good breeding. No Jewish girl could be obese enough for her intended.[15] As soon as a young girl was engaged, she was forcefed in order to make her plump. If she was already plump, she consumed large quantities of food to add sheer bulk until she reached the most desirable buxom state. Meats cooked in rich sauces, sweets, fenugreek seeds, and other fat-producing foods were used by women to induce obesity. Forty to fifty large pellets of bread crumbs were crammed down the gullet with the fingers as far as possible—much in the same way as one stuffs a goose—and washed down with sips of tea. This gorging regimen was done two or three times a day, and the twenty-day stretch before the actual wedding night was the period of most intense cramming, so that by the time a bride was led to the canopy she might weigh more than two hundred pounds.[16] This custom is no longer followed because today's Jewish men are more often attracted to slender women. In fact, the heavier girls have a more difficult time finding a groom.

A week before the wedding ceremony the Henna Festival commenced. Before entering the ritualarium with her entourage, the bride was given a candy to suck on in order to ensure a sweet life. The bride pasted a thick coat of henna dye on her hands and feet to symbolize happiness through fertility. The henna ceremonies lasted for several days. In former times, wedding festivities lasted over a month, and even today they are lavish affairs lasting twelve to fourteen days. The bride wore a loose dress called *kamizsa* that hung straight with no waist-line. She wore a headdress of gold coins, and her face was covered with a shroud-like veil called *sifsari*, which was clutched by hand or held in the teeth.[17]

Two unique traditions in the Jerban-Jewish lifecycle should be noted here. After the *brit millah* ceremony, the *mohel* exhibited his blood-spotted fingers in all directions. "The privilege of picking up the foreskin in a clay pot, of showing the tools of the operation to the assembled men, and of marking the threshold of the room with blood from the foreskin is then sold twice a year in the syna-gogue. It is a mitzvah, which benefits the person who acquires it; the proceeds go to the community's charitable works."[18] When the baby reached *bar mitzvah* age, he was called up to read from the Torah, and was sprayed with spiced water.[19]

In premodern times Jewish women, like their Muslim counterparts, wore a veil when out in public. However, Jewish women, unlike the Muslim women, refrained from tattooing themselves, because this is strictly forbidden by Jew-ish law. Jewish women wore red brimless caps that were adorned with distinc-tive gold and silver embellishments. This headgear was held in place by the woman's braids, which were pulled through slits in the side of the cap. Their outer garments were also of a different pattern from the Muslim women's.

Jewish men traditionally wore a red *chechia* (beret), which distinguished them from their Muslim neighbors, who wore black caps. Jewish and Arab men still wear the same kind of baggy Turkish trousers, called *sarwal arabi*. Over this, they wear hooded cloaks or long-sleeved striped robes. What distinguished Jew-ish men from the Muslim men on the island were their curly *peot* and the black stripes sewn around the cuffs of their pants.

The great Jewish philosopher Moses Maimonides, whose family fled to North Africa in the wake of the Almohades persecutions in Spain, observed that the Jews of Jerba were simple and pious folks, but also unlettered and quite superstitious.[20] The Jerban Jews must have taken the great Sephardi sage's opin-ion of them to heart. For many centuries thereafter, Jerba produced rabbis in greater proportion than other Jewish communities in North Africa. "Export-ing" rabbis and *kohanim* to the Maghrebian hinterland has been one of the Jerban community's chief activities. In recent times a Jerban rabbi was appointed chief rabbi of Tunisia. Jerba is also a North African center for the writing and pub-lishing of rabbinic tracts.[21] It is for these reasons that Jerba has been called "the Jerusalem of Africa." As everywhere else in North Africa, great rabbis of Jerba were believed to be wonder workers endowed with supernatural powers. They were revered as saints and their tombs were visited by pilgrims, Muslim as well as Jewish, from all over North Africa. Nevertheless, saint worship among the Jerban Jews was not quite as pervasive as it was in other places in North Africa. Harvey Goldberg posits that the "hagiolatry among the Jews of Jerba, [which focuses] on a synagogue rather than a saint [is] a 'compromise formation' representing Jewish accommodation to the Ibadi [local Muslim] rejection of saint worship."[22]

Rabbinic jurisdiction, the *beit din*, extended over every aspect of people's lives. For example, anyone derelict in synagogue attendance might be subject to corporal punishment (*malkut*). The actual responsibility of meting out punishment was delegated to the *mukadam*, or communal head. The *mukadam*, usually the wealthiest man in the community, was also responsible for upholding law and order and collecting taxes. He was a dictatorial ruler, accountable only to the *bey* or governor of the island. This position was abolished when Tunisia became a French Protectorate.

The Jews of Jerba were involved in a wide variety of traditional crafts but were renowned as goldsmiths. Some Jews were engaged in the trades, specializing in masonry and carpentry, and in mattress, saddle, and harness making. Some kept small shops, while others were wine merchants and itinerant peddlers. Still others bought crops and sheep's wool from farmers and sold them in the Houmt Souk. Many Jews owned land but did not farm the land themselves.[23] In the Houmt Souk there were designated Jewish streets marking separate Jewish trades. Since families were large, most Jews barely eked out a livelihood.

With the beginning of Tunisian independence in 1956 under President Habib Bourghuiba, the Jews were granted equal rights with the rest of the population. The Jews had been strong supporters of the nationalists in their struggle for independence from France, and a Jewish attorney was appointed to a ministerial post in the newly formed government. President Bourghuiba followed a path of moderation vis-à-vis Israel long before Anwar Sadat of Egypt did. It was Bourghuiba's criticism of the Arab League in 1965 on the Palestinian question and his advocacy of direct negotiations with Israel that led to a break in relations with Egypt. Even so, the staunchly religio-Zionistic Jerban Jews found themselves lured by the promise of Israel. Emigration commenced in 1948, and increased in wake of the 1967 Six Day War. The acceleration of the departures was propelled by the stoning of the Jerban Chief Rabbi's home during the heat of the Yom Kippur War in 1973 and the murder of two Jerban Jews in the aftermath of an Israeli bombing raid on Palestinian headquarters south of Tunis in 1985.

From Bourghuiba's time forward, Tunisia's leaders have always assured the Jewish community that they have no reason to be afraid of living there. Despite the freedoms they enjoy, the Jews have felt insecure in Tunisia because of Islamic fundamentalists and the menace of Palestinian terrorists. The PLO had its headquarters in Tunis until 1994, when it moved to the Gaza Strip.

Tunisian Jews are not allowed to go directly to Israel. They invariably make *aliyah* from Italy or France. In Israel, the Jerban Jews have formed distinct communities in the cities of Ashkelon, Beersheva, and in the Negev. Many have settled in *moshavim*, the largest of these being Moshav Eitan on the Beersheba road.

NOTES

1. Edouard Roditi, "North African Jews," *The Menorah Journal* (Spring–Summer 1955), p. 72.

2. Geoffrey Furlonge, *The Lands of Barbary* (London: John Murray, 1966), p. 50.

3. Nahum Slouschz, *Travels in North Africa* (Philadelphia: Jewish Publication Society, 1927), p. 273.

4. "The Ultimate Ghetto," *The New York Review of Books* (28 February 1985), p.14.

5. *Tunisia* (London: The Bodley Head, 1969), pp. 98–99.

6. On contemporary Jewish life in Jerba see Shlomo Deshen, "Near the Jerba Beach: Tunisian Jews, an Anthropologist, and Other Visitors," *Jewish Social Studies* New Series 3:2 (Winter 1997), pp. 90–118.

7. Slouschz, *Travels*, p. 257.

8. Ibid., p. 258.

9. Marion Woolfson, *Prophets in Babylon: Jews in the Arab World* (London: Faber and Faber, 1980), p. 73.

10. For a study of the conflict between the Touansa and Grana see Yaron Tsur, "The Two Jewish Communities of Tunis (Touansa and Grana) on the Eve of the Colonial Period," *Proceedings of the Ninth World Congress of Jewish Studies,* Division B, 3 (Jerusalem, 1986), pp. 67–73.

11. *Travels*, p. 265.

12. Dvorah Hacohen and Menachem Hacohen, *One People: The Story of the Eastern Jews.* (New York: Adama Books, 1986), p. 91.

13. Ibid., p. 92.

14. Lucette Valensi, "Religious Orthodoxy or Local Tradition: Marriage Celebration in Southern Tunisia," in *Jews Among Arabs: Contacts and Boundaries*, edited by Mark R. Cohen and Abraham L. Udovitch (Princeton, N.J.: The Darwin Press, 1989), pp. 70–71.

15. Graham Petrie, *Tunis, Kairouan, and Carthage* (London: William Heinemann, 1908), p. 142.

16. Ruth Gruber, *Israel Today: Land of Many Nations* (New York: Hill and Wang, 1958), p. 148.

17. Keren Tzionah Friedman, "I Am a Picture: Change and Continuity on the Island of Djerba," *Folklore and Mythology* 2:3 (December 1983), p. 4.

18. Abraham L. Udovitch and Lucette Valensi, *The Last Arab Jews: The Communities of Jerba, Tunisia* (London: Harwood Academic Publications, 1984), p. 53.

19. Hacohen and Hacohen, *One People*, p. 86.

20. For an analysis of Maimonides' statements regarding North African Jewry and the Jews of Jerba in particular see Udovitch and Valensi, *The Last Arab Jews*, pp. 11–13.

21. "Over the past hundred years," write Udovitch and Valensi, "the Jewish community of this island has produced close to 500 books. [I]t might in reality be much higher. These data would be of little significance...if it were not for the fact that the community we are talking about numbered, for most of this period, between 2000 and 3000 people...and that, until recently, none of its women could read or write. Furthermore, this is a community in which ninety percent of the males earn their livelihood by the sweat of their brow." Ibid., pp. 84–85.

22. "Jerba and Tripoli: A Comparative Analysis of Two Jewish Communities in the Maghreb," *Journal of Mediterranean Studies* 4:2 (1994), p. 292.

23. Margaret Wilder, *The Djerban Diaspora: A Tunisian Study of Migration and Ethnicity* (unpublished dissertation, University of Pennsylvania, 1980), pp. 58–59.

Part XIV

Jews from Quara, Ethiopia
Credit: Peggy Myers

The Queen of Sheba's Lost Children

BACKGROUND INFORMATION

The Federal Democratic Republic of Ethiopia is a landlocked highland country situated in the Horn of Africa. It lies at a geographical and cultural crossroads between Black Africa, Muslim North Africa, and the South Arabian Peninsula. The capital is Addis Ababa, and the official language is Amharic. Ethiopia has been referred to as the roof of Africa. With almost 450,000 square miles, it is nearly three times the size of California.

Ethiopia is one of the poorest and least developed countries in the world, according to the United Nations Food and Agricultural Organization. Ninety percent of the population lives in rural areas. Its fifty-five million people are perennially plagued by famine, disease, and civil strife. Known as Kush in biblical times and Abbysinia in the Middle Ages, Ethiopia (Greek for "land of the burnt faces") is one of the oldest civilizations in the world. According to local legend, Ethiopus was the son of Ham and grandson of Noah. Ethiopia has been described as a "museum of peoples, languages, and faiths."[1] This is due to numerous invasions and large-scale migrations into the region.

Ethiopians of the northern plateau are believed to be descended from indigenous Black Africans and an amalgam of peoples who invaded their land from around 2000 B.C.E. to the early centuries of the Common Era. The three main sources of external influence are the Kushitic peoples on the west, Semitic peoples on the east, and Mediterranean peoples on the north. The Ethiopians are an Afro-Arabian people, with the Kushitic grouping being absorbed by the less numerous but more culturally advanced and powerful Semitic elements.[2] By the beginning of the Common Era, one Semitized group known as the Amhara established a powerful kingdom in Ethiopia, with Axum as its capital.

The *Kebra Negast* or "Book of the Glory of the Kings" is the historical charter of Ethiopia. One modern scholar has described this chronicle as "a pastiche of legends conflated early in the fourteenth century" by court biographers intent on legitimizing the rule of a "restored" House of Solomon.[3] According to the *Kebra Negast*, before the advent of Christianity Judaism was widespread in the Ethiopian highlands—so much so that half the inhabitants worshipped the Mosaic God (the other half adored the Serpent King). In the fourth century, as a result of maritime commercial relations with the Byzantine Empire, Orthodox Christianity was introduced to the ruling class in Axum. During this epoch Christian Ethiopia was a mighty empire that colonized the South Arabian Peninsula. The Greek Bible was probably translated into Ge'ez, or classical Ethiopic, during this early period of Christian expansion.

"The . . . ancient legends on which Ethiopian tradition is based . . ." writes Polson Newman, "enshroud a little-known Christian country with a romantic glamour, carrying the mind back to stories of the Queen of Sheba, King Solomon, and the Ark of the Covenant; but when it is realized that the imagination of the Ethiopian people has been purposely stimulated all along the line for political purposes, a great deal of the glamour disappears to reveal indisputable facts of a very unromantic nature. Religious tradition has for centuries been utilised as a means of fostering the appearance of national unity, and the first thing every usurper has done has been to arrange through the Church a pedigree showing his descent from Solomon. Indeed the matter has been so overdone that it has reduced itself to a farce."[4]

To legitimize their claim to rule by divine right the Amharic Christian elites perpetuated a historical fiction that they were descended from an uninterrupted line of kings whose lineage traced back to Menelek I, the offspring of the mythical union of King Solomon and the Queen of Sheba. By aligning themselves with the House of Israel, they could trace their lineage from Shem rather than Ethiopus, the offspring of the accursed Ham.[5] In this way too they could buttress their claim to having been descended from people who practiced monotheism even before the advent of Christianity.[6] The last *negus* (monarch) of Ethiopia, Haile Selassie, ruled for forty-four years (1930–74) and referred to himself as the "Lion of Judah." Haile Selassie took pride in claiming to be the 225th emperor in the royal line from Menelek I.

Ethiopia's inaccessibility largely accounts for its resistance to Islam, which swept across North Africa in the seventh and eighth centuries. The old sea routes were severed, and Axum was cut off from Byzantium. On the wane by the ninth century, and reduced to a political nonentity by the twelfth century, the Axumite dynasty was overthrown by a federation of Kushitic tribes known as the Zagwe. In 1270 the original "Solomonic line" was restored. In the course of the next four centuries the Amharic Christian warlords engaged in sporadic wars with their Muslim, Agaw, and Beta Israel neighbors, in time subjugating them all. However, Ethiopia did not emerge from its isolation to become a unified modern state until the middle of the nineteenth century under Emperor Hailu Tewodros.

Until the Marxist revolution in 1974, the Ethiopian Orthodox Church was the official state religion. Orthodox Christianity is prevalent in the northern and central highlands. The Muslim element, mostly drawn from the Oromo (the country's largest single ethnic group), are predominant in the eastern or coastal regions and may, in fact, constitute the largest religious group in the country. The Shanqalla (Black African) population in the southern region held animistic beliefs.

Until 1950, the head of the Ethiopian Orthodox Church was the *abuna* (bishop) appointed by the Patriarch of Alexandria. The Ethiopian Orthodox Christian Church, although closely akin to that of Egypt's Coptic Church and following its lead implicitly on doctrinal matters (i.e., in its rejection of the Roman Catholic man/God duality of Christ), nevertheless has been accused by the latter of heretical (read: Jewish) tendencies. Rejecting the traditional Pauline Christian doctrine that claims that biblical law lost its binding force at the coming of Jesus, the Ethiopian church has retained many rites and customs of ancient Judaism. The Old Testament is as sacred as the New Testament, male children are circumcised on the eighth day, pork is forbidden, Saturday as well as Sunday is kept holy, and in former times, sacrifices were made throughout the year. The calendar is reckoned from Adam and Eve, not from Jesus. Churches are reputed to be built on the plan of King Solomon's temple, and the priests dance around the Holy of Holies like the *kohanim* of Biblical times.

THE BETA ISRAEL OF ETHIOPIA

> In Ethiopia, the distinction between Judaism and Christianity is so
> obliterated that when people say Christianity they might as well
> have Judaism in mind, or vice versa.
>   —Teshalo Tibebu, *The Making of Modern Ethiopia,*
>   *1896–1974* (1995)

If one accepts as axiomatic the view of some elements within the Orthodox rabbinate that the Beta Israel have been cut off from the main body of the
Jewish people since at least talmudic times, then the Beta Israel of Ethiopia certainly qualify as the "most lost" of the lost tribes of Israel dealt with in this book.
The Beta Israel lived in some 500 rural districts located in the most remote and
highest-altitude *ambas* (mountain fastnesses) of northwest Ethiopia. As a result,
the religion of the Beta Israel was tempered by their surroundings to a far greater
extent than other Jewish communities in other countries were affected by their
isolation.

The Beta Israel were strict proto-Mosaics who knew nothing of the talmudic traditions that have shaped normative Judaism for the last two millennia.
They knew nothing of the celebrations of Fast of Esther and Chanukah, which
were instituted in Palestine during the Second Commonwealth. They were never
known to have had knowledge of Hebrew. Until the mid nineteenth century,
because of their great isolation, the Beta Israel thought they were the only Jews
left in the world. But the Beta Israel's claims to Jewishness were—and are to
this day—viewed with much skepticism by world Jewry and many modern scholars. This dissension arises from the great antiquity of the Beta Israel's beliefs,
practices, and oral history, which predate written language. Archaeological
evidence, documentation, research results, and scientific findings all tend to be
inconclusive—leaving them open to varied interpretations. Each interpretation
and theory has significant arguments in its favor, as well as in opposition to its
validity. All the differences in opinion, however, have not shaken the Beta Israel's
conviction and assertion that they are, indeed, Jews.

The Beta Israel themselves do not know exactly when their Jewish ancestors came to Ethiopia. They believe that subsequent to Menelek I there were
many waves of migrations to Ethiopia. Each group arrived at a different period,
intermarried with the local people, and converted them to Judaism.

There are no clear records, from any time, anywhere, of Jewish migrations into Ethiopia. However, there are many fascinating theories about the

origins of the Beta Israel. Some are based entirely on oral traditions or myths. Others contain little more than a shred of historical truth. Still others seem scientifically more feasible, despite a great lack of documentation and archaeological evidence. In nearly every case, it is difficult to know where fact ends and fiction begins.

According to a legend handed down from Josephus in the second century C.E., Moses, in his pre-liberator incarnation, served as a general in an Egyptian army that waged war on the Ethiopians. Having defeated them in battle, Moses took as his bride an Ethiopian princess and ruled in Ethiopia. Their offspring became the progenitors of the Beta Israel.[7]

Far more famous, and more popular, is the saga of King Solomon and Makeda, the Queen of Sheba. This story is a creative spin on the biblical story in I Kings 10:1–13 and the Ethiopian national epic *Kebra Negast*, and is accepted as God's truth by Ethiopian Christians as well as by the Beta Israel. The Queen of Sheba, the story goes, with 900 camels laden with precious gifts, visited the wise king in Jerusalem "to prove him with hard questions."[8] Enchanted by her exquisite beauty and moral excellence, Solomon—who by the latest count already had four hundred wives and six hundred concubines—invited her to sleep with him in his palatial bedchamber. To Solomon's dismay, the virgin queen rebuffed his advances. Insulted by her rejection, but not willing to take her by force, Solomon made the Queen of Sheba swear that she would have to yield to his desires if she took anything in his possession without permission. That evening the guileful king served the Queen a ten-course dinner consisting of nothing but hot and spicy dishes ("with wise intent," the text remarks). Feigning sleep, he kept a vigilant eye on her. During the night the queen woke up with parched mouth and rushed over to the well to quench her thirst. "Aha! I've caught you stealing my water!" Solomon exclaimed, and the Queen of Sheba had no choice but to accede to his wishes.

After the Queen returned to Ethiopia she bore Solomon a son, Menelek. When the boy came of age, the queen sent him to live with his father in Jerusalem. Upon completing his education, Menelek was crowned King of Ethiopia in Jerusalem and then returned to his homeland with a retinue of 10,000 young men from the leading aristocratic and priestly families of Israel. These retainers married into the local population and succeeded in converting large numbers of the pagan population to the Jewish religion. According to legend, Menelek stole the Ark of the Covenant from King Solomon's temple. The Ark was later transferred to the holy city of Axum (the Jerusalem of Ethiopia), where the Amharic Christians claim it exists (under guard) to this very day.[9] As one historian explains, "The *Kebra Negast*'s messages are clear, Menelek had bested his father, in a way avenging [the Queen of Sheba's] humiliation, and God had consigned his covenant with man to Ethiopia, making it Israel's successor. Ethiopians became the chosen people, an honor reinforced by their acceptance of Christianity."[10] The Beta Israel also affirm that they are descended from a group of Jews who smuggled out the Ark of the Covenant, but this took place almost four hundred years later, in the time of the destruction of the First Temple. This action prevented the holy Ark from falling into the hands of Nebuchadnezzar.

Orthodox Jews, from the romantic traveler Eldad the Danite in medieval times up to the recent declarations of the Chief Rabbinate of today's State of Israel, have sporadically identified the Beta Israel with the Lost Tribe of Dan. According to one early belief, the tribe of Dan left en masse for Ethiopia via Egypt during the civil strife that occurred in Israel during Jeroboam ben Navat's reign (circa 950 B.C.E.). These refugees, the story goes, established an independent kingdom in Ethiopia.

From the Chief Rabbinate's perspective, however, the Beta Israel are a remnant of the Tribe of Dan who were lost when captured by the Assyrians in the eighth century B.C.E. This view has some basis in the Bible. An indication that there were Jews in Ethiopia before the Babylonian captivity is found in the prophecy of Zephaniah (circa 615 B.C.E.): "From beyond the rivers of Ethiopia my suppliants, even the daughter of my dispersed shall bring my offering" (Zephaniah 3:10); and in Isaiah 11:11, where the prophet speaks of the return of a remnant in the Land of Kush.

Some scholars have suggested that perhaps the Beta Israel are descended from a community of Jewish mercenaries who were stationed on the island of Elephantine, on the Nile River, around the fifth century B.C.E.[11] Papyri and potsherds discovered in the Elephantine during the first decade of the twentieth century show that these Jewish garrisons were employed by the Persian Emperor to defend the frontiers, help regulate the ports, and maintain the peace. The Jewish mercenaries at Elephantine were permanently settled on the land with their families and possessions, and became an integral part of the economic and social life of the local population.

In defiance of Deuteronomy they built an alternative temple at Syene, opposite Elephantine, and made sacrifices at the altar to the pagan god Khnum, in addition to Yahu (Yahweh). The demise of the garrison began with the destruction of the temple by Egyptian priests who, around 411 B.C.E., rebelled against the Persian imperialists. The Jewish troops were defeated and many eventually withdrew from the island.

According to this view, these Jews fled south through Meroe (Sudan) during the rebellion and found haven in the highlands of Ethiopia. The Beta Israel, then, would be the offspring of these Elephantine Jewish mercenaries and Agaw tribespeople. Historians who advocate this theory give it additional credence by stressing the existence of sacrifices and priests in both of these proto-Diasporic communities. They also argue that in neither place was Hebrew known to have been spoken.

What makes this theory less tenable is that the mercenaries from the Elephantine were practicing henotheists, meaning they believed in the worship of one god without denying the existence of other deities. In addition to Yahweh, the Elephantine Jews did not neglect the pagan gods worshipped by their Egyptian neighbors. The Beta Israel however, practiced a pure monotheistic form of Biblical Judaism. What's more, the Beta Israel, were strict Sabbath observers, whereas in Elephantine the Sabbath "appears to have been honored more in the breach than in the observance."[12]

Another theory suggests that it might be possible that this Egyptian element was absorbed by previous, or later, migrations of Jews, and that their idiosyncratic form of Judaism disappeared over time. Steven Kaplan of The Hebrew University makes quick shrift of this notion by pointing out the great difficulty of navigating the Nile River between Egypt and Ethiopia.[13]

Additional migrations to Ethiopia before the Common Era may have taken place after Ptolemy Lagos (322–285 B.C.E.) settled Jewish prisoners of war from Israel along the Egypt-Sudan border. Josephus Flavius informs us that five hundred of Herod's soldiers accompanied Aelius Gallus's expedition to Ethiopia (circa 25–24 B.C.E.). More may have arrived after the destruction of the Jerusalem Temple in 70 C.E.

Until recent times (roughly pre-1970s) the most acceptable theory among modern historians was the view propounded by the doyen of Western Ethiopianists, Edward Ullendorf. He proposes that the Beta Israel are not "ethnically" Jews but rather they are an element of the Agaw people who resisted conversion to Christianity when it became Axum's official religion in the fourth century.[14] Wolf Leslau takes a similar position but is convinced that the Beta Israel form of proto-Mosaicism had to predate mishnaic times.[15] Viewed from this perspective, the Beta Israel are even less Semitic than the classical semi-Semitic Amharas and Tigreans.[16]

Drawing from oral traditions as well as historical, anthropological, and ethnomusicological sources, some modern authorities argue that the antecedents of Beta Israel religion are not at all traceable to external Jewish influences or some archaic form of Judaism, but to the Orthodox Christian Church itself! Ethnomusicologist Kay Kaufman Shelemay, in the course of conducting fieldwork on the Beta Israel in Ethiopia for her meticulously researched doctoral thesis in the 1970s, comparing Beta Israel liturgical texts with those of Ethiopian Christianity, discovered that

> [t]he central credal statement of Jewish tradition is missing altogether from Falasha worship. Virtually every parallel to Jewish tradition that I was able to find in Beta Israel liturgy is also present in the prayers of the Ethiopian Orthodox Church. In contrast, the major elements of Jewish liturgy known to have been part of universal Jewish practice for nearly two millennia are simply not present in the Beta Israel prayer. I found other prayers of Ethiopian Christian origin in all Beta Israel rituals, as well as quotations and paraphrases from the New Testament.[17]. . . Considerable evidence also suggests observances of a baptismal rite among the Beta Israel.[18] . . . There was no old liturgy, only an Ethiopian liturgical tradition sharing the language, liturgical texts and orders, and even the music of the Ethiopian Church.[19]

Shelemay found no evidence in the Beta Israel liturgy and religious ceremonies that favors regarding them as Jews prior to their contact with Western Jews in the nineteenth century. The Beta Israel, she concludes, are a heretical ultra-monotheistic Christian-like sect that developed relatively late (fourteenth century) and whose religious elements are almost entirely derived from Ethiopian Christian Orthodoxy.[20]

Steven Kaplan and James Quirin advocate that the Beta Israel must be treated on their own terms—i.e., as indigenous people, the products of Ethiopian culture—and must be perceived in the context of a historically changing Ethiopian society (specifically, the critical period from the fourteenth to the sixteenth centuries when they evolved into the people known as the Falasha).

In an effort to determine their biological origins, chromosomal studies have been carried out in recent years. These indicate that the Beta Israel have a different DNA gene pool than Jews in other lands. According to Dr. Karen Bacon, Hpa/Morph 3 and Ava II/Morph 3 are essentially nonexistent in Yemenite and Ashkenazi Jews, but they are found in significant amounts among Ethiopian Jews and Africans.[21] From this standpoint too, the Beta Israel may not, as legend has it, be descended from the tribes of Judah, Levy, or Dan.

Resolution of the continuing provocative questions and unresolved claims may be possible through the efforts of twenty-first-century scientists, using technologies and resources not presently available. Or the debate may remain a current, tantalizing issue for centuries to come.

After carrying on raging battles with the Amharic Christians and Muslims for many centuries, the Beta Israel principality was dealt a deathblow by the Christians in the seventeenth century. However, regarding the notion of the Beta Israel as a persecuted foreign minority, James Quirin declares that this "does violence to their history, and to Ethiopian history, though it fits into an analogous outmoded view of Africa."[22]

To attribute the demise of the Beta Israel simply to Christian anti-Semitism is convenient, but also highly misleading. Ethiopian emperors and ecclesiasts certainly perceived the Beta Israel as a thorn in their side because the Beta Israel sometimes held the balance of power between the Christians and Muslims, who were mortal enemies. Equally threatening was the fact that some Christians were attracted to the Beta Israel religion. This, we are made to understand, "presented a challenge to the ruling dynasty's claim to embody the smooth and legitimate transfer of the right to rule from ancient Israel to Ethiopia."[23]

But a much greater threat to Christian hegemony was posed by the Oromo expansion from the southwest and from Islamic *jihad*ists, within and without Ethiopia. These occurrences nearly brought Amharic civilization to the brink of disaster. During the 350-year period of Amharic Christian expansion, consolidation, and hegemony (roughly from 1270–1620), the pagan Agaw, Qemant (a pagan-Hebraic tribe that lived alongside the Beta Israel), Shanqalla, and other tribal peoples were also violently resisting enforced acculturation, and were also eventually forced into submission.

"Although the clerical authors of the royal chronicles often attempt to portray their heroes' exploits in religious terms," Kaplan notes, "the composition of the forces aligned in battle raises serious doubts about this view."[24] Confrontations with the Amhara need to be interpreted in the context of wider imperial interests and concerns, and not as a holocaust against the Jews.[25]

Disenfranchised and relegated to the status of serfs and lowly artisans, the Beta Israel were stigmatized as *falashas* ("landless" or "uprooted ones") by their feudal landlords and consigned to the lowest rung in the Ethiopian caste system. This epithet has similar connotations to today's pejorative term "wetback" in reference to Mexican-Americans. Today's Ethiopian Jews, especially the younger generation, resent and reject the appellation Falasha. They refer to themselves as Beta Israel (House of Israel) or just plain Ethiopian Jews, and expect others to accord them dignity and respect in calling them by these names.

Before the last mass evacuation to Israel in 1991, known as Operation Solomon, the principal areas of Beta Israel concentration were the Semien Mountains of Gondar province, near Lake Tana, the principal source of the Blue

Nile; and the Tigre region in the northeast. When finally the last of the 3,000 so-called Jews in Quara (near the Sudanese border), who have been languishing since the early 1990s because they were left off official rosters of Ethiopian Jews approved for immigration, make *aliyah*; and some 30,000 Faias Mura (Beta Israel converts to Christianity) are finally permitted to reunite with their relatives in Israel, Jewish life in Ethiopia will have come to a dramatic end.

The Beta Israel were a powerful force in medieval times. In their heydey in the sixteenth and seventeenth centuries, they maintained a virtually independent principality in their difficult-to-penetrate enclaves and were led by valiant princes and princesses. Disasters such as conflagration, famine, and disease, as well as forced and voluntary conversions, eventually reduced their numbers from hundreds of thousands to a current total of approximately 65,000.

According to the Ethiopian chronicles, Judaism had been widespread in Ethiopia for more than thirteen centuries before the advent of Christianity. While there is no tangible evidence to confirm that either the ancient Israelites or the later Jews of the South Arabian Peninsula influenced Ethiopia directly, "linguistic and religious analysis strongly suggests that in Aksum there was a pre-Christian 'Jewish' element whose origin is obscure."[26] Despite the absence of tangible evidence, few scholars question the claim that small groups of Jews came from Arabia and elsewhere in the early centuries of the Common Era. "These Arabian Jews," Kaplan speculates, "had almost certainly assimilated members of the surrounding population through conversion and intermarriage. These processes of intermarriage and acculturation appear to have continued in the predominantly Agaw regions as well. While a significant portion of the Agaw accepted Christianity, others probably embraced a more Judaic faith."[27]

Around 331 C.E., according to the Ethiopian national epic, *Kebra Negast*, King Ezanas was converted to Christianity by the Syrian monk Frumentius. Most of the leading aristocratic clans followed the young king into the new religion, but a substantial minority remained staunchly adherent to their ancestral faith. Whether this nonconforming element was persecuted is not certain. The outright oppression of the Judaizers probably did not actually begin until the sixth century, after the Dhu Nuwas debacle in Himyar (Yemen) at the hands of Kaleb, the zealous Christian king of Ethiopia.[28] The Ethiopian invaders perpetrated violent attacks against the Jews of Himyar and many Himyarite Jews were sold into slavery. At this point, belief has it, the Judaizing elements in Ethiopia withdrew or were banished to the northern provinces, and they established an independent enclave there.

Local tradition holds that Kaleb abdicated power and donned monkish robes. He passed the kingly mantle on to his son Garb Masqal, but the transition was not a smooth one. An older son named Beta Israel, who may have represented the Judaizing faction within the ruling circle, attempted to usurp ascension to the throne. The anti-Christian forces were routed, and Beta Israel was killed. Another version has it that Beta Israel survived and he and his followers fled to the remote Semien mountains where their distant descendants would later be known as the Falashas.

Elements called *ayhud* in the Ethiopian chronicles fought alongside the surrounding Agaw pagan tribespeople in their internal struggles against the Axumites. The appellation *ayhud* is scornful and literally means "Jew," but in common usage it came to include a whole assortment of religious and political dissidents whom the ruling classes abhorred. Sometime around 960 C.E., these dissidents successfully rebelled against Amharic Christian rule. Led by the legendary beautiful warrior Queen Yodit (identified in popular lore as an *ayhud*), they routed Axum, killed four hundred leading members of the reigning Solomonic dynasty, annihilated thousands of monks and priests, and razed hundreds of churches and monuments. The Zagwe-Agaw dynasts "retained the Axumite social and political order," writes Marcus, but since they did not have the ethnic legitimacy of their predecessors, " . . . created myths that they descended from Moses."[29] According to legend, the first five Zagwe kings and queens practiced the Old Mosaic faith. The last six kings and queens returned to Christianity.[30]

In 1268, the Shewan warlord Yekuno Amlak overthrew the Zagwe king and conquered many Muslim territories. The reign of Yekuno Amlak marks the beginning of an Amharic cultural and religious revival that would make its imprint on Ethiopian life for the next 700 years. "As a usurper, the new monarch encountered considerable resistance and, in order to win over Tigray with its many Auxumite traditions, he and his supporters began to circulate a fable about his descent from King Solomon and Makeda, Queen of Sheba, a genealogy that . . . gave him traditional legitimacy and provided the continuity so honored in Ethiopia's subsequent national history."[31]

Amda Seyon I (1314–44), founder of the Ethiopian state, set about widening and consolidating his locus of power, first with intrusions into the southern and southeastern sections of the plateau, and then to the north. This "heroic age" of the Ethiopian Christians (1270–1632), "marked the beginning of the Falasha . . . as an identifiable named group, formed in response to the impact of a revived Christian state and proselytizing. . . . "[32]

These expansionistic incursions into their territories were tenaciously resisted by the *ayhud*. Amda Seyon also launched a major campaign against the hostile Islamic principalities. After subduing the Muslims, he dealt a devastating blow to a people who "were originally Christian but now denied Christ like Jews."

The reign of Yeshaq (1412–27) is considered to be the turning point in Beta Israel history. When the *ayhud* leader Gedewon refused to pay a tribute to the emperor and recognize his overlordship, Yeshaq invaded Gedewon's capital Wagara and defeated the *ayhud*. According to Beta Israel oral history, the war lasted seven years and was concluded only after some local Muslims betrayed Gedewon. Yeshaq decreed that all *ayhud* must convert or lose their land: "He who is baptized in the Christian religion may inherit the land of his father; otherwise, let him be a *falasi*."[33] In consequence of this decree, the *ayhud* withdrew into more isolated, less fertile regions in the Semien highlands. There they were able to maintain a degree of autonomy and offered asylum to other political and religious dissidents.[34]

Bitterly contested theological disputes that arose among several monastic sects fractured the state Church and threatened to impede an effort by the Orthodox Church Fathers to conform with Alexandrian doctrine. Some of these sectarian elements, in particular the Estifanosites and Ewostatewosites, protested the drift to Copticism by refusing to take vows. But they remained Christian, while even more radical factions held to an even more proto-Mosaic line. This latter group insisted on celebrating only the Saturday Sabbath and rejected the divinity of Christ outright. Some of these ascetics took their cause into friendly Agaw country where they established monasteries and preached their sectarian dogma. An ecumenical dialogue with their Agaw *ayhud* hosts resulted in some of these monks reformulating it to the "pure" Mosaic creed. Although some excommunicated heretics were later reabsorbed into the Orthodox Church, the extreme nonconformist elements, i.e., the Lovers of Moses, remained separate. And from "[o]ut of this melange of preexisting *ayhud* groups and new influences from Orthodoxy a community emerged known as the Falasha with a distinct religious, ethnic, and economic identity."[35]

Negus (Emperor) Zar'a Yaqob (1434–68) was a great reformer who further solidified Ethiopian territory. He was also a fanatical Christian who sought to literally stamp out all creeds that did not conform to what he considered the proper faith. "A decree was instituted ordering everybody to bear on his forehead and arms the protestation of his faith and renunciation of the Devil in the form of tattoo markings."[36] Called the "Exterminator of the Jews," Zar'a Yaqob pursued a relentless but not very successful campaign to forcibly convert the Falasha to Christianity. It appears that the Falasha submitted only outwardly, and upon the death of Zar'a Yaqob many reverted to their original *ayhud* faith. To combat this heresy, Zar'a Yaqob's son and successor Ba'eda Maryam (1468–

78), sent his troops into Beta Israel territory. For seven years, the Falashas staved off the Christian attacks, until they were worn down and forced to surrender. The Falashas were compelled to reconvert to Christianity and rebuild the churches they had destroyed.[37]

Early in the sixteenth century Muslims and Falasha forces regrouped for a major assault on their Christian overlords. Emperor Lebna Dengel (1508–40), with an army under the generalship of his son Claudius, and with assistance from Portuguese musketeers, routed the Turkish-backed armies of the great Muslim warrior Ahmad Gragn, the Sultan of Harar. The reign of Sarsa Dengel (1563–97) was spent waging battles on many fronts, including some ferocious attacks on the Falasha. According to Beta Israel oral tradition, Sarsa Dengel burned the Falasha holy books and committed the ultimate sacrilegious act of saying mass in their *mesgid* (house of worship).[38]

During the reign of the Falasha warlord Gedewon, the Jewish territory in Semien served as a hideout for royal pretenders plotting against the Solomonic throne. Sarsa Dengel's son Susneyos III (1606–32), a convert to Roman Catholicism, mobilized his troops to attack the Beta Israel. His army, supplied with muskets and other modern military firepower by his Portuguese allies, inflicted heavy losses upon the Falasha forces, who had only spears and swords to fight with. Thousands of Falasha men and women who refused to embrace Christianity were massacred, and their children were sold into slavery. Gedewon and his military cohorts slit each other's throats rather than surrender.

There were also heroic tales of Beta Israel women hurling themselves off cliffs or into abysses, with God's name on their lips, rather than be subjected to horrible abuse. This was the end of Jewish autonomy in the enclaves of Semien. Eventually, those who managed to survive were allowed to return to their ancestral faith, although their inherited land-use rights *(rist)* were repealed and they were forbidden to own land. The Beta Israel, along with the other subjugated minorities in the region, were incorporated into the Amharic caste system but were allowed to maintain their separate identity and practice their religion unhindered.

Dispersed to the north of the Lake Tana highland region, in tiny villages, and forbidden to own land, the Falasha lived a precarious existence as tenant farmers and artisans. The agricultural workers toiled as sharecroppers and shepherds, renting land from the parish church or a feudal landlord in exchange for an annual portion (generally about one-quarter) of the yield. During the reign of King Fasilides (1632–67), the new capital, Gondar, became an important commercial and cultural center. Beta Israel masons and carpenters were hired to build the rough-hewn stone churches, castles, and bridges characteristic of that age and helped accelerate the process of urbanization. Others became soldiers in the Ethiopian army and established a reputation as valiant warriors.

By serving the needs of their imperial and noble benefactors, the Beta Israel were able to reverse earlier processes of decline. An elite corps of Beta Israel artisans and *chewas* (professional soldiers) in Gondar attained upward mobility. They were granted *gult* (land and titles allocated to servants of the Crown) as payment for their work. *Gult* entitled its holder to exact tribute and corvee labor from the *rist* peasantry (i.e., the peasantry that had an ancestral claim to the land). "The Beta Israel were also rewarded for their military and artisanal skills with appointments to the titles of *azmach* and *bejrond*. These titles illustrate the process of incorporation and upward mobility that occurred. . . . As *azmaches*, they were advisors to the kings, according to their own traditions, but were not appointed to provincial governorships. As *bejronds*, they were chiefs of the workers, but were not guardians of the treasury, lions, or crowns. . . . "[39]

The near collapse of central government institutions and the wholesale destruction of the urban areas during the *zemana mesfinate* ("The Era of the Princes") (1769–1855) caused numerous intense problems for the Beta Israel. Worst was the depression of the construction industry, which brought about widespread unemployment. Their land grants lost, or stolen from them by the feuding warlords and *shifta* (roving bandits), and struggling to survive appalling hardship, most Gondarian Beta Israel withdrew to the rural areas, where they reverted to tenant farming and the crafts as sources of livelihood. Like the Yemenite Jews across the Red Sea, the Beta Israel craftspeople became a self-reliant group who monopolized specialized trades such as blacksmithing, weaving, leather working, and pottery and basket making. In these capacities, they were considered the finest in all of Ethiopia and were an indispensable part of agrarian society.

In Ethiopia, the Orthodox Church has traditionally cultivated contempt for people who engage in nonagricultural work. "Manual labor bears the stigma of slave labor," Edith Lord informs us.[40] In local folklore there is widespread belief that a class of people who work in handicrafts, especially those who fashion tools from iron, are *tabibs* (sorcerers and witches) who have mastered the black arts. *Tabibs* are possessed of *buda* (the evil eye), which is derived from the devil. *Tabibs*—used interchangeably with *budas*, or evil-eyed ones—have the power to turn themselves into hyenas at night and prey upon humans. The Ethiopian masses shunned the gaze of these "thin-blooded" people who were capable of bringing about all manner of misfortune.

In order to safeguard against their occult powers, the masses wore an assortment of charms and amulets around their wrists and necks. Although *budas* were believed to emanate from all low-status groups in Ethiopia, the Beta Israel, as the country's hereditary blacksmiths, were the most feared and despised caste of all.[41] On the one hand noted for their cleanliness, honesty, and meticulous work, there was also a pervasive belief among the rural Ethiopian people that the Beta Israel, by virtue of their occupation involving fire and water, were to blame for the frequent droughts, the rampant diseases, the unexplained deaths of children, and all the "slings and arrows of outrageous fortune." Occasionally, the superstitious masses would lash out against their imagined tormentors, killing and maiming them.

Generally, the Beta Israel lived in separate villages from their non-Jewish neighbors. If they did live in the same towns or villages, they inhabited quarters separated by stones or fences as a demarcation line between themselves and the Gentiles. In response to the hostile treatment accorded them by the dominant culture, the Beta Israel spiritual leaders, namely the monks and priests, set out to redefine their identity and devise certain defense mechanisms designed to perpetuate their separate peoplehood. Strict rules of conduct were enacted to insulate the Jews from their neighbors.

The issue of purity is one of the more conspicuous examples of perceived self-esteem and moral superiority. Any physical contact with non-Jews made the Beta Israel ritually impure. In the special Beta Israel section of the marketplace, they shielded themselves from contamination by sitting behind fences and in enclosures. Non-Jews who bought wares from the Beta Israel had to toss their coins into a dish of water, which cleansed them.[42] Any Beta Israel who had remained outside the village walls for a period of time was obligated to first seclude him or herself in an isolated hut for five or six days and eat only chickpeas (soaked in water, but not cooked) before entering the village. They were forbidden to eat food touched by a non-Beta Israel. For this reason, the Beta Israel were called *attenkun* ("touch-me-nots") by the other Ethiopians. Beta Israel who settled in the cities were considered unclean by the Beta Israel who lived in the villages.

According to Hermann Norden, who visited Ethiopia in the 1920s, it was a country where sexually transmitted diseases at times reached epidemic proportions. But the Beta Israel were virtually free of venereal infections.[43] Every Beta Israel village was located near a river or stream; their personal hygiene was intertwined with their religious obligations to carry out ritual ablutions. The unwashed Ethiopian masses would refer to the Beta Israel as "those who smell from water," because of their distinctive odor. "Christians were attracted to the Beta Israel religion because of its high standards of morality, holiness, and asceticism."[44]

Like the Christian Bible, the Beta Israel Orit was written in Ge'ez, or Old Ethiopic. Ge'ez, like Hebrew and Arabic, is a Semitic tongue. In addition to the Five Books of Moses, the Beta Israel possessed the Books of Joshua, Judges, Samuel, and Ruth. These Holy Books, together with apocryphal and pseudepigraphical texts such as the Books of Jubilees, Enoch, the Commandments of the Sabbath, and the Death of Moses, are called *Orit* (Ethiopic for Torah). Virtually all modern historians agree that the whole compendium of Beta Israel Holy Writ is derived from Orthodox Ge'ez sources (of course denuded of Christological content).[45] The Bible was interpreted literally. The Sabbath, festivals, and fast days were very strictly adhered to.

The blowing of the *shofar* was not included in the Beta Israel equivalent of the Rosh Hashanah service, and neither were booths built to celebrate the Sukkot holiday. Biblical and rabbinic commandments such as wearing *tzitzit* and *tefillin* and posting *mezuzot* are never known to have been observed. Until well into the twentieth century, the Beta Israel still practiced the paschal sacrifice. A number of Beta Israel customs that are anathema to normative Jewish teachings, such as tattooing, confessions, and the institution of monasticism, are derived from the surrounding culture. Over the course of centuries, "the combination of a common biblical ethos and a long history of contact and mutual acculturation between [Christian and Beta Israel] societies had resulted in their possessing religious systems and cultural identifications that were remarkably similar. The two groups shared biblical elements in their religion, a clear correspondence between their religious hierarchy of monks and priests, a corpus of literature and a common Israelite self-image."[46]

The *mesgid* or *beit makdas* was a simple structure that looked from the outside like the other Beta Israel dwellings, except that it was larger. Traditionally, a red earthen pot was placed on the pinnacle of the roof. In recent times, the *mesgid* was crowned with a Star of David. The interior was divided into two sections, one for the congregation and a separate chamber designated the *Queddesta Queddusan,* or Holy of Holies. In the *Queddesta Queddusan*, the *Orit* and ritual objects were preserved behind a curtain, and only the priests were allowed to enter. Worshippers removed their shoes upon entering the *mesgid*. During prayer services, the Beta Israel would prostrate themselves northeastward, toward Jerusalem. They would pray bareheaded; only the *qessotch* or priests wore turbans. Beta Israel prayer services could be conducted with fewer than ten men. Among the female population, only unmarried girls and old women were allowed to enter the synagogue. The women did not sit with the men; they either sat off on the side or behind a partition. Prayers were accompanied by dancing and the beating of drums and cymbals.

The institution of the rabbinate never existed in Ethiopia. Every village had a *qes* or priest who tended to the spiritual needs of the community. These *qessotch* were not of Aaronic descent, nor was the position hereditary. *Qessotch* were for the most part drawn from the general population, and each was selected based on his own merits. In addition to being well versed in prayers and the *Orit* and passing the ordination exam, a candidate had to be of good repute and come from a respectable family. Only the *qessotch* understood Ge'ez, the language of the *Orit*, which they translated for the masses in the *mesgid* on the Sabbath and holidays. Some of their other functions included chanting the prayers, slaughtering cattle, and sacrificing the paschal lamb. They officiated at community ritual events and blessed the sick, the newborn, and the newly wed. And, like their Christian counterparts, the *qessotch* took confessions from those who had sinned or were about to die, and administered absolution. The Beta Israel would offer the *qessotch* a portion of their crops and the firstborn of their flocks. Like the Ethiopian Orthodox priests, the *qessotch* could marry, but could not be divorced. If his wife died, a priest could not remarry. The *qessotch* were distinguished from the other Beta Israel by their beards, white turbans, and *jantillas* (ritual umbrellas). Assisting the *qessotch* as educators, musicians, and scribes were the learned men known as the *debtarotch* (deacons). These *debtarotch* "represented a secondary unconsecrated clerical group responsible for performing the liturgy. In general, a *debtera* was someone who was prevented from continuing in, or seeking elevation to, a higher religious position by some personal, physical, or familial flaw."[47]

In addition to the priesthood, the Beta Israel had until the twentieth century an institution unknown in any other Jewish community: a monastic order of monks and nuns. According to Beta Israel tradition, monasticism began with Aaron, the High Priest and brother of Moses. Aaron was married and had four sons, but upon donning the ecclesiastical vestments, he renounced the world "and lived in meditation in the shadow of the tabernacles."[48]

More tenable is the widely held view that the institution of monasticism was drawn from the Christian milieu. In Orthodox Church tradition, the Nine Saints who came from Syria sometime in the late fifth century are said to have introduced monasticism into Ethiopia.

One leading authority has argued that all the "Hebraic" traits of the Ethiopian Church result from the reforms instituted by emperor Zar'a Yaqob in the fifteenth century. "It is surmised that his zeal for reform might have caused him to re-establish a primitive Christianity that was closer to Biblical Judaism than the contemporary form."[49] Evidence indicates that virtually every major feature of the Beta Israel religion is traceable to renegade Christian monks and their disciples in the fourteenth and fifteenth centuries.[50] Qozmos, a renegade cleric and miracle-maker, is said to have joined the Beta Israel in the fifteenth century and copied the *Orit* for them. During this same epoch Sagga Amlak, the rebellious son of Negus Zar'a Yaqob, ran away from the royal court and embraced the religion of the Beta Israel. Together with Abba Sabra, another Christian monk who became a Beta Israel, he is said to have established monasteries throughout Beta Israel commuities. Sagga Amlak is also believed to be the one who instituted the Beta Israel laws of purity. More than anyone else, the Beta Israel monks were instrumental in guarding and preserving the heritage of their people in the face of a hostile outside world. Representing the "Old Guard," the monks tenaciously upheld Beta Israel traditions and were, after contact with Western Jewry, the element of Beta Israel society most resistant to the modernizing influences of the Talmud.

The Beta Israel were scattered throughout the northern escarpments in some 500 small rural districts with populations that generally did not exceed more than forty families. In terms of architectural design, Beta Israel villages were more or less indistinguishable from their neighbors'. A typical village consisted of *tukuls*, or cylindrically shaped huts, which might be described as looking like a cross between a teepee and a log cabin. *Tukuls* were made from local wood and straw and coated with mud. Each hut had a cone-shaped roof, which was thatched with reed and straw. There were no chimneys or windows. The door served as the only opening for light to penetrate within. Heaps of straw were strewn on the dirt floor to serve as beds. All cooking was done outside on an open fire. What distinguished the Beta Israel villages from the others were the *mesgid*, with its Star of David fashioned from corrugated metal, and special shelters designated for women who were menstruating and giving birth.

During their menstrual periods, women were considered unclean and were isolated outside the village walls in a special "hut of blood" called *yaras gojo*. The woman's family placed food in front of her, but did not allow her to touch the dishes and thereby contaminate them. When the bleeding stopped, the woman immersed herself in the river at sundown and returned to her home. A woman who had given birth stayed in the "hut of blood" for one week if the baby was male, and two weeks if it was female. After a ritual bath, she was transferred to a special "hut for the woman in childbirth" for thirty-two days after the birth of a boy and sixty-four days after the birth of a girl. During this period a nurse, usually a relative, tended to all her needs. Upon leaving the hut, the new mother shaved her head and body hair and immersed herself in water in the presence of two female witnesses. After sunset, she and her newborn returned home for a family celebration. The hut of conception was considered contaminated and was burned to the ground.[51]

When a child was born, it was doused with cold water and blessed by the priest. The circumcision was usually performed by a woman. Priests never performed circumcision, since doing so would have ritually polluted them. Like other Ethiopians, the Beta Israel performed clitorectomies on girls in infancy. The operation was performed by a woman called *kinterkoraj*. In addition to breast milk, infants were fed butter. Instead of being bathed, they were rubbed all over with butter.

Sometimes if the firstborn was a son, his parents would dedicate the prepubescent to a monastic life and place him under the aegis of the *meneign* (monks or nazirites). Beta Israel *meneign* renounced all worldly pleasures and spent much of their lives in the desert fasting, praying, meditating, and writing religious texts. Because of their saintliness and prophetic abilities, they were held in higher regard than the *qessotch*. The monastic institution is now extinct. The last of the Beta Israel monks, fifty-nine-year-old Abba Bayene, arrived in Israel during Operation Solomon and today lives in the back room of a synagogue in Ashdod.[52]

Belief in the efficacy of magic is widespread in Ethiopia. In addition to their own spiritual leaders, the Beta Israel, like other Agaw tribespeople, would turn to a variety of healers and mediums for protection from *saytan ganel*, or spirit-induced diseases, and from the malevolent genies that disrupt the universe. *Awakotseh* were consulted to foretell the probability of death or recovery from illness. *Ganien sabotseh* or *tankways* were called upon to exorcise the *zars* that possess humans, especially women, who have offended these spirits. "To the accompaniment of songs and dance and the burning of scented herbs, the victim is driven into a frenzy until the *zar*, speaking through his victim, ultimately reveals his name. Once this is known, he can be persuaded to depart in return for various offerings, such as meal and the sacrifice of a cock."[53] To protect themselves from the evil eye, Beta Israel women wore strings of charms and amulets around their necks.

In a land that has been described as "forcefully reminiscent of the Old Testament World,"[54] the Beta Israel were considered to be the most biblical of Ethiopians because they observed the Orit commandments literally. They were especially strict in observing the laws pertaining to the *Sanbat* (Sabbath) and the Festivals. Work came to a stop on Friday afternoon, at which time the Beta Israel would head to the river to wash their bodies and clothing. All food for the *Sanbat* was prepared in advance and eaten cold. The *Sanbat* fare included the special Beta Israel bread called *dabbo*, which was eaten with ground peas and a hot sauce called *wat* and washed down with *thella* (beer brewed from toasted barley). Each family would contribute foods to a feast that took place after services on *Sanbat* in the courtyard of the *mesgid*. It was a Beta Israel Sabbath custom for segregated groups of men and women to go out into the fields, lie down on the grass, and discuss religious matters.[55]

In contrast to talmudic teachings, Beta Israel law forbade profaning the *Sanbat* even for a critically ill child. However, if attacked on the *Sanbat,* the Beta Israel were permitted to defend themselves. Also in contrast with rabbinic Jewry, which considers Shabbat to be an especially auspicious time to perform the *mitzvah* of *proo irvoo* ("Be fruitful and multiply"), the Beta Israel abstained from sex on the Day of Rest.

Astasreyo, the Ethiopian equivalent of Yom Kippur, was a fast day strictly observed by Beta Israel over seven years old. It was not a day of atonement like Yom Kippur, but merely a day of remembrance of the dead. When *Astasreyo* came to a close, the Beta Israel would scatter corn on the roof of the *mesgid* and on the ground. This act symbolized the belief that humans must be compassionate toward anything that is weaker than themselves. It was also an act of prayer that God the Almighty might do likewise to themselves.[56] Blowing the *shofar* on *Berhan Seraqa* (Rosh Hashanah) and *Astasreyo* was forbidden in Ethiopia. The blowing of a ram's horn was a sign of the authority of the emperor. Blowing a *shofar* would have been construed as a sign of insubordination. The Beta Israel assert that they feared severe punitive measures from the authorities, and therefore only made verbal reference to the blowing of the *shofar*.[57]

*Tukul*s were thoroughly cleaned three or four days in advance of *Fassika* (Passover). During this time, the Beta Israel would eat nothing but roasted barley. *Fassika* began at sunset on the fourteenth of *Lissan* (Nissan) and was observed with paschal sacrifices on a stone altar in the courtyard of the synagogue. There was no *seder* ceremony among the Beta Israel. On *Fassika* the Beta Israel ate a pita-like unleavened bread made from wheat and water called *keeyta*. For reasons that are not clear, eggs, cheese, and leavening products were not eaten on *Fassika*. In the days when the Beta Israel maintained their autonomy, anyone caught eating leavening products on *Fassika* was thrown off a cliff or stoned to death.[58]

As in Temple times, the Beta Israel included animal sacrifices as part of the daily prayer services. At the urging of Dr. Jacques Faitlovitch, the great early-twentieth-century Jewish advocate for the Beta Israel, ritual sacrifices were sharply reduced. But this curtailment was accomplished over opposition from the monks and the more conservative *qessotch*. Only the paschal sacrifice has been maintained to this day.

Of the many unique festivals celebrated by the Beta Israel, *Seged* was and still is the most important. Held on the last day of the ninth moon, *Seged* commemorates Ezra's proclamations against the Babylonian wives. Led by their *qessotch* carrying Torah scrolls, the Beta Israel, clad in spotless white clothing, would ascend a hilltop carrying stones on their backs. Upon reaching the top of the hill they would cast away the stones, which symbolized sin.[59] The *qessotch* would exhort the people to follow God's ways. They would read from the Scriptures and recite prayers to commemorate the dead. After the services, the people would wind down the hill chanting prayers to the beat of drums. The entire village then partook of a communal feast, accompanied by singing and dancing. In Israel today, *Seged* is celebrated by the Ethiopian Jews as a day of unity and ethnic solidarity.

Beta Israel notions of a Messiah were similar to those of their Christian neighbors. The Messiah's name was Tewodros (Theodore), a direct descendent from the House of David, but they believed he would not arrive for another 10,000 years. It was said that during a cataclysmic war that would engulf the universe, Tewodros would arise and lead the Beta Israel back to the Holy Land.

The Beta Israel were described by Western missionaries as the most ethical and moralistic of all Ethiopian tribes. Crimes and transgressions were punished severely and required rigorous acts of repentance. The Protestant missionary J. M. Flad described the penitential process as he witnessed it in a Beta Israel village in the mid nineteenth century:

> An unmarried woman who has sinned is brought before the priest. . . . After she has confessed her sin, a fire is kindled in the sight of the whole congregation. The penitent must herself fetch the wood for this fire, bringing a burden of wood everyday for eight days, and piling it up in the neighborhood of the *Mesgeed*. She must then, her body being protected by only a slight covering, spring into the midst of the flame when the fire is at its height. Care is taken nevertheless that she not be materially injured; she is drawn out of the fire as quickly as possible. . . . After she recovers from the burns, she brings a kid as a sin-offering, bathes herself in water, and is sprinkled by a priest, after which she is again received into the congregation.
>
> If a man has sinned and is excommunicated he must, in order to be again recovered, fast for seven days, his only food being raw *Shimbera* (peas) and water. After the fast is ended, he brings two goats to the priest, as a sin-offering. The priest receives the goats and sends the penitent to cut seven rods, which he brings to the priest. The man then removes his up-

per garment, and falls at the feet of the priest. A lay person, who is appointed, then strikes the penitent with each of the seven rods . . . and dealing the seventh blow with all his force. After this penance the goats are offered as a sin-offering. The priest lays his right hand on the penitent's and his left hand on the offering, and absolves the man from his sin. He must then bathe himself and be sprinkled with holy water by the priest, after which he may enter the congregation and take part in the services.[60]

Stones played a major symbolic role in the life of the Beta Israel. To patch up a quarrel, each antagonist would lift up a stone and place it upon his back. Then they would hurl the stones away and kiss each other, and, it was hoped, the quarrel was resolved.[61]

The Beta Israel were serial monogamists and this monogamy began very early in life. The marriageable age was nine or ten for girls and fifteen for boys. Marriages were arranged by the parents without conferring with the young people. Festivities lasted up to ten days. Home-brewed beer and mead were consumed in large quantities. Before the end of the festivities, the bride was examined by the female elder of the community. If she was found not to be a virgin, the marriage was annulled, she was excluded from the community, and no Beta Israel was permitted to marry her.[62] During the holy matrimonial rites, the *qessotch* would beat drums and recite prayers and tie the *keshera*, a red and white band, around the groom's forehead. The white represented the festive quality of the celebration; the red represented the bride's virgin blood. The groom and his best men would then proceed to the bride's house to stay for the night, from whence they and two of the bride's male relatives would carry the new wife to the groom's house the next day.

As in most other pre-industrial societies, the Ethiopian Jewish community was built around the patrilocal extended family, which functioned as an independent economic unit. Work and domestic chores were divided among the family members, whose basic material, emotional, and social needs were provided by the family. Roles in the extended family were interchangeable in the sense that uncles and grandparents might function as parents, and cousins as brothers. "The relationship of children to their parents and particularly, the head of the family, was based on authority and respect. As soon as he [was] able to understand his wider world the child was made aware that individuals older than he, and all those in higher social positions, must be shown the utmost deference."[63]

Married Beta Israel women were distinguished from their Gentile neighbors by their short-cropped hair. Amharic women traditionally wore their long hair in braids sheened with a pomade of butter. As a sign of subjection to her husband, the Beta Israel wife always addressed her husband in the third person. Both men and women wore the *shamma*, a white, loose fitting, toga-type cloak made from cotton. The men wore a khaki-style shirt called *ej-tabab*, cotton trousers, and invariably carried a *dula*, or walking stick. The women wore embroidered cotton dresses that reached down to the ankles. They would loop the *shamma* around the upper part of the body to function as a sling for carrying a child, or wear it over their heads and faces to protect themselves from the sun. In recent times, they would embroider their dresses with Jewish symbols, such as the Star of David. Some people wore sandals; most, however, went barefoot. Children were expected to wash the feet of their parents and guests at night or after a journey. They would receive frequent blessings from their parents for these services.

The basic food in the Ethiopian diet is a large, spongy pancake-like bread called *injera*, which is made from *teff* and water. *Teff* is a vitamin-rich fine grain similar to millet and is indigenous to the Ethiopian highlands. *Injera* is usually eaten with ground chickpeas and spices. A favorite dish is *wat*, a very spicy vegetable-based stew made with beans, eggs, and pieces of chicken, beef, lamb, or no meat at all. *Thella*, beer brewed from toasted barley; *tej*, mead made from honey; and *katikalla*, a gin made from distilled grains, were the favorite alcoholic beverages. *Brundo* (raw meat), considered to be a delicacy among the Christian population, was eschewed by the Beta Israel. This kept the Beta Israel free of intestinal worms.[64] Among the Beta Israel, when people were on especially good terms with one another, they would hand-feed each other. The *qessotch* forbade their parishioners from smoking tobacco, which they saw as a Muslim vice. Anyone using cigarettes or snuff was forbidden to enter the *mesgid*.[65]

The ninth-century Jewish traveler Eldad the Danite, possibly of East African origin himself, claimed that his people, the Lost Tribe of Dan, was situated in the remote mountains of Kush.[66] The twelfth-century travelers Petachia of Ratisbon[67] and Benjamin of Tudela[68] brought back news of an independent kingdom in Ethiopia, but their information was probably based on hearsay. The first Ashkenazi Jew to reach the Beta Israel is believed to have been Solomon of Vienna in 1626. Emperor Susneyos, at the urging of his Portuguese allies, had him thrown out of the country for attempting to combat the Jesuits who were trying to convert the Beta Israel. His visit did little to draw the attention of European Jewry to the wretched condition of the Beta Israel. Of far greater significance were the contacts made by the Scottish explorer James Bruce, who lived in Ethiopia from 1768 to 1773.

Bruce was the first known European to discover the source of the Blue Nile. The results of his exploration and discovery were described in a five-volume work published in 1790.[69] It was the most comprehensive study of the history and ethnology of Abbysinia to that date. Included among his observations was the fact that the Lake Tana area, the source of the Blue Nile, was in great part inhabited by a "race" of black-skinned Jews. Bruce himself never actually entered the Jewish villages, but he managed to interview several Beta Israel while sojourning in Gondar. He inquired into their history, and, based on his studies, estimated the Beta Israel population at 250,000.

With the exception of a few concerned individuals, such as the young Italian-Jewish scholar Filosseno Luzzatto (1829–54), who inquired about the Beta Israel via correspondence, the world Jewish community paid scant attention to news of the discovery of lost brethren in the Horn of Africa. In 1805 Great Britain opened a diplomatic office in Ethiopia. On the heels of the diplomats and soldiers came an army of Christian missionary organizations. The London Society for Promoting Christianity among the Jews understood well the implications of the Jewish world's neglect of the Beta Israel. Beginning in the mid 1850s, the London Society carried on intensive work to spread the Gospel among the Beta Israel. Permission to do this was granted by the Emperor Tewodros, on condition that the Beta Israel be baptized into the Orthodox Church. The most notorious of the missionaries were two Jewish converts to Christianity, Joseph Wolff and Henry Aaron Stern. In trying to win over Jewish souls, these sophisticated missionaries would refer to themselves as White Falashas. They inveighed against certain archaic Beta Israel traditions such as the institution of monasticism, sacrifices, and the laws of purity. With their great scriptural learning and dialectical skills, they oftentimes made fools of the less sophisticated Beta Israel monks in theological debates.[70]

The missionaries distributed food and maintained schools for Beta Israel children. "From the beginning, the dream of Protestant missionaries to the Beta Israel had been not only to convert Jews to Christianity, but to use the new converts to revive the Ethiopian Orthodox Church, which was uniformly seen as unenlightened and backward, if not corrupt and morally bankrupt."[71] The material temptations the missions offered were too enticing for some of the more impecunious Beta Israel. The young who were more literate and upwardly mobile were also more likely to repudiate the ancestral faith.[72] Those who had submitted to baptism, or who had married non-Jews, were excommunicated from the Beta Israel community. But many of the Beta Israel converts retained their occupational caste and continued to identify as Falasha, and many who did convert eventually returned to their original Beta Israel faith. Even those who converted sincerely were generally held in contempt by their suspicious Christian neighbors. The overwhelming majority of Beta Israel, however, proved resistant to conversion. By 1908 only some 1,800 had converted to Christianity.[73]

The reign of Negus Tewodros II (1855–68) marked the end of a period of feudal anarchy in Ethiopian history known as the *zemana mesfinate*. After defeating all the other contenders, the former bandit turned emperor conducted a series of campaigns to bring most of the northern highlands under his control. Ethiopia began to make some contact with the outside world. A number of reforms were introduced in government, and experiments with modern technology and transport were applied to agriculture and industry. But sound, innovative projects of reform such as cleaning up corruption in the Church were combined with overly zealous measures to suppress local rebellions and Amharize the non-Christian populations. The arrival of the Protestant missionaries at the court of Tewodros in 1862 precipitated a fear of forced conversion among the Beta Israel. As a matter of policy, Tewodros was against forced conversions, and during his reign the total number of converts amounted to no more than fifty.[74] But the aggressive missionary activities (especially a campaign against sacrifices) that were given official support, combined with great poverty, hunger, and disease, evoked in the Beta Israel a messianic fervor for Zion. Led by the prophet Abba Mahari, thousands of Beta Israel abandoned their villages and headed northward to the Red Sea. They believed that God would duplicate the miracle He had performed for the Israelites in the Exodus and part the waters for them. The tortuous trek took them through barren mountains and torrid, waterless land where they encountered predatory wild animals and marauding thieves. They managed to get as far as Tigre, where most of them perished from disease or starvation. The more fortunate managed to straggle back to their villages, barely alive. Some were so demoralized that they voluntarily accepted conversion to Christianity.

European Jewry slowly became aware of the news of this Beta Israel tragedy. In 1864 Azriel Hildesheimer, a prominent German Orthodox rabbi, published a full-page appeal in the *London Jewish Chronicle* calling for a mission to rescue the Falashas before they were all converted. Alarmed by the glowing reports of the missionaries, the Paris-based Alliance Israelite Universelle was stirred into action. Joseph Halevy, a professor of Oriental Studies at the Sorbonne, was commissioned to lead an expedition into the Ethiopian highlands to investigate the plight of the newly discovered coreligionists.

At first Halevy was given a rather cool reception by the Beta Israel. They were convinced he was a merchant or, worse, a missionary who was trying to trick them into believing he was a Jew. In his "Travels in Abyssinia," Halevy described in very dramatic and moving terms his initial encounter with the Beta Israel:

> My approach was announced beforehand by some children who were tend-ing flocks of sheep. . . . Men and women cried out at the astonishment of my complexion and my dress. . . . They appeared uncomfortable, and when I wished to draw near, they drew back. Only two persons ventured to grasp my hand in a friendly manner, while the others called out 'touch us not.'
>   . . . After hesitating for a minute, the Falashas broke silence. "Sir," said they, "doubtless you require a knife or sword: you should buy them in a large town, for the instruments we make are of too rough a work-manship to suit a European." "Oh, my brethren," I replied, "I am not only a European; I am, like you, an Israelite. I come, not to trade in Abyssinia, but to inquire into the state of my co-religionists. . . . You must know my dear brethren, that I also am a Falasha! I worship no other God than the great Adonai, and I acknowledge no other law than the law of Sinai." These words, uttered slowly, and in distinct tones . . . had a striking ef-fect on the Falashas. Whilst some appeared to be satisfied, others shook their heads doubtfully, and looked at each other as if to inquire how I should be answered. At last several voices exclaimed, "What! you a Falasha! a white Falasha! You are laughing at us! Are there any white Falashas?"
>   I assured them that all the Falashas of Jerusalem, and in other parts of the world, were white; and that they could not be distinguished from the other inhabitants of their respective countries. The name of Jerusalem, which I had accidentally mentioned, changed as if by magic the attitude of the most incredulous. A burning curiosity seemed at once to have seized the whole company. "Oh, do you come from Jerusalem the blessed city? Have you beheld with your own eyes Mount Zion, and the House of the Lord of Israel, the holy Temple?" . . . I . . . was deeply moved on seeing those black faces light up at the memory of our glorious history. . . . [75]

Halevy managed to convince the Beta Israel that he was a fellow Jew who had come to investigate their circumstances. He promised them support in re-establishing bonds with world Jewry. But in spite of an auspicious beginning, the skeptical and color-prejudiced European Jewish world of the late nineteenth century soon lost interest in this "lost tribe" of dark-brown-skinned brethren in Ethiopia.

The invasion of Mahdist dervishes from the Sudan in 1888 was originally intended to be only an extended raid whose objective was to help fellow Muslims, forcibly converted to Christianity by King Yohannes, to return to their ancestral faith.[76] The extended raid turned into a holy war that laid waste large portions of northern Ethiopia. King Yohannes managed to repel the Muslim invaders (though he was killed in battle), but not before they had ravaged many Beta Israel villages in Gondar province. The dervish invasions, combined with drought, locust, rinderpest, and plagues, wiped out an estimated one-third to one-half of the Beta Israel population between 1888 and 1892. "Those who survived left their normal places of residence and scattered far and wide. Traditional village life and customary separation from non-Jews broke down in the face of danger of starvation."[77]

It was during this period, when the communal and cultural structure of the Falashas was rapidly breaking down, that their greatest patron and champion appeared on the scene. The arrival of Jacques Faitlovitch (1880–1955), a Polish-born Orthodox Jew, turned the tide for them. A gifted linguist, Faitlovitch had studied under Halevy in Paris. The paternalistic but well-meaning Faitlovitch single-handedly undertook the moral obligation to rescue the Falashas from the missionaries. He viewed their degraded status through the prism of classical European anti-Semitism, and the Falasha cause became his lifelong obsession. For half a century, the indefatigable Faitlovitch served in the capacity of "culture broker," working diligently to help reestablish contacts between the Falashas and world Jewry, to acquaint them with rabbinic Judaism, and to educate the young. In effect, to a large extent he reshaped them according to his image of what they should be.

With the financial assistance of Baron Edmond de Rothschild and the Chief Rabbi of Paris, the twenty-four-year-old Faitlovitch took the first of numerous trips to Ethiopia in 1904. The Falashas, wary of old missionary tricks, at first refused to believe he was a Jew. Initially, Faitlovitch was not permitted to enter their synagogue until he had meditated outside the village walls for seven days and had undergone ritual ablution. He lived among them for a year, battling the missionaries and instructing the young. Upon returning to Europe, Faitlovitch requested assistance from the Alliance to build schools in Beta Israel villages. The Alliance was at first ambivalent, but decided to send a representative to Ethiopia to check out Faitlovitch's report. Rabbi Chaim Nahum of Constantinople, who would eventually become Chief Rabbi of Turkey, and then of Egypt, was chosen to investigate. Upon returning from his two-month trip in 1908, Nahum published a report of his own. Based on his findings, Nahum concluded that the Falashas were not Jewish by blood (they were originally Greeks from Egypt), they were content to be where they were, and it was not worthwhile to teach them an updated form of Judaism. In short, he concluded, there was no need for Jewish organizations to assist them.[78]

Undeterred, Faitlovitch established pro-Falasha support committees with branches in Europe, Palestine, and the United States. Outstanding rabbis from forty-four communities, including the first Ashkenazi Chief Rabbi of Palestine, Abraham Isaac Kook, endorsed the committees' efforts. In 1921, Rabbi Kook called on world Jewry to "save our Falasha brethren from extinction and contamination . . . and to rescue 50,000 holy souls of the House of Israel from oblivion."[79] Pro-Falasha committees sponsored forty Beta Israel boys with scholarships to study in Palestine and Western Europe. Later they returned to Ethiopia, where some served as educators and religious leaders.

A few of Faitlovitch's students served in the Ethiopian government. The most prominent were Professor Taamrat Emmanuel, a diplomat and political advisor to Emperor Haile Selassie, and his nephew Tadesse Yacob, Ethiopia's finance minister in the early 1920s (and a convert to Christianity). "Yet all in all," writes Robert L. Hess, "his school was a failure for it did not succeed in training young men who would then serve the Falasha community as teachers and pull the Falasha out of their stagnation."[80] A notable exception was Yonah Bogale (1920–87) from Gondar. He was a relative of Taamrat and Tadesse. Bogale was an educator and civil servant who mastered ten languages, including Yiddish. For many years he was the leading spokesman for the Ethiopian Jewish community in Israel.

The pro-Falasha committees raised funds to open a school in Addis Ababa. When the Italians occupied Ethiopia in 1935, the school was forcibly closed. During the Italian invasion some Jewish villages were attacked. Most Beta Israel proved their loyalty to the emperor by serving in the Ethiopian armed forces or as guerrillas in the anti-Fascist underground. In reprisal, some Beta Israel villages were wiped out by the Italians. After Mussolini aligned himself with Hitler in 1940, the Italian Fascists tried to stir up the populace against the Jews by dropping leaflets in Amharic accusing them of being *buda*.[81]

During the 1960s, Ethiopia went through a period of economic and political upheaval. These acute crises, combined with Emperor Haile Selassie's mishandling of the country's famine, caused an estimated 300,000 people to starve to death, leading to the revolution of 1974. After forty years of autocratic rule, Selassie was overthrown, the monarchy was abolished, and Ethiopia was declared a Marxist state. A provisional governing committee called the Dargi, composed mostly of young noncommissioned officers, took the helm.

From this clique, a ruthless young lieutenant colonel, Haile Mengistu Mariam, rose to become the committee's chairman.

The Marxist military regime that overthrew Emperor Haile Selassie should theoretically have improved the lot of the Beta Israel. Major revolutionary reforms were implemented and all nationalities and religions were proclaimed to be equal. The Ethiopian toiling masses, including the Beta Israel, were now supposedly the masters of the land they plowed, and were given the right to self-determination. Initially, the Beta Israel had welcomed the land reform measures. But the reforms were not successful. In fact, the Beta Israel's problems were in many ways exacerbated by the revolution. Dispossessed landlords often resorted to violence in attempts to retrieve their property. Roving bandits, known as *shifta*, hired by former members of the aristocracy, attacked Beta Israel villages, looting, maiming and raping the inhabitants. Beta Israel villages were oftentimes caught in the crossfire between government troops and secessionist forces.

"By mid [twentieth] century," Shelemay writes, " a campaign had been launched to ensure formal recognition of the Falashas as Jews by religious authorities in Israel. To buttress the case for recognition, supporters romanticized and mythologized the Beta Israel past, proposing connections with diverse peoples and places in Jewish antiquity. Even among scholars speculation based on tenuous evidence replaced evenhanded inquiry. . . . Beta Israel origins were considered to be separate from those of other Ethiopians, despite the fact that the Ethiopian Christian majority also traced its descent to King Solomon."[82]

The young State of Israel made no significant effort on behalf of Ethiopian Jewry. There were less than two hundred Beta Israel in Israel when Menachem Begin was elected prime minister in 1977. Ethiopia and Israel enjoyed close relations from 1948 until the Yom Kippur War in 1973, when Ethiopia broke relations with Israel due to enormous pressure from Muslim African states. Because of the dynamics of realpolitik, Labor Party governments did not wish to antagonize a rare regional ally. For his part, Emperor Haile Selassie was less than enthusiastic about allowing the Beta Israel to leave. He regarded them as loyal citizens of his reign, and feared that a mass exodus would unleash an uncontrollable tide of other tribal minorities clamoring to leave the country. The Israeli attitude toward the Beta Israel is best summed up by Yehuda Shapiro:

> While Israel spent millions in a largely useless effort to encourage aliyah from America, Western Europe, and South Africa, the Israel Embassy in Addis Ababa was coldly turning away groups of Ethiopian Jews—especially young Ethiopians who made the arduous journey from distant vil-

lages to plead for help in emigrating to Israel. Despite the fact that Chief Rabbi Isaac Herzog reaffirmed the Beta Israel's Jewishness in 1954, many in high positions—few of them particularly religious or learned in Jewish law—cast doubt on the halachic status of the Ethiopian Jews. And incredible as it may seem, it is reliably reported that when Yisroel Yeshayahu, the longtime Speaker of the Knesset, visited Ethiopia in the 1950s and was petitioned by a group of Beta Israel to save them from a life of persecution and degradation in Ethiopia, he recommended instead that the Jews of Ethiopia consider solving their problem through conversion to Christianity. . . . Some Beta Israel took the time honored route of "illegal aliyah" by disguising themselves as Ethiopian Christians and taking their chances with the immigration authorities. (Happily, the Jewish state had not entirely lost its Jewish heart, and no Beta Israel "illegals" were ever deported.)[83]

It was not until 1973 that the status of the Beta Israel was authenticated by the Israeli Chief Rabbinate. That year the Sephardi Chief Rabbi, Ovadiah Yosef, basing his decision on the legal precedence established by Rabbi David Ben Abi Zimra (a.k.a. Radbaz, 1479–1573), ruled that the Beta Israel were indisputably Jews, ignorant of rabbinic Judaism "like a child raised among idolaters," but nevertheless an integral part of the Jewish people.[84] He concluded that the Beta Israel were descended from the Tribe of Dan who went southward to Ethiopia. "It is our duty," Rabbi Yosef wrote, "to redeem [them] from assimilation, to hasten their immigration to Israel, and to educate them in the spirit of our holy Torah and to make them partners in the building of our sacred land." Three years later the Ashkenazi Chief Rabbi Shlomo Goren concurred in this ruling. These rulings were vital, and in 1975 an interministerial committee drawn from the Departments of Justice, Immigrant Absorption, Religion, and Interior ruled that the Beta Israel were eligible to immigrate under the Law of Return. This law, adopted by the Knesset in 1950, automatically gave the right to every Jew to immigrate to Israel. It was now the responsibility of the Jewish Agency to facilitate this process.

Rabbi Yosef declared that no formal conversion was necessary, but to forestall any lingering doubts he insisted on ritual immersion for women and the ceremonial *hattafat dam brit* for males *giyur lechumrah* (strict conversion). For the men, this meant undressing and having a drop of blood drawn from their already circumcised penises. Yosef defined this ritual as an "act of renewing the covenant with the Jewish people and not a conversion." The concern in rabbinic circles was that over the centuries non-Beta Israel and slaves of the Beta

Israel might have married into the community without proper (i.e., normative Jewish) conversion. As Peter Schwab explains it, "The Chief Rabbinate maintained there was no way to tell whether Ethiopians had committed adultery, were married or divorced according to Jewish law, or whether married women had children in marriage following an invalid divorce, thus stigmatizing their children and calling into question their status as Jews."[85] There was a *safek* (possibility) that these *mamzairim* (bastards) subsequently would have intermarried with the general Beta Israel population, casting doubt upon the status of their relatives.[86]

The great majority of Beta Israel did not think that European-style rabbinic orthodoxy should be imposed upon them to qualify them as Jews.[87] Nevertheless, the Israeli Chief Rabbinate compelled several thousand immigrants to undergo the quasi conversion. To the Beta Israel the ritual immersion smacked of baptism, and the drawing of blood from the penis was a severe insult and the denial of an identity they had tenaciously preserved in a hostile Christian environment. To hammer home a message about how they felt about their treatment, Beta Israel parents refused to let their children swim in the sea, and one Beta Israel refused to perform a religious ceremony at a local community center because there was a swimming pool on the premises. After a year of marches, and a six-week sit-down demonstration at the Chief Rabbinate's headquarters, the Chief Rabbinate relented. An agreement was eventually reached between the government and the Chief Rabbinate that called for the religious status of each Ethiopian Jew to be considered on its own merits. The problem was solved when a member of the Sephardi Chief Rabbinate's council was appointed the official marriage registrar for Ethiopian Jewry, and was allowed to marry them without symbolic conversion. Under David Chelouche, the Chief Rabbi of Netanya, all men who through a combination of written documentation and oral evidence could prove their eligibility to marry were exempted from the requirement of ritual immersion. Still, many rabbinical courts have tended to be extremely cautious in deciding these cases.

In 1975 the Israeli government formally recognized members of the Ethiopian community as Jews under the Law of Return, though it was only after the Likud government came to power in 1977 that Prime Minister Menachem Begin set out to rescue the Ethiopian Jews. This was a process that came at a difficult time: The region was suffering from a series of droughts and famines, and Ethiopia was plunged into a civil war with Arab-backed forces in Ogadon, Eritrea, and along the Sudanese border. An arms deal in exchange for Ethiopian Jews was concluded, but for public consumption both governments vehemently denied cooperating. For its part, the Ethiopian government could not afford to alienate its major supplier of military aid, the Soviet Union. The Israelis also did not want the fact publicized because of possible repercussions in the United States, which had broken diplomatic relations with the Marxist regime of Ethiopia.

Hopes were very high in the Beta Israel community when two planes carrying a total of 120 Beta Israel passengers arrived in Israel. But then, in Zurich on February 6, 1978, Foreign Minster Moshe Dayan made a stupefying announcement to the press that Israel was helping to arm Ethiopia in its struggle against Somalia. Furious with Israel for Dayan's breach of secrecy, Addis Ababa expelled all Israeli advisors and put a halt to further Jewish emigration. Nevertheless, foreign agencies, specifically the American Association for Ethiopian Jewry, found ways to enable small numbers of Ethiopian Jews to slip out and make their way to Israel.

During Ethiopia's "Red Terror" of 1977–78, there was a campaign by the extremely insecure neo-Stalinist regime to terrorize the urban population. Anyone suspected of antigovernment activities was subject to arbitrary arrest and unspeakably brutal measures by the ubiquitous police. Gondar province was turned into a virtual battlefield. The revolution, the civil war, the struggle for secession in Eritrea, and the Ogadon war with Somalia, in addition to the famine, caused an estimated one million Ethiopians to flee to neighboring Sudan, Kenya, and Somalia. Hundreds of Beta Israel were killed in the crossfire between rebel groups and the revolutionary government. Under Major Melaku, the Jewhating governor of Gondar province, the provincial government not only cracked down on individual Beta Israel who wanted to emigrate to Israel, but it conducted a campaign of terror against the entire community. Teaching Hebrew and espousing Zionism were made a crime punishable by imprisonment. During Governor Melaku's rule, hundreds of Beta Israel were rounded up and imprisoned.[88]

With the onset of a severe famine and the escalation of the civil war, hundreds of thousands of Ethiopians fled to refugee camps across the Sudanese border. Among these refugees were some Beta Israel. "The [Beta Israel] benefited from the European memory of Jewish persecution, and their plight . . . galvanized the attention of the international media across all spectra of beliefs, political orientation, and ideology."[89] Spurred on by the American Association for Ethiopian Jewry, the Beta Israel began leaving their homes in Gondar and Tigre provinces for Sudan. Thousands left their villages and made the dangerous two-week trek on foot, dodging government soldiers, armed robbers, and wild animals. Many died en route. Those fortunates who survived the hazardous journey arrived at makeshift camps in the Sudan, where they lived in abominably wretched conditions. In 1979, at Prime Minister Menachem Begin's behest, the Mossad began smuggling Ethiopian Jews to Israel via the Sudan and Kenya. By early 1984, more than 5,000 Ethiopian Jews had slipped into Israel under an official cloak of secrecy.

By late 1984, sickness in the refugee camps in Sudan had reached epidemic levels. Tens of thousands of refugees were suffering from starvation and inadequate medical care. Three thousand Jews died of starvation, dehydration, and illnesses such as typhoid and malaria, with 2,000 of them dying in the summer of 1984 alone. When it became clear that thousands more would perish if nothing were done, the Israeli government mounted a rescue operation.

A dramatic clandestine mission, code-named Operation Moses, was undertaken by the Mossad and the CIA, with the assistance of the reluctant Sudanese strongman Gaffar al-Nimeiri (who agreed to cooperate after being promised half a billion dollars in foreign aid by the Reagan administration). Eight thousand Beta Israel were transported to Israel via Belgium, Switzerland, and Italy. This four-week operation, totaling more than thirty-five flights, lasted from November 1984 to January 1985. On January 6th, at the height of this rescue, details of the operation were prematurely leaked to the media by two Jewish Agency heads. At once, the other Arab countries began to apply intense pressure on Sudan to halt the flights. As a result, the Sudanese government withdrew its cooperation and the rescue mission was abruptly suspended before it could be completed.[90]

The premature suspension of Operation Moses left hundreds of Beta Israel stranded in the Sudan. There were cases of Beta Israel existing in the Sudanese refugee camps for as long as eight years. In March 1985, Operation Sheba, with the use of U.S. planes, rescued approximately 700 Ethiopian Jews from the Sudanese camps. Those who were not evacuated either returned to Ethiopia, died in the camps, or somehow managed to find their way to Europe, the Americas, or other third world countries. Most of those remaining in the Beta Israel villages in Ethiopia were women, young children, and old people. Tremendous guilt and despair over having left behind their loved ones during Operation Moses drove more than fifty Ethiopian Jews in Israel to commit suicide between 1986 and 1991.[91]

In 1986, the Ethiopian government embarked on what it called a "villageization" program. This entailed the abandonment of dispersed settlements in the countryside and in their place the creation of villages where the peasantry of a given region would be obliged to reside.[92] In areas where the Beta Israel lived, this meant that any cooperative of 500 Christian and Muslim families had to include ten to fifteen Jewish families from previous all-Jewish villages. The villageization program, deeply unpopular throughout Ethiopia, had the effect of uprooting Jewish life that was already in upheaval, and forcing the Beta Israel to reside among non-Jews who were often hostile toward them.

In November 1989 the Ethiopian government reestablished diplomatic relations with Israel, and an Israeli embassy was opened in the capital. This news quickly spread by word of mouth to the 500 villages in which the Jews resided. At the instigation of workers from the American Association for Ethiopian Jewry (AAEJ), thousands of Beta Israel embarked on the 500-mile trek to Addis Ababa. Some were robbed and killed by armed bandits on the way. Because the mass exodus was spontaneous and sudden, the Beta Israel left almost all their possessions behind. Some 20,000 displaced Ethiopian Jews crammed into a tiny area near the Israeli embassy compound. Having just restored relations with Addis Ababa, however, Jerusalem had no intention of becoming involved in an alleged mass transfer of a host population. By plopping thousands of Jews down on the Israeli embassy compound, the AAEJ hoped to force the Israeli government's hand.

Western volunteer doctors who arrived under the auspices of the Joint Distribution Committee (JDC) were appalled at the physical condition of the malnourished refugees. One such volunteer, Professor Emanuel Friedman of the University of California, San Francisco, Medical School, who spent four weeks in Addis Ababa in late 1990, describes the seemingly indescribable living conditions of the Beta Israel he witnessed near the Israeli compound:

> They would rent out anything that had four walls. A chicken coop would house a family of eight. A tiny room would house ten or more. There were no sanitary conditions, whatsoever. Only about fifty percent of their living spaces actually had outdoor latrines. There was no running water. A small earth mound covered with an old blanket would be the bed. Cooking and everything else was done in that little room. They might or might not have one small hole in the wall for light and air. Generally it was just an entrance. They had to go to a central area some distance just to get water.[93]

Many became seriously ill, and 250 died, mostly from pneumonia and bronchitis. In August 1990, Dr. Theodore Myers of Stanford University set up a full-scale medical clinic in Addis Ababa and, together with Drs. Friedman, Eli Schwartz, and other healthcare workers, instituted infant and childhood nutrition programs that dramatically reduced the death rate. The Beta Israel were registered and given ID cards, and a mass immunization campaign was carried out. Makeshift *tukuls*, schools, and *mesgids* were built on the embassy ground. Food and blankets were distributed, and each family was given a monthly stipend.

Meanwhile, a major escalation in the fighting took place between the Ethiopian government forces and the separatist rebel groups in Tigre and Eritrea. The United States joined the talks, offering to broker a peace conference between Mengistu and the rebel forces if the Beta Israel were allowed to emigrate. But then the rebel forces scored a series of major victories. President Mengistu fled the country and was succeeded by General Tesafye Gabre Kidan. With the major stumbling block now out of the picture,

> Prime Minister Yitzchak Shamir decided that the rescue operation could brook no further delay. Rebel forces were closing in on the capital and the Jews were a potential target for revenge attacks. . . . Mengistu had sought to use the Ethiopian Jews as bargaining chips to obtain Israeli weaponry. . . . Shamir refused to do business with him. . . . His succesor, General Tesafye Gabre Kidan, reportedly demanded a $100 million payment, but settled for thirty-five million, paid into a New York bank. . . .[94]
> A committee of Jewish Agency representatives and local Ethiopian Jews spread the word among the community in Addis Ababa, many of whom had been waiting a year for rescue. Fearing that deserting soldiers and jealous peasants would incite a pogrom against the relatively well-treated Jews, some several hundred plainclothes Israeli soldiers were poised to safeguard the operation.[95]

In one extended swoop lasting thirty-three hours and totaling forty planeloads, the Israeli government under an extremely tight security net evacuated more than 14,000 Jews out of Ethiopia. The Beta Israel could not take anything but the clothes on their backs and a few personal religious objects. One Boeing 747 set an all-time record, packing in 1087 passengers, or more than twice its normal number. Seats had been removed and the floor of the entire cabin was covered with mattresses. Five women gave birth during the journey. Two-thirds of the passengers were under the age of eighteen.

After the last Operation Solomon flight departed from Addis Ababa, there were still some 6,000 Beta Israel left in Ethiopia. Some had missed the airlift because they were caught in rebel-held territory. One group from the remote mountain region of Quara, in northern Ethiopia's Gondar province, did not learn about Operation Solomon in time. Additionally, there were thousands of Falas Mura left behind—Ethiopian Jews who had converted to Christianity but nevertheless wished to be reunited with their loved ones in Israel.

Today, Ethiopian Christians with some Beta Israel ancestry are believed to number in the hundreds of thousands. These were the Falas Mura, or Maryam

Wodet (Lovers of Mary), Ethiopians whose ancestors, or themselves, had converted to Christianity. According to Dr. Kaplan, they had converted "for educational opportunities, social advancement, and the possibility of gaining rights to win land."[96] Many converted for their own personal reasons, on their own volition. Simon Messing, who did a study of the Ethiopian Jews in the early 1960s, estimated the Christianized Beta Israel population at 50,000.[97] The *Oritawi* (Torah-observing) Beta Israel treated the Falas Mura as Gentiles whose touch polluted, and they were forbidden to enter the Beta Israel *mesgids*.[98] Many Falas Mura insist that they never attended Christian churches, continued to practice Judaism in private, and married exclusively among themselves.[99] During Operation Solomon, some 4,000 Falas Mura camped outside the Israeli compound in Addis Ababa awaiting permission to emigrate. Those Falas Mura who converted for love and money were written off as traitors by staunch Beta Israel. Some of those who were clamoring to go to Israel were believed to be not Jewish at all, but Christians posing as Jews. Nevertheless, writes Daniel Friedman, "Today in Israel, the Ethiopian Jewish community tends to support the Falas Mura's demand to be able to immigrate to Israel, despite its past hostility to converts."[100] Many Falas Muras were trying to reunite with relatives in Israel. Israel's two Chief Rabbis favored bringing the legitimate marranos out of Ethiopia, examining each claim on a case-by-case basis, so that those who could prove Jewish descent would be admitted under Israel's Law of Return, which guarantees citizenship for Jewish immigrants. A specially appointed Israeli ministerial committee decided early in 1993 to admit only those Falas Mura who had immediate family in Israel. But they were not admitted as Jews under the Law of Return. Only those Falas Mura who reconvert are automatically considered for immigration under the Law of Return. As of summer 1999 there are some 5,000 Falas Mura living in Ethiopia. There are about 30,000 more in Ethiopia, where they have been receiving humanitarian aid from the American Jewish Joint Distribution Committee.

Marcia Kretzmer says that the Beta Israel, like other Ethiopians, "have a boundless capacity for bearing suffering with resignation and fortitude."[101] In January 1996 a stunned Israeli public witnessed a spectacle given prime time on the international cable networks. More than fifteen thousand Ethiopian Jews (New York Times figure) had converged on the prime minister's office in Jerusalem and were sprayed with tear gas and water cannons when the protest turned violent. The ostensible reason for the demonstration was the galling revelation that Mogen David Adom (the national blood bank) had adopted a policy of routinely discarding all blood received from Ethiopian donors because of an unsubstantiated claim that the Operation Solomon immigrants were fifty times more likely to carry HIV than the rest of the Israeli population. (No studies have been produced to back up this claim.)[102] The authorities felt it would be less insulting to reject the blood than to reject the donor. This was the proverbial straw that broke the camel's back. The *edah* (ethnic community) that had heretofore been viewed as docile and utterly lacking in *sabra chutzpah* had come out in full force to vent their collective spleen at the Israeli government and society for much more than just this one grievance that was not being redressed.

In a 1986 article in *Moment Magazine*, Jeff Halper of The Hebrew University made the following observation: "In the back of the Israeli public's collective mind—not to mention the minds of the absorption workers and policy makers themselves—are 'the mistakes of the '50s,' when immigrants from Muslim countries were treated as cogs in the bureaucratic wheel, stripped of their own cultural identity and channeled into the economic and social margins of Israeli society. That danger still exists, but many workers and activists are determined to see that the Ethiopians . . . find their rightful place in Israel's rough-and-tumble society."[103] Lamentably, Israel has learned little from "the mistakes of the '50s." It is thirteen years since this article was published, and the situation for many Ethiopian Jews is as grim and depressing as ever.

When the Beta Israel from the pre-Operation Solomon period arrived in Israel, the Ministry of Immigration embarked on a policy of placing no more than fifty or sixty Beta Israel families in a single neighborhood, in order not to ghettoize them. Although it was more difficult for them to adjust to Israeli life than other *edot*, many of these earlier Beta Israel arrivals overcame insurmountable problems, made a radical adjustment, and found their niche in the Israeli mosaic. Their unemployment rate was less than the national level. According to Tesheme Wagaw, an Ethiopian Christian scholar who conducted extensive field work in Israel in the late 1980s, this wave experienced little overt racism, and the general attitude toward the Israeli government, despite problems with housing and jobs, was generally positive.[104]

The arrival of the Operation Solomon wave coincided with a mass influx of hundreds of thousands of Jews from the former Soviet Union, which created an acute crisis in housing and job opportunities. Many thousands of Ethiopian families were able to utilize generous mortgage terms offered by the *Suchnut* (Ministry of Absorption), which enabled them to move into permanent settlements. Thousands more are still isolated from the rest of Israeli society and are still living in ramshackle caravan trailer parks or in absorption centers. These centers, Israeli researcher Esther Hertzog argues, "develop social distance and power-dependence relations, and promote segregation."[105]

The authority structure of the Beta Israel extended family system (*zamed*), in which the elders were traditionally revered, is rapidly being undermined in

Israel. The Beta Israel fear secularization, rising juvenile delinquency, and the erosion of their Ethiopian Jewish heritage and cultural values. The difficulty of integrating into Israeli society, and having to rely on the government for hand-outs, has had a demoralizing effect on the older generation of Beta Israel. Family life has been turned upside down because of the reversals of roles played by parents in relation to their children. The young are out in the world, quickly learning the languages and habits of a modern lifestyle, and they must serve as the representatives for their elders to the outside world. The elders, who are linguistically and occupationally handicapped, have become totally dependent on their children for advice and support.

There are estimated to be close to 75,000 Ethiopian Jews in Israel today. Eighty-five percent of Ethiopian immigrant families live below the poverty line.[106] Many of those who are employed are performing predominantly menial tasks. Ethiopian students have been placed in inferior religious schools, and collectively steered into vocational studies programs that offer little opportunity for higher education and little hope of getting a job.[107] A number of concerned journalists and social activists have expressed fear that the Beta Israel will supplant the Palestinians as a source of cheap labor, thereby creating a polarized society with an American-style Black underclass.[108]

As recently as 1993 an African-American researcher with a self-described Afro-centric worldview declared that the "data suggest that discrimination on the basis of skin color is not a problem in Israel."[109] Yet many young Ethiopian Jews are feeling increasingly marginalized because of their swarthy pigmentation. "For an alienated minority," writes the prominent Israeli journalist Yossi Klein Halevy, "a Black African identity is becoming a substitute for a failed sense of Israeliness—an ironic reversal of their parents' insistence on being Jews, not Ethiopians."[110] When the first Beta Israel arrived in the early 1980s, many successfully competed for places in the Israeli Army's elite paratrooper units. Even today, the Ethiopian community is represented disproportionate to their numbers in the armed forces. A very disturbing statistic is this: While the Ethiopian Jews make up just four-tenths of one percent of the soldiers in the Israeli Defense Forces, they comprise ten percent of its suicides.[111]

However, there is some consolation in knowing that the next generation, sons and daughters of goatherds and bead stringers who never left the proverbial four cubits of their birth, is quickly learning to cope with ATM machines, malls, public transportation, and the internet. An increasing number of young Ethiopian Jews are enrolled in institutions of higher learning and succeeding in the professions. They are contributing significantly to, and benefitting from, Israel's prosperity. With Israeli and world Jewry's vigilance and greater aware-

ness of the struggles of these African Jews, they may yet be integrated into Israeli society.

NOTES

1. Jean Doresse, *Ethiopia* (New York: F. Ungar, 1959), p. 222.

2. The Somali, Oromo, and Agaw tribespeople—of whom the Beta Israel are
considered an integral part—together with the Nubian tribes of Southern Egypt, are all
classified as Kushitic.

3. Harold Marcus, *A History of Ethiopia* (Berkeley: University of California Press,
1994), p. 17. For theories of an earlier dating of the Kebra Negast, see David W. Johnson,
"Dating the Kebra Negast: Another Look," in *Peace and War in Byzantium: Essays in Honor
of George T. Dennis*, edited by Timothy Miller and John Nesbitt (Washington, D.C.:
Catholic University of America Press, 1995), pp. 197–208.

4. Polson Newman, *Ethiopian Realities* (London: G. Allen and Unwin, 1936), p. 13.

5. A. H. M. Jones and Elizabeth Monroe, *A History of Ethiopia* (Oxford: Clarion
Press, 1962), p. 17.

6. Robert L. Hess, *Ethiopia: The Modernization of Autocracy* (Ithaca, N.Y.: Cornell
University Press, 1970), p. 37.

7. Tessa Rajak, "Moses in Ethiopia: Legend and Literature," *Journal of Jewish Studies*
29:2 (Autumn 1978), pp. 111–22.

8. Sir Ernest A. Wallis Budge, one of the outstanding authorities in the early
20th century on the history of Ethiopia, writes that it is "very likely that some enterprising 'queen of the south' did make a journey to Jerusalem and interview Solomon. . . .
Many eminent scholars have accepted the story as historical, and I think on the whole
they were right. . . ." *A History of Ethiopia*, vol. 1 (London: Anthropological Publications, 1970, Reprint of 1887 edition), pp. x and 193.

9. For an imaginative and entertaining account of the Ark of the Covenant see
Graham Hancock, *The Sign and the Seal: The Quest for the Lost Ark of the Covenant* (New
York: Simon and Schuster, 1992).

10. Marcus, *A History*, p. 18.

11. David Kessler, *The Falashas: The Forgotten Jews of Ethiopia* (New York:
Schocken Books, 1985), pp. 41–47. On the Jewish military colony of the Elephantine
see Bezalel Porten, *Archives from Elephantine* (Berkeley and Los Angeles: University of
California Press, 1968).

12. Cited in Steven Kaplan, "The Two Zions and the Exodus from Ethiopia," in
Jewish Messianism in the Modern Era: Meaning and Metaphor, edited by Jonathan Frankel
(New York: Oxford University Press, 1991), p. 301.

13. Steven Kaplan, The Beta Israel (Falasha) of Ethiopia (New York: New York University Press), p. 27.

14. *The Ethiopians: An Introduction to Country and People* (London: Oxford University Press, 1960), pp. 11–112.

15. *Falasha Anthology* (New Haven: Yale University Press, 1979), p. xli.

16. Paul Henze, *Ethiopian Journeys* (London: Ernest Benn Ltd., 1977), p. 181.

17. *A Song of Longing: An Ethiopian Journey* (Urbana: University of Chicago, 1991), pp. 138–39.

18. *Music, Ritual, and Falasha History*, 2nd ed. (East Lansing: Michigan State University Press, 1989), p. 205.

19. *A Song of Longing*, p. 142.

20. Ibid., pp. 137–52.

21. "A Biochemical Response to an Halakhic Challenge: The Case of the Ethiopian Jews," *Torah U-Madda Journal* 3 (1991–92), p. 6.

22. James A. Quirin, *The Evolution of the Ethiopian Jews: A History of the Beta Israel (Falasha) to 1920* (Philadelphia: University of Pennsylvania Press, 1992), p. xi.

23. Ibid., p. 59.

24. *The Beta Israel (Falasha) of Ethiopia*, pp. 65 and 161.

25. Ibid., p. 161.

26. Quirin, *The Evolution*, p. 15. Similarly, Kaplan writes: "The overwhelming impact of biblical and Hebraic patterns on early Ethiopian culture is undeniable." See *The Beta Israel*, p. 17.

27. *The Beta Israel*, p. 40.

28. "Leadership and Communal Organization Among the Beta Israel (Falasha): An Historical Study," *Encyclopaedia Judaica Yearbook* 1986–87 (Jerusalem: Keter, 1988), p. 154.

29. Marcus, *A History*, p. 12.

30. Otto A. Jager, *Antiquities of Northern Ethiopia* (Stuttgart: F. A. Brockhaus, 1965), p. 18. Most modern scholars reject the notion that the Zagwes were Jewish. The Zagwe are considered to have been devout Christians. See Kaplan, *The Beta Israel*, p. 48.

31. Marcus: *A History*, p. 16.

32. Quirin, *The Evolution*, p. 40.

33. Taddesse Tamrat, *Church and State in Ethiopia, 1270–1527* (Oxford: Clarendon Press, 1972), p. 205.

34. James A. Quirin, *The Beta Israel (Falasha) in Ethiopian History: Caste Formation and Culture Change, 1270–1868* (unpublised dissertation, University of Minnesota, 1977), p. 258.

35. Quirin, *The Evolution*, p. 40.

36. Doresse, *Ethiopia*, p. 121.

37. Kaplan, *The Beta Israel*, pp. 59 and 184.

38. Quirin, *The Evolution*, p. 74.

39. Ibid., p. 109.

40. *Queen of Sheba's Heirs* (Washington, D.C.: Acropolis Books, 1970), p. 39.

41. Frederick C. Gamst, *The Qemant: A Pagan-Hebraic Peasantry of Ethiopia* (New York: Holt, Rinehart, and Winston, 1969), p. 53.

42. Quirin, *The Beta Israel*, p. 232.

43. *Africa's Last Empire: Through Abyssinia to Lake Tana and the Country of the Falasha* (London: H. F. & G. Witherby, 1930), p. 202.

44. Quirin, *The Evolution*, p. 162.

45. Shelemay, *Music, Ritual*, p. 57; Kaplan, *The Beta Israel*, p. 73; Quirin, *The Beta Israel*, p. 65.

46. Kaplan, *The Beta Israel,* pp. 110–11.

47. Ibid., p. 128.

48. Joseph Halevy, "Travels in Abyssinia," in *Miscellany of Hebrew Literature,* vol. 2, second series, edited by A. L. Lowy (London: Trubner and Co., 1877), p. 231.

49. Ephraim Isaac, "An Obscure Component in Ethiopian Church History," *Le Museon,* 85 (1972), p. 232.

50. Shelemay, *Music, Ritual*, pp. 79–80; Kaplan, *The Beta Israel*, pp. 158–59.

51. Leslau, *Falasha Anthology*, p. xv.

52. Yossi Klein Halevi, "The Last Jewish Monk," *The Jerusalem Report* 3:19 (28 January 1993), pp. 22–23.

53. Richard Cavendish, editor-in-chief, *Man, Myth, and Magic: The Illustrated Encyclopedia of Mythology, Religion, and the Unknown*, vol. 15 (New York: Marshall Cavendish, 1994), p. 2078.

54. Edward Ullendorf, *Ethiopia and the Bible* (London: Oxford University Press, 1968), p. 3.

55. Norden, *Africa's Last Empire*, p. 199.

56. Simon Messing, *The Story of the Falashas: Black Jews of Ethiopia* (New York: Balshan Press, 1982), p. 49.

57. Pamela Kidron, "In a New Light," *The Jerusalem Post Entertainment Magazine* (29 September 1989), pp. 2–3.

58. Kaplan, "Leadership," p. 157.

59. *The Peoples of Africa* (New York: Marshall Cavendish, 1978), p. 79.

60. *The Falashas (Jews) of Abyssinia* (London: William Macintosh, 1869), p. 56.

61. *The Peoples of Africa*, p. 79.

62. Leslau, *Falasha Anthology*, pp. xvii–xviii.

63. Chaim Rosen quoted in Amy Avgar, "The Ethiopian Parents and Children in Israel," *Na'amat Woman* (January-February 1993), p. 7.

64. Simon Messing, "Journey to the Falashas: Ethiopia's Black Jews," *Commentary* 22 (1956), p. 37.

65. Flad, *The Falashas*, p. 58.

66. Elkan N. Adler, ed., *Jewish Travellers in the Middle Ages: 19 Firsthand Accounts* (New York: Dover Publications, 1987), p. 6.

67. Ibid., p. 71.

68. Ibid., p. 61.

69. James Bruce, *Travels to Discover the Source of the Nile*, 2nd ed. (Edinburgh: G. G. J. and J. Robinson, 1790).

70. Steven Kaplan, "The Beta Israel Encounter with Protestant Missionaries: 1860–1905," *Jewish Social Studies* 49:1 (Winter 1987), p. 31.

71. Quirin, *The Evolution*, p. 179.

72. Quirin, ibid., pp. 183–84.

73. Kaplan, "The Beta Israel (Falasha) Encounter," p. 34; Quirin, *The Evolution*, p. 182.

74. Quirin, *The Evolution*, p. 155.

75. Halevy, "Travels," pp. 215–16.

76. Richard A. Caulk, "Yohannes IV, the Mahdists, and the Colonial Partition of North-East Africa," *Trans African Journal of History* 1:2 (July 1971), p. 30.

77. Kaplan, "Leadership," p. 159.

78. On Nahum's report of his mission to the Beta Israel see Esther Benbassa, *Haim Nahum: A Sephardic Chief Rabbi in Politics* (Tuscaloosa, Alabama: University of Alabama Press, 1995), pp. 119–44; Tudor Parfitt, "Rabbi Nahoum's Anthropological Mission to Ethiopia," in *The Beta Israel in Ethiopia and Israel: Studies on Ethiopian Jewry*, edited by Tudor Parfitt and Emanuela Trevisan Semi (Surrey, England: Curzon Press, 1999), pp. 1–14.

79. Cited in Kessler, *The Falashas*, p. 144.

80. "An Outline of Falasha History," *Proceedings of the Third International Conference of Ethiopian Studies* (Addis Ababa: Institute of Ethiopian Studies, 1969), p. 111.

81. Messing, "Journey," p. 39.

82. *A Song of Longing*, p. 37.

83. "We Are All Falashas," *Response* 12 (Summer 1979), p. 36.

84. Cited in Don Seeman, "Ethnographers, Rabbis, and Jewish Epistemology: The Case of the Ethiopian Jews, *Tradition: A Journal of Orthodox Jewish Thought* 25:4 (1991), p. 15.

85. "Israel and the Ethiopian Jews," *Jewish Currents* 41:8 (September 1987), p. 7.

86. On determining the status of the Ethiopian Jews from an Orthodox halakhic point of view, see Hershel Schachter, "Determining Jewish Identity: Ethiopian Jewry," *The Journal of Halacha* 9 (Spring 1985), pp. 143–60; J. David Bleich, "Black Jews: A

Halakhic Perspective," *Tradition: A Journal of Jewish Thought* 15:1 (1975–76), pp. 48–79; Michael Corinaldi, *Jewish Identity: The Case of Ethiopian Jewry* (Jerusalem: The Magnes Press, The Hebrew University, 1998), esp. pp. 110–119.

87. Notable exceptions are Qes Rafael Hadane and his son Yosef, a yeshiva-ordained rabbi, who fear that perpetuating the proto-Mosaic Judaism practiced by the Beta Israel would marginalize them and make them a separate sect like the Samaritans and the anti-talmudic Karaites. See Yossi Klein Halevi, "The Struggle of the Kessim," *The Jerusalem Report* 3:12 (22 October 1992), pp. 19–20.

88. Claire Safran, *Secret Exodus* (Prentice Hall Press, 1987), p. 45; *Los Angeles Times* (12 November 1981), p. 1B. See also Galia Sabar Friedman, "Religion and the Marxist State in Ethiopia: The Case of the Ethiopian Jews *Religion in Communist Lands* 17:3 (Autumn 1989), pp. 247–256.

89. Teshome G. Wagaw, "The International Ramifications of Falasha Emigration," *The Journal of Modern African Studies* 29:4 (1991), p. 558.

90. For various accounts of Operation Moses and the repercussions of the "leak" see Tudor Parfitt, *Operation Moses: The Story of the Falasha Jews from Ethiopia* (London: Weidenfeld and Nicolson, 1985), esp. pp. 89–107; Claire Safran, *Secret Exodus*, esp. pp. 133–39; Louis Rapoport, *Redemption Song: The Story of Operation Moses* (San Diego: Harcourt Brace Jovanovich, 1986), esp. pp. 130–51; Graenum Berger, *Rescue the Ethiopian Jews: A Memoir, 1955–1995* (New Rochelle, N.Y.: John Washburn Bleeker Publishing Co., 1996), pp. 143–158.

91. William Recant, "The Journey Home: An Insider's Account of Operation Solomon," *The Jewish Monthly* (June–July 1991), p. 15; Marcia Kretzmer, "The Pain of Separation," *The Jerusalem Post Magazine* (10 March 1989), p. 8.

92. Arch Puddington, "Ethiopia: The Communist Uses of Famine," *Commentary* 81:4 (April 1986), p. 34.

93. Interview with Dr. Friedman, March 1995.

94. David Horovitz and Micha Odenheimer, "Precious Cargo," *The Jerusalem Report* 1:34 (6 June 1991), p. 11.

95. Ibid., p. 12.

96. "Falasha Christians: A Brief History," p. 20. See also Messing, *The Story*, p. 98.

97. Messing, *The Story*, pp. 94–5 and 99.

98. "The Beta Israel in Ethiopia never saw the Falas Mora as brothers," a Beta Israel spokesperson in Israel told journalist Tom Sawicki in 1993. "In fact, many saw them as traitors." *The Jerusalem Report* 4:1 (20 May 1993), p. 20.

99. Messing, *The Story*, p. 99.

100. "The Case of the Falas Mura," in *The Beta Israel in Ethiopia and Israel: Studies on Ethiopian Jewry*, edited by Tudor Parfitt and Emanuela Trevisan Semi (Surrey, England: Curzon Press, 1999), p. 73. " . . .[A]ccording to halakhah, Jewish identity is

secured and transmitted via the mother and cannot be annulled by conversion. In the eyes of the rabbinate, since the Falashas had scarcely mixed with the neighboring population, they were still Jewish. The Rabbinate thus suggested that the Falas Mura should be given a Jewish education and reconverted, which they were encouraged to do and which occurred in an initiation ceremony presided over by Rabbi [Menachem] Waldman." Ibid., p. 79.

101. "The Pain of Separation," p. 8.

102. According to *The Jerusalem Report* only one percent of all Ethiopian Jews were tested as HIV-positive, a rate that is lower than major Western European countries. Yossi Klein Halevi, "Lost Tribe," *The Jerusalem Report* 3:2 (30 May 1996), p. 15.

103. "From Gondar to Ashdod," *Moment* (January-February 1986), p. 43.

104. "The Emigration and Settlement of Ethiopian Jews in Israel," *Middle East Review* (Winter 1987/88), p. 48; "The International Ramifications of Falasha Emigration," p. 580; *For Our Soul: Ethiopian Jews in Israel* (Detroit: Wayne State University, 1993), p. 240.

105. "The Bureaucratic Absorption of Ethiopian Immigrants in Israel: Integration or Segregation?" in Steven Kaplan et al., eds., *Between Africa and Zion: Proceedings of the First International Congress of the Society for the Study of the Ethiopian Jews* (Jerusalem: Ben-Zvi Institute, 1995), p. 189.

106. Micha Odenheim, "Blood and Other Libels: Israel's Ethiopian Dilemma," *Tikkun* 11:2 (1996), p. 46.

107. *The Jerusalem Report* 2:28 (7 May 1992), p. 13.

108. Shula Mula, "What Happens to a Dream Deferred?" *The Jerusalem Report* 6:10 (21 September 1995), p. 58; Tom Sawicki, "Frozen Out," *The Jerusalem Report,* 5:1 (19 May 1994), p. 20.

109. Durrenda Ojanuga, "The Ethiopian Jewish Experience as Blacks in Israel," *Journal of Black Studies* 24:2 (December 1993), p. 151.

110. "Lost Tribe," p. 15.

111. *Northern California Jewish Bulletin* (4 April 1997), p. 22A.

Selected Bibliography

Adler, Elkan N., ed. *Jewish Travelers in the Middle Ages: 19 Firsthand Accounts*. New York: Dover Publications, 1987.

Ahroni, Reuben. *The Jews of the British Crown Colony of Aden: History, Culture and Ethnic Relations*. Leiden: E. J. Brill, 1994.

———. *Yemenite Jewry: Origins, Culture, and Literature*. Bloomington, Ind.: Indiana University Press, 1986.

Alcalay, Ammiel. *After Jews and Arabs: Remaking Levantine Culture*. Minneapolis: University of Minnesota Press, 1993.

Altshuler, Mordechai. *The Jews of the Eastern Caucasus: The History of the Mountain Jews from the Beginning of the Nineteenth Century*. Jerusalem: Ben-Zvi Institute for the Study of Jewish Communities of the East—The Hebrew University of Jerusalem, 1990. [Hebrew]

Arbel, Rachel and Lily Magel. *In the Land of the Golden Fleece: The Jews of Georgia: History and Culture*. Tel Aviv: Beth Hatfutsoth, 1992.

Ashkenazi, Michael and Alex Weingrod, eds. *Ethiopian Jews and Israel*. New Brunswick, N.J.: Transaction Books, 1987.

Baazova, Lily, et. al. "Georgia: The Land and the Jews," *Ariel* 96 (1994): 5–26.

Bahloul, Joëlle. "The Sephardic Jew as Mediterranean: A View from Kinship and Gender." *Journal of Mediterranean Studies* 4:2 (1994): 197–207.

Barer, Shlomo. *The Magic Carpet*. London: Secker and Warburg, 1952.

Baron, Salo W. *A Social and Religious History of the Jews*. Vol. 18. *The Ottoman Empire, Persia, Ethiopia, India, and China*. 2nd ed. New York: Columbia University Press, 1983.

Ben-Am, Issacher. *Saint Veneration among the Jews of Morocco*. Detroit: Wayne State University, 1998.

————. *The Sephardi and Oriental Jewish Tradition.* Jerusalem: Magnes Press, The Hebrew University, 1982.

Benet, Sula. *How To Live To Be 100: The Lifestyles of the People of the Caucasus.* New York: Dial Press, 1976.

Benjamin of Tudela. *The Itinerary of Benjamin of Tudela.* Critical text, translation and commentary by Marcus Nathan Adler. New York: Phillip Feldheim, 1907.

Benjamin, I. J. *Eight Years in Asia and Africa, from 1846 to 1855.* 2nd ed. Hanover: n.p., 1863.

Benzoor, Nina, ed. *Azerbaijan: Mountain Jews, Urban Jews.* Exhibition Catalogue. Haifa: Museum of Music and Ethnography, 1992.

Ben-Zvi, Itzhak. *The Exiled and the Redeemed.* Philadelphia: Jewish Publication Society, 1957.

Bergl, Hetty, ed. *Facing West: Oriental Jews of Central Asia and the Caucasus.* Zwolle: Waanders, 1997.

Berman, Colette and Yosef Miller. *The Beautiful People of the Book.* Jerusalem: Millhouse Publishers: 1988.

Bleich, J. David. "Black Jews: A Halakhic Perspective." *Tradition: A Journal of Jewish Thought* 15:1 (1975–76): 48–79.

Bonne-Tamir, Batsheva. "Oriental Jewish Communities and their Genetic Relationship with South-West Asian Populations." *Indian Anthropologist* (1985): 153–170.

Bowman, Steven B. *The Jews of Byzantium 1204–1453.* University of Alabama Press, 1985.

Brauer, Eric. *The Jews of Kurdistan.* Completed and edited by Raphael Patai. Detroit: Wayne State University Press, 1993.

————. "The Jews of Afghanistan." *Jewish Social Studies* 4:2 (April 1942): 121–138.

Brutzkus, Y. "Di Geshichte fun di Berg Yiden oif Kavkaz," Vilna: *YIVO Historische Shriften* 2 (1937): 26–42. [Yiddish]

Buck, Pearl S. *Peony.* New York: John Day, 1948.

Budge, E. A. Wallis. *The Queen of Sheba and Her Only Son, Menyelek.* London: Oxford University Press, 1930.

Bukhara, Musical Crossroads of Asia. Recorded, compiled and annotated by Ted Levin and Otanazar Matykubov, with an introduction to the recordings. Washington, D.C.: Smithsonian/Folkways, 1991. (SF 40050)

Caspi, Mishael M. *Daughters of Yemen.* Berkeley: University of California Press, 1985.

————, ed. *Jewish Tradition in the Diaspora: Studies in Memory of Walter J. Fischel.* Berkeley, C.A.: Judah Magnes Museum, 1981.

Chenciner, Robert. *Daghestan: Tradition and Survival.* New York: St. Martin's Press, 1997.

Chouraqui, Andre N. *Between East and West: A History of the Jews of North Africa.* New York: Atheneum, 1973.

Cohen, Hayyim J. *The Jews of the Middle East, 1860–1972.* Jerusalem: Israel Universities Press, 1973.

Cohen, Mark R. and Abraham L. Udovitch, eds. *Jews Among Arabs: Contacts and Boundaries.* Princeton, N.J.: The Darwin Press, 1989.

Connolly, Arthur. *Journey to the North of India: Overland from England through Russia, Persia and Affghanistan.* London: Richard Bentley, 1838.

Corinaldi, Michael. *Jewish Identity: The Case of Ethiopian Jewry.* Jerusalem: The Magnes Press, The Hebrew University, 1998.

Cowen, Ida. *Jews in Remote Corners of the World.* Englewood Cliffs, N.J.: Prentice Hall, 1971.

d'Beth Hillel, David. *Travels from Jerusalem Through Arabia, Kurdistan, Part of Persia and India to Madras.* Madras: n.p., 1832.

Daniel, Ruby and Barbara Johnson. *Ruby of Cochin: An Indian Jewish Woman Remembers.* Philadelphia: Jewish Publication Society, 1995.

Daum, Werner, ed. *Yemen: 3000 Years of Art and Civilization in Arabia Felix.* Innsbruch: Pinguin-Verlag, 1987.

De Felice, Renzo. *Jews in an Arab Land: Libya 1835–1970.* Austin: University of Texas, 1985.

de Leeuw, Henrik. *Crossroads of the Mediterranean.* Garden City, N.Y.: Hanover House, 1954.

Deshen, Shlomo. *The Mellah Society.* Chicago: University of Chicago Press, 1989.

Deshen, Shlomo and Walter P. Zenner. *Jewish Societies in the Middle East: Community, Culture and Authority.* Lanham, N.Y.: University Press of America, 1982.

————. *Jews Among Muslims: Communities in the Precolonial Middle East*, New York: New York University Press, 1996.

Eber, Irene. "Kaifeng Jews Revisited: Sinification As Affirmation of Identity." *Monumenta Serica* 41 (1993): 231–247.

Elazar, Daniel J. *The Jewish Community of Iran.* Jerusalem and Philadelphia: Center for Jewish Community Studies, 1975.

————. *People and Polity: The Organizational Dynamics of World Jewry.* Detroit: Wayne State University Press, 1989.

Eliav, A. L. *Between Hammer and Sickle.* Philadelphia: Jewish Publication Society, 1969.

Encyclopaedia Judaica. Jerusalem: Keter, 1971–1973.

Eraqi Klorman, Bat-Zion. *The Jews of Yemen in the Nineteenth Century: A Portrait of a Messianic Community.* Leiden: E. J. Brill, 1993.

Faith and Survival: Ethiopian Jewish Life 1983–1992. Photographs by Peggy Myers. Text by Dr. Ted Myers. Berkeley, C.A.: Judah L. Magnes Museum, 1992.

Farago, Ladislas. *Arabian Antic.* New York: Sheridan House, 1938.

Fischel, Walter J. "Cochin in Jewish History: Prolegamena to a History of the Jews in India." *Proceedings of the American Academy for Jewish Research* 30 (1962): 37–59.

————. "The Contribution of the Cochin Jews to South Indian and Jewish Civilization," In *Commemoration Volume.* Edited by S. S. Koder, et al. Cochin: Kerala Historical Association, 1971.

————. "Israel in Iran." In *The Jews: Their History, Culture, and Religion.* Edited by Louis Finkelstein. 3rd ed. Philadelphia: The Jewish Publication Society. 1960.

————. *Jews in the Economic and Political Life of Medieval Islam.* Vol. 22. London: Royal Asiatic Society, 1937.

———. "The Jews in Mediaeval Iran from the 16th to the 18th Centuries: Political, Economic, and Communal Aspects." *Irano-Judaica* 1 (1982): 265–291.

———. "The Jews of Central Asia (Khorasan) in Medieval Hebrew and Islamic Literature." *Historia Judaica* 7 (1945): 29–50; and (1946): 66–67.

———. "The Jews of Kurdistan a Hundred Years Ago." *Jewish Social Studies* 6 (1944): 195–226.

———. "The Jews of Persia (1795–1940)." *Jewish Social Studies* 12:2 (April 1950): 119–60.

———, ed. *Unknown Jews in Unknown Places: The Travels of Rabbi David D'Beth Hillel (1824–1832)*. New York: Ktav Publishing House, 1973.

Friedman, Keren Tzionah. "I Am a Picture: Change and Continuity on the Island of Djerba." *Folklore and Mythology* 2:3 (December, 1983): 3–6.

Gamliel, Shalom Ben Sa'adya et. al. *Yemenite Paths*. Jerusalem: Shalom Research Center, 1984. [In Hebrew with English summaries]

Geertz, Clifford et al. *Meaning and Order in Moroccan Society: Three Essays in Cultural Analysis*, Cambridge: Cambridge University Press, 1979.

Gellner, Ernest. *Saints of the Atlas*. Chicago: University of Chicago Press, 1969.

Gilad, Lisa. *Ginger and Salt: Yemeni Jewish Women in an Israeli Town*. Boulder: Westview Press, 1989.

———. *Yemeni Jewish Women*. Unpublished dissertation, Cambridge University, 1982.

Gitelman, Zvi. *A Century of Ambivalence: The Jews of Russia and the Soviet Union, 1881 to the Present*. New York: Schocken, 1988.

———. "Ethnic Identity and Ethnic Relations Among the Jews of the Non-European U.S.S.R." *Ethnic and Racial Studies* 14:1 (January 1991): 24–42.

Godbey, Allen H. *The Lost Tribes A Myth—Suggestions Towards Rewriting Hebrew History*. Durham, N.C.: Duke University Press, 1930.

Goitein, S.D. *From the Land of Sheba*. New York: Schocken Library, 1947.

———. "Jewish Education in Yemen as an Archetype of Traditional Jewish Education." *Commentary* 12 (1951): 109–146.

———. "The Jews of Yemen." In *Religion in the Middle East: Three Religions in Concord and Conflict*. Vol. 1. *Judaism and Christianity*. Edited by A. J. Arberry. Cambridge: Cambridge University Press, 1969.

Goldberg, Harvey E. "Anthropology and the Study of Traditional Jewish Societies." *Journal of the Association for Jewish Studies* 11:1 (Spring 1990): 1–22.

———. *Cave Dwellers and Citrus Growers: A Jewish Community in Libya and Israel*. Cambridge: Cambridge University Press, 1972.

———. "Introduction: Culture and Ethnicity in the Study of Israeli Society." *Ethnic Groups* 1 (1977):163–186.

———. *Jewish Life in Muslim Libya: Rivals and Relatives*. Chicago and London: The University of Chicago Press, 1990.

————, ed. *The Book of Mordechai: A Study of the Jews of Libya*. Philadelphia: Institute for the Study of Human Issues, 1980.

————, ed. *Sephardi and Middle Eastern Jewries*. Bloomington: Indiana University Press, 1996.

Goldstein, Darra. *The Georgian Feast: The Vibrant Culture and Savory Food of the Republic of Georgia*. San Francisco: HarperCollins Publishers, 1993.

Gottreich, Emily R. *Jewish Space in the Moroccan Mellah of Marrakech, 1550–1930*. Unpublished dissertation, Harvard University, 1999.

Green, Warren. "The Fate of the Crimean Jewish Communities: Ashkenazim, Krimchaks and Karaites." *Jewish Social Studies* 46:3–4 (Summer-Fall 1984): 169–176.

Grossman, Grace Cohen. *The Jews of Yemen: An Exhibition Organized by the Maurice Spertus Museum of Judaica*. Chicago: Spertus College of Judaica Press, 1976.

Hacohen, Dvora and Menachem Hacohen. *One People: The Story of the Eastern Jews*. New York: Adama Books, 1986.

Halevy, Joseph. "Travels in Abyssinia." In *Miscellany of Hebrew Literature*. Vol. 2. Second Series. Edited by A. L. Lowy. London: Trubner and Co., 1877.

————. *Travels in Yemen: An Account of Joseph Halevy's Journey to Najran in the Year 1870*. Written in Sa'ani Arabic by his Guide Hayyim Habshush. Edited by S. D. Goitein. Jerusalem: Hebrew University Press, 1941.

Hancock, Graham. *The Sign and the Seal: The Quest for the Lost Ark of the Covenant*. New York: Simon and Schuster, 1992.

Hess, Robert L. "Toward a History of the Falasha." *Eastern African History*. Edited by David F. McCall, Norman R. Bennett, and Jeffrey Butler. New York: Frederick A. Praeger, 1969.

Hirschberg, H. Z. *A History of the Jews of North Africa*. 2 vols. Leiden: E. J. Brill, 1981.

————. "The Oriental Jewish Communities." In *Religion in the Middle East: Three Religions in Concord and Conflict*. Vol. 1. *Judaism and Christianity*. Edited by A. J. Arberry. London: Cambridge University Press, 1969.

Hourani, Albert. *A History of the Arab Peoples*. New York: Warner Books, 1991.

Hyman, Mavis. *Jews of the Raj*. London: Hyman Publishers, 1995.

Isaac, Ephraim. "An Obscure Component in Ethiopian Church History." *Le Museon* 85 (1972): 225–258.

Isenberg, Shirley B. *India's Bene Israel: A Comprehensive Inquiry and Sourcebook*. Berkeley, C.A.: Judah L. Magnes Museum, 1988.

Israel, Benjamin J. *The Bene Israel of India: Some Studies*. New York: Apt Books Inc., 1984.

————. *The Jews of India*. New Delhi: Centre for Jewish and Interfaith Studies, 1982.

Jews in Old China: Some Western Views. Compiled and with an Introduction by Hyman Kublin. New York: Paragon Book Reprint Corp., 1971.

The Jews of Ethiopia: A People in Transition. Tel Aviv: Beth Hatfutsoth, Nahum Goldmann Museum of the Jewish Diaspora, 1984.

The Jews of Kaifeng—Chinese Jews on the Banks of the Yellow River. Tel Aviv: Beth Hatfutsoth, 1984.

The Jews of Kurdistan: Daily Life, Customs, Arts and Crafts. Exhibition Catalogue, no. 216. Jerusalem: The Israel Museum, 1981.

The Jews of San'a; As Seen by the Researchers Hermann Burchett and Carl Ruthjens. Tel Aviv: Beth Hatfutsoth, The Nahum Goldmann Museum of the Jewish Diaspora, 1982.

Johnson, Barbara C. *Our Community in Two Worlds: The Cochin Paradesi Jews in India and Israel*. Unpublished dissertation, University of Massachusetts, 1985.

Jung, Leo, ed. *Jewish Leaders (1750–1940)*, New York: Bloch, 1953.

Kaplan, Steven E. T*he Beta Israel (Falasha) in Ethiopia*. New York: New York University Press, 1992.

————. " 'Falasha' Religion: Ancient Judaism or Evolving Ethiopian Tradition? A Review Article." *Jewish Quarterly Review* 79 (July 1988): 49–65.

————, Trevisan Semi, and Tudor Parfitt, eds. *Between Africa and Zion*. Proceedings of the First International Congress of the Society for the Study of the Ethiopian Jews. Jerusalem: Ben Zvi Institute, 1995.

Kashani, Reuben. *The Jews of Afghanistan*. Jerusalem: n.p., 1975. [In Hebrew and English]

Katz, Nathan and Ellen S. Goldberg. "Jewish 'Apartheid' and a Jewish Gandhi." *Jewish Social Studies*. Vol. L: 3–4 (Summer-Fall 1988/93): 147–176.

————. *The Last Jews of Cochin: Jewish Identity in Hindu India*. Columbia, S.C.: University of South Carolina Press, 1993.

Katz, Nathan, ed. *Studies of Indian Jewish Identity*. New Delhi: Manohar Publishers, 1995.

Kehimkar, Haeem S. *The History of the Bene Israel of Bombay*. Tel Aviv: Dayag Press Ltd., 1937.

Kessler, David. *The Falashas: A Short History of the Ethiopian Jews*. London: Frank Cass, 1995.

Khazanov, Anatoly. *The Krymchaks: A Vanishing Group in the Soviet Union*. Research Paper No. 71. Jerusalem: The Hebrew University, 1989.

Krinsky, Samuel. *The Glassmakers: A Jewish Odyssey*. New York: Hippocrene Books, 1991.

Lancet-Miller, Aviva. *The Jews of Bukhara*. Jerusalem: Israel Museum, Catalog no. 39, Winter 1967–68.

Landshut, Siegfried. *Jewish Communities in the Muslim Countries of the Middle East: A Survey*. London: The Jewish Chronicle, 1950.

Laskier, Michael M. *North African Jewry in the Twentieth Century*. New York: New York University Press, 1994.

————. *The Alliance Israelite Universalle and the Jewish Communities of Morocco 1862–1962*. Albany: State University of New York, 1983.

Leslau, Wolf. *Falasha Anthology*. New Haven: Yale University Press, 1979.

Leslie, Donald D. "Persia or Yemen? The Origin of the Kaifeng Jews." *Irano-Judaica* (1982): 101–111.

————. *The Survival of the Chinese Jews*. Leiden: E. J. Brill, 1972.

Levin, Theodore. *The Hundred Thousand Fools of God*. Bloomington: Indiana University Press, 1996.

Levy, Avigdor. *The Sephardim in the Ottoman Empire*. Princeton, N.J.: The Darwin Press, 1992.

Lewis, Bernard. *The Arabs in History*. New York: Harper and Row, 1960.

———. *The Jews of Islam*. Princeton, N.J.: Princeton University Press, 1984.

Lewis, Herbert S. *After the Eagles Landed: The Yemenites of Israel*. Boulder: Westview Press, 1989.

Littman, David. "Jews Under Muslim Rule: The Case of Persia." *The Weiner Library Bulletin* 32 (1979): 2–15.

Loeb, Laurence D. "Folk Models of Habbani Ethnic Identity." In *Studies in Israeli Ethnicity: After the Ingathering*. Edited by Alex Weingrod. New York: Gordon and Breach Science Publishers, 1985.

———. *Outcaste: Jewish Life in Southern Iran*. New York: Gordon and Breech Science Publishers, 1977.

Loewe, Michael. "The Jewish Presence in Imperial China." *Jewish Historical Studies* 30 (1987–88): 1–20.

Loewenthal, Rudolf. "The Extinction of the Krimchaks in World War II." *The American and East European Review* 10 (April 1951): 130–36.

———. *The Jews of Bukhara*. Washington, D.C.: Central Asian Collectanea, 1961.

———. "The Judeo-Tats in the Caucasus." *Historia Judaica* 14–15 (1952–53): 61–82.

Lord, Henry J. *The Jews in India and the Far East*. Westport, C.T.: Greenwood Press Reprint, 1976.

Maatuf Saadia Ben Yitzchak. *Habban (Hadramaut) Jewry in the Last Generations*. Master's Thesis, Department of History, Bar Ilan University, Ramat Gan, Israel, 1984. [In Hebrew with English summary]

Malcioln, Jose V. *The African Origin of Modern Judaism: From Hebrews to Jews*. Trenton, N.J: Africa World Press, 1996.

Mandelbaum, David G. "The Jewish Way of Life in Cochin." *Journal of Jewish Social Studies* 1: 4 (October 1939): 423–60.

———. *Society in India*. 2 Vol. Berkeley: University of California Press, 1970.

Marcus, Harold. *A History of Ethiopia*. Berkeley: University of California, 1994.

Masliyah, Sadok. "Persian Jewry—Prelude to Catastrophe." *Judaism* 116, 29:4 (Fall 1980): 390–404.

———. "The Bene Israel and the Baghdadis: Two Indian Communities in Conflict." *Judaism* 43:3 (Summer 1994): 279–293.

Menashri, David. "The Jews of Iran: Between the Shah and Khomeini." In *Anti-Semitism in Times of Crisis*, edited by Sander L. Gilman and Steven T. Katz. New York: University Press, 1991.

Mendelsohn, Rebekah Z. *The Bokharan Jewish Community of New York City*. Master's Thesis, Anthropology, Columbia University, 1964.

Mendelssohn, Sidney. *The Jews of Asia, Especially in the Sixteenth and Seventeenth Centuries*. London: Kegan Paul, Trech, Traubner, 1920.

———. *The Jews of Africa; Especially in the Sixteenth and Seventeenth Centuries*. London: Kegan Paul, Trech, Traubner, 1920.

Messing, Simon. *The Story of the Falashas: Black Jews of Ethiopia*. New York: Balshan Press, 1982.

Mishkowsky, Noach. *Etiopia: Yidn in Afriki un Azieh*. New York: Borochov Yugent Bibliotek, 1936. [Yiddish]

Moreen, Vera B. *Iranian Jewry's Hour of Peril and Heroism: A Study of Babai Ibn Luft's Chronicle (1617–1662)*. New York: The American Academy for Jewish Research, 1987.

Moshavi, Baruch. *Customs and Folklore of 19th Century Bucharian Jews in Central Asia*. Unpublished dissertation, Yeshiva University. Ann Arbor: University Microfilms, 1974. [In Hebrew with English summary]

Moskovich, V. and B. Tukan. "The Krimchak Community: History, Culture and Language." *Pe'Amim: Studies in the Cultural Heritage of Oriental Jewry* 14 (1982): 5–31. [Hebrew]

Muchawsky-Schnapper, Esther. *The Jews of Yemen: Highlights of the Israel Museum Collection*. Jerusalem: The Israel Museum, 1994.

Muthiah, S. *The Splendour of India*. New Delhi: UBS Publishers' Distributors, 1992.

Nahai, Gina B. *Cry of the Peacock*. New York: Crown Publishers, 1991.

Naim, Janet. *Libya: An Extinct Jewish Community*. Tel Aviv: Beth Hatfutsoth, The Nahum Goldmann Museum of the Jewish Diaspora, 1980.

Needle, M. Patricia, ed. *East Gate of Kaifeng: A Jewish World Inside China*. Minneapolis: University of Minnesota China Center, 1992.

Negbi, Zohar and Bracha Yaniv. *Afghanistan: The Synagogue and the Jewish Home*. Jerusalem: Center for Jewish Art—The Hebrew University of Jerusalem, 1991.

Ness, Brenda J. *The Children of Jacob: The Bene Israel of Maharashtra*. Unpublished dissertation, University of California at Los Angeles, 1996.

Neumark, Ephraim. *Journey to the Lands of the East*. Edited by Abraham Ya'ari. Jerusalem: Levine Epstein Bros., 1947. [Hebrew]

Newby, Gordon D. *A History of the Jews of Arabia: From Ancient Times to Their Eclipse Under Islam*. Columbia, S.C.: University of South Carolina Press, 1988.

Nini, Yehudah. *The Jews of Yemen 1800–1914*. Chur, Switzerland: Harwood Academic Pub, 1991.

Onolemhemhen, Durrenda N. and Kebede Gessesse. *The Black Jews of Ethiopia: The Last Exodus*. Lanham, M.D., and London: Scarecrow Press, 1998.

Ozeri, Zion M. *Yemenite Jews: A Photographic Essay*. New York: Schocken Books, 1985.

Pankhurst, Richard K. *A Social History of Ethiopia: The North and Central Highlands from Medieval Times to the Rise of Emperor Tewodros*. Addis Ababa: Addis Ababa University, 1990.

Parasuram, T. V. *India's Jewish Heritage*. New Delhi: Sagar Publications, 1982.

Parfitt, Tudor. *Operation Moses: The Story of the Exodus of the Falasha Jews from Ethiopia*. London: Weidenfeld and Nicolson, 1985.

————. *The Road to Redemption: The Jews of Yemen 1900–1950*. Leiden: E. J. Brill, 1996.

————. *The Thirteenth Gate: Travels Among the Lost Tribes of Israel*. Bethesda, M.D.: Adler and Adler, 1987.

————, and Emanuela Trevisan Semi, eds. *The Beta Israel in Ethiopia and Israel: Studies on Ethiopian Jews*. Surrey, England: Curzon Press, 1999.

Passow, Meyer. *Exotic and Vanished Jewish Tribes*. Tel Aviv: WIZO, 1974.

Patai, Raphael. *Jadid al-Islam: The Jewish "New Muslims" of Meshhed*. Detroit: Wayne State University, 1997.

————. *The Seed of Abraham: Jews and Arabs in Contact and Conflict*. Salt Lake City: University of Utah Press, 1986.

————. *Tents of Jacob—Yesterday and Today*. Englewood Cliffs, N.J.: Prentice-Hall, Inc., 1971.

————. *The Vanished Worlds of Jewry*. New York: Macmillan, 1980.

Plaks, Andrew H. "The Confucianization of the Kaifeng Jews: Interpretations of the Kaifeng Stelae Inscriptions. In *The Jews of China*. Vol. 1. *Historical and Comparative Perspectives*. Edited and with an introduction by Jonathan Goldstein. Armonk, N.Y.: M. E. Sharpe, 1999.

Points East: A Publication of the Sino-Judaic Institute. Menlo Park, C.A.

Pollak, Michael. *Mandarins, Jews and Missionaries: The Jewish Experience in the Chinese Empire*. Philadelphia: Jewish Publication Society, 1980.

————. *The Torah Scrolls of the Chinese Jews*. Dallas: Bridewell Library, 1975.

————. "The Revelation of a Jewish Presence in Seventeenth-Century China: Its Impact On Western Messianic Thought." A Study Presented at the Symposium "Jewish Diasporas in China: Comparative and Historical Perspectives." *John K. Fairbank Center for Asian Research,* Harvard University (16–18 August 1992): 1–27.

Pundak, Nahum. "The Jewish Silversmiths from the Yemen." *Ariel* 15 (Summer 1966): 21–27.

Quirin, James A. *The Beta Israel (Felasha) in Ethiopian History: Caste Formation and Culture Change, 1270–1868*. Unpublished dissertation, University of Minnesota, 1977.

————. *The Evolution of the Ethiopian Jews: A History of the Beta Israel (Falasha) to 1920*. Philadelphia: University of Pennsylvania Press, 1992.

Rabinowitz, Louis I. *Far East Mission*. Johannesburg: Eagle Press, 1952.

————. *Jewish Merchant Adventurers: A Study of the Radanites*. London: Edward Goldston, 1948.

Rafael, Chaim. *The Sephardi Story: A Celebration of Jewish History*. London: Vallentine Mitchell, 1991.

Rapoport, Louis. *Redemption Song: The Story of Operation Moses*. San Diego: Harcourt Brace Jovanovich, 1986.

————. *The Lost Jews: Last of the Ethiopian Falashas*. New York: Stein and Day, 1980.

Ro'i, Yaacov and Avi Beker, eds. *Jewish Culture and Identity in the Soviet Union*. New York: New York University Press, 1991.

Robinson, Nehemiah. *Persia and Afghanistan and Their Jewish Communities*. New York: Institute of Jewish Affairs, 1953.

Rodrigue, Aron. *Images of Sephardi and Eastern Jewries in Transition: The Teachers of the Alliance Israelite Universalle, 1860–1939*. Seattle and London: University of Washington Press, 1993.

Roland, Joan G. *The Jewish Communities of India: Identity in a Colonial Era*. 2nd ed. New Brunswick, N.J.: Transaction Publishers, 1998.

Rosen, Lawrence. *Bargaining for Reality: The Construction of Social Relations in a Muslim Community*. Chicago: University of Chicago Press, 1984.

Ross, Dan. *Acts of Faith: A Journey to the Fringes of Jewish Identity*. New York: St. Martin's Press, 1982.

Sabar, Yona, ed. *The Folk Literature of the Kurdistani Jews: An Anthology*. New Haven and London: Yale University Press, 1982.

Salamon, Hagar. *The Hyena People: Ethiopian Jews in Christian Ethiopia*. Berkeley: University of California Press, 1999.

Samuel, Shellim. *Treatise on the Origin and Early History of the Beni Israel of Mahashastra State*. Bombay: Iyer and Iyer, 1963.

Schachter, Hershel. "Determining Jewish Identity: Ethiopian Jewry." *Journal of Halacha* 9 (Spring 1985): 143–160.

Schechtman, Joseph B. *On Wings of Eagles: The Plight, Exodus, and Homecoming of Oriental Jewry*. New York: T. Yoseloff, 1961.

Schindler, Ruben and David Ribner. *The Trauma of Transition: The Psycho-Social Cost of Immigration to Israel*. Aldershot, England: Avery, 1997.

Schroeter, Daniel J. *Merchants of Essaouira: Urban Society and Imperialism in Southwestern Morocco, 1844–1886*. Cambridge: Cambridge University Press, 1988.

———. "Orientalism and the Jews of the Mediterranean." *Journal of Mediterranean Studies* 4:2 (1994): 183–196.

Schwartz-Be'eri, Ora. "Jewish Weaving in Kurdistan." *Kurdish Times* 6:1–2 (Summer-Fall 1991): 86–96.

———. "Kurdish Jewish Silvercraft." *The Israel Museum Journal* 7 (Spring 1988): 75–86.

Seeman, Don. "Ethnographers, Rabbis and Jewish Epistemology: The Case of the Ethiopian Jews." *Tradition: A Journal of Orthodox Thought* 25:4 (1991): 13–29.

Segev, Tom. *1949: The First Israelis*. New York: The Free Press, 1986.

Sered, Susan S. *Women as Ritual Experts: The Religious Lives of Elderly Jewish Women in Jerusalem*. New York: Oxford University Press, 1992.

Sergew Hable Selassie. *Ancient and Medieval Ethiopian History to 1270*. Addis Ababa: United Printers, 1972.

Shai, Donna. "Wedding Customs among Kurdish Jews in (Zakho) Kurdistan and in (Jerusalem) Israel." *Folklore Research Center Studies* 4 (1974): 253–266.

Shapiro, Sidney, ed. *Jews in Old China: Studies by Chinese Scholars*. New York: Hippocrene Books, 1984.

Shelemay, Kay Kaufman. *A Song of Longing: An Ethiopian Journey*. Urbana: University of Illinois Press, 1991.

———. *Music, Ritual and Falasha History*. 2nd ed. East Lansing: Michigan State University Press, 1989.

Shivtiel, A., et al. "The Jews of San'a." In *San'a: An Arabian Islamic City*. Edited by R. B. Serjeant and Ronald Lewcock. London: World of Islam Festival Trust, 1983.

Shokeid, Moshe and Shlomo Deshen. *Distant Relations: Ethnicity and Politics Among Arabs and North African Jews in Israel*. New York: Praeger, 1982.

Simon, Rachel. *Change Within Tradition Among Jewish Women in Libya*. Seattle: University of Washington Press, 1992.

———. "The Sephardi Heritage in Libya." *Shofar* 10:3 (1992): 90–112.

Simons, Geoff. *Libya: The Struggle for Survival*. New York: St. Martin's Press, 1993.

Sitton, David. *Sephardi Communities Today*. Jerusalem: Council of Sephardi and Oriental Communities, 1985.

Slapak, Orpa, ed. *The Jews of India: A Story of Three Communities*. Jerusalem: The Israel Museum, 1995.

Slouschz, Nahum. *Travels in North Africa*. Philadelphia: Jewish Publication Society, 1927.

Soroudi, Sorour S. "Jews in Islamic Iran." *The Jerusalem Quarterly* 21 (Fall 1981): 99–114.

Spector, Daniel. *A History of the Jews of Persia*. Unpublished dissertation, University of Texas. Ann Arbor, Mich.: University Microfilm, 1975.

Spencer, Edward. *Turkey, Russia, The Black Sea and Circassia*. London: George Routledge, 1854.

Stern, Henry. *Wanderings among the Falashas of Abyssinia*. 2nd ed. London: Frank Cass Reprint, 1968.

Stillman, Norman. *The Jews of Arab Lands: A History and Sourcebook*. Philadelphia: Jewish Publication Society, 1979.

———. *The Jews of Arab Lands in Modern Times*. Philadelphia: Jewish Publication Society, 1991.

Strizower, Schifra. *Exotic Jewish Communities*. London and New York: Thomas Yoseloff, 1962.

———. *The Children of Israel: The Bene Israel of Bombay*. New York: Schocken, 1971.

Studies of the Chinese Jews: Selections from Journals East and West. Compiled and with an introduction by Hyman Kublin. New York: Paragon Book Reprint Corp., 1971.

Tibebu, Teshalo. *The Making of Modern Ethiopia*. Lawrenceville, N.J.: The Red Sea Press, Inc., 1995.

Timberg, Thomas A., ed. *Jews in India*. New York: Advent Books, 1986.

Tobi, Jacob. *West of Eden: A Survey of the Aden Jewish Community*. Netanya, Israel: Association for Society and Culture, 1994.

Tobi, Yosef. *The Jews of Yemen: Studies in their History and Culture*. Leiden and Boston: E.J. Brill, 1999.

Trevisan Semi, Emanuela. "The Beta Israel (Falashas): From Purity to Impurity." *Jewish Journal of Sociology* 25 (1985): 103–114.

Udovitch, Abraham L. and Lucette Valenti. *The Last Arab Jews: The Communities of Jerba, Tunisia*. London: Harwood Academic Publications, 1984.

Ullendorf, Edward. *Ethiopia and the Bible*. London: Oxford University Press, 1968.

———. *The Ethiopians: An Introduction to Country and People*. 3rd ed. London: Oxford University Press, 1973.

Wagaw, Teshome G. "The International Ramifications of Falasha Emigration." *Journal of Modern African Studies* 29:4 (1991): 557–581.

———. *For Our Soul: Ethiopian Jews in Israel*. Detroit: Wayne State University, 1993.

Waldman, Menachem. *The Jews of Ethiopia*. Jerusalem: Ami Shav, 1985.

Weil, Shalva. *The Jews from the Konkan: The Bene Israel Communities in India*. Tel Aviv: Beth Hatfutsoth, 1981.

Weingarten, Michael A. *Changing Health and Changing Culture: The Yemenites in Israel*. Westport, CT: Greenwood, 1992.

Westermarck, Edward. *Ritual and Belief in Morocco*. 2 vols. London: MacMillan, 1926.

Westheimer, Ruth and Steven Kaplan. *Surviving Salvation*. New York: New York University Press, 1992.

Wexler, Paul. *The Non-Jewish Origins of the Sephardi Jews*. Albany, N.Y.: State University of New York Press, 1996.

White, William. *Chinese Jews*. 3 vols. Toronto: University of Toronto Press, 1942.

Wigoder, Geoffrey, ed. "Jews from the Land of Frankincense." *Israel* 5 (Spring 1973): 124–131.

———. *New Encyclopedia of Israel and Zionism*. 2 vols. Madison, New Jersey: Fairleigh Dickenson University Press, 1994.

Williams, Joseph L. *Hebrewisms of West Africa*. New York: The Dial Press, 1931.

Willner, Dorothy. *Nation-Building and Community in Israel*. Princeton, N.J.: Princeton University Press, 1969.

Ye'or, Bat. *The Dhimmi: Jews and Christians Under Islam*. London: Fairleigh Dickenson University Press, 1985.

Yehoshua-Raz, Benzion D. *From the Lost Tribes in Afghanistan to the Mashhad Jewish Converts of Iran*. Jerusalem: Mosad Byalik, 1992. [Hebrew]

Zand, Michael. "Bukhara." *Encyclopaedia Judaica Year Book 1975/6*, pp. 183–192. Jerusalem: Keter, 1976.

Zand, Michael. "Bukharan Jews." *Encyclopedia Iranica*. Vol. 4, pp. 530–545. London: Routledge and Keegan Paul, 1990.

Appendix A
Ethno-geographic Breakdown of Four Major Jewish Groupings

Each group is identified by its unique religious customs, ceremonies, and observances. Some of the mores and folkways, including the superstitions, are often adaptation from the surrounding non-Jewish milieu.

MIZRACHIM

a) Mista' arvim, or ancient Oriental Jewish communities of the Middle East and North Africa, who lived in a Muslim milieu and spoke a regional Judeo-Arabic dialect, in addition to Arabic. The great centers of Talmudic learning that shaped Judaism in the first millenium after the exile were situated in Baghdad, Kairouan, Fustat, and Fez. Mista'arvi civilization was, to a large extent, gradually subsumed by the Sephardim who had migrated to the Eastern Mediterranean after the expulsion of 1492.

b) Disparate and isolated ancient Jewish communities on the African and Asian Jewish periphery ("Ten Lost Tribes"), including fringe enigmatic communities such as the Beta Israel of Ethiopia and the Bene Israel of Bombay. In many places the Jews spoke a pidgin tongue that was a mixture of the local language and Hebrew i.e. Judeo-Persian in Central Asia, Judeo-Berber in the Atlas Mountains, Juhuru (Judeo-Tat) in the northeastern Caucasus.

SEPHARDIM

Primarily Judeans, who first migrated to North Africa and Babylonia after the destruction of the two Temples (586 B.C.E. and 70 C.E.); later, in early Medieval times settled in large numbers on the Iberian Peninsula. During the "Golden Age" (roughly 950–1391) many Sephardim distinguished themselves as theologians, doctors, poets, businessmen, and diplomats. After the massacres of 1391 and the Expulsion Decree of 1492 the Sephardim were concentrated in the Ottoman Empire, North Africa, and the New World. Spoke a Spanish-Jewish dialect called Ladino, with regional nuances.

ROMANIOTES

Palestinian Jews driven into Roman lands after the destruction of the 2nd Temple and the Bar Kochba revolt, whose communal life was molded in the backdrop of a Byzantine Orthodox-Christian milieu. Their culture now almost extinct, these Greek-speaking Jews were absorbed into the Sephardi milieu when the Iberian Jews settled in the Ottoman Empire after 1492.

ASHKENAZIM

Jewish communities originally from Italy and Byzantine lands who first settled in Western and Central Europe (Rhineland) in the Middle Ages. Later, in the 15th Century, they migrated in large numbers to Eastern Europe, primarily Poland. In the Slavic lands these Ashkenazi (French-German) Jews encountered remnants of the Jewish Khazars who had fled from the Crimean peninsula during the Mongol invasions. Together they laid the foundations for the Jewish communities of Eastern Europe. Spoke a German-Jewish dialect called Yiddish.

Appendix B
Jewish Communities on the African and Asian Jewish Periphery

GENERAL CHARACTERISTICS OF THESE COMMUNITIES

1. Having inhabited these regions for millennia, the Jews were more or less indistinguishable from the surrounding peoples.
2. They retained traditions discarded or long forgotten by Sephardim and Ashkenazim.
3. In many cases, they embraced mores and folkways of the dominant culture that were at great variance with "normative" Judaism.

Country	Traditional Habitat	Arrival	Milieu	Est. Pop.	In Israel
N. Yemen	towns, villages	BCE	Shiite	500(?)	200,000
S. Yemen	oasis towns	CE	Sunni	0	1,600
Ethiopia	mt. villages	?	Eth. Orthodox	*0	75,000
Atlas Mts., Moroc.	mt. villages	BCE	Sunni	0	50,000
Jerba, Tunisia	isl. villages	BCE	Sunni	1,000	10,000
Tripolitania, Libya	mt. caves	BCE	Sunni	0	1,500
Bombay, Ind.	coastal villages	BCE	Hindu	5,000	40,000
Cochin, Ind.	jungle towns	BCE	Hindu	20	5,000
China	port cities	CE	Confucian	**200	0
Cent. Asia (Bukhara)	oasis towns	CE	Sunni	5,000	70,000
Afghanistan	oasis towns	CE	Sunni	0	50,000
Iran	oasis towns	BCE	Shiite	27,000	200,000
Kurdistan	mt. villages	BCE	Sunni	0	125,000
Georgia	fuedal towns	CE	Orthodox	5,000	75,000
Daghestan	mt. villages	CE	Sunni	15,000	60,000
Crimea	mt. villages	BCE	Sunni	500	?

*status of 30,000 Falas Mura still pending

** descendants of Jews

Index

ABOUT THE AUTHOR

Ken Blady, Jewish educator, writer, and Yiddish translator, was born in Paris, France and grew up in Chassidic Brooklyn, where he attended yeshiva and rabbinical seminary. A San Francisco Bay Area resident since 1972, Ken has a B.A. in History from the University of California at Berkeley, and an M.A. in Clinical Counseling from California State University, Hayward. He is the author of *The Jewish Boxers' Hall of Fame* and translator of *The Journeys of David Toback*. Ken is a popular lecturer on a variety of Jewish themes at colleges, synagogues, elder hostels, and adult educational institutions. He has been featured on local cable TV and on radio talk shows, including "The Voice of Israel."